UPDATE

A HISTORY

OF THE

UNITED STATES

SINCE

1945

Daniel F. Davis is chairman of the Social Studies Department at Stoughton, Massachusetts, Secondary Schools. Much of the material for this book was developed from a course on the postwar period he has taught for 10 years. He obtained his Ph.D. at Ohio State University, his M.A. from City University of New York at Brooklyn College, and his B.S. from State University of New York at Oswego. He has coauthored two world history textbooks.

Norman Lunger is a professional writer living in rural Pennsylvania. He has done graduate study in international relations at Columbia University in New York City and at Centre Européen Universitaire in Nancy, France. He has a B.A. from Texas Christian University. He was coauthor of the Scholastic American Citizenship Program, and also coauthored a high school geography textbook.

Publisher: Eleanor Angeles
Editorial Director: Carolyn Jackson
Special Editor: John Nickerson
Production Editor: Michael Corby
Art Director and Designer: James Sarfati
Photo Researcher: Rosalyn Sohnen
Maps by David Lindroth.
Cover: Artist's conception of a satellite under construction in space. Inset, from *Out of the Forties*, by Nicholas Lemann.

CONTENTS

BY DANIEL F. DAVIS, PH.D. AND NORMAN LUNGER
SCHOLASTIC INC.

The American Scene in 1945

SUPPOSE YOU WAKE UP one morning and find out that it's 1945. You're still you, the same age you were when you went to bed last night. But the world around you is quite different.

First, there are no music videos. In fact, if there's a television in your house, you're part of a very small minority. But that's not all. There's not even any rock 'n' roll. How did anyone manage to get along in 1945?

Americans in 1945 got along pretty well, actually. As Winston Churchill observed shortly after the end of World War II: "America stands at this moment at the summit of the world." Churchill was right. To be an American in 1945 was to be a citizen of a nation wealthy beyond belief in a world that had otherwise been ripped apart by war.

The United States counted only a little more than 400,000 war dead, nearly all of them members of the military. Central Europe, East Asia, and the Soviet Union had lost more than 15 million lives to the war. Britain and France together had lost a million soldiers as well as civilians. America had escaped the horrible aerial bombings that had wasted the other two continents.

Not only had the United States emerged relatively untouched from World War II, but had been in some ways blessed in the process. Real wages were up 44 percent during the war. Since war-time rationing left Americans with little to spend their money on, they put more than $136 billion into war bonds and savings accounts. This huge financial reserve helped fuel a tremendous economic boom that followed the end of the war. It also provided for one of the easiest postwar transitions the world had ever seen.

The people of the United States enjoyed a much larger share of the world's wealth than people elsewhere. In the aftermath of the war, U.S. factories produced *more than half* of the planet's manufactured goods. U.S. foundries and refineries churned out *almost two thirds* of the world's steel and oil. Americans drove *three fourths* of the world's automobiles. Their incomes were *15 times greater* than those of the average person overseas.

GROWING PAINS

In 1945 the United States was a nation of 145 million people. The heaviest center of population had developed in the so-called eastern corridor, a path of urban settlement that reached down the Atlantic coast from Maine to Virginia. The collection of towns and cities fringing the Great Lakes and the Mississippi River formed a second population center. New York, Chicago, and Philadelphia were the nation's three largest cities.

But the population was shifting. Even before World War II, California had become the nation's fifth most populous state. Between 1940 and 1945, the state had added another 1,900,000 residents. By 1950, California would have more than 10 million inhabitants, second only to New York.

Another shift was that of people from farms and villages to the nation's growing towns and cities. This shift had been taking place for more than half a century. Before 1880, the majority of Americans had been farmers. The Industrial Revolution had helped to change that. By 1945, farmers made up only about 15 percent of the population.

The movement from farms to cities was keenly felt in the nation's most heavily agricultural region, the South. In 1945 the South remained something of a nation within a nation. It had only a few major cities, and was only beginning to develop large industries. Average income in the South was barely half that of the national average.

The lower standard of living in the South encouraged a massive migration starting as early as 1920, toward the cities of the Northeast and Midwest. Millions of southerners found jobs in Cleveland's refineries, Pittsburgh's steel mills, and Detroit's auto plants. This migration was as important in its own way as the immigration that had brought millions of Europeans to America between 1880 and 1910. Most significant about the great exodus from the South was that most of the migrants were blacks.

These Americans were hardly welcomed with open arms in northern cities. Certain jobs were closed to them. They had to live in certain neighborhoods, often in the most run-down parts of town. During the war several major clashes had erupted between black and white workers in defense plants. In Detroit a race riot had claimed 34 lives in 1943.

Yet the great migration of black Americans would soon help to bring issues of racial discrimination to national attention. For generations after the U.S. Civil War, millions of white Americans had been able to convince themselves that this problem was limited to the South. Discrimination was viewed as a regional curiosity, simply "the way they do things *down there*." Now, North as well as South looked racial discrimination in the face. Some did not like what they saw. The seeds of change slowly began to take root.

ADVANCES IN SCIENCE

The war had brought vast changes to America. Scientists of several countries had worked around the clock to devise new weapons and improve old ones. Among the many new developments of the war years had been jet airplanes, helicopters, radar, guided missiles, and the atomic bomb.

But in addition to weapons, some scientists had worked on developing products that had as much impact after the war as they did in aiding the Allied victory. During the war, technicians had worked on new ways to provide food that was nutritious and edible for millions of soldiers stationed around the world. After the war, precooked frozen foods became stock items in grocery stores across America.

The war had proved the usefulness of the early wonder drugs, such as sulfapyradine and penicillin. These drugs had enabled doctors to combat infection among the wounded. War research led to another category of drugs—antibiotics. The first of these, streptomycin, was used to control tuberculosis, kidney infection, and several other diseases.

In 1945, researchers were poised on the verge of still other scientific breakthroughs. At Bell Laboratories in New Jersey, electrical engineers were studying materials known as semi-conductors. Their efforts would lead in 1947 to the development of transistors, tiny transmission units that cut the cost and size of radios (and later, television sets and computers) up to half, almost overnight. Radio-listeners of the future would be able to tune in to everything from the Beach Boys to Beethoven to even the Beastie Boys while strolling down suburban sidewalks, thanks to the transistor. But that dims in comparison with the effect the development would have on television. As television sets became more affordable, they became as much a staple in the home as a table and chairs. The TV set also came to hold great power over Americans, influencing everything from which frozen food they bought to which presidential candidate they voted for.

At research facilities at the University of Pennsylvania in Philadelphia, physicists John Eckert and John Mauchly were busy putting together a gigantic machine. They called it an Electronic Numerical Integrator and Calculator, or ENIAC. When completed in 1946, ENIAC would become the world's first all-electronic digital computer.

THE QUEST FOR SECURITY

Yet most Americans in 1945 knew little of what was happening in the nation's research labs. Most were too busy rebuilding their own lives. Whether they knew it or not, they stood on the threshold of a "gadget revolution." Among the new devices which would soon appear were steam irons, electric lawn mowers, even electric guitars. There was a ready market for these devices. The nation's birth rate soared in the five years after the war's end. "The veterans and their wives grabbed for the good things as if there were no tomorrow," one contemporary journalist later recalled. "They wanted everything at once—house, car, washing machine, children."

One could hardly blame them. Young adults of 1945 had grown up in the midst of a terrible economic depression. They had come of age during the most destructive war in all of world history. It was little wonder, then, that theirs was a generation that prized security above most other values.

AMERICA: THE WORLD'S POLICEMAN

Between 1915 and 1945, America had twice become involved in major conflicts. After World War I, the United States had tried to withdraw from world leadership, but such a retreat had just not worked. After the end of World War II, it became clear to the nation's leaders that their country would have to occupy a central role on the world political stage. On December 4, 1945, the U.S. Senate voted overwhelmingly to join a new world organization, the United Nations.

While the United States was without peer as a world leader, one country promised to be a major rival—the Soviet Union. In 1945, despite the devastation suffered by the U.S.S.R. during World War II, its production of steel, oil, and manufactured goods dwarfed that of all nations except for the United States. These two nations were so vastly superior to all others in military and economic strength that they were already being called superpowers.

Tensions between the superpowers had begun long before World War II. When the Russian tsar (emperor) was overthrown by the Communists in 1917, Americans viewed the new government with distrust. Indeed, the United States had not recognized the Soviet Union for the next 16 years.

Suspicions had been raised by two basic differences. The first was political: the United States was a democracy, whereas the Soviet Union was headed by a dictator. The second difference was economic. The United States followed a system of free enterprise known as capitalism. The Soviet Union practiced communism, a theory that called for ownership of all land and businesses by everyone together. At the time of the Russian Revolution, its Communist leaders promised to put an end to capitalism.

Thus, the leadership of each country tended to regard its counterpart as the main cause of all that was wrong with the world. Tensions between the two countries would become a constant feature of world affairs for decades to come.

A NEW POLITICAL REALITY

At the same time, a new factor had arisen to keep such tensions in check: the development of atomic weapons. The dawn of the Nuclear Age had instantly changed the rules of international politics. The age that had begun with the utter destruction of the cities of Hiroshima and Nagasaki signaled to humankind that it could potentially destroy itself.

The implications of this concept were not lost on those who had helped develop the atomic bomb. U.S. scientist J. Robert Oppenheimer, upon witnessing the first test-explosion of an atom bomb in the New Mexico desert, was reminded of a passage from ancient Hindu scripture: "I am become Death, the shatterer of worlds."

The existence of nuclear weapons was about to have a dramatic impact on American politics. For the first 170 years of its history, the United States had enjoyed the military security provided by two vast oceans and friendly neighbors at its northern and southern borders. But these barriers offered no protection against nuclear weapons. By 1949, the Soviet Union had developed an atomic bomb. In the 1950's, Great Britain had one too. France and China developed their own nuclear bombs in the 1960's. It seemed likely that India, Israel, and South Africa also had built nuclear weapons. In the Nuclear Age, the United States was clearly a giant. But as we will see, it could be a vulnerable giant.

Suppose you had been a teenager in 1945. Today you would be middle-aged, probably a parent, maybe even with children the age you are now. You would have lived to witness some of the most exciting moments in the history of the nation and the world, as well as some of the most tragic. You might be concerned about nuclear arms buildups, or it's likely that such issues and events get shuffled and lost in your routine.

History in the making does not always demand our attention. It is often much more subtle. That's one reason history books are useful. They serve to remind us that history is happening all the time, all around us.

U.S. POPULATION GROWTH,
1940 – 1980.

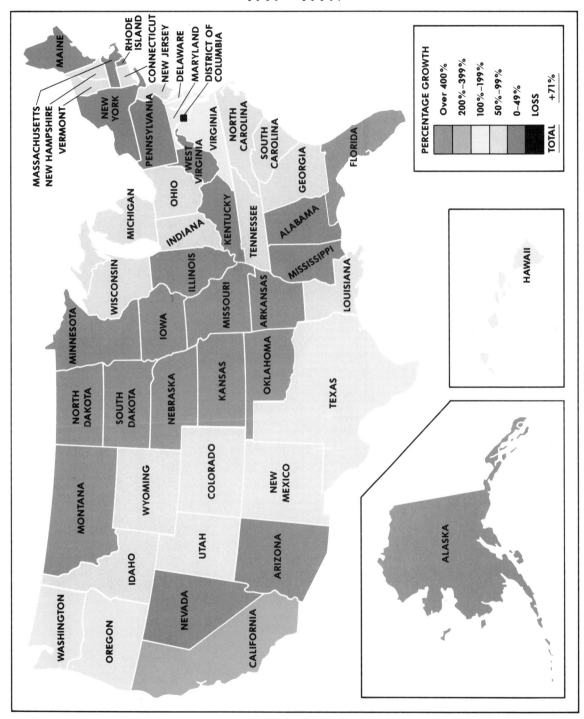

CHAPTER 1

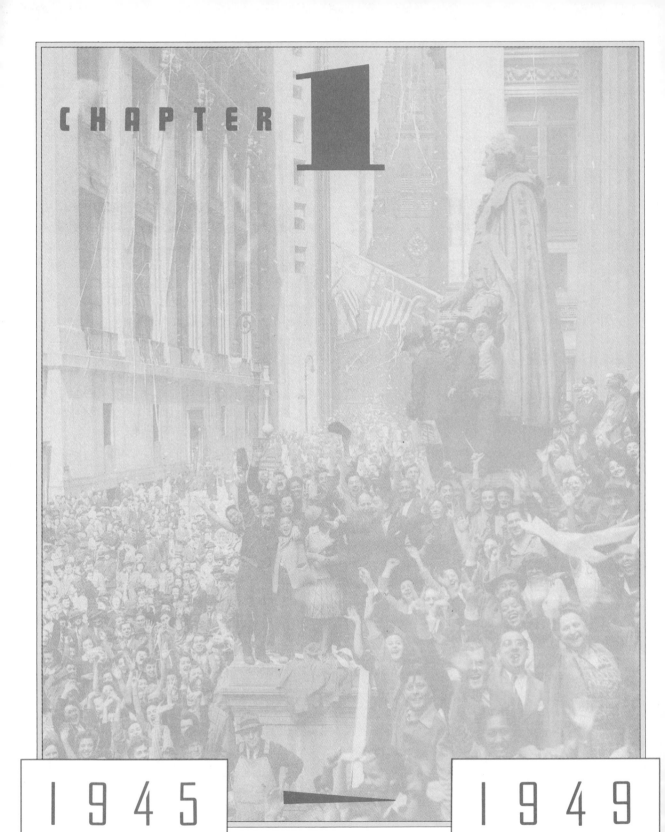

1945   —   1949

The Postwar World Takes Shape

April sunshine poured through the windows of the clapboard cottage in Warm Springs, Georgia. It splashed across the shoulders of a silver-haired man reading his mail at a desk. He was dressed rather formally — white shirt, red tie, vest. He wore a wool cape, carefully arranged by an artist who sat nearby painting his portrait.

Franklin Delano Roosevelt felt at home in Warm Springs. He had come here often after being stricken with polio at the age of 39. Long before becoming the nation's 32nd President, he had spent many hours exercising in the naturally heated waters of a local pool. Now, in the spring of 1945, he was back to regain his strength.

Although few Americans were aware of it, the recent months had taken a serious toll on the President's health. The decisions had been difficult; many involved arrangements affecting the outcome of World War II. In spite of high blood pressure and a heart ailment, Roosevelt had made a 14,000-mile voyage to Yalta in the Soviet Union that winter to confer with Soviet and British leaders. When he returned, he had followed doctor's orders and gone to Warm Springs for a rest.

Even as Roosevelt posed for a watercolor painting on April 12, events were rushing head-long toward a climax in Europe and Asia. U.S., British, and Russian armies had beaten back the forces of Nazi Germany and were headed toward the German capital, Berlin. In the Pacific, the U.S. Tenth Army was engaged in its bloodiest encounter with Japan on the island of Okinawa. In San Francisco, city officials were preparing to host the first meeting of the United Nations. A shipment of uranium 235 was moving toward Los Alamos, New Mexico, where the metal would be tested in a powerful new weapon, the atomic bomb.

At Warm Springs, however, the morning had been tranquil. Near one o'clock Roosevelt placed a cigarette into a long holder and lit it with a match. Then he returned to the mail. Suddenly the artist saw his hand fall. For a moment she thought he had dropped the cigarette. Instead, he pressed his left hand to his temple and said, "I have a terrible headache." He slumped in his chair, unconscious. A physician raced to the cottage but arrived too late to help. Within three hours Franklin Roosevelt lay dead of a cerebral hemorrhage (bleeding in the brain).

Unfinished portrait of President Roosevelt.

When the news reached the White House in Washington, D.C., Roosevelt's assistant, Stephen Early, took charge. He summoned the President's wife, Eleanor, then put in a call to Vice President Harry Truman on Capitol Hill. When Truman arrived at the White House, he was directed to Mrs. Roosevelt's sitting room. Mrs. Roosevelt walked up to him and put her hand on his shoulder. "Harry," she said, "the President is dead."

At first, Truman was speechless. Then he responded: "Is there anything I can do for you?"

The First Lady returned the question graciously: "Is there anything we can do for you? You're the one who's in trouble now."

Truman, 60, had been vice president for only 83 days. His career could hardly have been more different from that of the man he was about to succeed. Franklin Roosevelt had been born to a socially prominent family from New York. Truman had come from a farm family in Missouri and had gone broke in a men's clothing store business before entering politics. Roosevelt had graduated from Harvard College and Columbia Law School. Truman's formal education after high school had consisted of some law courses he had taken in night school. Roosevelt had been a gifted orator whose speeches and radio talks had moved the nation. Truman was a plain-spoken person who wasted no words getting to his point.

Yet as U.S. senator from Missouri between 1939 and 1945, Truman had been a loyal supporter of the Democratic party and of Roosevelt's New Deal. Although the senator's political career had begun with the backing of a

President Roosevelt's funeral was held in the White House.

corrupt political machine, he himself was a man of obvious integrity. During the war he had chaired a watchdog committee which saved the government $15 billion. He was known for his knowledge of American history and was both liked and respected on Capitol Hill. He had won the Democratic nomination for vice president as a compromise candidate acceptable to all elements of his party. Now he was about to become the seventh vice president to inherit the nation's highest office.

Members of Roosevelt's cabinet began arriving at the White House. Chief Justice Harlan Fiske Stone hurried over from the Surpeme Court building, forgetting his judicial robes in his haste. Truman met with the cabinet members and asked all of them to stay on at their posts for the immediate future. When the meeting was concluded, Truman stood with his wife Bess, while Chief Justice Stone administered the oath of office. Afterward, Truman met briefly and in private with Secretary of War Henry L. Stimson, who mentioned that the United States was developing a new weapon of incredible force.

The new President still seemed somewhat dazed when he greeted the press the next day. "Boys, if you ever pray, pray for me now," he told reporters. "I don't know whether you fellows ever had a load of hay fall on you, but when they told me yesterday what had happened, I felt like the moon, the stars, and all the planets had fallen on me. I've got the most terribly responsible job a man ever had."

Later the same week Chief Justice Stone mused about these events in a letter to a friend. "Truman's succession," he predicted, "may well mark the end of one epoch and the beginning of another."

1 World War II Comes to a Divisive End

Stone's prediction later proved to be correct. Yet the epoch of postwar America emerged gradually from the epoch that had passed. Franklin Roosevelt had left a long shadow, longer still because he had been the only president in American history to serve a full three terms and be elected to a fourth. In 1945 few young Americans could remember living under any other president.

Roosevelt had taken office in 1933 amid the Great Depression. Millions of men and women were out of work, and a great many of them were hungry and desperate. Roosevelt pledged himself "to a new deal for the American people." He proposed to let the government stimulate the economy, and Congress passed most of his ideas into law in two bursts of legislation in 1933 and 1935. The New Deal reduced unemployment but did not end it. Nevertheless, it ended the worst hardships of the Depression years and restored America's confidence in itself.

During the 1930's, the United States sought to steer clear of alliances with European or Asian nations, a policy known as *isolationism*. In Europe, however, ominous events were taking place. In 1933 an Austrian-born rabble-rouser, Adolf Hitler, became chancellor of the

German government. Soon thereafter, he and the members of his Nazi party turned Germany into a *totalitarian* state (a government with complete power over the people). In Italy, meanwhile, Benito Mussolini had secured a hold on government back in the 1920's. In 1935 Mussolini's armies invaded the independent African nation of Ethiopia, using strong-arm tactics that Hitler would later employ.

In East Asia, military leaders had gained strength within the Japanese government, and sought an Asian empire of their own. In 1931 Japan had invaded the Chinese province of Manchuria and taken it by force. Six years later Japan attacked the five northern provinces of China proper. By the end of 1938, the Japanese controlled nearly all of eastern China.

OUTBREAK OF WORLD WAR II

The use of force had yielded some easy victories, and no one excelled at shows of force more than Hitler. In September 1939, the German army pounced upon Poland and devoured it in less than a month. Two days after the invasion began, Britain and France declared war on Germany, touching off World War II. Hitler soon conquered the Netherlands and Belgium and knocked France out of the war. In September 1940 Germany, Italy, and Japan joined in a 10-year alliance.

The three, known as the Axis powers, continued to bully their neighbors. In June 1941, while battling Britain in the West, Hitler struck the Soviet Union on Germany's east. The following December the Japanese staged a surprise attack against the U.S. Pacific fleet at Pearl Harbor, Hawaii. The United States quickly entered the war on the side of Britain and the Soviet Union.

World War II had several turning points. In Eastern Europe, the Russians won their first major victory in 1942. At Stalingrad (now Volgograd) on the Volga River, Soviet forces repulsed the Germans in a five-month siege that took one million lives. After this battle, Soviet forces grew strong, fueled by the increased output of Russian factories and by massive aid from the United States. While U.S. and British pilots bombed German factories, rail lines, and shipyards, the Soviets pushed the Germans westward by land. Nazi troops were driven from the Ukraine by March 1944.

For many months Soviet Premier Josef Stalin had urged the United States and Britain to open up a second, western front against Germany. In June 1944 Allied forces did so, landing on the coast of France and making their way eastward toward the German border. After this D-Day landing, Germany was doubly imperiled, and Soviet troops could make still greater gains in the east. In January 1945 the Russians entered the Polish capital of Warsaw. They were rapidly approaching eastern Germany itself.

FRIENDSHIP TO FRICTION

As world leaders met at Yalta in February, goodwill toward the Russians had reached a high-water mark. Like the United States, the Soviet Union had entered the war as the result of unprovoked attack. The Soviet people had shown great courage in defending their

Leaders of the Big Three from left to right: Prime Minister Winston Churchill, President Harry Truman, Premier Josef Stalin.

homeland with a great sacrifice in lives. The perseverance of Russian troops had further captured the admiration of many Americans. No one could doubt that victory was near.

Yet there was a darker side to American attitudes toward the Russians. The United States believed in free enterprise, while the Soviet Union followed Communist doctrines in which most land and business were controlled by the state. The United States was democratic in its principles. The Soviet Union, like war-time Italy and Germany, was a totalitarian state.

Soviet Premier Josef Stalin was not the sort of man democratic people could easily trust. He was a shrewd, repressive dictator who had long ago put his rivals to death. He had ordered some 10 million people into work camps,

the full horror of which would not be known for decades. Hitler had copied Soviet work camps in planning German "death camps" where six million Jews and other people had been executed.

In spite of Stalin's reputation, Franklin Roosevelt thought he had room for bargaining at Yalta. The war showed no sign of ending in Asia, and the two allies needed each other's help to bring victory. After the war, the Soviet government would want additional U.S. aid to rebuild. Under the circumstances, Roosevelt was confident that he could talk Stalin into agreeing to U.S. terms for peace.

Roosevelt was as aware as anyone that Stalin held control in the Eastern European countries taken by Soviet troops. The President was ready to concede to the Soviet Union a *sphere of influence* in that area. (A sphere of influence is a territory in which an outside nation exercises some control over internal affairs.) What Roosevelt did not want was the establishment of a set of puppet states with strings pulled by Moscow. At Yalta he bargained to allow Eastern European peoples to choose their own governments in free elections.

Particular attention focused on Poland. The British had declared war on Germany to defend Polish independence. Having almost won the war in Europe, the British feared that they would lose what they had gone to war to gain. The Russians believed, however, that Soviet control of Polish borders was vital to their own national security. Twice in this century the Soviet Union had been invaded through Poland, and it had no intention of allowing another invasion. From the Soviet viewpoint, Anglo-American efforts to achieve a measure of freedom for Poland verged on interference in Soviet affairs.

With feelings so high, the Big Three powers could reach only a vague declaration that promised "free and unfettered" Polish elections "as soon as possible."

Returning from Yalta, Roosevelt remained optimistic about the shape of the postwar settlement. In the last weeks of his life, though, his optimism gave way to misgivings, then mistrust. The Soviets signaled that they planned to control affairs in another Eastern European country, Rumania. They sent up no signs of loosening their grip over Poland.

THE POLISH QUESTION

Soon after taking office, Harry Truman realized that Roosevelt's attitude toward the Soviet Union had been stiffening. Ten days into his presidency, Truman met with Soviet Foreign Minister Vyacheslav Molotov in Washington. Truman made it clear that he and British Prime Minister Winston Churchill wanted a Polish government that would include all segments of public opinion. Molotov said that his government wished to cooperate with the United States. Truman told him that the United States wanted the Soviet Union to honor the agreements reached at Yalta. Molotov claimed that the Soviet government was

Celebrating the end of World War II in Times Square, New York. The statue is the flag raising at Mt. Surabachi and later became the Marine Monument.

honoring its commitments, and so it went. Growing impatient, Truman abruptly ended the conversation by dismissing Molotov. The foreign minister hurried away, appearing to have been offended.

Truman believed that the Russians should be handled firmly. He later said that he had given Molotov a "straight one-two to the jaw." U.S. Ambassador to Moscow W. Averell Harriman, by contrast, worried about Truman's bluntness.

Germany surrendered on May 8, 1945, ending the war in Europe. Axis attempts at world domination had cost the lives of more than 35 million Europeans, including some seven million Russians and five million Germans. Europe had driven itself to complete exhaustion. In the words of one observer, it had become "a vast, dilapidated slum and poorhouse."

Yet in the United States, sentiment for ending massive aid to Europe was already building in Congress. Three days after victory in Europe, Truman responded to congressional pressure by halting some shipments of supplies to Europe. The order affected both Britain and the Soviet Union, and Stalin raged that the action had been taken in a "scornful and abrupt manner."

THE POTSDAM CONFERENCE

As good will continue to crumble, Truman and Stalin came face-to-face two months later. They met at a conference of the Big Three powers in the town of Potsdam outside the former German capital, Berlin. By then, Stalin had apparently determined to remake Eastern Europe into a Soviet-controlled

buffer between his country and the West.

Truman tried to salvage what he could from the alliance. He addressed his most important points to Stalin, who reminded him of a Missouri political boss with the ability to look an adversary straight in the eye. Yet Truman grew impatient after two weeks of trying to get the Russians to bend on the future course of Europe. "You never saw such pig-headed people as the Russians," he wrote his mother.

In the end, the Big Three agreed on just enough points to keep the alliance together. They divided Germany into four occupation zones, one each for the United States, the Soviet Union, Britain, and France. They recognized Soviet occupation of German lands to the east of the Oder River. If the Soviet Union did not get all it wanted, neither did it yield on Eastern Europe. On the matter of the Polish government, Stalin stood firm.

THE ATOMIC BOMB

While at Potsdam, Truman received word that an atomic bomb had been tested successfully in the New Mexico desert. The British had taken an active role in developing the bomb, but the Russians had not yet been officially informed of it. Now Truman told Stalin that the United States had perfected "a very powerful explosive which we are going to use against the Japanese."

U.S. and British scientists had begun work on such a bomb in 1941. After the United States entered the war, the top-secret project had been assigned to the U.S. War Department under the code name of the Manhattan Engineering District. Few atomic physicists who worked on the program knew the details of what their colleagues were doing.

As work on the bomb went forward, U.S. forces were slowly drawing ever-nearer to Japan. In early 1945 U.S. strategists began planning an invasion of the Japanese islands, known as Operation Downfall. The plans called for the use of thousands of ships, tens of thousands of planes, and more than four million troops.

The course of the Pacific war made it very plain what an invasion of the home islands meant. The losses in the battle for Okinawa, 360 miles to the southwest of Japan, were only one indication. Between April and June, the U.S. Tenth Army had struggled mightily to take the island. Japan had fought off these forces with heavy air attacks, including the use of suicide planes. The United States had lost 11,260 troops in this single engagement, and the Japanese had lost 110,000 men.

The use of the atomic bomb was viewed by government officials as a possible way of reducing the death toll in invading Japan. With the bomb's successful test, President Truman seemed to lose all interest in whether or not Soviet leaders declared war on Japan. Instead, he saw to it that the United States, Britain, and China made one final, direct appeal to the Japanese.

From Potsdam, the Big Three sent Japan a proclamation stating Allied terms for surrender. It called for the occupation of Japan and the punishment of war criminals, but it promised that the Japanese people would not be destroyed. The proclamation made its most important point without mentioning the bomb: "The alternative [to surrender] is prompt and utter destruction."

As it happened, Japanese diplomats were already pressing for peace through the Russians. Soviet leaders were not reporting such efforts to Washington or London, because they still had plans for declaring war on Japan themselves. When the Japanese received the Potsdam proclamation, they chose to fight on. They feared that surrender on Allied terms would mean that their emperor — a god in their eyes — would be treated as a war criminal. Besides, they had no specific idea of what "prompt and utter destruction" meant.

CATACLYSM AT HIROSHIMA

On the morning of August 6, an American Superfortress bomber took off from the island of Tinian, carrying a bomb containing uranium 235. At 8:15 A.M., the plane dropped the 10-foot-long bomb on the military post of Hiroshima. The device exploded almost 2,000 feet above the city in a blinding flash. Thousands of people near the center of the city were incinerated in an instant. The blast that followed leveled every building within two miles of the bomb's center. Above the city a huge, mushroom-shaped cloud appeared, bringing rains which fell in a black, greasy downpour. The cloud would later seem a grim symbol of the nuclear age. Finally, a powerful fire wind blew toward the city's center. Many of those who had found safety in water were drowned by the waves the wind created.

About 100,000 people were dead. Tens of thousands more were dying of burns and other injuries. Many survivors were deformed

A Boeing B-29, the *Enola Gay,* lands after dropping the atomic bomb on Hiroshima.

beyond recognition. A vast section of a major city had simply disappeared.

Two days after the bombing, the Soviet Union declared war against Japan. On August 9, another U.S. plane dropped a second bomb, made from plutonium, on the city of Nagasaki, killing an additional 70,000 people. Five days later the Japanese emperor made a radio broadcast appealing to his people to stop the fighting. With his imperial decree, the fighting finally ended.

Some critics have suggested that the bombs were dropped to keep the Soviet Union from any further war gains. Others have argued that Truman decided to end the war with a tremendous display of American power that might compel the Soviets to be more flexible in Europe. Truman himself believed that he had saved thousands, even millions, of Americans and Japanese lives. "I regarded the bomb as a military weapon," he later wrote, "and never had any doubt that it should be used."

Whatever the reasons for the decisions, the two explosions soon made it apparent that human beings had the capacity to destroy not only their enemies, but the entire human race. The possibility gave thoughtful people everywhere cause for meditation.

SECTION RECAP

1. What is a *totalitarian state?*

2. What are two differences between American and Soviet political and economic systems?

3. What is the difference between a *sphere of influence* and a *puppet state?*

4. Why did the United States use the atomic bomb against Japan?

2 Reconversion America

Meeting with reporters at the White House at seven P.M. on August 14, Truman announced the nation's victory over Japan. He proclaimed a two-day holiday for government employees, and a V-J (victory over Japan) celebration began across the land. In California jubilant crowds played leapfrog down Hollywood Boulevard. In Salt Lake City, giddy westerners did a snake-dance in the pouring rain. In New York City, merry-makers fell back on a famed tradition. They shredded their telephone books into confetti, then sent a blizzard of paper swirling through the streets.

The President replaced a model-gun paperweight on his desk with a miniature plow. The plow was a sort of reminder that the first order of business was to put the nation back on a peace-time footing, a process known as *reconversion*. U.S. troops were insisting that they be brought home as quickly as possible. Eager relatives bombarded Congress with mail, and Congress passed the pressures along to the Department of War.

DEMOBILIZATION

Soon American troops began arriving back in the United States at the incredible rate of 35,000 a day. Many of them flashing grateful smiles, they thronged down the gangplanks of transport ships. Douglas MacArthur, Supreme Commander of the Allied Powers in the Pacific, pleased troops further by announcing that the force needed to occupy Japan would

General MacArthur promoted rapid demobilization.

be less than half that originally projected. His announcement had not been cleared with the War or State Departments, and it created more pressure to *demobilize*, to "bring the boys home."

Truman and General Dwight D. Eisenhower, U.S. commander in Europe, worried that rapid demobilization would make the nation look weak to the Russians. The process slowed somewhat in early 1946, but it continued nonetheless. Less than a year after V-J Day, seven million men and women had been demobilized. By 1947, there were only 1.6 million U.S. forces on active duty worldwide.

Congress had already anticipated some of the problems that might face returning troops. In June 1944 it had passed the Servicemen's Readjustment Act, otherwise called the GI Bill of Rights. This law provided funds for veterans to attend colleges or vocational schools, and loans for building homes, running farms, or starting up new businesses. The GI Bill also entitled servicemen and women to medical treatment at veterans' hospitals and made rehabilitation available for the wounded.

DEPRESSION OR INFLATION?

On the surface at least, the America that GIs returned to was not very different from the America they had left. The war years had been a period of considerable self-sacrifice at home. Cars and electrical appliances had remained in short supply. There had been little new construction since building materials had been scarce. The Office of Price Administration had issued rationing books limiting the amount of meat, butter, coffee, and gas individuals could purchase. The government had even recycled silk stockings into gunpowder bags.

How was the nation to go from such wartime austerity to a peace-time economy with a minimum of friction? Would the result be rampant *inflation*, the process by which the prices of goods and services rise ever higher? Or would the economy turn downward, producing unemployment?

In the summer of 1945, Americans could not be certain what lay ahead. Some pondered the possibility of another depression for sound reasons. Hundreds of thousands of GIs were returning home without jobs. Meanwhile, the government was halting production of planes and other war goods, throwing many laborers

A returning soldier receives a warm welcome.

out of work. A month after the war ended, the government cancelled war contracts worth $35 billion. As a result, about 10 million people were laid off from war-related jobs. After years of constraints, however, the economy was booming. By mid-1946, the United States was at full employment.

Far more bothersome was the problem of inflation. Chronic war-time shortages of consumer goods had forced people to save their money. Now they were eager to spend it on whatever they had done without. Of course, it would be a while before industry could gear up to manufacture enough consumer items. Since such goods were still in short supply, prices threatened to go up and up.

Consumers were not the only people hungry for improvements in the standard of living. Labor unions wanted higher wages, business leaders sought higher profits, and farmers called for higher prices on their crops. The various demands of these groups often brought them into conflict with one another. When meat prices were kept low, for example, farmers held their beef off the market. When controls were lifted, meat was plentiful, but prices skyrocketed. The New York *Daily News* captured the dilemma in a headline:

PRICES SOAR, BUYERS SORE, STEERS JUMP OVER THE MOON

President Truman wanted to curb inflation and protect consumers by maintaining price controls imposed during the war. Business leaders wanted the controls lifted. Higher prices, they argued, would spur production of more goods. In 1946 Congress lifted controls on everything but sugar, rice, and rents. In less than two years, prices rose 33 percent.

LABOR UNREST

During the war, labor unions had kept their pledge not to strike against industries essential to the war. Meanwhile, prices crept steadily upward, raising the cost of living. Union members believed that they deserved higher wages and more benefits, and they were willing to strike to get them. In the first year after the war, five million union workers were involved in 4,500 work stoppages. Coal miners and workers in steel, automotive, and meat-packing plants were most strike-prone.

Government officials tried to keep a lid on union demands. They predicted that wage increases would lead to even higher prices and more inflation. These officials also worried that a strike could create a crisis of its own. Their worst fears were realized in May 1946 when railroad engineers and trainmen walked off their jobs. This paralyzed the shipping of food and other essential items.

Truman went on the radio to denounce the unions' leaders as men who put their own interests above the national welfare. He then asked Congress to give him the power to declare a national emergency whenever stoppages occurred in a major industry under federal control. Workers who kept on striking in such an emergency would lose their jobs. They could also be drafted into the army.

The strike was settled before Congress could act. Yet the President's request aroused protests from labor and management alike. These critics believed that Truman's proposal endangered basic democratic freedoms. His supporters replied that something had to be done to prevent strikes from becoming a threat to national security.

AN AGE OF ABUNDANCE

Such controversy aside, there could be little doubt that America's working classes were moving upward. The three years following the war were a period of gradually developing abundance, shared by almost all. Gone were the lean years of the 1930's and the austerity of the early 1940's. Beef shortages were frustrating simply because ordinary Americans could afford to eat meat four or five nights a week.

One item was particularly abundant: babies. As GIs returned to their wives, the na-

Symbols above the refrigerator show how many hogs it took for a farmer to buy a refrigerator in 1940 and 1948.

tion's birth rate suddenly soared. In 1946 there were half a million more babies than the year before. The next year the number swelled by an additional 400,000. The trend continued into the mid-1950's. Children born in that decade would later be called baby boomers.

Parents of the previous generation had been told to put babies on a strict schedule and not to "coddle" them. Now came a new set of rules for raising children set down by a physician named Benjamin Spock. In his runaway best-seller, *Common Sense Book of Baby and Child Care*, Spock advised parents to feed babies when they were hungry and pick them up when they cried.

Growing families only added to another dilemma then facing the nation — a housing shortage. Between 1932 and 1945, only about 300,000 new housing units were built a year. As soon as materials became available after the war, the construction industry tried to make up for lost time. Such efforts took months, however, and for a time some families found themselves without any housing they could afford. They crowded into converted Army barracks or trailer camps, or doubled up with relatives or friends.

Much of the new housing in the late 1940's was built in towns and villages around the fringes of large cities. The suburbs, once mainly the playground of the wealthy, were increasingly the "bedroom communities" of the middle class. Family estates of many acres gave way to tract housing on lots of an acre or less in size.

In Southern California, groves that had once yielded oranges and lemons now held ranch-style houses by the score.

NEW BUILDING METHODS

In the spring of 1947, William Levitt began building tract houses in a Long Island potato field. He experimented by using assembly-line production and materials that were *prefabricated* (partly put together in a factory rather than at a housing site). The historian William Manchester described how Levitt applied assembly line techniques to the build-

ing of housing: "Convoys of trucks moved over the hardened pavement, tossing out prefabricated sidings at 8 A.M., toilets at 9:30, sinks and bathtubs at 10, sheetrock at 10:45, flooring at 11." Levitt's methods were effective in cutting costs, and other builders soon adopted them, bringing great changes in the way houses were built.

Levitt's homes were modest. Each had a kitchen, two bedrooms, and a living room with a fireplace, and sold for $6,990 in 1948. Although critics complained that these dwellings looked too much alike, buyers paid little attention. Newlyweds found Levittown an ideal alternative to the cramped quarters of city apartments.

A *Harper's Magazine* article explained the

A shopping center in Levittown, Long Island.

attraction of life in the suburbs: "These communities have none of the social problems of older towns, such as slums, crowded streets, vacant lots that are both neighborhood dumps and playgrounds. . . . Instead, everything is new. Dangerous traffic intersections are almost unknown. Grassy play areas abound. Shops are generally located under one roof. . . . Everybody lives in a 'good neighborhood'; there is . . . no 'wrong side of the tracks.' Outwardly there are neither rich nor poor. . . ."

RETURN TO CONSUMERISM

Housing was not the only item in demand in the postwar years. Americans were free to resume their love affair with the automobile. New cars became so prized that buyers were willing to make "under-the-table" deals to obtain them.

American consumers also renewed their prewar flirtation with electric appliances such as stoves, refrigerators, and radios. At the same time, they eagerly grabbed up an array of gadgets. Electric blankets warmed up the chilled, and electric air conditioners cooled off the overheated. Automatic washers and dryers put an end to drudgery in the laundry, and electric dishwashers made life easier in the kitchen. There were steam irons, freezers, garbage disposal units, and the list went on and on. The use of such gadgets required more electric power than ever before, and electric utility companies rushed to meet the demand.

The people who benefited most from household gadgetry were the nation's homemakers.

THE ROLE OF WOMEN

Many women found electric appliances particularly useful because they also had jobs outside the home. The percentage of women in the labor force had been climbing steadily throughout the century. Then, during the war, it took a sudden spurt. More than four million women had hung up their aprons and put on coveralls, uniforms, or office clothes. By 1945 one out of every three members of the national work force was female.

After the war, Fannie Hurst, a novelist with feminist sympathies, thought she saw a distressing development. "A sleeping sickness is spreading among the women of the land," she told her audiences. "They are retrogressing into . . . that thing known as The Home." If giving up a weekly paycheck in order to raise a family meant moving backward, many women were only too happy to "retrogress." The roles of wife and mother seemed primary functions to many women of these years.

Some women did stay on in the workplace, and many of them were in for a disappointment. During the war, defense plants had paid equal wages for equal work, but these standards were discarded. Working women were often unable to join labor unions. Many found they were earning less than men and had less opportunity for advancement.

One factory worker told what happened to her in an interview years later: "Well, the war ended. The black man went first, and I went second, and everybody else remained. We were laid off within a day of each other. . . . I finally ended up going to an office. I readjusted, but I never really liked it."

BLACK MIGRATION

The woman's story could not have seemed unusual to black Americans. Many of them had known economic uncertainty for as long as they could remember. Most blacks had supported the war effort. Yet they had been aware of the irony of defending a way of life that excluded them from the opportunities open to white Americans.

In the South, laws still segregated blacks and whites in schools, hotels, public rest rooms, and on buses. While such laws did not exist in most of the North, blacks faced discrimination there, too. They were seldom welcome in the suburbs. White families often fled city neighborhoods when a black family moved in.

Even so, World War II accelerated a trend that had been building since World War I. That trend was the "Great Migration" of black people from the South to the industrial North. During the 1940's one million black southerners had pulled up stakes to take jobs in cities such as Boston, Chicago, and Detroit. By 1950 about one in three black Americans lived outside the South.

Unlike most black southerners, the black people of the North were free to exercise their right to vote, and their votes could make a difference on election day. Increasingly, they supported civil rights groups such as the National Association for the Advancement of Colored People (NAACP) and the newly formed Congress of Racial Equality (CORE). The NAACP's membership grew from 50,000 to 500,000 during the war.

Hoping to end discrimination on a national level, the NAACP had tried to persuade U.S. leaders of the importance of the black vote. Up to 1945 this campaign had largely failed. Although the Roosevelt administration had responded sensitively to acts of prejudice of a personal nature, it had done very little to advance black rights on a national scale. Not until 1944, for example, had blacks been assigned to combat units — and then those units had been all-black.

ADVANCES FOR CIVIL RIGHTS

In 1946 President Truman appointed a committee to look into discrimination based on race and religion. The committee issued its report, *To Secure These Rights*, the following year. It found that southern law officials often looked the other way when blacks were injured or killed in clashes with racists. The committee recommended laws to provide equal oportunities in education, employment, and housing.

When Congress proved unwilling to go along, the President encouraged the Department of Justice to aid individuals in civil rights cases. In the summer of 1948, he also issued an executive order calling for equal treatment and opportunity in the armed services. At first, military authorities seemed to ignore this directive, but gradually, segregation among the nation's servicemen and women began to fade.

Two other developments of the late 1940's pointed the way to gains for black Americans. The first occurred rather quietly. In 1947 a predominantly black congressional district on Chicago's South Side sent to the U.S. House of Representatives its first black member in 16 years. The representative, William Dawson, was soon followed by two additional black lawmakers, one from the Harlem area of New York City, and the other from Detroit.

The second development caused much more fuss, for it concerned the national pastime, baseball. Traditionally, black atheletes played in their own segregated baseball league, far from the big-time status of the major leagues. But for blacks, the postwar years were a time of growing acceptance, and Branch Rickey, general manager of the Brooklyn Dodgers, moved matters along. In 1946 he signed up a

26-year-old black athlete, Jackie Robinson, to play with one of the Dodgers' minor-league teams. The next year he brought Robinson to Brooklyn to play first base for the Dodgers.

Some fans jeered Robinson, and some of his fellow players called him names. Yet the plucky Californian kept "turning the other cheek" and scoring more runs. With his powerful assistance, the Dodgers won the pennant in 1947. Robinson was named "Rookie of the Year." The team won five more pennants before Robinson retired in 1956. By that time, most Americans were accustomed to watching black athletes on the playing field.

Brooklyn Dodger Jackie Robinson coaching a youngster.

EXTENDING THE NEW DEAL

Civil rights issues represented perhaps the most important unfinished business of the New Deal. As his presidency lengthened, Truman urged completion of other items as well.

Labeling his proposals a second bill of rights, Truman called for additional public housing, firmer protection against unfair employment practices, and a raise in the minimum wage from 40 to 65 cents an hour. He also went out on a limb by recommending a sweeping plan for national health insurance. In Truman's view, a health insurance program would protect Americans from the "economic fears" caused by illness.

The 1945 Buick,
a highly desirable consumer purchase.

Given the war-weary mood of the late 1940's, it is not surprising that most of these reform efforts fell on deaf ears. The only "new deal" that interested many Americans then was to purchase scarce automobiles and appliances. The 79th Congress, elected in 1944, balked at a larger role for government. Although Truman did eventually win a major victory on housing, a *coalition* (temporary combination) of Republicans and conservative Democrats in both houses blocked many of his other ideas.

CONTROL OF THE ATOM

Even so, Congress did agree to shift control of research and development of atomic energy from the War Department to a civilian (non-military) agency. Responsibility for the atom was given to a five-member Atomic Energy Commission. Working with this organization would be a Military Liaison Committee. (The word *liaison* means coordination.) The act also gave the president the sole authority for deciding if and when to use the bomb for military purposes.

In the autumn of 1946, campaigns began for the first congressional election of the postwar era. Truman was blamed for inflation, strikes, wage and price controls, and shortages of consumer goods. Republicans sensed the dissatisfaction and coined the slogan: "Had enough?" When the votes were counted, the Republicans took control of both houses for the first time since 1928.

DIVISION OF POWER

Now power was divided between a Democratic President and a Republican-dominated Congress. Despite obvious differences, the 80th Congress cooperated with Truman on most matters of foreign policy. It also passed the National Security Act, which combined the Departments of War and of the Navy into a single Department of Defense. In addition, this law set up a National Security Council made up of the president, certain cabinet members, and other advisers on foreign policy and defense. The council was given an information-gathering arm, the Central Intelligence Agency (CIA), which soon evolved into a "cloak-and-dagger" organization.

On more ordinary matters, however, Congress went its own way. Its legislation included a tax cut of $6.5 billion that reduced all personal income tax rates. Congress passed this law over Truman's third veto. It showed even more muscle in its handling of a major public issue, labor's right to strike.

THE TAFT-HARTLEY ACT

The work stoppages of late 1945 had enraged labor's foes and even many of labor's friends. Some politicians even claimed that strikes and other actions had been promoted by Communists. A great many Americans began to say the right to strike should be curbed.

Congress responded to this pressure with a law best known by the names of its Republican sponsors, Senator Robert A. Taft of Ohio and Representative Fred A. Hartley, Jr., of New Jersey. The Taft-Hartley Act was intended to reverse some provisions of a major New Deal law, the Wagner Act of 1935. This law granted unions the right to bargain collectively and to strike. Opponents of organized labor believed that the Wagner Act had given unions too much power.

The Taft-Hartley Act banned *closed shops* (workplaces where employers were forced to hire union workers) and made unions open to lawsuits for breaking contracts. It allowed the president to appoint a fact-finding committee to decide if a threatened strike might create a national emergency, gave him the power to impose an 80-day "cooling-off" period if it did, and directed federal mediators to try to solve the dispute during this period. Furthermore, it required union officers to pledge that they

were not members of the Communist party.

The Taft-Hartley bill soon became an issue in itself, dividing friends of the New Deal from its foes. Union officials denounced it as a "slave labor law." Senator Taft replied that the bill "simply reduces special privileges granted to union leaders." In spite of his concern over labor unrest, Truman vetoed the bill. But Congress quickly overrode Truman's veto, and the bill became law.

The nation's legislators seemed to have turned their backs on the President. Throughout his 1948 campaign, Truman would attack the 80th as a "do-nothing" Congress. Yet the President had basic support on matters more critical. Such support was important, for the United States had already entered the Cold War.

SECTION RECAP

1. What benefits did veterans receive from the "GI bill of rights"?

2. What are *baby boomers*? What advice did Benjamin Spock offer parents in his *Common Sense Book of Baby and Child Care*?

3. What methods did William Levitt introduce to the housing industry after the war, and what impact did they have?

4. List two examples of progress toward equal treatment made by blacks after the war. What were the chief civil rights organizations of the period?

5. What was the overall purpose of the Taft-Hartley Act? Why was it controversial?

Senator Tom Connally signs the United Nations Charter
as President Truman looks on.

3 The Cold War Begins

All during World War II, Americans had debated the nation's war aims and wondered about the outcome. Returning from a journey to Russia and China in 1942, former presidential candidate Wendell Willkie thought he had found a "reservoir of good will" that could unify the world's peoples "in the human quest for freedom and justice." Willkie's book, *One World*, became a best-seller, and a great many Americans applauded its ideas. Some of them remembered Woodrow Wilson's proposal for a League of Nations to keep the peace after World War I. They called for the creation of a world organization to protect the peace following World War II.

In the summer of 1944, diplomats from the

United States, the Soviet Union, Britain and China met at Dumbarton Oaks, an estate on the outskirts of Washington, D.C. Their aim was to continue their wartime alliance by converting it into a peace-time organization, the United Nations. Over a period of eight weeks, they bargained with one another until they had agreed on everything that seemed acceptable to that point. Further arrangements were worked out at the Yalta Conference in February 1945. The United States and the Soviet Union agreed to a meeting in San Francisco in April 1945 to draw up a United Nations Charter.

Diplomats from 50 nations, representing three fourths of the world's people, attended that meeting. They hammered out a charter with a preamble that explained the purposes of the organization: "We the peoples of the United Nations, determined to save succeeding generations from the scourge of war . . . to promote social progress and better standards of life in larger freedom . . . have resolved to combine our efforts to accomplish these aims . . ." The following summer the United States Senate voted to join the new organization. Harry Truman signed the charter three days after the bombing of Hiroshima.

At the outset hopes for the United Nations ran high. The United Nations did provide a forum for discussing world issues, but it generally lacked authority to keep the peace. The U.N. organization might have played a larger role in keeping world order if the major powers had been able to agree on a way to do so. However, the United States and the Soviet Union kept drifting further apart.

AREAS OF DISAGREEMENT

As we have seen, postwar tensions arose from a number of causes. Stalin remained unwilling to allow a freely elected government in Poland and tightened his hold on other Eastern European states, especially Rumania and Bulgaria. On the other hand, the United States remained unwilling to extend loans to the Soviet Union to help it rebuild. Neither President Truman nor Congress showed much interest in aiding an ally that was on the way to becoming an international foe.

Late in 1945 Soviet leaders made their rivalry more apparent. They applied pressure on two countries of the Middle East:

Iran. During the war, the Big Three had stationed troops in Iran to prevent its takeover by Germany. They had agreed to remove their troops within three months after the war's end. Late in 1945 local revolts occurred in two Iranian provinces near the Soviet border. Russian leaders gave these uprisings their support. Meanwhile, the U.S. and Britain withdrew their troops on schedule. Soviet troops remained, however, resisting Iranian efforts to end the local uprisings.

Turkey. Since 1936 Turkey had been in sole control of the Dardanelles, one of two straits connecting the Black Sea to the Mediterranean. As a country bordering the Black Sea, the Soviet Union had long desired to share in this control. Now the Soviets put pressure on the Turkish government to get what they wanted. They also demanded the right to lease naval bases in the area.

In February 1946 Stalin took his case against his former allies to the Russian people. In a speech to boost the output of Soviet farms and factories, he explained that the Soviet armed forces had to remain strong to deter any "capitalist" threat. He urged his people to be ready for "any eventuality."

U.S. leaders turned for guidance to a scholarly American with first-hand knowledge of Soviet affairs. George Kennan had been a staff member of the U.S. Embassy in Moscow off and on since the 1930's and had watched Stalin's harsh rule with horror. Asked for his opinion of Soviet aims, Kennan argued that Soviet leaders were haunted by a fear of *encirclement*, the surrounding of their country by enemies.

In their quest for security, Soviet leaders believed it was to their advantage to disrupt "the internal harmony of our society," Kennan wrote. They also sought to break "the international authority of our state." For these reasons, the Soviet Union posed a vital threat to U.S. interests all around the globe. Yet the threat could be countered by using "firmness" and "vigor," Kennan argued. When the Soviets met "strong resistance," he added, they usually withdrew.

Kennan's point about firmness was not lost on the Truman administration. The nation's diplomats began moving toward a "harder line" with Moscow.

"IRON CURTAIN" SPEECH

The next month Truman went to Fulton, Missouri, with former British Prime Minister Winston Churchill. At Westminster College, Churchill delivered a speech that echoed some of Kennan's ideas. Churchill had a flair for drama that few world leaders could match. He described the impact on Stalin's territorial gains in Eastern Europe in commanding tones: "From Stettin in the Baltic to Trieste in the Adriatic, an iron curtain has descended across the continent Europe."

The people who lived behind this "curtain," he said, were under Moscow's control. He warned that unless Western nations stood up to the Russians, they would continue to expand throughout Europe. Nevertheless, he added, he did not believe that the Soviets wanted war. In his opinion, "there is nothing they admire so much as strength, and there is nothing for which they have less respect than for weakness, especially military weakness."

Churchill's remarks frightened some Americans and touched off widespread debate. Stalin called the British leader a "firebrand of war." Harry Truman, who had privately considered the speech "admirable," refused to take sides in public. As tensions continued, Churchill's views seemed more and more in keeping with the times. The words "iron curtain" became a catchphrase seen in the American press.

In the spring of 1946, the United States took its protests over the presence of Soviet troops in Iran to the United Nations. At one point in the proceedings, Soviet representative Andrei Gromyko walked out to show his disgust. Shortly thereafter, however, Soviet leaders did recall their troops from Iran.

Winston Churchill addressing the Virginia legislature with General Eisenhower to his right.

ATOMIC STALEMATE

In response to urging by the United States, the United Nations had formed its own Atomic Energy Commission. At the time, the United States was the only nation that had atomic bombs. It said it was willing to share its atomic secrets with the new organization on several important conditions. One was that a way be found to inspect member-nations for signs of atomic testing. Another was that the commission be able to punish any nation that broke the organization's agreements.

Although the world did not yet know it, the Soviet Union had already embarked on its own atomic program. Stalin apparently feared that the U.S. proposal would throw up obstacles to Soviet progress in building a bomb. Instead, Soviet diplomats suggested that the United States should destroy all its atomic weapons. They further called upon the United Nations to outlaw the production and use of all such weapons everywhere. U.S. officials regarded the Soviet position as impractical, and by the end of 1946 it was clear that talks were getting nowhere.

TRUMAN DOCTRINE

Meanwhile, pressures of other kinds were building in Europe. Amid the remote mountain villages of northwestern Greece, Communist rebels were trying to overturn the national government. For a time the British had kept a lid on the rebellion by stationing troops in the area. As the British began leaving Greece in 1946, however, rebellion flared again, aided now by three Communist neighbors — Albania, Yugoslavia, and Bulgaria.

The British, exhausted by their efforts in World War II, could no longer be much help.

Early in 1947 Americans in Greece reported that the government was about to topple. In Washington, U.S. officials linked Communist pressures in Greece to the continuing Soviet pressure against nearby Turkey . They feared that Communist victories in the eastern Mediterranean might give the Soviet Union an opening on three continents — Europe, Africa, and Asia. In the view of Under-Secretary of State Dean Acheson, the Soviets were "playing one of the greatest gambles in history." He claimed that "we and we alone were in a position to break up the play."

Guided by such thinking, Truman took strong action. In March he asked a joint session of Congress for $400 million in military aid for both Greece and Turkey. As a matter of policy, he said, the United States should "support free peoples who are resisting attempted subjugation [conquest] by armed minorities or by outside pressures." This pledge came to be known as the Truman Doctrine. Congress approved the President's aid request within 10 days, and Greece and Turkey remained outside the Soviet sphere of influence.

POLICY OF CONTAINMENT

By now, the United States had rejected isolationism, but it had not yet replaced it with a new set of foreign policy objectives. With the Truman Doctrine, though, came a new policy, formulated by planners such as George Kennan. In an article in the June 1947 issue of *Foreign Affairs* magazine, Kennan advised

President Truman denounces communism in his inaugural address.

"long-term, patient, firm, and vigilant containment of Russian expansive tendencies." Before long, the word *containment* was being used to describe the new policy.

Truman wanted to avoid the mistakes of the prewar period. In the 1930's the leaders of Western Europe had failed to stand up to the expansion of Germany and Italy, and a disastrous conflict had resulted.

Nevertheless, containment had its critics. Foreign affairs analyst Walter Lippmann criticized Kennan's article in his newspaper column for an entire month. Any plan to face down the Soviets at every point would require endless acts of American intervention, said Lippmann. The key to improving Soviet-American relations, he claimed, was settling the dispute over Europe.

Lippmann collected these columns and published them as a book. In naming the book he chose the English translation of a phrase used by the French to describe Hitler's "war of nerves" immediately before World War II. The title was *The Cold War*, and the phrase soon became embedded in the American language. Today it is the term most commonly used to describe Soviet-American relations from 1945 to the present.

THE MARSHALL PLAN

Whether or not Europe was at the center of Soviet-American quarrels, it lay, for the moment, in the afterwash of war. In the cities, many thousands of people lived in cellars of bombed-out buildings. In the countryside, women and children begged for potatoes or whatever food could be had. Destruction was everywhere—smashed bridges, downed power lines, disrupted railroads, factories that were only shells. Some Europeans sought solace in radical solutions. In France and Italy, Communist parties experienced remarkable growth.

To add to the agony, the winter of 1947 was the coldest and snowiest in Europe in 50 years. The weather brought further suffering to those already short of food, fuel, clothes, and housing. Remaining farms were abandoned; remaining factories, closed. "I doubt if things in Europe have ever been worse," said Harry Truman, "in the Middle Ages, maybe, but not in modern times."

What could be done? One American who proposed an answer was former General George Marshall, then secretary of state. In a speech on June 7, 1947, he suggested that each of Europe's governments should work out a recovery program and advise the United States on how it could help the most. Marshall promised "full cooperation" to any government willing to join in such an effort.

His speech led directly to the European Recovery Program. Nicknamed the Marshall Plan, it ultimately delivered $12.5 billion to 17 European nations. More than half of those funds went to areas hardest hit by war. In France food rationing soon ended, and Parisians could once more buy warm loaves of fresh bread by the score. Idle factories reopened, and output soared 50 percent above prewar levels. The *London Economist* described the plan as "the most . . . generous thing that any country has done for another."

Similar aid was offered to the Soviet Union

and Eastern Europe, but Stalin spurned it and forced Eastern European leaders to reject it, too. Claiming that the Soviet economy was strong enough to restore Eastern Europe, Stalin unveiled his own aid program, the Molotov Plan. It was never heard of again.

BERLIN BLOCKADE

A few weeks before Congress voted to fund the Marshall Plan, Communists wrested power from the pro-Communist but independent government of Czechoslovakia. A democratic nation was transformed into a totalitarian regime in less than a month. The Czech coup sent up an alarm to much of the non-Communist world. It reminded Western Europe of the importance of its defenses and the need to decide on the future of Germany.

Postwar Germany contained U.S., Soviet, British, and French zones of occupation. For some months the United States, Britain, and France had talked of converting their zones into a single, self-governing West German republic. Stalin opposed plans to reunite Germany. When plans were announced for a West German government on June 7, 1948, Stalin demonstrated his displeasure.

The former German capital, Berlin, was located near the center of the Soviet zone. Each of the four powers governed a sector of the city, with the U.S., British, and French sectors known collectively as West Berlin. On June 23, Stalin blockaded the city, cutting off all road and rail access from the West.

Suddenly the 2.5 million people of West Berlin were hostages to the Cold War. If the West could be forced to abandon Berlin, Euro-

pean confidence in the United States would be badly undermined. U.S. leaders wanted to avoid a direct clash with the Soviet army, but were determined not to abandon the city. Truman summed up the American position in one clipped sentence: "We are going to stay, period." To show that he meant business, he ordered two squadrons of B-29 bombers to Britain and West Germany. They were the only aircraft capable of carrying atomic bombs.

BERLIN AIRLIFT

Although ground traffic was halted into West Berlin, air traffic was not. In a heroic show of ingenuity, the Americans and British took to the skies. Every three minutes around the clock a C-27 cargo plane carrying food, coal, and other necessities, touched down in-

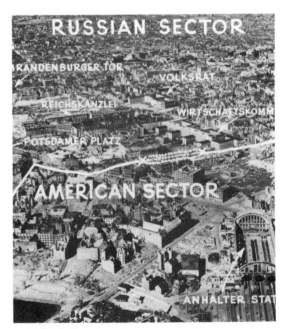

Berlin divided.

side West Berlin. On their return flights, pilots carried sick and undernourished children to the safety of hospitals in the West. Air Force fliers came up with a saying that was half-slogan and half-quip: "The difficult we do immediately. The impossible takes a little longer."

Outmaneuvered, Stalin lifted the blockade after 231 days and 277,264 flights. The United States had shown Western Europeans that it would stand by them in a crisis. The Soviet Union, by contrast, had gained very little, not even the ability to thwart German unity. On May 23, 1949, the Federal Republic of West Germany came into existence with its capital in the town of Bonn. As a countermeasure, the Soviets established a German Democratic Republic in eastern Germany the next October.

NATO AND DETERRENCE

After the crisis, Truman called for a defensive alliance between the United States and interested governments in Western Europe. In July 1949, the United States joined the North Atlantic Treaty Organization (NATO), the first peacetime alliance in its history. Dwight D. Eisenhower, the general who had commanded U.S. forces in Europe in World War II, was named commander of all NATO forces.

NATO was based on the principle of *collective security*. An attack upon any one of its members would be treated as an attack on all. Fundamental to its success was the strategy of *deterrence*, which held that fear of swift American counterattack would deter Soviet aggression. Such a strategy relied almost exclusively upon U.S. air power. In the event of war, planners hoped that NATO's ground forces would hold armies east of the Elbe River while bombers of the United States Strategic Air Command (SAC) attacked the Soviet Union.

NATO and the strategy of deterrence strengthened America's policy of containment. With the admission of Greece and Turkey to NATO in 1952, U.S. power protected most of Europe in an arc from the North Sea to the Eastern Mediterranean. Although members of the alliance sometimes quarreled with one another, the alliance itself endured. The Truman adminstration had put in place a foreign policy that would carry the nation into the 1980's.

SECTION RECAP

1. What was the aim of the United Nations? What was the major obstacle to its success?

2. Who was George Kennan and how did he advise that the United States deal with the Soviets?

3. What was the Truman Doctrine? What word came to sum up the new American foreign policy?

4. What was the Marshall Plan, and what impact did it have on Europe?

5. Why did Stalin blockade Berlin? How did the West respond?

6. What was NATO, and how did it represent a new U.S. course?

4 The Presidential Election of 1948

President Truman boards a train
to Washington after defeating
Thomas Dewey in the 1948 election.

In the spring of 1948, Harry Truman had been in the White House for three momentous years. Over that period he had made some fast friends, but also some bitter enemies. The liberal wing of the Democratic party thought he had not taken a strong enough hand in his efforts to extend the New Deal. Southern Democrats criticized his position on civil rights. Other Americans expressed a more general disappointment. The St. Louis *Post Dispatch*, the leading newspaper in Truman's home state, sensed the growing mood of uneasiness. According to its editors, Truman lacked the "stature, the vision, the social and economic grasp or the sense of history required to lead the nation in a world crisis."

The nation had not had a Republican president for 16 years. Even so, most political analysts gave the Grand Old Party (GOP) a better-than-even chance of capturing the presidency in 1948. When the Republicans met at their national convention in June, they chose debonair Thomas E. Dewey, governor of New York, as their nominee. Dewey had run against Franklin Roosevelt in 1944 and lost. As for Truman, Republican Representative Clare Boothe Luce of Connecticut labeled him "a gone goose."

The Democrat's convention the next month was something of a brawl. Some southern Democrats noisily protested Truman's stand on civil rights. "We're just mild about Harry" they sang. In the end, all the delegates from Mississippi and some from Alabama stormed out of the convention, waving a Confederate flag. When Truman stepped up to the podium to accept his nomination, one of the delegates let loose a flock of white pigeons, symbolizing doves of peace. Birds went flapping everywhere, even onto the speaker's platform, where Truman stood waiting in a white linen suit.

Undaunted, the President went on to deliver an electrifying speech. He charged that the Republican-controlled 80th Congress had failed to act in what he thought was the na-

tion's welfare. In conclusion, he announced that he was going to call Congress back into special session to see if it would pass some of the laws endorsed by the Republican platform. Democrats praised the speech for its courage, but Republicans ridiculed it as desperate. (Congress did meet in special session but accomplished almost nothing.)

MINOR PARTIES' CHALLENGE

Not only was the President under attack from the Republicans but also from two important minor-party candidates. Both threatened to draw popular support from the Democrats.

The most conservative anti-civil rights groups formed the States' Rights party, also called the Dixiecrats. They opposed every recommendation of the President's civil rights committee, including the elimination of poll taxes and an end to segregation. Most of all, they opposed what they considered to be federal intervention in state and local issues. Their candidate was South Carolina Governor J. Strom Thurmond.

The liberal challenge to the Democrats came from the Progressive party. The Progressives of this campaign were a combination of radicals and idealists who believed that Truman had strayed too far from the politics of Franklin Roosevelt. Party leader Henry Wallace, who had been Roosevelt's vice president in 1940, called for a more even-handed policy toward the Soviet Union. Within his party was a small group of Communists who managed to direct the party's platform toward their aims.

WHISTLE-STOP CAMPAIGN

But the party still had its greatest asset: Harry Truman. The "forgotten man" took to the campaign trail with a fervor few presidential candidates have matched. He crossed the nation by rail on the "Truman Special," to seek a term as President in his own right. Because his train paused at many small towns and crossings, his tour was known as a "whistle-stop campaign."

At stop after stop, he hammered away at Republicans as "gluttons of privilege" who intended to make American a "colony of Wall Street." He warned Iowa farmers that Republicans were "sticking a pitchfork" in their backs. He told consumers that Republicans opposed rent controls. He reminded black Americans of his stand on civil rights. By October the crowds were growing larger and friendlier. Some of his supporters shouted "Lay it on 'em" and "Give 'em hell, Harry." The man who had looked like a "lame duck" in the spring was winning points for his willingness to fight for what he wanted.

Tom Dewey also campaigned by railroad, but he traveled half as far and spoke to half the crowds. He had been accused of attacking Roosevelt too savagely in 1944, so now he avoided mentioning his opponent by name. The result was that his campaign lacked gusto. The Louisville *Courier-Journal* parodied Dewey's positions as, "Our rivers are full of fish" and "You cannot have freedom without liberty."

Nevertheless, many analysts were sure that Dewey would win. In late October, *Life* magazine ran an article on Dewey with the caption, "The Next President Travels by Ferry Boat over the Broad Waters of San Francisco Bay." *Newsweek* polled 50 political experts, all of whom predicted a Dewey landslide. Many pollsters stopped surveying two months before the election.

ELECTION RESULTS

On election night, reporters, analysts, and pollsters refused to accept the numbers. Late in the evening, news broadcaster H. V. Kaltenborn was still predicting that Dewey had "the best chance." By morning, however, it was clear that Truman had pulled off the most amazing upset in presidential history. He had 24 million popular votes to Dewey's 22 million. Truman had won 303 electoral votes to Dewey's 189.

The Dixiecrats carried only four southern states, the Progressives none. Truman had captured the labor vote, the black vote, and the votes of many who had "sat on the fence" until the last weeks of the campaign.

SECTION RECAP

1. What two groups threatened to draw support away from the Democratic ticket in 1948? What did each stand for, and who were their candidates?

2. Contrast Truman's and Dewey's styles in the 1948 campaign.

3. Why was the presidential election of 1948 one of the greatest upsets in American history?

4. What groups supported Truman in the 1948 presidential election?

APRIL 1945	JULY 1945	MARCH 1946	JUNE 1947	MAY 1949

A	B	C	D	E	F	G	H	I	J

MAY 1945	AUGUST 1945	MARCH 1947	JUNE 1948	JULY 1949

1. Chapter One covers the history of the early years of the Cold War. Ten events from that period are listed below. On a separate piece of paper, number from 1 to 10.

Referring to the time line above, indicate the letter (A–J) of the period in which each event occurred.

1. Winston Churchill makes Iron Curtain speech.

2. Big Four meet at Potsdam.

3. President Truman asks Congress for $400 million for military aid to Greece and Turkey.

4. Germany surrenders.

5. Stalin cuts all road and rail access to West Berlin.

6. The Federal Republic of Germany (West Germany) is born.

7. Truman becomes President.

8. The United States joins NATO.

9. George Marshall suggests a massive aid program to rebuild Europe.

10. United States drops atomic bomb on Hiroshima.

2. Define these terms: *coalition, collective security, closed shop, demobilize, deterrence, encirclement, inflation, isolationism, liason, prefabricated, reconversion, sphere of influence, totalitarian.*

3. How did the United States resist the expansion of the Soviet Union and the spread of communism after World War II?

4. What changes occurred in American society in the years after World War II?

CHAPTER 2

1949 — 1953

An Age of Anxiety

THE PEOPLE WHO MINGLED in the lobby of New York City's Majestic Theater on April 7, 1949, had come for an evening in which art mirrored hope. They were attending the opening of a new musical comedy, *South Pacific*, that had already run up the largest advanced ticket sale in the history of Broadway. The show had been created by the popular music-and-lyrics team of Richard Rodgers and Oscar Hammerstein II and playwright Joshua Logan. It was set in a fictional corner of the Pacific Ocean during World War II.

Outside, the world seemed safe but unpredictable. Harry Truman had begun his second term as President. The United States remained the unquestioned leader of what was now being called the free world. Yet there was a certain anxiety in the national mood, about atomic weapons, about Soviet conduct, about this or that event around the globe. Along with the anxiety ran an overriding optimism that decent human beings could find solutions to whatever divided them and somehow build a better world.

Inside the Majestic, the same spirit of optimism prevailed. *South Pacific* mainly concerned a French planter named Emile De Becque (played by opera star Ezio Pinza) and a Navy nurse, Ensign Nellie Forbush (played by musical comedy star Mary Martin). Forbush came from Little Rock, Arkansas, and revealed her all-American innocence in such

Mary Martin
in *South Pacific*.

observations as "Gosh, I had no idea people lived like this right out in the middle of the Pacific Ocean." De Becque was older, wiser, and lonelier.

For more than two hours, Nellie and Emile carried on a war-rattled romance. The visible enemy, the Japanese Navy, was defeated in an off-stage battle. An invisible enemy, racial prejudice, was shown to be hurtful to the people who harbored it. In the final scene Nellie and Emile were reunited, and the audience left the theater humming tunes such as "Some Enchanted Evening" and "Bali Ha'i."

South Pacific was one of a dozen or more productions that made the early postwar years a "golden age" of American musical comedy. Earlier shows had included *Brigadoon* (1947), *Finian's Rainbow* (1947), and *Kiss Me Kate* (1948). Ever since Jerome Kern's *Show Boat* in 1928, musicals had been moving away from their roots in vaudeville.

What set the Rodgers and Hammerstein show apart from other musicals was its seriousness of purpose. Unlike most musical comedies, *South Pacific* dealt with contemporary themes in a contemporary setting. It won the coveted Pulitzer Prize for drama in 1950.

Nellie Forbush became a symbol of wide-eyed American goodwill. Night after night, she won the hearts of audiences with her rosy outlook on the world:

> I hear the human race
> Is falling on its face
> And hasn't very far to go,
> But every whippoorwill
> Is selling me a bill
> And telling me it just ain't so!

In the years that *South Pacific* played to packed houses, the human race did sometimes appear to be "falling on its face." In the autumn of 1949, the Soviet Union exploded its first atomic device. A few months later President Truman announced that the United States was developing a hydrogen bomb with far more destructive power than the atomic one dropped on Hiroshima. Meanwhile, the Cold War continued to create new anxieties at home and abroad. In the summer of 1950, the United States became directly involved in a military conflict in Asia.

1 The Cold War in Asia

When Franklin Roosevelt and Josef Stalin met at Yalta in 1945, they agreed upon spheres of influence in Asia after the war. Once Germany had surrendered, Stalin promised to enter the war against Japan. In return, the Soviet Union would receive the Kurile Islands in the North Pacific and would occupy the northern half of the Korean peninsula. The United States would take control of Japan and most of the islands of its former empire. China would become a buffer zone between Soviet and American spheres.

A Tokyo train station during the American occupation.

The Soviet Union declared war against the Japanese in August, and the Yalta agreement soon took effect. The Japanese formally surrendered on September 2, 1945, aboard the U.S. battleship *Missouri* in Tokyo Bay.

MacARTHUR'S OCCUPATION

When American soldiers first occupied Japan, the nation was both physically and spiritually burnt out. In four years of fighting, nearly two million Japanese had died. Vast sections of major cities had been reduced to rubble by U.S. firebombs. Millions of people were homeless, and the rice supply was dangerously low. The people themselves, in the words of writer John Gunther, were "dazed, tottering, and numb with shock."

Douglas MacArthur, the general who had commanded United States forces in East Asia during the war, took charge of the battered nation. Although he reported to the President, MacArthur had been promised by Truman that "your authority is supreme." A willful and imperious leader, MacArthur nonetheless had a strong sense of justice and a firm command of history. He turned these qualities to his advantage, while fending off all Russian influence in the occupation.

MacArthur's first step was to get Japan back on its feet. He established army kitchens for the hungry and ordered millions of tons of food from America. He organized repair crews to get trains and telephone lines working again. He emphasized, however, that the United States did not intend to do for the Japanese what they could do for themselves. Much of the rebuilding was left to the home-

President Truman with General MacArthur.

less who put up new houses on the sites of the old.

Far from retreating sullenly from the rule of the conquerors, the Japanese people seemed to welcome it. They found self-satisfaction in obeying MacArthur's new orders. Before long, borrowings from American culture began to appear. A Tokyo newspaper ran the comic strip, *Blondie*, translated into Japanese. A "Last Chancu" gas station opened near Kyoto.

CONSTITUTION OF 1947

The crowning achievement of the occupation was Japan's new constitution. The Japanese referred to it as the MacArthur Constitution because the general had apparently written parts of it. This fundamental law took the form of a long amendment to the constitu-

Generalissimo Chiang Kai-shek.

tion of 1889. It was approved by the emperor, by the *Diet*, or Japanese legislature, and by Japanese voters. It took effect May 3, 1947.

The new constitution was so far-reaching that it seemed radical to other Asians and even to some Americans. It did away with all notions of divine rule by proclaiming that the government was a "sacred trust of the people" with authority "derived from the people." It assured basic human rights such as freedom of religion and assembly. It lowered the voting age from 25 to 20. It guaranteed labor's right to bargain collectively, and called for "essential equality" of the sexes.

Most remarkable, however, it announced that "the Japanese people forever renounce war as a sovereign right of the nation." It promised that military forces would never be maintained for offensive purposes.

The occupation ended in 1951. Japan and the United States signed a peace treaty and a mutual security pact on the same date. The latter allowed the United States to base troops in Japan indefinitely for the continuing defense of both nations. In less than a decade, former enemies had become allies.

THE CHINA TANGLE

The Japanese invasion of China in 1937 had brought a temporary truce to civil war there. Nationalist forces, led by General Chiang Kai-shek, had battled Communist forces, led by Mao Ze-dong, since the 1920's. The two factions put aside their differences to drive out the Japanese. When the United States entered the war in 1941, it contributed millions of dollars for weapons, food, and medicine.

This aid did little to improve the spirit of Chiang's already exhausted armies. Some of the money found its way into the pockets of corrupt Nationalist officials. Chiang won no major victories against the Japanese. Instead, he hoarded U.S. weapons for the impending postwar showdown with the Communists, who controlled much of northern China.

CHOOSING SIDES

As World War II drew to a close, both United States and Soviet officials avoided locking themselves into a firm position on China's future. In discussions with U.S. diplomats, Stalin shrugged off Mao's rebels as not being "genuine" Communists. Whatever the Soviet dictator's motives, he seemed ready to welcome Chiang as China's leader. Meanwhile, many U.S. Foreign Service representatives reported that the Communists were true democrats who had the confidence of the Chinese people.

The Truman administration had been advised that abandoning Chiang would be tantamount to handing China to the Communists. On the other hand, the President was determined at all costs to avoid becoming involved in an Asian land war. He felt that it would lead to an unnecessary loss of life.

Several efforts were made to coax the rivals into a coalition. In 1945, the United States flew Mao to Chonquing to confer with Chiang. But Mao wanted to retain control of northern China, and Chiang insisted upon controlling the whole country. Neither man would budge.

Between December 1945 and January 1947 General George C. Marshall worked in China to avoid civil war. Although he achieved a cease-fire, Chiang and Mao hardened their positions. Marshall finally denounced both sides and came home. The United States withdrew almost all its military forces from China.

Now the civil war resumed in earnest. In Manchuria, the Soviets supplied Mao's forces with armies captured from the Japanese. Entire divisions of Chiang's Manchurian forces were cut off from Nationalist armies to the south and deserted to the Communists. As the Communists moved south, order gave way to chaos in the cities and farms.

In September 1947, U.S. General Albert C. Wedemeyer warned Truman that Communist control of China would endanger American interests in all of East Asia. He admitted that Chiang's regime was corrupt, repressive, and did not have popular support. Nevertheless,

General Marshall inspecting Chinese Communist troops with future Chinese premiers Mao Ze-dong (far left) and Zhou En-lai (second from left).

he saw possibilities for reform, provided Chiang had solid U.S. support. The Truman administration continued to concentrate on Europe, and kept the report from the American people.

Mao's forces went right on gaining new ground. In August 1949, the U.S. State Department issued a 1,054-page *white paper* (detailed government report) warning of the impending Nationalist collapse. Secretary of State Dean Acheson argued in a separate letter that nothing the United States "did or could have done . . . would have changed the results." The only possible alternative to Communist victory was a U.S. ground war against Mao's forces.

In December 1949, Chiang Kai-shek and his staff fled to the island of Taiwan (sometimes called Formosa) off the southeastern coast of China. Chiang still considered himself the true leader of the Chinese people. He vowed to regain the mainland some day. Meanwhile, Mao and the Communists established their government, the People's Republic of China, in the ancient capital of Beijing.

Once the Communists swept into power, they forgot earlier U.S. efforts to settle China's problems peacefully. What they remembered was the aid the United States had given their sworn enemy. They set out to drive Americans from China.

DEBATE OVER CHINA

America's ties to China predated the United States Constitution. For many decades, Protestant missionaries had returned from Asia telling how they had converted Chi-

nese to Christian beliefs. To be sure, the United States had not exactly welcomed Chinese immigrants in the mid-19th century and had barred them ever since 1882. Nevertheless, Americans had long pictured the Chinese as a friendly people drawn irresistibly to the American way of life.

Now the old romantic notions had been shattered, and new questions had taken their place. Why couldn't the country which helped defeat Nazi Germany and Imperialist Japan have helped Chiang overcome a ragtag peasant army? On the other hand, if Chiang's government was so corrupt and inefficient, if his cause was so hopeless, why had the Truman administration given him billions of dollars?

The questions came tumbling forward, some of them raised by a so-called China lobby. (A *lobby* is a pressure group organized to influence legislative or executive decisions.) Financed partly from Taiwan, this lobby promoted the Nationalist cause. Its members complained that the United States had "sold China down the river."

Until the early months of 1950, President Truman's foreign policy had enjoyed *bipartisan* (two-party) support. As a result of the China debate, however, Republican enthusiasm for this policy faded.

Harry Truman had been backed into a corner. He had once grumbled that Nationalist leaders "were all thieves, every last one of them." Now, however, he was forced to recognize Chiang's regime as the legitimate government of China. Beijing Communists protested the right of the Nationalist government to represent China in the United Nations.

They soon signed a treaty of mutual assistance with the Soviet Union, placing their country within the Soviet sphere of influence.

The Cold War had divided China from Japan in much the same way it had split Eastern from Western Europe. Secretary of State Acheson declared a new foreign policy toward East Asia in mid-January 1950. Henceforth, he said, the United States would limit its protection along a line extending through Japan and the Philippines. This *defensive perimeter* (outer boundary) would presumably exclude Taiwan, Korea, and Southeast Asia. People who lived beyond the perimeter would have to arrange for their own defense, possibly with the aid of the United Nations.

Acheson's announcement only created a further furor. Prominent Republicans called upon the secretary of state to resign. Some of Acheson's opponents even suggested that he was acting in the Soviet Union's behalf. Such an accusation was the cruelest sort of falsehood, but cruel accusations were now in style.

SECTION RECAP

1. Describe the mood of the nation at the beginning of the postwar period. What part of that mood was captured by *South Pacific*?

2. What parts of Asia came into the Soviet sphere of influence immediately after the war? The U.S. sphere of influence?

3. What was most remarkable about the MacArthur Constitution?

4. What factions fought in the Chinese civil war? Who were their leaders? Who won?

 # The Enemy Within

According to a Hollywood wisecrack, Jack L. Warner had been a speaker at so many banquets that he automatically started talking at the sight of half a grapefruit. Actually, the head of the Warner Brothers movie studio didn't need grapefruits to come through loud and clear. In November 1947 he told some members of Congress about "termites" (Communists) that had gnawed their way into the nation's businesses. "My brothers and I will be happy to subscribe generously to a pest removal fund . . . to ship to Russia the people who . . . prefer the communistic system to ours," Warner asserted.

Warner was a witness before the House Un-American Activities Committee (HUAC). Amid the sort of publicity normally reserved for a movie premiere, the committee was conducting hearings on communism in the motion picture industry. The committee had summoned 41 filmmakers of varied political leanings. Nineteen of the 41 had refused to cooperate. They became known as the Hollywood 19, and all of them were widely believed to have been members of the Communist party during the 1930's and early 1940's.

Warner expressed an indignation widely felt by Americans in the late 1940's. The uncovering of a Soviet spy ring in Canada had raised new suspicions about similar operations in the United States. Was it possible that American Communists and *fellow travelers* (Communist sympathizers) had helped the Soviets to gain an upper hand in Eastern Europe and elsewhere?

Jack Warner testifies before the House Un-American Activities Committee.

SECOND RED SCARE

In the months immediately following World War I, fear of Communists and aliens had led to the harassment of many innocent Americans. Historians referred to this period from 1919 to 1920 as the Red Scare. Now, it seemed, a Second Red Scare was in the making.

In a sense, it began within the White House. By early 1947, President Truman had grown concerned by reports about spies in Canada. Not wanting to appear "soft on communism," he decided on action against any possible *espionage* (spying) within the federal government. He issued an executive order requiring checks on the loyalty of more than three million federal employees. One measure of loyalty was whether or not a person had belonged to any organization defined by the Department of Justice as *subversive*. (A subversive person or group is one that tries to destroy institutions by weakening people's faith in them.)

FILM INDUSTRY BLACKLISTING

Hardly had this loyalty check begun when the House Un-American Activities Committee opened hearings on the film industry. A parade of producers, directors, writers, and actors went before newsreel cameras to discuss what they knew of communism in Hollywood. Ten of the 19 witnesses who had refused to answer the committee's questions were sentenced to prison for contempt of Congress. In a joint statement, film producers suspended or fired all 10. This action set off a round of *blacklisting* (denying employment to people, in this case because of their alleged political views).

To a good many Americans, blacklisting

seemed out of step with the ideas of the nation's founders. These critics pointed out that the United States had long valued freedom of thought and association. Humorist E. B. White, for example, thought it a "wistful idea" that blacklisters might exercise restraint. "If I must declare today that I am not a Communist," he warned in a letter to the *New York Herald Tribune*, "tomorrow I shall have to testify that I am not a Unitarian. And the day after, that I never belonged to a dahlia club."

Such opposition might have tempered the anti-Communists, but events kept getting in the way. Now the HUAC threw its spotlight on suspected subversion in government. In August 1948 the committee summoned its key witness, a pudgy, middle-aged, magazine editor named Whittaker Chambers.

Alger Hiss (top left corner) listens as Whittaker Chambers testifies against him.

THE HISS CASE

By his own confession, Chambers had at one time been a true believer in communism. He had also spied for the Soviet Union before losing faith in the movement in the 1940's. Now he had come before the committee to identify Communists in government. One of the names he mentioned was that of a former State Department employee, Alger Hiss.

As dapper as Chambers was dowdy, Hiss had spent a lifetime building solid connections. A graduate of Johns Hopkins University and Harvard Law School, he had held various important posts in the Roosevelt administration. In 1948 he became head of a private foundation, the Carnegie Endowment for International Peace, but continued to be a close associate of Secretary of State Acheson.

At first Hiss denied knowing Chambers and sued him for libel. A number of prominent Americans rallied to Hiss's defense. President Truman dismissed the case as a "red herring" (something that detracts attention from the real issue.) After the Democratic election victory in November, it was widely assumed that the HUAC would simply drop the case.

Late in 1948, however, Chambers claimed that Hiss had also been a Soviet spy. He produced State Department documents allegedly retyped by Hiss so that Chambers could pass them along to Soviet officials. The witness then led House investigators to his Maryland farm where he dramatically removed three rolls of microfilm from a hollowed-out pumpkin. He charged that these "pumpkin papers" had been gathered by a spy ring that included Hiss.

Some of the documents produced by Chambers were still so top-secret that they could not be shown to the press. Yet the government could not charge Hiss with espionage because his alleged activities had taken place so long ago. For that reason, a federal grand jury took a different course. On December 15, 1948, it indicted Hiss for *perjury* (lying under oath).

The first trial lasted six weeks. By now, Hiss was admitting that he had once known Chambers under another name. Still, if Chambers was lying, Hiss could provide no convincing explanation why. When the first trial ended without a verdict, a second trial was held. This time the evidence against Hiss seemed insurmountable. The jury found Hiss guilty, and he was sentenced to five years in prison.

RESULTS OF THE HISS CASE

The verdict aroused all manner of emotions. Many college-educated eastern Democrats were disappointed. A number of them refused to accept the verdict, and some who did accept it felt somewhat betrayed. Most Republicans saw the outcome as a victory. They thought it proof that there *had* been Communists in the New Deal, and that some of them *had* spied for the Soviet Union.

One California Republican claimed special credit for pursuing Hiss. Richard M. Nixon, still in his 30's, had pressed the case while serving on the HUAC. For Nixon, the Hiss affair "was only a small part of the whole shocking story of Communist espionage in the United States."

Meanwhile, other courtroom dramas had been unfolding. In 1949 the Truman administration sought and won the conviction of 11 Communist leaders in the case of *Dennis* v. *United States*. The government charged the 11 with violating the Smith Act of 1940, which outlawed the teaching or advocating of revolution.

Reminders of the Cold War seemed to turn up almost everywhere. In February 1950 the British government announced that atomic scientist Klaus Fuchs had confessed to spying for the Soviet Union. Some experts suggested that Fuchs's activities had hastened Russian production of an atomic bomb by at least a year. A British court convicted Fuchs and sentenced him to 14 years in prison. His confession soon led to the arrest of alleged members of his spy ring, including an American couple, Ethel and Julius Rosenberg.

Investigators suspected the Rosenbergs of supervising spying at the Los Alamos atomic laboratory in New Mexico. The two were arrested in 1950 and put on trial the next year. A federal jury convicted them of atomic espionage, and a judge sentenced them to death. They were electrocuted on June 15, 1953, maintaining their innocence to the end.

INTERNAL SECURITY ACT

The Hiss, Dennis, and Rosenberg cases, together with the Communist victory in China and the Soviet testing of an atomic bomb set off a new sense of alarm. Congress scrambled to protect the government from further subversion. In the summer of 1950, it debated and passed an internal security bill.

The bill ordered Communist and Communist-front organizations to register with the government. There was nothing criminal in belonging to these organizations, and the bill said as much. Yet members of such a group could sacrifice certain civil liberties. They could be denied employment in defense plants or passports for traveling abroad. They could be subject to internment in national emergencies.

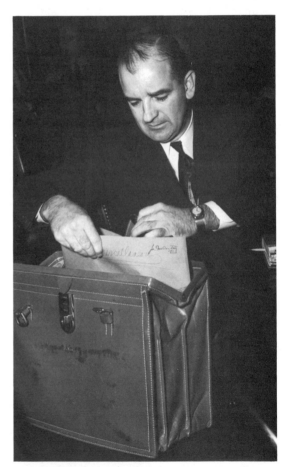

Senator McCarthy with a briefcase full of State Department documents.

Truman vetoed the bill, saying that it "was as practical as requiring thieves to register with the sheriff." Congress overrode the veto, however, and soon state and local governments were passing similar laws.

The Internal Security Act was not the only danger to civil liberties. Blacklisting was growing in the entertainment industry. School teachers and college professors risked firings because of their political views. In union halls and school auditoriums, people waved accusing fingers at their neighbors. A Bartlesville, Oklahoma, librarian was fired because she had subscribed to three general-interest periodicals.

In *Harper's Magazine*, columnist Bernard DeVoto grumbled that the United States was becoming a "nation of common informers." He stood aghast at the increase in invasion of privacy. "I like a country where we do not have to stuff the chimney against listening ears. . . . We had that kind of country only a little while ago and I'm for getting it back."

THE RISE OF JOE McCARTHY

Still, the anti-Communist crusade kept gaining strength. In the winter of 1950, it found a leader in Republican Senator Joseph R. McCarthy of Wisconsin. As McCarthy's biographer, Richard Rovere, later put it, no politician ever had "a surer, swifter access to the dark places of the American mind."

McCarthy came from a large farm family, part-Irish and part-German. As a boy, he was known as sulky but likable, a youngster with a blind drive to succeed. He left school briefly at the age of 14, then returned to finish his last four years in one, while holding down two jobs. At Marquette University, he continued to take academic short cuts, earning a degree in law. For a few years he practiced law in a local firm.

At 31, McCarthy ran for circuit judge and won. After the Japanese attack on Pearl Harbor, he joined the Marine Corps, where he was mainly tied to a desk job in the South Pacific. Nonetheless, he later called himself Tail-gunner Joe, implying that he had been an aerial gunner on bombing missions. The nickname was only one early indication that McCarthy had a talent for invention.

After the war, McCarthy was reelected as a circuit judge. In 1946 he ran for the U.S. Senate. After narrowly defeating the incumbent senator in the Republican primary, he easily defeated his Democratic opponent.

Once in Washington, the bull-shouldered, bushy-browed McCarthy irritated some important lawmakers of both parties with his brashness. He was accused of unethical conduct by entering his Senate race while serving as judge. A survey of Washington news reporters picked him as the nation's worst senator.

McCARTHY AND COMMUNISM

By the beginning of 1950, McCarthy was worried about getting reelected. In four years in the Senate he had not shown much conviction on any political issue, but now he needed a focus for his campaign. He arranged a meeting with a political science professor, a Washington lawyer, and a Roman Catholic priest. The priest was Father Edmund Walsh, a regent of the School of Foreign Service at Georgetown University. He ventured the opinion that the most important issue was the threat communism posed to democratic governments.

McCarthy brightened. "The government is full of Communists," he said. "The thing to do is to hammer at them." One of his other advisers urged him to get the facts before tackling the issue. McCarthy promised that he would.

McCarthy's career as an anti-Communist began on February 9, 1950. In a speech before a Republican women's club in Wheeling, West Virginia, he lashed out at the "traitorous actions of those who have been treated so well by this nation." Who were they? "The bright young men who are born with silver spoons in their mouths are the . . . worst." And which bright young men? The ones in the State Department, led by the most dangerous official of them all, that "pompous diplomat in striped pants," Dean Acheson.

Capping his overheated rhetoric with a dramatic flourish, the senator held up a piece of paper. He reportedly said: "I have here in my hand a list of 205 people that were known to the secretary of state as being members of the Communist party, and who, nevertheless, are still working and shaping the policy of the State Department." Actually, the senator's list was a hoax.

He used the same technique in a speech in Salt Lake City the next day. This time, however, there were 57 Communists in the State Department, not 205. He gave the last of three speeches in Reno, Nevada, and sent President Truman a telegram demanding action. Then he boarded another plane and returned to Washington.

McCarthy's charges did not draw national attention until the *New York Times* published them a few days later. The Truman administration rushed to deny them, but Senate leaders chose a Foreign Relations subcommittee chaired by Maryland Democrat Millard Tydings to look into the matter.

To the floor of the Senate, McCarthy took 81 files that he had never seen before on State Department employees. For nearly six hours, he riffled through these files, commenting somewhat absently on this or that individual. His presentation led nowhere, and Republican Senator Robert A. Taft called it a "reckless performance."

Reckless or not, McCarthy's stand against communism brought him some wholehearted support. Political contributions rolled in, and local civic groups gave him awards. Republican senators who had once shunned him now appeared to pay him their respect. The senator had unquestionably touched a raw nerve in American politics.

McCARTHY AND THE PRESS

McCarthy developed his own techniques of dealing with the press. He rigged phone conversations while interviews were underway. He built suspense by calling one press conference in the morning to announce another in the afternoon. He encouraged news photographs of himself sleeping on an office couch. For a time, many members of the press corps doted on such antics. McCarthy was, in the words of the profession, "good copy."

**Senator McCarthy before the Senate
Foreign Relations Committee.**

Press coverage brought him more and more recognition, and according to George Gallup, half the people polled thought that McCarthy was helping the country. (Twenty-nine percent did not approve of the senator, and another 21 percent had no opinion.) Meanwhile, supporters kept their cards and contributions coming in.

Responding to the Wheeling speech, the Tydings subcommittee reported that McCarthy had been guilty of deliberate falsehoods. When asked about the report, McCarthy responded, "I don't answer charges, I make them." Meanwhile, the charges he was making grew steadily wilder. Now he said he was ready to name "the top Russian espionage agent" in the United States.

The person he had in mind was a college professor named Owen Lattimore. Yet McCarthy stopped short of naming Lattimore, leaving reporters to dig for the name themselves. Then, as they gathered their information, McCarthy quickly shifted his ground. Instead of being a "top agent," Lattimore became the "chief architect" of Asian policy and a government "risk." In fact, Lattimore was an obscure non-Communist expert on Asia who had occasionally counselled the State Department on Asian matters, but his advice had rarely been taken.

And so it went with McCarthy — sensational accusations followed by bluster and backtracking, without much attention to the facts. What was happening in Congress disturbed some of its members. Republican Senator Margaret Chase Smith spoke out. She said it was time to remember "that the Constitution, as amended, speaks not only of the freedom of speech but also of trial by jury instead of trial by accusation." She was "not proud of the way we smear outsiders . . . and still place ourselves beyond criticism on the floor of the Senate."

Yet no one seemed able to stop McCarthy. In the autumn of 1950, he stormed into Maryland to attack Senator Tydings, who was up for reelection. McCarthy took with him a photograph doctored to show Tydings with the head of the Communist party. Tydings lost the election, and the meaning was clear to other members of Congress: stay out of McCarthy's way.

The echoes of the Second Red Scare kept reverberating — in libraries, schools, churches, union halls, radio and television studios. Hundreds of entertainers soon found themselves unable to get work — sometimes without understanding why.

SECTION RECAP

1. Why did Jack L. Warner testify before the House Un-American Activities Committee? Of what were the Hollywood 19 accused?

2. Who were Alger Hiss and Julius and Ethel Rosenberg? Of what were they accused and convicted? How were they punished?

3. What impact did the Internal Security Act have on civil liberties?

4. How did Senator McCarthy manipulate public opinion?

 # War in Korea

On June 24, 1950, Harry Truman returned to Independence, Missouri, for a weekend rest. He had just finished Saturday night dinner when the telephone rang. On the other end of the line was Secretary of State Acheson. "Mr. President," said Acheson, "I have some very serious news. The North Koreans have invaded South Korea."

Truman was stunned. He said he would fly back to Washington immediately, but Acheson advised him not to. The government still did not know whether the attack was a raid or a full-fledged invasion. If Truman returned too quickly, he could touch off a war scare.

By next morning, it was clear that the fighting was no raid. Artillery shells had been fired across the border, followed by North Korean planes. Then North Korean troops had crossed the border. A war was underway, one with important consequences for the United States.

Truman returned to Washington on Sunday afternoon. For most of the flight, he remained alone, mulling over what had happened and what might next occur.

Because of its location on the eastern edge of northern Asia, the Korean peninsula had long served as a pawn in the chess game of regional politics. Three Asian nations had taken an interest in Korea for decades. The first was China, which had controlled the peninsula until 1895. The second was Russia, which had interests in northern Korea as early as the 1890's. The third was Japan, which set up a *protectorate* there in 1905. (A

Exhausted American troops rest in the Korean mud.

protectorate is a government controlled by outside powers.) Japanese domination of Korea lasted until the end of World War II.

DIVISION OF PENINSULA

At that time Korea became a ward of the United Nations. It was "temporarily" divided at 38° North parallel of latitude into North and South Korea. Soviet troops occupied North Korea, the more industrialized section. The United States dominated the more agricultural and more populous South.

Within four years both powers withdrew their forces from the peninsula. As they did, Koreans established separate governments for North and South. In North Korea a Com-

munist dictatorship was set up under a Korean named Kim Il Sung. South Koreans organized a government under strong-man Syngman Rhee. Each dictator was a fierce nationalist determined to reunite Korea under his own banner.

In the winter of 1950, the U.S. Central Intelligence Agency began reporting that troops of Korean descent trained by Mao's Chinese Communist forces were flooding into North Korea. U.S. officials did not find these reports alarming. Acheson had already appeared to exclude Korea from the defensive perimeter of the United States. He had not, however, ruled out the possibility of U.S. action through the United Nations.

FOREIGN POLICY OPTIONS

Aboard the presidential plane *Independence* that summer Sunday, Truman measured the choices before him. Like his key officials, he assumed that the Soviet Union had masterminded the attack on South Korea to test American resolve. Up to now, Stalin had confined his testing to Europe, where it had been met without producing wider war. In Asia, however, the risks of broad-scale conflict were greater.

Discontent among Asians had two main sources: poverty and the hatred of Western rule. By getting involved in Asian conflicts, Truman and Acheson feared stirring resentment among the very people they wished to aid. Yet Truman's critics were charging that he had been "soft on communism" since the Communists took China. In the face of such charges, could Truman possibly avoid taking a strong stand on Korea? And if he took such a stand, how would the Koreans react?

Similar questions confronted diplomats at the United Nations. After all, a U.N. terri-

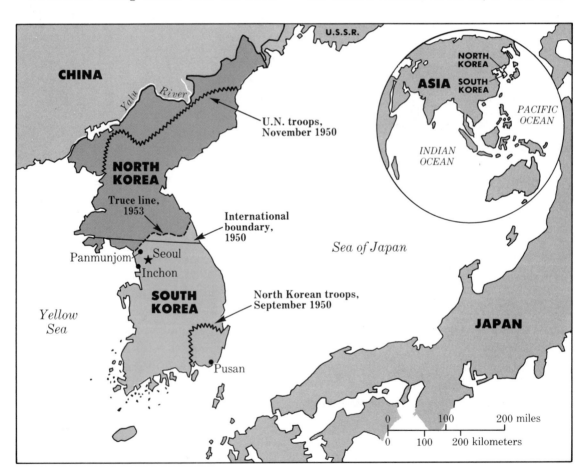

tory was under attack. Had the situation been slightly different, the United Nations might have been paralyzed. The main decision-making body of the U.N., the Security Council, could not act if any of its five permanent members cast a veto. One member, the Soviet Union, almost certainly would have done so. But Soviet diplomats were boycotting Security Council sessions to protest the organization's refusal to allow the People's Republic of China to become a member. Without the Soviets, the Security Council was free to act.

Even before Truman landed, the United States had put before the council a resolution calling for a cease-fire. The resolution also called upon member-nations to "render every assistance to the United Nations" in this regard. This move was the first sign that U.S. officials intended to stand firm in Korea. The resolution passed the Security Council by a majority vote.

AID TO SOUTH KOREA

Back in Washington, Truman huddled with his key advisers Sunday night and off and on Monday. By Tuesday, the government had agreed to lend the South Koreans air and naval support while asking the Security Council to call on member-nations to help drive back the North Koreans. With Soviet diplomats still absent from the council, the U.S. resolution passed. For the first time in history, a world organization had voted to repel aggression with force.

While decisions were being reached, Communist forces took the South Korean capital of Seoul. Frightened residents of the area clogged the roads leading south. General Mac-Arthur soon arrived for a first-hand look at the situation. He reported that South Korean troops were confused and unprepared for attack by air. He urged that the United States put combat troops into South Korea.

At first, Truman had been reluctant to commit U.S. ground forces to Korea. He feared that the Soviets might send troops, too. By now, however, U.S. officials had been assured that the Soviets had no plans to become directly involved in the fighting. At 5 A.M. on June 30, Truman ordered one U.S. regiment into combat, and he committed other troops later the same day.

Truman and his advisers had involved the United States in major military combat without consulting Congress. Some critics pointed out that the Constitution gives war-making powers to Congress and Congress alone. At a news conference in the first week of the crisis, Truman insisted a bit defensively that the nation was not at war. When a reporter asked if it would be correct to call the fighting a "police action," Truman responded: "Yes, that is exactly what it amounts to."

UNITED NATIONS COMMAND

The following week the Security Council called for the setting up of a unified U.N. military operation. It specified that the commander of this operation should be chosen by the United States. The next day, Harry Truman selected General MacArthur for this role. "If Washington only will not hobble me," MacArthur boasted, "I can handle it with one arm tied behind my back."

Despite the general's self-confidence, the job required two fists. North Korean forces kept pushing South Korean troops into retreat. Within weeks, U.N. soldiers had been pushed southward almost all the way to Pusan at the tip of the peninsula. MacArthur's strategy was to "trade space for time." He needed precious weeks to bring in soldiers and supplies. Without them, he could not regain lost territory. As U.N.-occupied land shriveled, the situation seemed grim. Yet within the Pusan area, U.N. troop strength and stores of supplies were growing with every passing week.

INCHON LANDING

Then MacArthur executed one of the most daring maneuvers of his military career. He struck at Inchon, a port near Seoul (see map on page 60). Inchon had no sandy beaches suitable for landing soldiers or supplies. Instead, it had mud flats, breakwaters, heavy currents, and incredibly strong tides. Nonetheless, before dawn on September 15, 1950, U.S. Marines began scrambling ashore. In a single day, 18,000 U.N. troops moved several hundred miles behind enemy lines.

MacArthur's troops proceeded to Seoul, where they cut the enemy's supply lines. Pinned between one U.N. army to the west and another to the south, many North Korean troops retreated north of the 38th parallel. As they fled, MacArthur cleared all of South Korea of remaining Communist forces in only 15 days.

MacArthur's victory seemed breathtaking. Now Truman saw the possibility of unifying all of Korea under non-Communist control. He authorized the general to move north all the way to the Yalu River, dividing Communist China from North Korea. The United Nations General Assembly endorsed the plan.

The Chinese Communists, meanwhile, watched with alarm as U.N. troops stormed ever closer to their border. Zhou En-lai, the Chinese foreign minister, sent word through U.N. diplomats that if MacArthur's forces continued to advance northward, China would enter the war.

ENTRY OF THE CHINESE

On Thanksgiving Day, 1950, MacArthur opened what he expected to be the last campaign of the war. Two days later the Chinese Communists came into the fighting "with both feet." In a series of bloody engagements, almost one million Chinese troops pushed U.N. forces back into South Korea. The U.N. command did not recover until the Communists were again 70 miles south of Seoul.

An embarrassed Truman administration soon changed course. Gone was talk of unifying Korea. Gone were orders to take the offensive north of the 38th parallel. By January 1951, MacArthur's troops had regained their position along the former border, and Truman was content to keep them there. Although he was not yet saying so, the United States was embracing the concept of *limited war*. (A limited war is one kept to a specific area and fought without nuclear weapons.)

Frustrated, MacArthur publicly contradicted this concept. He complained that the enemy was being given *sanctuary* (a safe or

Marine Major General Oliver P. Smith greeting General MacArthur at Inchon.

protected place) across the Yalu in China. He argued that wars were fought to be won. He grumbled that he lacked the weapons he needed for a victory. Yet he was pressing his views on officials who no longer wanted to hear them.

In March, U.S. diplomats floated a proposal for peace talks among the Allies. After learning of the idea, MacArthur went public with a statement that China must now be aware of its "complete inability" to conquer Korea. The general's threatening words torpedoed the administration's peace moves. Acheson called the statement "a major act of sabotage."

Privately fuming, Truman kept his patience. The administration tried to muzzle MacArthur, but he would not be stilled. In

April he concluded a letter to a Republican member of Congress: "As you point out, we must win. There is no substitute for victory."

DISMISSAL OF MacARTHUR

When these remarks were read on the House floor, they produced a national furor. Many Democrats charged that MacArthur was making foreign policy — and announcing it through the opposition party. European diplomats requested an explanation. The President's patience finally ran out.

Truman polled his senior advisers. When they voted for dismissing the general, Truman said that was exactly what he had in mind. On April 11, Truman announced that "with deep regret" he was relieving MacArthur of his duties. Another general, Matthew B. Ridgway, would take his place.

Truman's decision prompted the most impassioned protest of his presidency. The legislatures of California, Florida, and Michigan censured him. The Illinois Senate called the firing irresponsible and capricious. In the White House mail room, letters against the dismissal outnumbered those favoring it by about 20 to 1. Some Americans talked of impeaching the President and his secretary of state.

MacArthur returned home for the first time in 14 years. Tens of thousands greeted him at Hickam Field in Hawaii. Well-wishers nearly trampled him in San Francisco. In Washington, the general spoke before a joint session of Congress. "War's very object is victory — not prolonged indecision," he proclaimed.

In testimony to the Senate Foreign Relations and Armed Services committees, he said that he could see only three ways of ending the war. The first was to "pursue it to victory." The second was to "surrender to the enemy." The third choice was, in his view, least desirable — "to go on indefinitely and indefinitely, neither to win or lose."

CRITICISM OF MacARTHUR

Truman's key military advisers thought otherwise. General Omar Bradley, chairman of the Joint Chiefs of Staff, told senators that MacArthur's strategy "would involve us in the wrong war, at the wrong place, at the wrong time, and with the wrong enemy." The United States was not fighting to unify Korea but to deter aggression.

Truman defended his firing of MacArthur on the ground that the general had been trying to make policy. Such activities, Truman wrote in his memoirs, were out of step with American traditions. "If there is one basic element in our Constitution," he maintained, "it is civilian control over the military. Policies are to be made by the elected political officials, not by generals or admirals. . . ."

The furor finally subsided, and the United States committed itself further to limited war in Korea. U.N. forces dug in along a line that ran north of the 38th parallel. Peace talks opened in July 1951, but after first appearing to succeed, hit snags over dealing with prisoners of war. The Communists broke off the talks in October 1952.

Although Americans had been staunchly behind the war effort when it first began, now they were not so sure. A 1952 Gallup poll revealed that 51 percent of them thought the United States had made a mistake in getting into the war. Such misgivings would later seem minor compared to doubts about another limited war — the one still to come in Vietnam.

SECTION RECAP

1. Why did the Security Council approve United Nations intervention in support of South Korea?

2. What impact did MacArthur's landing at Inchon have on the fighting? Why did the Chinese come into the war?

3. Why did Truman fire MacArthur? How did General Bradley view MacArthur's strategy?

Edward R. Murrow, one of television's early serious journalists.

4 Television Comes of Age

Millions of Americans had watched Douglas MacArthur's address to Congress in the flickering light of television sets in their homes, offices and neighborhood gathering places. By 1951, television's popularity had mushroomed.

As late as 1947, only about 14,000 American homes had television sets. Screens were still small, and the greenish pictures were often blurred with "snow." Then, in 1948, the phenomenon began. More than 200,000 television sets were sold *each month*. In January 1950, the nation had three million television owners. By the end of the year, the number of owners had more than tripled.

DEVELOPMENT OF TELEVISION

Television had been a brainchild of the great age of invention in the second half of the 19th century. Soon after Thomas Edison developed an incandescent light bulb, a German scientist, Paul Gottlieb Bipkow, started tinkering with a whirling disk that scanned images. From his tinkering, Bipkow devised a mechanical way to transmit moving pictures. Several American inventors, including Philo T. Farnsworth and Vladimir Zworykin, then found an electronic way to do the same thing. In 1929 the Russian-born Zworykin produced a cathode-ray tube known as a *kinescope*. This kinescope had the main features of what was later called a picture tube.

Chicago youngsters watch a Hopalong Cassidy movie.

Two radio-broadcasting companies took a special interest in the new medium. One was the Columbia Broadcasting System (CBS), which conducted an experimental telecast as early as 1931. The other was the Radio Corporation of America (RCA), parent organization of the National Broadcasting Company (NBC). In 1936 RCA installed TV receivers in 150 New York City homes. NBC's local station then carried experimental telecasts, opening the blurry adventures of Felix the Cat.

Television sets remained crude by later standards. RCA sold them with five- and nine-inch screens for $200 to $600 a set. Installation crews hitched up antennae incor-

rectly. Skilled repair services were scarce. Owners of sets faced technical problems galore.

Even when television sets worked, viewers did not always know what they were watching. In 1939 some New Yorkers got a glimpse of the first televised sportscast, a college baseball game. Producers used only one camera, planted on the third base line. When a batter had a hit, the camera had to search the field for the ball. "We got so we were praying for all the batters to strike out," a sportscaster later remarked. "That was *one* thing we knew the cameras could record."

During World War II, most technicians abandoned television to help the government develop a super-secret new device, radar.

Right after the war, though, there was a major improvement in TV transmission. Because television waves are sent at much higher frequency than standard AM radio waves, television waves do not bend. Therefore, they could not be received over long distances without a relay system. The system used was *coaxial cable*, a conductor wrapped in an insulated tube which, in turn, was wrapped in more conducting material. In 1946, 225 miles of this cable was laid between New York and Washington, D.C. The new hook-up meant that live programs could be transmitted between two cities.

The Washington-New York connection opened the way for more extensive TV coverage of national politics. Early promoters of the medium such as RCA President David Sarnoff had predicted that TV would have a momentous impact on election campaigns. "Political candidates may have to adopt new techniques," said Sarnoff. "Their dress, their smiles, their gestures . . . may determine . . . their popularity."

Political events became part of the meat-and-potatoes of early television because they were inexpensive to produce. Stations were not yet earning large advertising revenues.

The drive for low-budget productions took cameras to boxing arenas, ball parks, and roller derbies. It also led them to wrestling matches, where they made an early celebrity of a golden-haired wrestler named Gorgeous George. G.G., as his fans called him, came equipped with 88 satin costumes and an opera diva's ego. Before each match, his valet sprayed the surroundings with perfume.

Higher budgets came to television in 1948 with the arrival of two shows. The first was an hour of vaudeville presided over by a slapstick clown named Milton Berle. Berle sang, danced, made silly faces, and did nearly anything for a laugh. Before long, he held three-quarters of the entire TV audience spellbound every Tuesday night.

The second show was a variety hour conducted by a newspaper columnist, Ed Sullivan. While Berle begged the camera for attention, Sullivan seemed eager to run the other way. He was rarely funny and didn't sing or dance. Still, Sullivan had a knack for presenting talented performers, be they ballet stars, stand-up comics, or trained seals.

Early television offered something for almost everyone. For shoot-'em-up fans, there was *Hopalong Cassidy*. For younger viewers, there was a charming puppet show, *Kukla, Fran, and Ollie*. For people who preferred gentle comedy, there was *The Goldbergs*, a radio transplant about a phrase-bending Jewish housewife from the Bronx. ("If it's nobody, I'll call back.") Such shows were broadcast live or from motion-picture film.

As late as May 1949, a majority of Americans had never watched TV. Most viewers lived in major metropolitan areas of the East Coast or California, where audiences were large enough to make telecasting worthwhile. In 1948, however, the coaxial cable began moving westward, opening up new viewing areas along the way.

Meanwhile, the quality of reception was improving. TV sets got bigger and less "snowy." There was a boom in TV sales in

1950, the year of the first rectangular TV picture tube. The networks' investments were beginning to pay off. Advertising income rose to $100 million, four times larger than the year before.

IMPACT OF TELEVISION

Television had already begun to make inroads into the home life of its viewers. "The television is the best nurse in the world," raved one Manhattan mother. "I talked with a man who had seen his teen-age daughter for the first time in two months," said one CBS executive. "He bought a set, and now she brings her boyfriends home." Yet the new appliance did not necessarily promote family harmony. Critic Louis Kronenberger observed that family members "sit now for hours, side by side, often shoulder to shoulder, scarcely exchanging a glance. Or if they do address one another, they do so crossly, campaigning for this program or that."

Meanwhile, television was cutting into time people once spent reading, going to movies, or, especially, listening to radio. High-budget radio shows were living on borrowed time. Network executives poured profits from radio into new productions for television. Yet radio had some advantages television could not offer. "In radio," funny-man Fred Allen commented, "a writer could create any scene that the listener could picture mentally. In television, a writer is restricted by the limitations imposed on him by the scenic designers and the carpenter . . . all the poor man had left was his imagination. Television has taken that away from him."

COAST-TO-COAST CABLE

On September 4, 1951, 40 million viewers watched President Truman address the Japanese Peace Treaty Conference in San Francisco. The program was the first carried coast-to-coast by coaxial cable and microwave relay and was telecast by 94 local stations. Soon afterward, networks began enlisting some of these stations as affiliates, and big-budget productions got underway.

In November, reporter Edward R. Murrow opened a new television series, *See It Now*. It came from CBS Studio 41 in the Grand Central Terminal Building in New York. As the program began, viewers could see two television monitors, both carrying live images. One was of the Atlantic, the other, the Pacific. The scenes kept shifting, but twin shots remained — New York's Brooklyn Bridge and San Francisco's Golden Gate, the Statue of Liberty and Telegraph Hill.

The great age of television had arrived, and Murrow understated it in his customary way. "No journalistic age was ever given a weapon for truth with quite the scope of this fledgling television."

SECTION RECAP

1. How did the inventions of Paul Gottlieb Bipkow and Vladimir Zworykin advance the development of television?

2. Who were Milton Berle and Ed Sullivan? How did they influence early television?

3. How did television viewing affect family life in America? How did it affect other forms of entertainment?

5 Literature: The Individual and Society

Levittown, Long Island, homes displayed a conformity widespread in the 1950's.

In a sense, television hastened a process already underway. The cultural variety of America had, in fact, been blurring for decades as people of all regions, classes, and ethnic groups competed for roles in the larger society. Now they watched the same telecasts, whistled the same jingles, and bought the same items from grocery shelves. The sameness affected everything from laundry detergents to automobiles.

As buying habits became more standardized, the nation was changing in other ways.

In the early 1800's a great majority of Americans had been self-employed. By 1870, however, only one third of all workers were in that category. By the early 1950's, salaried employees made up more than half of the nation's work force. These employees were primarily white-collar workers, members of an expanding middle class.

WHITE-COLLAR AMERICA

Most of them conducted their business from offices, the citadels of the emerging economy. Yet some critics complained that American offices were too cold and impersonal, that they robbed workers of their feeling of worth as human beings. C. Wright Mills drew a bleak picture of an office in his book, *White Collar* (1951): "At rows of blank-looking counters sat rows of blank-looking girls with blank, white folders in their blank hands, all blankly folding blank papers."

Mills and other critics asked some disturbing questions: Were Americans placing too much emphasis on status and material wealth? Were standardization and uniformity creating a drab society? What was happening to traditional American values? Was the worth of the individual slipping slowly away?

David Riesman, a professor of sociology at Harvard University, explored middle-class social values in his book, *The Lonely Crowd* (1950). As societies become more technologically advanced, Riesman argued, parents give up some of their authority to other institutions such as schools, the mass media, and *peer groups* (people of a person's own age). Riesman called this new society *other-directed*.

Riesman maintained that other-directed societies lead to stability and tolerance, but also fostered conformity and loss of individuality. He illustrated the point by telling the story of a boy who, when asked if he would like to fly, replied, "I would like to be able to fly if everybody else did."

DEATH OF A SALESMAN

Meanwhile, other writers were exploring social values through art. One of the most moving statements on the subject was made by Arthur Miller in his 1949 play, *Death of a Salesman*.

The play concerns Willy Loman, a scarred veteran of 20 years of sales trips. He started making those trips in the 1920's, when business was booming and selling merchandise seemed a sure path to success. Willy never made a fortune, but he refused to relinquish his puffed-up dream.

He raised two sons, Biff and Happy, to believe that all they needed for success was a winning style and an eye for a fast deal. His sons seem no closer to success than Willy himself. Happy is a cheap hustler, and Biff cannot hold a steady job.

Willy is tired and losing his grip. Bothered by his forgetfulness while driving, he asks to be transferred to a sales job where he doesn't have to travel. Instead, he is fired outright.

Actor Lee J. Cobb starred in the role of Willy Loman opposite Mildred Dunnock, who played his wife.

Soon afterwards, Biff tells his father that he is nothing but a "hard-working drummer who landed in the ash can like the rest of them." In an emotional frenzy, Willy takes his own life.

A friend delivers the funeral oration: "Willy was a salesman . . . . He's the man way out there in the blue riding on a smile and a shoe-shine. And when they start not smiling back, that's an earthquake . . . . A salesman is (sic) got to dream, boy. It comes with the territory."

Death of a Salesman drew immediate acclaim as a masterpiece of American theater. Willy Loman came to seem a classic example of the "little man" who thinks he can turn smiles into diamonds. The play won the Pulitzer Prize for drama in 1949.

THE CATCHER IN THE RYE

Two years later there appeared a short, often comic first novel by a writer named J.D. Salinger. In *The Catcher in the Rye*, Salinger explored social values in a very different way.

The hero is prep-school student Holden Caulfield, the kind of youngster who is often told by his peers to "grow up." Holden's trouble is partly that he hasn't yet decided whether he wants to grow up or not. Expelled from school for lack of attention to his studies, he travels home to New York City. Instead of returning to his parents' home, he strikes out in search of answers to his problems.

What he finds is that the adult world is often bitterly disappointing. He reveals his opinion of adults by telling his younger sister what he thinks of his father's profession, the law:

"Lawyers are all right, I guess — but it doesn't appeal to me," I said. "I mean they're all right if they go around saving innocent guys' lives all the time, and like that, but you don't *do* that kind of stuff if you're a lawyer. All you do is make a lot of dough and play golf and play bridge and buy cars and drink Martinis and look like a hot-shot. And besides. Even if you *did* go around saving guys' lives and all, how would you know if you did it because you really *wanted* to save guys' lives, or because you did it because what you *really* wanted to do was be a terrific lawyer, with everybody slapping you on the back and congratulating you in court . . . ? How would you know you weren't being a phony? The trouble is, you *wouldn't*."

Holden does not resolve his problems. After a while, he simply goes home to an adult world he does not completely trust. Yet his adventures say a great deal about the worth of the individual in American society. They also remind readers how vulnerable every individual can be.

SECTION RECAP

1. How did television affect cultural diversity in the United States?

2. List one positive and one negative attribute of David Riesman's "other directed" society.

3. Who wrote *Death of a Salesman*? What is Willy Loman's recipe for success?

4. Who was Holden Caulfield? How did he view the adult world?

1. The founders of our government added the Bill of Rights as the first 10 Amendments to the Constitution to protect our freedoms. As you read in this chapter, many of our freedoms were challenged during the 1950's. The First and Fifth Amendments helped many citizens protect their rights during that time. Read the text of these two amendments and the list of five freedoms below. Then number from 1 to 5 on a separate piece of paper. Indicate on the paper which amendment protects each freedom.

Amendment 1: Congress shall make no law respecting an establishment of religion or prohibiting the free exercise thereof; or abridging the freedom of speech, or of the press; or of the right of the people peaceably to assemble, and to petition the government for a redress of grievances.

Amendment 5: No person shall be held to answer for a capital, or otherwise infamous crime, unless on a presentment or indictment of a grand jury, except in cases arising in the land or naval forces, or in the militia, when in actual service in time of war or public danger; nor shall any person be subject for the same offence to be twice put in jeopardy of life or limb; nor shall be compelled in any criminal case to be a witness against himself, nor shall be deprived of life, liberty, or property, without due process of law; nor shall private property be taken for public use, without just compensation.

1. Forbids trying an accused person twice for the same crime

2. Allows membership in the Communist party

3. Protects a person from having to testify against herself or himself

4. Permits picketing

5. Allows newspapers to print editorials attacking the government

2. Define these terms: *Diet, white paper, lobby, bipartisan, espionage, subversive, blacklisting, perjury, protectorate, sanctuary.*

3. What changes did the Constitution of 1947 bring to Japan?

4. How was democracy in the United States challenged during the Second Red Scare?

5. What is *limited war*? How did this idea bring President Truman and MacArthur into conflict?

6. List three ways television affected American society in the 1950's.

CHAPTER 3

1953

1957

A General in the White House

Former General
Dwight D. Eisenhower
proved to be a popular campaigner.

PRESIDENT TRUMAN'S PEPPERY temper was working overtime that Tuesday morning in January 1953. It was his last morning in the White House. The final minutes were sifting slowly away. As he waited to leave for the inauguration of President-elect Dwight D. Eisenhower, Truman was working up to a slow boil.

To many Americans, General Eisenhower, or Ike, as the headline writers called him, was a hero. His success as commander of the Allied invasion of France in 1944 had won him wide affection and respect. "I Like Ike" buttons had sprouted on the lapels of many Americans during the 1952 election campaign.

But Truman did not like Ike. Years later, he would call Eisenhower "one of the most . . . difficult people I have ever encountered in my life."

What had stirred Truman's ire this morning of January 20, 1953, was a little dispute over presidential protocol. By tradition, the president and the president-elect rode together to the inauguration. But who rode with whom? Eisenhower had proposed that Truman stop by Eisenhower's hotel to pick him up. Truman flatly refused. In Truman's view, it was the President-elect who should stop by the White House to pick up the outgoing President. Rank did have its privileges, after all.

When Ike's car pulled up at the door, Truman waited for the President-elect to get out of the car to greet him. Eisenhower kept his seat. Tight-lipped and angry, Truman slipped in beside the general. They rode off in stony silence.

No doubt political rivalry played a part in Truman's tiff with Eisenhower. The incoming President was a Republican; Truman, a Democrat. In his campaign speeches, the general had attacked "the mess in Washington." He had accused the Democrats of having "abandoned China" and botched the war in Korea. And Eisenhower had talked of men in high office who were "too big for their britches and too small for their jobs." Short, quick-tempered Harry Truman must have bristled at that.

Perhaps, too, Truman was sensitive that a long era in American life was coming to an end. After 20 years with Democrats in the White House, a Republican was moving in.

"Twenty years of treason," said Republicans like Joe McCarthy, the Red-hunting senator from Wisconsin. McCarthy went too far for Eisenhower; McCarthy would now become a thorn in Eisenhower's side as he had been in Truman's. But still, the change in eras was what made this morning in 1953 so electric.

In a few hours Eisenhower was President. To the cheers of well-wishers, he rode down Pennsylvania Avenue in a gala inaugural parade, then watched as the marching bands and floats and elephants moved past the reviewing stand. Yes, elephants — symbol of the Republican party. No one could miss the point: The Republicans were back in town.

The Eisenhower Style

Eisenhower came to office at a time when the Republicans wished to distinguish themselves sharply from the Democrats. In their party platform, the Republicans promised new departures in foreign and domestic policy. They blasted the Democrats for doing too little to fight communism. The Republicans promised to be bolder. They would drop the policy of containment and work to roll back the iron curtain. The Republicans also warned against "socialism" at home — a phenomenon they blamed largely on the New Deal. The Republican platform promised to wipe out budget deficits and boost free enterprise.

As President, Eisenhower would abandon neither containment nor the social policies of the New Deal. Thus, he would not make the sharp break with the past that many Republicans wanted. His presidency would bring continuity more than change.

In part, this was because of the nature of the problems facing the United States of the 1950's. Eisenhower could find no workable alternative to containment. He would conclude that New Deal policies such as Social Security were essential to the well-being of the American people — and too popular to be dropped.

There was also a second reason for the continuity between the Roosevelt-Truman and the Eisenhower years: Eisenhower's own personality. Eisenhower saw himself as a unifier and healer, as a figure above petty politics. For years it had been hard to pin a party label on Eisenhower. Was he a Republican or a Democrat? In 1948 both Democrats and Republicans had tried without success to make him their party's choice for president. Only in 1952 did Eisenhower make his choice clear.

After years of military service, Eisenhower saw his duty in terms of national, rather than party, interests. His quick mind, ready smile, and easy-going manner had helped him rise through the ranks. By the late 1930's, he was a lieutenant colonel on the staff of General Douglas MacArthur in the Philippines. Promoted to general, he directed the Allied invasion of North Africa in late 1942. In early 1944 Eisenhower took command of all Allied forces in Western Europe. "Ike" was now a household word. The name flashed across the front pages of newspapers as Allied troops stormed ashore on D-Day and began pushing the Germans back toward Germany. Many Americans gave much of the credit for the ultimate Allied victory to General Eisenhower himself.

After the war, Eisenhower commanded U.S. occupation forces in Germany. He returned to Washington as chief of staff, then resigned in 1948 to become president of Columbia University in New York City. In 1952 he returned to military life as commander of NATO forces in Europe, a post from which he resigned to run for president.

WINNING THE PRESIDENCY

Eisenhower did not win the presidential nomination without a struggle. The Republican party was a split into conservative and

"I Like Ike" buttons were everywhere.

moderate wings. The conservatives, known as the Old Guard, had backed the rival candidacy of Senator Robert A. Taft of Ohio. Taft's rock-hard conservatism won a wide following, especially in the Midwest and South. But Republicans in large, eastern states considered Taft an isolationist. Even worse, they considered him a loser. The Republican convention picked Eisenhower on the first ballot.

For his running mate, Eisenhower chose a man with strong conservative credentials. Richard M. Nixon had risen to prominence in the anti-Communist investigations of the late 1940's and early 1950's. His presence on the ticket seemed likely to patch up Ike's differences with the Old Guard.

But trouble flared when the liberal *New York Post* broke a story about a "millionaire's club" that had helped to finance Nixon's political career. Nixon rejected the charge that the money was for his personal use. He said he

had become the target of a left-wing smear. Nonetheless, some Republicans began to suggest that Nixon should withdraw as a candidate. Concerned that Eisenhower himself would request such a step, Nixon made a nationally-televised speech in his own defense.

With great feeling, Nixon declared that the entire $18,000 fund had been used to expose the corruption and "communism" in the Truman administration. Nixon said he had not benefited personally. He did mention one personal gift — a dog named Checkers — but added that "the kids . . . love the dog, and . . . we're going to keep it." The Checkers speech, as it came to be known, provoked an outpouring of support for Nixon. Eisenhower praised Nixon as a man of courage, and the storm blew over.

The Democratic candidate, Illinois Governor Adlai Stevenson, was thoughtful and witty, a man of unshakable integrity. Yet his eloquent speeches seemed to annoy as many voters as they pleased. Eisenhower supporters called Stevenson an egghead, or intellectual, who could only be understood by other eggheads. On election night, the Eisenhower-Nixon ticket swept to victory. The Republicans even managed to chip away at the "Solid South," winning the electoral votes of four southern states that normally backed Democrats. What's more, the Republicans won a majority in the House of Representatives, and won an even split in the Senate.

Vice presidential candidate Richard Nixon surrounded by his family—daughter Julie (left), wife Pat, and daughter Tricia—with Checkers.

GETTING DOWN TO BUSINESS

To Eisenhower — and to many other Republicans — the federal government was like a business. It should be run on sound business principles. Who would know better than a business person how to run it? To serve in his cabinet, therefore, Eisenhower picked business executives. The only member from outside the business world was the secretary of labor, Martin P. Durkin, a leader of the plumber's union. A columnist humorously summed up the new cabinet as "eight millionaires and a plumber."

One of the "millionaires" was a woman, Oveta Culp Hobby, from a Houston newspaper publishing family. In April 1953 she took over the newly created Department of Health, Education, and Welfare (HEW). Some conservatives thought health, education, and welfare were not the responsibility of the federal government. Eisenhower, it appeared, disagreed. But he did hope that HEW would streamline government programs and make them work more efficiently.

Social policy was one of many issues on which Eisenhower and the Old Guard differed. Eisenhower argued that the Republican party had to take a "progressive" line on social issues if it hoped to win elections. He used terms like "middle-of-the-road" to describe his own policies. Frustrated by conservative opposition in Congress, he once described the Old Guard as "the most ignorant people now living in the United States." Needless to say, conservative opinions about Eisenhower were not always flattering either.

Eisenhower ran the White House on the military staff system. In order to see the President, a government official had to make an appointment with the White House chief of staff, Sherman Adams. Even cabinet members had to go "through channels."

Eisenhower found it easier to deal with his subordinates than with the press. At news conferences, his answers often rambled on until both he and the reporters seemed to have forgotten the original point. One of Eisenhower's aides later described him as "a little like a debate come to life." The public didn't seem to mind, however. Year after year, Eisenhower scored high in the opinion polls.

He won active public sympathy in September 1955, when he suffered a heart attack while on vacation in Colorado. For a time, people wondered if Vice President Nixon might have to take over. But Eisenhower's staff system kept the wheels of government turning smoothly, and the President made a full recovery.

SECTION RECAP

1. Identify two reasons the Eisenhower presidency did not bring about the changes the Republican party wanted in 1952.

2. What was the Old Guard?

3. Why was Richard Nixon considered a good running mate for Eisenhower? Why did he deliver his Checkers Speech, and what was its effect?

2 "New Look" Foreign and Defense Policies

President Eisenhower addresses the United Nations
General Assembly on the peaceful use of nuclear energy.

Republicans had made sweeping charges against the foreign and defense policies of the Democrats: Roosevelt had "sold out" Poland at Yalta; Truman had "lost" China to the Communists and had bogged down in a "no-win" war in Korea; Communists were advancing, the free world was retreating; and American taxpayers were groaning under the high taxes needed to finance massive military spending and foreign "giveaways." The Republicans pledged to take a "new look" at such policies and seize the initiative in world affairs.

To preside over the State Department, President Eisenhower appointed an international lawyer named John Foster Dulles. For six and a half years, until his death in 1959, Dulles put his own distinctive stamp on U.S. foreign policy.

BRINKMANSHIP

Dulles was an experienced diplomat long before becoming secretary of state. In 1945 he had been a U.S. delegate to the San Francisco conference that created the United Nations. In 1951 he had been the chief architect of the U.S.-Japanese peace treaty.

Dulles took a sternly moralistic view of world affairs. The son of a Presbyterian minister, he saw the Cold War as a spiritual as well as ideological clash. On one side stood Soviet communism, based on "an atheistic, Godless premise." On the other side stood the forces of freedom and faith.

Dulles saw the policy of containment as a futile attempt to live with the Communist peril rather than try to end it. In his 1950 book *War or Peace*, Dulles wrote: "It is time to think in terms of taking the offensive in the

Civilian Defense observers in special glasses watch the explosion of an atomic bomb in the Nevada desert seven and a half miles away.

world struggle for freedom and rolling back the engulfing tide of despotism."

In the 1952 Republican platform, which he helped to shape, Dulles assailed "the negative, futile, and immoral policy of 'containment.'" The platform promised to "revive the contagious, liberating influences which are inherent in freedom." And it pledged to "repudiate all commitments contained in secret understandings such as Yalta which aid Communist enslavements."

Many conservatives were convinced that Roosevelt had made secret agreements with Stalin at Yalta in 1945. They thought Roosevelt had thus cooperated in the "enslavement" of Poland and Eastern Europe. Upon becoming secretary of state, Dulles searched government files for evidence of such accords. He found none, and dropped the subject.

Likewise, the new administration eventually came to reluctant acceptance of containment as the lesser of two evils. It concluded that *rollback* — the policy of working to roll back the iron curtain — was more likely to lead to a devastating world war than to an expansion of freedom.

Nonetheless, U.S. foreign policy did take on a new look in 1953. Dulles lost no opportunity to berate the Soviets or to reaffirm the U.S. commitment to "liberation." Neither did he shy away from open confrontation with Communist (especially Chinese) power. In a controversial 1956 interview, Dulles citied three instances in which, he said, U.S. threats of military force had caused the Chinese Communists to back down. "You have to take chances for peace," he said. "The ability to get to the verge without getting into war is the necessary art. . . . We walked to the brink and we looked it in the face." From then on, observers applied the term *brinkmanship* to Dulles's methods of militancy and confrontation. The methods sharply divided the U.S. public. Some praised Dulles for his courage and others denounced him as reckless and dangerous.

A BIGGER BANG FOR THE BUCK

Hand in hand with brinkmanship went a stronger emphasis on nuclear weapons. The Eisenhower administration wanted to boost U.S. power while cutting costs. Therefore, it slashed the size of ground forces and built up the U.S. bomber fleet. An Air Force Academy opened in Colorado to prepare for the new stress on air power. Dulles warned that the United States would not hesitate to use nuclear weapons to respond to *any* Communist aggression. This policy was known as *massive retaliation.*

For most people, the new policy was summed up by the slogan, "A bigger bang for a buck." Democrats such as Stevenson complained that the administration was putting dollars before defense.

The nuclear arms race was much on people's minds during the early 1950's. In November 1952 the United States tested its first hydrogen bomb — hundreds of times more powerful than the atomic bomb dropped on Hiroshima. Soon the Soviets had tested an H-bomb. Britain had developed its own A-bomb, and French and Chinese scientists were hard at work on A-bombs too. Experts warned against the dangers of *nuclear proliferation* — the spread of nuclear weapons. The more countries that had such weapons, the greater the danger of nuclear war, the experts said.

At a desert testing site in Nevada, and on isolated islands in the Pacific, U.S. officials set off the new bombs to test their effects. Residents of desert cities learned to live with the dull thuds and flashes of nuclear tests. Some took advantage of their nearness to the test sites to sell "nuclear souvenirs" and "uranium burgers." But many people worried about the dangers of nuclear war. Sales of backyard bomb shelters soared.

During test explosions, soldiers huddled in trenches as close as two miles to ground zero. They gazed in awe at the brilliant fireball that towered high in the air. They detected a raw, metallic taste and a smell like that of overheated electric wires. Authorities assured the men that they had nothing to fear from radiation, and ordered them to charge forward into the swirling dust.

U.S. officials felt that such tests and maneuvers were crucial to defense. In 1955 a classified report declared: "The public will need indoctrination to accustom themselves to the fact that low levels of radiation can and must be lived with." But some scientists disagreed. They argued that radiation in any amount posed a danger. During the 1970's and 1980's, U.S. courts would begin to weigh the claims of soldiers and civilians who sued the government, saying they had developed cancer and other ailments because of exposure to radiation during the tests of the 1950's.

TRUCE IN KOREA

During his campaign, Eisenhower had pledged to go to Korea and to bring the war to "an early and honorable end." Soon after the election, and before becoming President, Eisenhower did fly to Korea. He met with U.S. commanders and discussed various strategies.

Eisenhower and Dulles settled on a "peace or else" policy. Early in 1953 they ordered stepped-up air attacks on North Korea. Meanwhile, they privately dropped hints to Chinese leaders that if progress toward a truce didn't come soon, the United States might send its bombers across the Chinese border — perhaps armed with nuclear weapons.

In June 1953 the warring sides agreed to a truce. After three years of fighting and perhaps a million deaths, including those of 33,000 U.S. soldiers and 400,000 Korean civilians, the fighting halted with neither side able to claim victory. Korea remained divided roughly at the 38th parallel.

Although peace talks went on, no final peace treaty was ever signed. Hostile armies continued to face each other across a narrow demilitarized zone. The United States kept some 40,000 soldiers in South Korea. The soldiers were still there in the late 1980's.

The Eisenhower-Dulles policy toward Korea set a pattern for the years that followed. Tough talk and negotiations would go hand in hand.

EYES ON ASIA

Many Republican conservatives had accused the Truman administration of ignoring Asia while lavishing U.S. aid on Europe. They had questioned the value of the NATO alliance. They had mourned the loss of China to the Communists.

Republican conservatives hoped that Chiang Kai-shek's Nationalist forces would invade mainland China. The Nationalists had a large army in Taiwan, bolstered by U.S. aid. At the start of the Korean war, the United States had stationed its Seventh Fleet between Taiwan and the mainland. The fleet was there partly to protect the Nationalists and partly to keep Chiang from invading the mainland and touching off a wider war.

Chiang's supporters wanted the Seventh Fleet pulled back. They were certain Chiang could now oust the Communists. At the very least, they felt, Chiang could tie down Chinese troops so they would no longer cause trouble in Korea or elsewhere. Chiang's supporters called for U.S. leaders to "unleash" Chiang.

Early in 1953, fulfilling a promise in the Republican platform, Eisenhower ordered the Seventh Fleet not to interfere with any Nationalist operations against the mainland. However, Chiang was not so strong as his supporters believed. He made limited attacks along the fringes of the mainland.

In late 1954 and early 1955, a major crisis erupted when Chinese Communist troops began bombarding some small, Nationalist-held islands in the Formosa Strait, between the mainland and Taiwan. The main islands under attack were Quemoy and Matsu. In response, the United States signed a long-planned mutual defense treaty with Chiang's Nationalists. But it insisted on "releashing"

Chiang by assuming a veto over Nationalist attacks on the mainland. Early in 1955 Congress approved the Formosa Resolution granting the President power to use U.S. armed forces "as he deems necessary" to defend the Chinese nationalists. In time, the bombing ended and the crisis died down.

VIETNAM: CHAPTER ONE

Meanwhile, U.S. attention had been drawn to another part of Asia: the French-held territory of Indochina. Indochina consisted of three parts — Vietnam, Laos, and Cambodia. The Japanese had occupied it during World War II. In 1945, before the French could regain control, a Vietnamese nationalist group known as the Vietminh had issued a declaration of independence, which France refused to recognize. French leaders sent troops to put down the Vietminh, but it was not easy. Although poorly armed and sometimes barefoot, the Vietminh more than held their own. By

1954 they surrounded the main body of French troops in the fortress of Dienbienphu.

At the end of World War II, U.S. leaders had been hostile to French colonial rule in Asia. Those attitudes changed, however. The Vietminh leader, Ho Chi Minh, was an outspoken Communist. U.S. leaders saw the Vietnam fighting as part of a worldwide Communist offensive. In 1950 they began sending military aid to the French troops. By 1954 the United States was footing 78 percent of the bill for the French war effort in Vietnam.

What would happen if Vietnam, like China, fell to the Communists? Eisenhower told a news conference in 1954 that the effects might be far-reaching. Vietnam was the first of a row of dominoes. If it fell, it would tip over the next domino, then the next, and the next. The *domino theory*, as it was called, foresaw the rapid communization of much of Asia if even one domino should fall.

U.S. officials worked up a variety of plans for rescuing Dienbienphu. They contemplated

Vietnamese troops cross a bridge in Tonkin.

using U.S. ground troops or even nuclear weapons. But congressional leaders were reluctant to support U.S. intervention. Thinking that Congress might change its mind if Britain and the United States intervened jointly, Dulles asked Britain for help. However, British leaders did not believe in the domino theory. They saw the war against the French as a limited Vietnamese nationalist and Communist uprising and said no. The United States did not directly intervene.

On May 7, 1954, Dienbienphu surrendered to the Vietminh. At an international conference in Geneva, Switzerland, shortly thereafter, France agreed to Vietnamese, Cambodian, and Laotian independence. Vietnam would be split in two. North Vietnam would be under Vietminh control. South Vietnam would be ruled by the French-backed, anti-Communist government of Ngo Dinh Diem. The Geneva agreements specified that free elections would be held in 1956 to reunite the two parts. Then Vietnam would be independent.

Before the end of 1954, the United States organized the Southeast Asia Treaty Organization (SEATO), an anti-Communist alliance. The members were Australia, Great Britain, France, New Zealand, Pakistan, the Philippines, Thailand, and the United States.

Meanwhile, the United States relieved France as the protector and supplier of anti-Communist forces in Vietnam. In 1956 the South Vietnamese government, aware of the weakness of of its support, refused to hold reunification elections. Soon guerrilla warfare broke out against the Diem government in South Vietnam. U.S. military advisers helped train South Vietnamese soldiers, but the United States did not send combat troops.

By 1959, U.S. intelligence agents were reporting growing North Vietnamese support for the guerrillas. On July 8, 1959, a guerrilla tossed a bomb into a South Vietnamese military base, and two U.S. soldiers died. They were the first U.S. fatalities in what would later become a major war. As long as Eisenhower was in office, however, U.S. involvement in South Vietnam would remain limited.

DEALING WITH ALLIES

In trying to line up support for U.S. actions, Secretary of State Dulles sometimes stepped on toes. His brusk manner and relentless anti-communism often annoyed the leaders of allied powers such as Britain and France. During the Dienbienphu crisis of 1954, British Foreign Secretary Anthony Eden complained that "Americans may think the time past when they need consider the feelings or difficulties of their allies. This tendency . . . is creating mounting difficulties for anyone in this country who wants to maintain close Anglo-American relations."

In most cases, Dulles managed to soothe ruffled feelings and win agreement on a common course of action. In 1954 he persuaded NATO to admit West Germany, despite ingrained French fears of German strength. The NATO allies agreed to West German rearmament, with certain safeguards. In response, the Soviet Union formed a military alliance called the Warsaw Pact with seven of Eastern Europe's Communist nations in 1955.

John Foster Dulles, who designed much of U.S. foreign policy during the Eisenhower years.

CRISIS IN THE MIDEAST

The great test for allied unity came the next year, when a crisis shook the Mideast. That area had been a hotbed of trouble ever since World War I, when the Ottoman (or Turkish) Empire crumbled and Britain and France picked up the pieces. The British took over an area known as Palestine, which contained some of the holiest places of Judaism, Christianity, and Islam.

Between 1917 and 1948, large numbers of Jews migrated to Palestine from Europe and Asia. They hoped to reestablish a Jewish homeland in the biblical land of Zion. At first, British officials encouraged the Zionist movement, as it was called. But Arab Muslims and Christians, already living in Palestine, feared that they would be pushed aside. In the face of Arab protests, Britain began to restrict the influx of Zionists in the late 1930's. Communal violence erupted in Palestine. Both Arabs and Jews resorted to terrorism, and each group formed underground armies. Turmoil grew as thousands of Jewish immigrants, fleeing the Nazi death campaign of World War II, evaded British patrols and found refuge in Palestine.

Finally, Britain dumped the problem in the lap of the United Nations. In 1948 the General Assembly recommended partition (division) of Palestine into Zionist and Arab states — a solution that Arabs rejected. Over Arab objections, Britain withdrew, and Zionist leaders announced the creation of the Jewish state of Israel. Both the United States and the Soviet Union granted recognition.

Almost at once neighboring Arab countries joined Arab Palestinian armies in attacking

Israel. Israel won the war of 1948, expanding its territory to include more of Palestine. But hundreds of thousands of Arab Palestinians became refugees, vowing one day to reclaim their homeland. Arab-Israeli tensions remained high. Arab leaders vowed never to accept Israel.

By the mid-1950's, one of the most outspoken Arab leaders against Israel was Gamel Abdel Nasser, the military ruler of Egypt. In ringing speeches broadcast over Radio Cairo, Nasser urged all Arabs to unite in one great nation. Nasser's doctrine of "pan-Arab nationalism" had a wide appeal among Arabs. Nasser professed two main goals. One was to destroy Israel and win back the Palestinian homeland. The other was to free the Arab world of Western colonialism.

Although Nasser described himself as neutral in the Cold War, both the United States and the Soviet Union tried to win his sympathy. The United States offered to help pay for a major Egyptian project, the Aswan High Dam. But in July 1956, Secretary of State Dulles withdrew the offer after Nasser had bought arms from Communist Czechoslovakia and recognized Communist China. Angrily, Nasser declared Egypt would pay for the dam itself. It would *nationalize* (assume ownership of) the Suez Canal and use the revenues from the canal's tolls.

Thus began the Suez Crisis of 1956. Although the Suez Canal passed directly through Egypt, the waterway had been under British and French control since it was built in the 1870's. British arms guarded the canal, which was a vital lifeline for oil shipments from the Persian Gulf to Western Europe. By taking over the canal, Nasser could claim to be striking a blow against colonialism. He could also claim to be acting under international law.

British and French leaders took Nasser's action as a direct challenge. They argued that the canal was too important to fall into non-Western hands. Israeli leaders, too, were worried that Nasser was growing stronger and might soon challenge Israel militarily. Therefore, Britain, France, and Israel cooperated in a joint attack on Egypt. On October 29, 1956, Israeli troops invaded from the east. British and French forces launched bombing raids, then landed along the canal. They were too late, however, to prevent Egypt from sinking ships to block the canal.

Dismayed, Eisenhower and Dulles denounced the joint attack. Eisenhower called the allied action at Suez unlawful and demanded that Britain, France and Israel withdraw their troops. Other nations also voiced outrage. Soviet leaders threatened rocket strikes. Faced with such wide condemnation, the invading nations halted their attack. A United Nations Emergency Force separated the warring forces, and the invaders, urgently in need of oil, agreed to withdraw. Nasser maintained control of the canal.

U.S. relations with the British and French had suffered a major setback. In time, however, the wounds healed. With Soviet help, Egypt would complete the Aswan High Dam by 1971. The Middle East remained a hot spot, and the United States became the most important Western influence there.

An Egyptian ship being overhauled
while Egypt controlled the Suez Canal.

RISE OF THE THIRD WORLD

Nasser was one of a new breed of leaders emerging in Asia and Africa, in what came to be called the Third World. Colonial rule was crumbling. Newly independent countries such as Indonesia were appearing. Old countries like Egypt were asserting their independence more forcefully.

The colonial nations of Western Europe no longer had the power to maintain their empires. Britain had begun to prepare many of its colonies for independence. France was willing to allow the independence of Morocco and Tunisia. After losing Indochina, however, France was determined to hold the North African territory of Algeria with its large numbers of French settlers. A war of independence broke out there in 1954.

In 1955 Nasser joined the leaders of 28 other Asian and African countries at a conference in Bandung, Indonesia. The participants declared that "colonialism in all its manifestations is an evil which should speedily be brought to an end." They vowed to oppose colonialism while taking a neutral position in the Cold War.

U.S. leaders viewed the Bandung Conference with suspicion — partly because Communist China was an active participant. Was "neutralism" a front for pro-communism? Many Americans thought so. In 1956 Secretary of State Dulles declared: "Except under very exceptional circumstance, [neutralism] is an immoral and shortsighted conception."

HOLDING THE LINE

In Dulles's eyes, the Cold War conditioned all aspects of world diplomacy. He wanted to woo as many nations as possible to sign mutual defense pacts with the United States. By the time Dulles died, the United States was bound by such pacts to defend 42 nations around the world. Critics accused him of "pactomania." Was it wise, they asked, for the United States to undertake to defend so many nations? Dulles insisted that it was essential; the pacts were an important way to hold the line against Communist expansion.

Under Eisenhower and Dulles, the United States also undertook covert (secret) actions to overthrow governments it considered to be pro-Communist. U.S. agents helped to overthrow the premier of Iran in 1953 and restore the control of the Iranian emperor, or shah. In 1954 U.S. agents supplied Guatemalan rebels, who overthrew an elected government that U.S. officials considered pro-Communist. In each case, officials publicly denied any U.S. involvement.

Much later, when U.S. covert actions became public knowledge, Americans were divided. Some argued that the actions had been wrong. They accused U.S. leaders of imposing repressive governments on other nations, of stifling needed social reforms in the name of

The Big Four—Soviet Premier Nikolai Bulganin, Eisenhower, French Premier Edgar Faure, and British Prime Minister Anthony Eden—at Geneva in 1955.

anti-communism. Others argued that such covert actions had been necessary to block outright Communist takeovers. They said the United States must be alert to the danger of Communists masquerading as social reformers in developing nations.

THAW IN THE COLD WAR?

While concern about communism remained high, signs were appearing of a possible thaw in the Cold War. Josef Stalin, the Soviet dictator, died in March 1953. His successors seemed eager to make a new beginning. They began to talk about the possibility of "peaceful coexistence" between the two superpowers.

Dulles was profoundly suspicious of Soviet intentions. He described Communist peace talk as phony and urged that the United States keep the pressure on. Eisenhower, however, was willing to explore ways of easing tensions. Responding to appeals from U.S. allies in Europe, he agreed to meet Soviet leaders in four-power talks at Geneva in July 1955.

The Geneva Summit, as it was called, marked the first real lessening of Cold War tensions. But the "Spirit of Geneva" had little practical effect. U.S. and Soviet positions remained far apart on such issues as the future of Germany and the nuclear arms race.

A new burst of tension occurred in 1956. One cause was the Suez invasion, which provoked Soviet threats against Britain and France. A second cause was a revolt that broke out about the same time in the Communist East European nation of Hungary. A reform-minded Communist government came to power and announced that it would pull Hungary out of the Soviet-led Warsaw Pact. Unwilling to permit such defiance, Soviet leaders sent troops and tanks into the Hungarian capital, Budapest. The U.S.-financed Radio Free Europe urged Hungarians to resist, but U.S. officials made no move to intervene with force. Soviet troops soon crushed the rebellion and arrested its leaders.

Had the administration abandoned its desire to promote the "liberation" of "captive nations"? No, not at all. But U.S. leaders had become very cautious. By 1956 it was apparent to all that the United States had lost its nuclear monopoly. Both superpowers were so heavily armed that the world now lived in what was being called a balance of terror. Under the circumstances, U.S. leaders concluded that open intervention in East European affairs would bring too high a risk of all-out war.

SECTION RECAP

1. What was the Eisenhower/Dulles policy on the Korean War? How did it affect the outcome?

2. What was the *domino theory*? What events prompted the United States to first become involved in the Vietnam War?

3. Why was the Suez Canal important to Western Europe? Why did Egyptian President Nasser want to control it?

4. What are *covert actions*? What were the arguments for and against the United States taking part in such activities?

3 The Domestic Scene

President Eisenhower relaxing on the golf course.

After the urbane activism of Franklin D. Roosevelt and the middle-class pluck of Harry S. Truman, "old soldier" Dwight D. Eisenhower seemed bland and unexciting to many people. He brought no sweeping vision of social change to the White House. Rather, he brought a set of golf clubs and a bookshelf of Wild West tales — or so it seemed. Writing in May 1953, a reporter described the popular conception of Eisenhower as that of "a man whanging golf balls at the White House back fence while history flows about him."

Many at the time felt that assessment to be unfair, and historians later agreed. Eisenhower had his own vision of America's future, and he worked hard to bring it about. Eisenhower believed, as did businessmen with whom he played golf and traded jokes, that the U.S. government had become bloated and oppressive. He wanted it trimmer, leaner. His administration would find "things it can stop doing rather than new things for it to do," he said.

CREEPING SOCIALISM

Eisenhower deplored some government programs as signs of "creeping socialism." He sought — with limited success — to cut back public power programs like the Tennessee Valley Authority (TVA). In place of public power, Eisenhower promoted private power. Over Democratic opposition, he got Congress to end a government monopoly on nuclear technology that dated to the early 1940's. In 1954 the people of Shippingport, Pennsylvania, saw work begin on the nation's first commercial nuclear power plant.

Moreover, Eisenhower insisted on major cuts in the national budget, laying off federal workers and slashing military spending. In 1954 the Republican-led Congress thoroughly revised the federal income tax code. It introduced deductions for medical expenses and raised other deductions, thus lowering taxes for both individuals and businesses. For the next several decades, the 1954 law set the basic framework for U.S. tax procedures.

But Eisenhower was not one of those Old Guard Republicans who wanted to "repeal the New Deal." In his 1952 campaign, he had praised "the social gains achieved by the people of the United States." Those gains, he said, "are not only here to stay, but here to be improved and extended."

Eisenhower worried that many voters still blamed "do-nothing Republicans" for the Great Depression of the 1930's. Under Eisenhower, the government would continue to address social and economic problems. This was especially so after 1954, when a brief recession (business slump) threw a scare into economic forecasters — and the administration. In the elections that year, Democrats regained control of Congress.

During Eisenhower's first four years, he supported — and Congress approved — a major federal housing program and a $25 billion, 10-year highway program. Started in 1956, the highway program created a nationwide system of interstate roads that helped to revolutionize Americans' travel habits. In the years that followed, travelers would abandon railroads in favor of quick, easy travel by car.

The Eisenhower administration also obtained congressional approval of a joint Canadian-American project for a canal between Montreal and Lake Erie. This St. Lawrence Seaway opened in 1959, making it possible to ship goods from the Atlantic Ocean all the way to Lake Superior.

In addition, Eisenhower pushed through Congress a major expansion of the Social Security system. The 1954 Social Security Act brought more workers, including farmers, under the system. Further extensions of Social Security passed Congress in 1956, 1958, and 1960.

Eisenhower's actions outraged many Old Guard Republicans, including his own brother, Edgar Eisenhower. Edgar wrote to the President and complained that his policies were no better than Truman's — and just as unconstitutional.

Replied the President: "Should any political party attempt to abolish Social Security, unemployment insurance, and eliminate labor laws and farm programs, you would not hear of that party again in our political history."

A disappointed Missouri farmer beside his 12-year-old auto reads that the President vetoed a farm bill.

DOWN ON THE FARM

President Eisenhower did not want to abolish farm programs, but he certainly wanted to shake them up. In his view, the Democrats' farm policies had brought disaster. Farmers were turning out record crops, yet their incomes were falling behind their costs. Each year, hundreds of thousands of farmers and farm workers gave up and moved to cities. Meanwhile, the federal government was buying up farm surpluses and stuffing them into already-bulging warehouses, at great cost to the taxpayers.

Eisenhower blamed the system of price supports begun in the 1930's. In return for taking part of their land out of production to hold down surpluses, farmers were guaranteed a fair price for their crops. If the market price fell below the fair price, the government made up the difference.

But what was a "fair" price? The traditional measure was a concept called *parity*. This took the "golden age of agriculture" (1910-1914) as a standard. It sought to guarantee farmers the same percentage return on investment as they would have made during the golden age. Say that in 1910-1914 an average wheat farmer earned $100 for every $90 invested in seeds, fertilizers, mortgage payments, and other costs. Obviously, costs had risen since then. To maintain parity, income would have to rise proportionally, keeping the same 100 to 90 ratio (in this example). Thus, a wheat farmer who now earned $200 against expenses of $180 would be matching the 100:90 ratio and thus would be earning 100 percent of parity. Few farmers were so lucky, however. Government aid brought their income up to only 90 percent of parity in the early 1950's.

Eisenhower did not propose abolishing parity or the price-support system, but at his bidding Congress did make some major changes. First, it ended rigid price supports. Instead of being set at exactly 90 percent, price supports could fluctuate between 75 and 90 percent. This aimed to cut government costs. Second, a new law introduced a "soil bank" program that paid farmers for taking land out of production for long periods. This aimed to reduce crop surpluses.

Like all farm programs, Eisenhower's stirred controversy. Some farmers, generally those who had smaller farms, called for higher rather than lower price supports. They said Eisenhower's policies threatened to wipe out the family farm. Other farmers applauded the new policies. They shared Eisenhower's view that farmers needed a stiffer dose of free-market competition.

To Eisenhower's dismay, however, his farm program provided no long-term solutions. The "chemical age" had come to farming, and chemical fertilizers and pesticides were boosting crop yields enormously. Farmers could produce more and more on fewer acres. During the 1950's, crop surpluses declined only slightly. Federal spending on agriculture soared, the soil bank benefited mainly those with large farms, and the number of family farms kept dropping.

BURSTING McCARTHY'S BUBBLE

Eisenhower wanted to end the divisive hunt for subversives in government. But he wanted to avoid antagonizing Senator McCarthy and his millions of supporters.

McCarthy still wanted a purge of State Department employees that he called "Acheson's architects of disaster." Although Dulles did fire many employees, McCarthy continued to investigate "disloyalty" and to demand further actions.

Eisenhower became increasingly angry at McCarthy and privately deplored the senator's tactics. But the President refused to issue a public criticism. He told his advisers, "I just will not — I refuse — to get into the gutter with that guy."

Early in 1954, McCarthy took on the U.S. Army in a series of congressional hearings. McCarthy charged that the Army had promoted possible Communists. When an Army general gave answers that McCarthy considered unsatisfactory, the senator charged that the general did not have "the brains of a five-year-old child." Later, Eisenhower obliquely critized McCarthy at a news conference. McCarthy responded by saying: "If a stupid, arrogant, or witless man . . . is found aiding the Communist party, he will be exposed."

By then, more and more people were alarmed at McCarthy's methods. One of them was Edward R. Murrow, still appearing on his weekly program, *See It Now*. Months earlier, Murrow had used the program to show how an innocent family had been hurt by unfounded accusations of disloyalty. On March 9, 1954, he turned his spotlight on McCarthy himself.

Viewers saw one film clip after another of Senator McCarthy in action. Here he stated one number of "proved" Communists in government. There he offered a different number. Time after time, the senator waved papers that he said contained proof of his charges. But no one got to examine the papers. What "proof" did they contain?

Murrow remained silent as the films rolled by. At the end, he offered his opinion. "We cannot defend freedom abroad by deserting it at home," he said in part. The following week *See It Now* showed more scenes of McCarthy in action.

Some Americans were outraged at the Murrow programs. Others applauded them, saying they showed McCarthy as a threat to American freedoms. McCarthy himself called Murrow "the leader and the cleverest of the jackal pack which is always found at the throat of anyone who dares to expose individual Communists and traitors."

In the weeks that followed, daytime television viewers had their first chance to see live coverage of the Army-McCarthy hearings. As usual, McCarthy dominated the proceedings. President Eisenhower now openly resisted McCarthy, however. He ordered executive-branch officials not to testify to McCarthy's committee about advice they had given the President. This was a sweeping claim of *executive privilege* — a president's right to refuse to cooperate with Congress. McCarthy urged public officials to defy the President.

The climax of the Army-McCarthy hearings came when the senator tangled with the Army's special counsel, Joseph N. Welch. One of Welch's legal assistants had once belonged — briefly and almost accidentally — to a subversive organization. Welch was aware of this membership and was unperturbed by it. To protect the younger lawyer from controversy, however, he had gotten McCarthy to agree not to mention the matter in public.

Army Counsel Joseph N. Welch (left) after his angry exchange with Senator Joseph McCarthy (right).

In the eighth week of the hearings, McCarthy suddenly broke his promise and raised the issue on nationwide television. An irate Welch then turned on McCarthy himself. "Let us not assassinate this lad further, Senator," Welch said with great disgust. "You have done enough. Have you no sense of decency, sir, at long last? Have you no sense of decency?"

Many viewers seemed to ask the same question. The hearings trailed off into trivia. McCarthy's bubble was beginning to burst. A few months later, the Senate popped it for good. In December 1954, by 67 to 22, it approved a historic censure motion. The motion condemned McCarthy for conduct that "tends to bring the Senate into disrepute." McCarthy's power was broken, and anti-subversive investigations took a new, quieter tone.

CRISIS IN BLACK AND WHITE

Every weekday morning, Linda Brown picked up her schoolbooks and walked for half a mile. Then she boarded a bus. Two miles down the road, she got off and entered Monroe Elementary School to greet her third-grade classmates and teacher. A few blocks from Linda's home was another school, Sumner. Linda could easily have walked to Sumner. There, she could have been with her friends, but Sumner was for white children, and Linda was black. In Topeka, Kansas, in 1951, blacks and whites attended separate schools. Kansas was among 21 states that sanctioned or required racially segregated schools. Most of them were southern.

In 1951 Linda's father and several other black parents filed a lawsuit against the school board. Similar lawsuits were being filed elsewhere. For more than 50 years the National Association for the Advancement of Colored People (NAACP) had been encouraging such suits as a way of breaking down barriers to black equality. The NAACP had managed to chip away at a few of the barriers, but blacks remained second-class citizens. In much of the country, they were barred from "white" schools, "white" restaurants, "white" churches, and all but the most menial jobs. In the South they were even barred from the voting booth.

Then came the lawsuit known as *Brown* v. *Board of Education of Topeka, Kansas.* A district court rejected the arguments of Topeka's black parents, and the parents appealed. In 1954 the U.S. Supreme Court handed down a unanimous decision that was to reverberate through U.S. life for years to come. The Court ruled that racially segregated schools were unconstitutional. In doing so, the Court overturned its own 1896 ruling in *Plessy* v. *Ferguson,* that states could require "separate but equal" facilities for people of different races. "Separate educational facilities," the Court now held, "are inherently unequal."

Reaction to the Court's ruling was sharply divided. Blacks — and many whites — rejoiced. But other whites angrily denounced both the decision and the Court. Senator Richard Russell, a Georgia Democrat, spoke of "a flagrant abuse of judicial power." Other southern officials pledged "massive resistance" to what they described as a violation of states' rights.

President Eisenhower, too, did not agree

with the Court, although he disapproved of segregation. In private the President would later remark: "I am convinced that the Supreme Court decision set back progress in the South at least 15 years. . . . The fellow who tries to tell me that you can do these things by force is just plain nuts." In public, however, he declared: "The Supreme Court has spoken and I am sworn to uphold the constitutional processes in this country; and I will obey."

Although the Court held in 1955 that desegregation should take place "with all deliberate speed," speed was rare. As late as 1958 not one black child was in school with whites in Virginia, Alabama, Mississippi, Georgia, Florida, or South Carolina. The NAACP filed suit after suit to force local officials to comply with the law.

REPERCUSSIONS

Nonetheless, change was occurring both above and beneath the surface of American life. In many communities, whites and blacks became more willing to speak out about what they perceived as injustices. Hazel Brannon Smith, a white newspaper publisher in Lexington, Mississippi, wrote a front-page editorial against a sheriff who shot a young black man in the back. As a result, her husband lost his job, and the paper lost much of its advertising. Mrs. Smith would later win a Pulitzer Prize for her crusading spirit.

Blacks began to find new ways to assert their claims to equal rights. One tactic was the *boycott* — the withdrawal of patronage from a business to force changes. Already in 1953, the blacks of Baton Rouge, Louisiana, had

Rosa Parks rides at the front of a Montgomery public bus a year after the famous boycott.

staged a boycott of city buses in protest of segregated seating. Late in 1955, national attention focused on another bus boycott, in Montgomery, Alabama.

The Montgomery boycott began when a quiet, dignified woman named Rosa Parks refused to yield her bus seat to a white man. Police came to arrest her. Mrs. Parks was what many southern whites would have described as an agitator. She was the longtime secretary of the local branch of the NAACP. She had worked with black youths who had tried to borrow books from "white" libraries and sit in "white" seats on buses. Rather than pay her $10 fine, Mrs. Parks joined ministers, women's leaders, and others in setting up a massive boycott to force the bus company to end segregated seating. They organized a car pool to help blacks get to work without using

Dr. King in Birmingham jail.

buses. Their leader was a 26-year-old Baptist minister named Martin Luther King, Jr.

Dr. King helped to set the style of a protest movement that would soon spread to other parts of the South and North. Blacks, he declared, wanted justice. They would accept nothing less. If they had to, they would break unjust laws and go to jail for their cause. But Dr. King instructed his followers to use only nonviolent methods. He compared the movement for black civil rights to the movement for independence that Mohandas K. Gandhi had led in India in the 1930's and 1940's.

Dr. King wanted to integrate blacks more fully into American society, but not all blacks agreed. Some believed that whites would never accept blacks as equals, and urged blacks to build their own, separate society. A leading exponent of that belief was a man who called himself Elijah Muhammad. His organization, popularly called the Black Muslims, expanded rapidly after 1954, especially in the crowded black slums of large northern cities.

Meanwhile, white opponents of integration were organizing too. Some joined groups like the White Citizens Council and the Ku Klux Klan. Others helped to organize private, all-white schools for students who refused to attend classes with blacks. Segregationist whites often found elected officials more than willing to aid their cause. In the South, several states tried to ban the NAACP as Communist or subversive — and, for a while, some succeeded.

Racial tensions had been building for years. After 1954, those tensions burst forth across the land. For years to come, Americans would wrestle with the pent-up pressures that the *Brown* decision had let loose.

SECTION RECAP

1. What was the Eisenhower Administration's approach to housing? Transportation and commerce? Agriculture?

2. Explain how the following contributed to the downfall of Senator McCarthy's "Red Hunt": President Eisenhower, Edward R. Murrow, Joseph Welch, the Senate.

3. What was the U.S. Supreme Court decision in the case *Brown* v. *Board of Education of Topeka, Kansas* ? What were the President's private and public reactions to the decision?

4. What were the goals of Dr. Martin Luther King, Jr. and his followers? What tactics did they use?

4 The Triumph of Mass Culture

Powerful engines, long, sleek bodies, and heavy chrome were features of the most desirable automobiles of the 1950's.

In the mid-1950's, Americans had much on their minds besides the Cold War, politics, and race relations. For large numbers of people, life was good. Paychecks were fatter than ever. Food was abundant. At night, one could flop down before a television set, devour a TV dinner, and forget one's troubles watching *I Love Lucy*.

GALLOPING CAPITALISM

One day in 1954, a salesman named Ray Kroc pulled up at a drive-in restaurant in San Bernardino, California. Kroc was curious. No other restaurant had ever ordered eight of his special milkshake machines — machines that could each turn out five shakes at a time. "I had to see what kind of an operation was making 40 at one time," Kroc said later.

The small, eight-sided building bore a sign that read "McDonald's Famous Hamburgers." Kroc gaped at the long lines of customers. He watched the workers bustling "like ants at a picnic." He took note of the careful specialization — hamburgers at this window, French fries at that. Before long, Kroc had talked the owners, Maurice and Richard McDonald, into setting up a nationwide chain of McDonald's restaurants.

The new business would work on the franchise system. Kroc would sell franchises (marketing licenses) to individual entrepreneurs all over the country. The entrepreneurs would build and run their own restaurants. But the restaurants would all look alike. They would follow standard procedures and use standard equipment, furnished by headquarters.

The first of the new chain's outlets opened in Des Plaines, Illinois, on a cloudy day in April 1955. Hamburgers cost 15 cents each, French fries a dime. Sales that first day totaled $377.12. Within five years there were 228 McDonald's, and by 1961 Kroc was able to buy out the McDonald brothers for $2.7 million. The dawn of the great franchise chains had arrived in America.

Franchise operations had existed for years, but mostly for car dealerships and soft-drink bottlers. Before Kroc, there were only scattered chains of franchised restaurants (Howard Johnson, which began in the 1920's) and motels (Holiday Inn, 1952). Kroc set off a great boom that would soon dot U.S. highways with names like Dunkin' Donuts and Midas Mufflers (both started in 1956).

The new franchise chains were symbolic of an era of seemingly unbounded optimism. Americans were rich and getting richer. The minor recession of 1954 gave way to a quick recovery. American corporations were churning out goods of which the prewar generation could only have dreamed. There were electric pencil sharpeners, stereo radios, push-button phones, vinyl flooring; the list went on and on. As one observer put it, the era of "galloping capitalism" had arrived.

During this period, the U.S. corporation was taking on new and larger dimensions. One firm, General Motors, had grown so big that its budget now equaled that of Poland. Many firms were expanding their investments in other parts of the world. In the Mideast, where British and Dutch firms had once dominated oil production, U.S. firms now led.

Business leaders were eager to put U.S. prosperity on display for people in other lands to see. The Advertising Council prepared an exhibit setting the sleek, modern home of 1956 beside the crude log cabin of 1776. The traveling exhibit, which toured four continents, included an array of the latest labor-saving appliances. It went under the title "People's Capitalism." Display cards announced that 60 percent of Americans owned their own homes and that 10 million people owned shares in U.S. businesses. "In the United States," said the cards, "almost everybody is a 'capitalist.'"

Not quite everyone, in fact. A smaller percentage of Americans owned stock in companies now than in the 1930's. And four fifths of all stock was held by less than one percent of U.S. families. Still, the figures and the fancy appliances were impressive. No other nation could boast such widespread wealth.

CHANGING LABOR SCENE

American workers shared in that wealth through wages that were among the highest in the world. Labor unions were negotiating new and innovative contracts. Part of a worker's compensation now often came in the form of employer-paid health insurance and pension plans. Auto and steel workers made a new breakthrough in 1955. For the first time, their contract promised them a guaranteed annual wage. This meant that they would receive a set percentage of their regular wage even if they should be laid off. (The employer would add to the amount the worker received from a state unemployment system.)

In 1955 labor's two major organizations merged. The American Federation of Labor (AFL) and the Congress of Industrial Organizations (CIO) joined to create one giant federation, the AFL-CIO. The new body contained almost 90 percent of the nation's 17.8 million union members. The labor movement seemed to be riding high.

But broad economic trends were working against that movement. Labor unions were most successful at organizing factory workers — women and men who wore "blue collars." From 1956 onward, however, white-collar workers outnumbered blue-collar ones, as service industries grew faster than manufacturing industries. Labor union membership reached its all-time high in 1956. After that, it slipped into a slow decline.

INVENTING THE TEENAGER

Before the 1950's, kids on their way to adulthood passed quietly through a stage called adolescence. Gawky girls and pimply boys had no desire to linger, and no one encouraged them to do so. If they'd just hurry and grow up, they could get jobs and marry and get on with the serious business of life.

During the 1950's, adolescents suddenly gained a new status. People began to call them teenagers. In a booming economy, they found jobs, often at fast-food chains. With money in their pockets, teenagers became a target of advertisers with products to sell — cream to erase or hide those pimples, mouthwash to give self-assurance, shampoo, perfume, phonograph records.

Teenagers bought lots of phonograph rec-

ords — mostly 45's, mixed in with some long-playing 33's called LP's. The music, by performers like Frank Sinatra and Rosemary Clooney, tended to soothe rather than excite. The main exception was R&B, or rhythm and blues — music with a beat, which originated with black musicians and appealed mainly to black audiences. In 1951, a Cleveland disc jockey named Alan Freed decided to play R&B on a "white" radio station. The listeners loved the music that Freed called rock 'n' roll. Soon white performers were bouncing to a new beat, and black performers were winning a wider audience.

Meanwhile, in the black night spots along Beale Street in Memphis, Tennessee, a white youth was tapping his feet to jazz, R&B, and other styles of music. Jiving with the musicians, trying out their tunes on his guitar, young Elvis Presley developed a style that would soon be known throughout America and around the world. In 1955, Presley signed a recording contract. Soon his songs — "Heartbreak Hotel" was the first — shot to the top of both pop and country music charts.

Mothers and fathers gasped in horror. For Elvis didn't just sing and strum — he swiveled. He wriggled his hips and pouted his lips and . . . well, in the America of 1955, one just didn't make those motions in public. But Elvis did. The fans loved it, and they squealed and screamed and mobbed the stage. In some cities, radio stations banned Elvis's records and fired disc jockeys who played them. And sometimes parents smashed Elvis's records. But the singer in the gold lamé suits just kept gaining new fans and selling more records.

Elvis Presley, King of Rock 'n' Roll.

Rock 'n' roll and performers like Elvis helped to drive a wedge between teens and their parents — to create what came to be called the generation gap. How could two generations reach such different conclusions about something so simple as music? To many teens, the new music was a statement of independence. They saw nothing wrong with Elvis's statement to *Look* magazine: "I just act the way I feel." What could be wrong with self-expression? Most adults, however, had been brought up to believe that one acted the way one was supposed to act, not the way one felt. To many, the new music was outrageous and Elvis was downright vulgar. What ever happened to self-control?

The teen subculture that developed in the middle and late 1950's would grow in the years to come. So would the generation gap. The stage was being set for explosive confrontations in the 1960's.

WE ALL LIKE IKE

For all the furor over rock 'n' roll, Americans seemed relatively content with their lives in the mid-1950's. Oh, people had their worries, of course. The nuclear arms race nagged at the back of the mind. Popular magazines were drawing attention to a problem called juvenile delinquency. And some worried that too many people were being riddled with bullets on TV shows. What kind of impact would all that killing have on impressionable youngsters?

Genial and fatherly, President Eisenhower seemed to have few doubts about where America was headed. In 1956, he and Vice President Nixon ran for reelection on a platform of "Peace, Progress, and Prosperity." Adlai Stevenson, given a second chance as the Democrats' nominee, seemed tired and listless. Eisenhower won by a landslide. Normally, such a victory would have pulled along enough congressional candidates to elect a Republican Congress. In 1956, however, the Democrats managed the unprecedented trick of winning a majority in both houses even while losing the presidency.

As Eisenhower entered his second term in 1957, optimism reigned among most Americans. Wasn't the United States the envy of the whole world? Didn't it lead all other nations in technological achievements and military strength? Within months, startled Americans would be wondering if the answers to both questions might not be so self-evident as they had seemed.

SECTION RECAP

1. In the mid-1950's, what was happening that helped franchises, and corporations in general, to boom?

2. What did the state of the labor movement appear to be in the mid-1950's? How was it deceptive?

3. What fostered new attention on adolescents in the 1950's? What was the "generation gap"?

4. What was ironic about President Eisenhower's landslide election victory in 1956?

1. In 1952, Eisenhower ran for president on the Republican ticket. Republicans promised to take a new look at the foreign and defense policies of the past. However, Eisenhower's presidency brought more continuity than the change the Old Guard wanted. He described some of his own policies as "middle of the road." On a sheet of paper, make three columns, and label them New Look, Middle of the Road, and Continuity. From the list below, decide under which column each item fits best. Be prepared to explain each choice.

   1954 Social Security Act

   Formosa Resolution

   brinkmanship

   1955 Geneva Summit

   parity

   containment

2. Define these terms: *rollback, brinkmanship, boycott, massive retaliation, nuclear proliferation, domino theory, nationalize, Third World, parity, soil bank, executive privilege.*

3. What was the long-term result of President Eisenhower's farm program? What agricultural development of the 1950's greatly influenced the effectiveness of his program?

4. What were Secretary of State Dulles's views on containment? How did these views manifest themselves in U.S. foreign policy regarding China? Vietnam? the Mideast? Iran? Guatemala?

5. What role did television play in the career of Senator Joseph McCarthy?

6. President Eisenhower's 1956 reelection platform was "Peace, Progress, and Prosperity." Was this an appropriate summation of what was achieved during his first term of office?

7. What covert actions did the United States take against other nations during the Eisenhower administration? How were they justified by Eisenhower and Dulles? Do you agree that they were justifiable? If so, why? If not, do you think overthrow of another government is ever justifiable? If so, under what circumstances?

CHAPTER 4

1957 — 1961

America on the Spot

THE BLOW TO AMERICAN PRIDE fell on October 4, 1957. From the near-edges of space chirped a faint radio signal: "Beep, beep, beep, beep . . ." On and on, monotonously, the signal spread the news that the United States had fallen behind in the race into space. A Soviet rocket had gotten there first, placing into Earth's orbit a sphere about the size of a basketball and weighing 184.3 pounds. The Russians called it *Sputnik* — "fellow traveler."

U.S. officials put up a brave front. Race into space? What race? One White House adviser referred to *Sputnik* as "a silly bauble." Said a general: "It's just a hunk of iron."

But the Soviet satellite was no silly bauble. It had not just floated up to an orbit 560 miles from the earth's surface. A Soviet rocket had put it there — a mighty rocket that could just as easily have carried a nuclear bomb around the world and blasted away an American city. That was the real threat of the Soviet achievement. The Soviets had beaten the United States into an era of ICBMs — of intercontinental ballistic missiles.

As Americans tried to absorb the sudden shock, cries of alarm echoed across the land. Some said the United States had suffered a second Pearl Harbor. *Life* magazine proclaimed *Sputnik* "really and truly 'the shot heard round the world.'"

To Americans, who for years had been convinced of their great technological superiority, it seemed like a disaster. Soviet leader Nikita Khrushchev was crowing that America's weapons belonged in museums. How had it happened? Why? And what should be done about it? With an intensity that verged on panic, Americans debated where their nation was going, where it fell short, and how to restore confidence — their own and the world's — in American superiority. Eventually, the debate would lead to a renewed sense of national purpose and rebirth of pride, but not right away.

Sputnik's Impact

No sooner had *Sputnik*'s first beep-beep been heard than the nation's legislators rushed for solutions to "the *Sputnik* crisis." Most of the solutions involved money — lots and lots of it. The United States should greatly increase its military strength. It should start a crash program to send people to the moon. It should pour federal money into education to turn out more scientists and engineers.

President Eisenhower wasn't convinced. "Suddenly we seem to have an hysterical approach," he told his cabinet. " . . . We want to cure every ill in two years, in five years, by putting in a lot of money. To my mind, this is the wrong attack." For the rest of his term, Eisenhower struggled to keep the lid on spending in the face of mounting pressure for new and bigger federal programs.

The pressure came from many groups. Research scientists wanted more federal support for basic research. Educators wanted massive federal aid for education. Military leaders wanted more missiles and bombers — and more people to run them. Big corporations wanted a piece of the action too, in contracts for missiles or space hardware.

Of course, party politics helped to frame the national debate. Democrats were quick to blame the Republican administration for letting the Soviets score such a resounding victory. Republicans, in turn, pointed to the Truman years. They asked why the Democrats hadn't mounted a larger missile-research program in the late 1940's and early 1950's.

From the haze of partisan debate, a national consensus eventually began to emerge. The federal government would have to assume major new duties. But what duties?

WHY ISN'T JOHNNY SMARTER?

Many critics suggested that young Americans were not getting a proper education. Maybe the schools were not turning out the scientists, engineers, and other leaders of tomorrow. That feeling found expression in the title of a book: *Why Johnny Can't Read*, by Rudolf Flesch. When the book came out in 1955, few people noticed it. After *Sputnik*, experts rushed forward to say it was all too true. No, Johnny — and Janie — could not

read as well as they should. Neither could they work math problems or speak foreign languages as well as Russian or Japanese young people. The experts noted that schools in the Soviet Union and Japan were far more rigorous and demanding.

Some critics said U.S. schools had too many easy courses, offered too many electives, didn't give enough homework. They blamed "progressive education." Others said U.S. schools paid teachers too poorly and devoted too little attention to science. Still others said that schools were geared to middle-class students and ignored the needs and potentials of the less affluent.

Despite disagreement on what was wrong, the critics managed to agree on a cure — federal aid to education. Up to that time, education had been considered to be primarily a state and local matter. Federal aid to education had been proposed before. But such proposals stumbled over questions of states' rights, religion (should parochial students get aid?), and race (would the federal government gain a new tool to force integration?).

In the wake of *Sputnik*, President Eisenhower proposed and Congress approved the National Defense Education Act (NDEA) of 1958. The NDEA set up a program of loans to college students. It also began a system of matching grants to state governments for science and foreign language facilities such as laboratories. Educators wanted more, and they kept the pressure on Congress. During the 1960's, the federal government would become a massive force in U.S. education. The NDEA would be just a start.

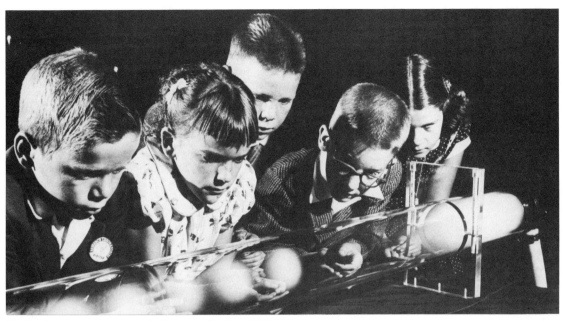

Pittsburgh students tour a research laboratory after *Sputnik's* launch.

DISCOVERING "GAPS"

Much of the post-Sputnik furor dealt with defense. Why didn't the United States have its own intercontinental ballistic missile? When would it get one? How vulnerable were U.S. cities to missile attack?

Democrat Lyndon Johnson of Texas, the Senate majority leader, conducted a series of hearings into U.S. satellite and missile programs. He had no trouble finding military officials to testify that their own particular service or program was starved for money. Administration officials insisted, however, that *Sputnik* had little military significance. They said the United States was ahead in most of the things that counted — bombers, electronics, warhead design, and all but the largest missiles.

Many Democrats saw matters differently. As early as 1956, Democrats had raised the specter of a "missile gap." That is, they had claimed that the United States lagged behind the Soviet Union in development of nuclear missiles.

Now Senator Johnson expanded on that charge. Wrapping up his hearings in January 1958, Johnson declared that the United States had fallen behind the Soviet Union not only in missile development but also in space flight and in numbers of submarines. In addition, he said, the nation lagged in research, and training scientists and engineers. Major new programs were essential, Johnson claimed. For the rest of the Eisenhower years, Democrats would repeat the warning that the United States was on the short end of dangerous "gaps."

Wernher von Braun and a 1952 model space vehicle.

AIMING FOR SPACE

Long before *Sputnik*, the Eisenhower administration had started its own space program, made up of three separate teams working on rocket and satellite programs. There was an Army team, a Navy team, and an Air Force team, and they were bitter rivals. A cartoonist caught the mood of rivalry by showing a U.S. military officer gazing up at *Sputnik* and mopping his brow. "Whew!" he was saying. "At first I thought it was sent up by one of the other services."

U.S. leaders had given the Navy project priority, mainly to emphasize the civilian face of U.S. space efforts. The Army and Air Force projects used military missiles as booster rockets. The missiles were destined to become part of a U.S. arsenal of ICBMs. The Navy rocket, on the other hand, was originally developed to do high-altitude scientific research. It was a civilian rocket. To U.S. leaders, that was important, for the non-military status helped to deflect criticism that the U.S. space program was warlike.

Actually, the blending of military and non-military aspects in space was unavoidable. Any rocket that could boost a satellite into orbit could also carry a warhead. Furthermore, satellites themselves had military uses. U.S. and Soviet leaders wanted desperately to have "spy" satellites that could peer down into their adversaries' backyards.

German expatriate Wernher von Braun was a leader of the Army's rocket team, and he was irked. He was sure that his team could launch a satellite quicker than the Navy team. Top U.S. leaders had decided, however, that speed was secondary. More important was that the first U.S. satellite be "peaceful." Then the Soviet Union would be less likely to argue that the orbiting satellite was violating its territory. The space age would be a whole new ball game, requiring a new set of rules, and one of the rules U.S. leaders wanted to establish was that national boundaries did not reach into space. (As it turned out, the issue was moot. Having sent up the first satellite, the Soviets accepted the argument that space was for everyone.)

In the weeks and months that followed the orbiting of *Sputnik*, the pressure for a U.S. comeback grew stronger. In November 1957, the Soviets sent up a second *Sputnik*. This

A successful launch from Cape Canaveral.

one carried a live dog named Laika. The Soviets as yet had no means to get the dog down, so it died in orbit. Even so, experts said the dog's presence showed that the Soviets were advancing toward manned space flight.

A month later, a highly-publicized U.S. space shot fizzled. The Navy's *Vanguard* rocket rose four feet off the launch pad, then blew up. "Flopnik," some people called the effort. "Stayputnik," others sneered.

BACK IN THE RACE

Army and Navy teams raced to get a satellite into space. Finally, on January 31, 1958, von Braun's Army team succeeded. A *Jupiter* rocket blasted off from Cape Canaveral, Flor-

ida, carrying a 31-pound satellite named *Explorer I*. Suspense mounted as officials waited for word from tracking stations that would confirm that *Explorer* was in orbit. Finally came the coded message: "Goldstone has the bird." At last, Americans were back in the space race.

U.S. space teams had reason to be proud of their work. *Explorer I* provided a wealth of scientific information. It discovered that two vast belts of radiation (the Van Allen belts) girdle the globe. The satellite's tiny size, requiring that instruments be restricted to the smallest space possible, helped to give the United States a lasting lead in miniaturized electronics. The months that followed saw other U.S. space shots (the Navy's *Vanguard* succeeded in March 1958), and other important discoveries. By 1960 the United States led the Soviet Union in numbers of satellites, 28 to 8. By the end of that year, both nations had ICBMs ready to fire.

To manage the U.S. space effort, Congress created the National Aeronautics and Space Administration (NASA). NASA is a civilian agency that works in parallel with military space agencies. Late in 1958, NASA started Project Mercury with the aim of putting the first human into space orbit. NASA hoped to get ahead of the Soviets in starting manned space flight. The agency desperately wanted to boost U.S. prestige, which was widely believed to have slipped because of *Sputnik*.

The U.S. space program was turning out to be bigger than President Eisenhower had planned, but smaller than many scientists and political leaders wanted. National space policy would be a burning issue for years to come. Nonetheless, space policy was only part of a larger issue — the proper relationship between government and society. After *Sputnik*, large numbers of people demanded that the United States win the space race by any means necessary. If that meant pouring federal money into education, or space technology, or new military hardware, so be it.

Such demands profoundly disturbed President Eisenhower. The President warned that the ideal of limited government was becoming endangered. Americans, he said, faced a difficult dilemma. On the one hand, modern technology was so complex that a large government role seemed indispensable, if only to pay for the necessary research and development. On the other hand, as the government's role grew larger, the realm of free enterprise and individual freedom of decision would shrink. It was a theme to which Eisenhower would return again and again.

SECTION RECAP

1. How did *Sputnik* stir up changes in the U.S. educational system?

2. Why was it thought important that the first U.S. satellite be considered peaceful?

3. Name two scientific advances contibutable to the satellite *Explorer I*.

4. What is NASA? What was the purpose of Project Mercury?

2 Foreign Affairs: Groping for Accommodation

War breaks out between the superpowers — no one is quite sure how. There is a quick spasm of destruction, and the fighting is cover. A few people survive in Australia, far away from the nuclear blasts, but it is only a matter of time until massive fallout (radiation) will wipe out life there, too. Waiting to die, the survivors send a submarine to the West Coast of the United States to check a mysterious radio signal. Investigators find nothing — only a soft-drink bottle, snagged in a window shade, tapping against a telegraph key. In the deserted street waves a forlorn Salvation Army banner: "There Is Still Time Brother."

That is how Stanley Kramer's 1959 film *On the Beach* (based on a novel by English author Nevil Shute) dramatized the popular perception that doomsday might lie just around the corner. It was a perception that President Eisenhower and other world leaders shared. In the 1950's, negotiators for the superpowers met time after time to try to find ways of taming the nuclear arms race before it was too late. Before, suspicion and distrust had blocked chances of an accommodation. Was anything different now?

THE ARMS RACE

The United States and the Soviet Union approached the problem of taming the arms race from different directions. U.S. proposals emphasized a need for inspection and controls:

A scene from the movie *On the Beach.*

First, let's set up a system to makes sure no one cheats on an agreement; then let's make the agreement. Soviet proposals started from the other direction: First, let's stop developing our weapons; then we can work out an inspection system. Neither side would agree to the other's approach. Neither trusted the other to carry an agreement through.

The U.S. approach was embodied in a plan that Eisenhower put forward at the Geneva Summit of 1955 — the "Open Skies" plan. It provided that both the United States and the Soviet Union would "give to each other a complete blueprint of our military establishments." Each nation would provide bases to the other, from which airplanes could take off to make aerial photographs of the host country. In such a way, Eisenhower declared, each nation would be able to inspect the other and make sure it did not make preparations for a surprise attack. Soviet leader Nikita Khrushchev quickly rejected the Open Skies plan as a plot for U.S. spying.

Khrushchev's approach could be seen in a speech he made at the United Nations in 1959. In it, the Soviet leader proposed the complete abolition of all arms, nuclear and non-nuclear, over a period of four years. The proposal had no provision for inspection or supervision. U.S. leaders treated the speech as nothing more than a propaganda ploy.

Only one aspect of arms control seemed to hold out any prospect of an early agreement — the idea of a ban on nuclear weapons tests. Such tests produced fallout that was carried around the world by high-altitude winds. By the late 1950's it was clear that fallout was a danger to human health. Scientists had learned that small amounts of radiation could eventually cause diseases such as cancer.

The Soviet Union began a campaign for a nuclear test ban, attracting support in many countries and at the United Nations. Then, in March 1958, Khrushchev announced that the Soviet Union would stop its testing unilaterally — without waiting for U.S. agreement. In the jockeying for propaganda advantage that followed, U.S., British and Soviet leaders agreed to begin detailed discussions on a test ban. For the first time since the start of the Cold War, serious arms-control talks began later in 1958 in Geneva. Both the United States and Britain followed the Soviet Union in announcing a halt to nuclear tests while the talks went on. However, no agreement could be reached during Eisenhower's term of office.

TACKLING OTHER ISSUES

Eisenhower had always tended to be more conciliatory toward the Soviet Union than his secretary of state, John Foster Dulles. During Eisenhower's second term, a battle with cancer kept Dulles from playing as active a role in policy-making as before. Eisenhower's conciliatory manner came to the fore.

One minor issue on which the superpowers could agree was a treaty to assure that the empty continent of Antarctica was used only for peaceful purposes. The United States proposed such a treaty in 1958. A year later, the two superpowers and 10 other nations signed it. The signers agreed to freeze any claims to territory in Antarctica for 30 years.

Major issues, however, resisted easy settlement. None was tougher than deciding the future of divided Germany. The issue had lain

dormant for a few years, but in 1958 Soviet leader Khrushchev issued an ultimatum. He said the four-power occupation of Berlin that dated back to 1945 was now outdated. The Soviet Union had decided to sign a treaty turning its powers in the city over to the East German government. Knowing the Western powers would object, Khrushchev set a deadline of six months for working out some alternative solution.

To Western leaders, Khrushchev's ultimatum raised the specter of a new Berlin blockade, similar to that of 1948 and 1949. If the Western powers refused to deal with East Germany, a country they did not officially rec-

Soviet Premier Nikita Khrushchev pats a cow at the government's experimental farm at Beltsville, MD.

ognize, the East Germans might cut off access across the 110-mile corridor that separated Berlin from West Germany. President Eisenhower bruskly rejected any solution imposed by one side. He pointed out that U.S., British, and French rights in Berlin were based on agreements with the Soviet Union made at Yalta in 1945. Those rights were to remain in effect until a final peace treaty could be signed — preferably with a united Germany.

For a time it seemed that a major crisis might be brewing. Six months came and went, however, and the Soviets did not act. Instead, the foreign ministers of the four powers gathered in Geneva to discuss what to do about Germany. As in the past, neither side would agree to major concessions.

AN EXCHANGE OF VISITS

For some time, Khrushchev had been dropping hints that he would like to visit the United States. At first, President Eisenhower ignored the hints. Then he began to consider the idea seriously. Why not an exchange of visits by the leaders of the two superpowers? Khrushchev could come to the United States and see the high standard of living, the many freedoms that Americans enjoy. Eisenhower could go to the Soviet Union and appeal for understanding between the two peoples.

John Foster Dulles, who opposed such an exchange, died in the spring of 1959. That summer, President Eisenhower issued Khrushchev an official invitation. The Soviet leader quickly said yes. He came for 12 days in September 1959.

Khrushchev's visit made colorful copy for the media. He made speeches. He tramped around cornfields. Grumpily, but with a twinkle in his eyes, he fielded questions from reporters. The Soviet leader visited a Hollywood movie studio and showed distaste at can-can dancing. ("Immoral," he called it.) To Khrushchev's regret, he was not allowed to go to Disneyland while he was in California. "Do you have rocket launching pads there?" Khruschev grumbled. No, no, not that, said U.S. officials. The amusement park was such a maze, they said, that they could not guarantee the Soviet leader's safety.

Khrushchev spent the last two days of his visit at Camp David, the presidential retreat in the Maryland mountains. There, Khrushchev agreed to drop his ultimatum on Berlin. At the same time, Eisenhower agreed to a four-power summit meeting in Paris the following June. The leaders agreed that Eisenhower should visit the Soviet Union either before or after the summit, but the visit never took place.

THE U-2 INCIDENT

Ever since 1956, U.S. pilots had been flying across the Soviet Union to photograph military installations, industrial plants and cities. U.S. designers had created a sleek, black plane called the U-2 precisely for this purpose. The plane was not particularly fast. It could not have outrun a jet fighter if one had challenged it. With wings that were twice as long as its fuselage, however, the U-2 could fly at more than 70,000 feet — or 13 miles. That was too high for fighters to climb. It was

**Pilot Francis Gary Powers
with a model of a U-2 plane upon his return.**

also, CIA leader Allen Dulles told President Eisenhower in 1956, too high for Soviet surface-to-air missiles (SAMs) to reach.

President Eisenhower felt serious qualms about the overflights. He granted Dulles's argument that reconnaissance (spy) flights were essential if the United States was to keep an eye on Soviet military preparations. Such flights could help spot preparations for any surprise attack. They could keep U.S. analysts informed about new Soviet missiles and satellites. But the Soviet Union would undoubtedly consider the flights to be a serious provocation — close to an act of war, Eisenhower told his aides. U-2 planes did not just dart across a frontier and back again, as

other U.S. reconnaissance planes had done for years (and as Soviet planes also did). The U-2s would fly from one side of the Soviet Union to the other. What if one should go down deep within Soviet territory?

Allen Dulles was reassuring. It was unlikely the Soviets could ever shoot down a U-2. If one of the planes did come down, it would almost certainly disintegrate. The Soviets had virtually no chance of capturing a pilot alive, Dulles declared.

Eisenhower thought about Dulles's arguments. In the end, he decided the risk would be worth taking. Until U.S. spy satellites were ready, U-2 overflights seemed the best way of keeping an eye on the Soviets. But Eisenhower insisted that the U-2s be piloted by civilians and that a plausible "cover story" be worked out. If one of the planes should come down, U.S. leaders would have to deny that it was spying. Publicly, therefore, the U-2s were "weather planes," collecting information about high-altitude winds. That was the same cover story used since the late 1940's for Air Force and Navy balloons that soared through the skies, snapping pictures of the Soviet countryside.

The U-2 did its job well. Pilots brought back enough film each trip to cover a four-lane highway 30 miles long. Processed in a secret lab over an auto repair shop in a run-down section of Washington, D.C., the film provided information that was invaluable for U.S. leaders. It showed hidden missile-testing sites and bombers lined up at secret airstrips. The film also suggested that in early 1960 the Soviets still had no functioning missile bases for ICBMs. In all likelihood, the "missile gap" did not exist after all.

Eisenhower kept the U-2s on a close leash. He insisted on authorizing most flights across the Soviet Union himself. After stopping the flights during Khrushchev's visit to the United States, he allowed them to resume. He authorized one for late April or early May 1960. It was to be the last flight before the four-power summit meeting that was to begin May 16 in Paris.

In the early hours of May 1, 1960, U-2 number 360 soared high above the city of Sverdlovsk, in the Ural Mountains deep within the Soviet Union. At its controls, Francis Gary Powers flipped the switches that operated the engine and the cameras. Powers was an experienced pilot who had quit the Air Force to fly for the CIA. He had been

travelling four hours since leaving a U.S. base in Pakistan, near the Soviet Union's southern borders. His destination was Norway, far to the north and west.

Suddenly, Powers later related, he heard a dull whoomp. A bright orange flash lit the cockpit. "I've had it now," the pilot said to himself. The plane spun out of control. Powers managed to break free of the craft and open his parachute. He landed in a farm field, near a village school. Soon a crowd of curious adults and children gathered to gawk at the bedraggled pilot. Before long, Powers had been whisked to Moscow to be questioned by Soviet authorities.

AN END TO INNOCENCE

From Norway, word that the plane was overdue flashed quickly to Washington. "Our boy isn't there," the CIA told the State Department. But what had happened? Puzzled, U.S. officials waited two days, then released their cover story: A NASA weather plane, collecting data about air turbulence, was missing. The search was concentrated in eastern Turkey.

Soviet Premier Khrushchev knew better. He waited two more days, then announced his news in a speech to the Soviet parliament. Soviet defenders had shot down a U.S. plane engaged in the "aggressive act" of invading Soviet air space. Had President Eisenhower been responsible? Were "Pentagon militarists" acting on their own? Either way, Khrushchev said, "aggressive circles" in the United States seemed to want to "torpedo the Paris summit."

From Khrushchev's point of view — as from Eisenhower's — the incident had come at an awkward moment. Khrushchev had been pushing for a relaxation of tensions with the United States. Hard-liners in the Soviet establishment had criticized him for getting too cozy with Eisenhower and for cutting back Soviet defenses. Chinese leaders were saying that Khrushchev had gone "soft." In denouncing U.S. "aggression," Khrushchev added: "I do not doubt President Eisenhower's sincere desire for peace." He seemed to be trying to dissociate Eisenhower from what U.S. pilots were doing.

U.S. leaders stuck to their own story. "There was absolutely no — N, O — no deliberate attempt to violate Soviet air space. There never has been," said a State Department spokesman. Then, after waiting for two more days, Khrushchev dropped his bombshell. "When I made my report two days ago," he declared, "I deliberately refrained from mentioning that we have the plane — and we also have the pilot, who is quite alive and kicking."

"Unbelievable!" President Eisenhower exclaimed when he heard the news. What followed was even more unbelievable. U.S. officials issued a series of new statements, inching closer to the truth, as Soviet leaders made further charges and a political storm crashed about President Eisenhower's head.

First, the story was that spy flights did take place, but no such flight as Khrushchev described had been authorized. Officials stressed a need for such flights (by "unarmed civilian U-2 aircraft") to penetrate Soviet se-

crecy and fend off any surprise attack. Critics were quick to ask how an unauthorized flight could have taken place. Didn't U.S. leaders control the CIA?

Finally, President Eisenhower decided to shoulder full responsibility. Intelligence-gathering, the President declared, was "a distasteful but vital necessity," He himself had authorized U-2 flights over the Soviet Union. The implication was that such flights would continue. But the President insisted the United States had done "nothing that could be honestly considered provocative." He accused the Soviets of purposely blowing a minor incident into a crisis.

A crisis it certainly was. Up to that point, Khrushchev had left open the question of Eisenhower's visit to the Soviet Union. Now he slammed the door shut. The President would no longer be welcome.

The Paris summit meeting barely got off the ground. Khrushchev refused to hold serious discussions unless Eisenhower made a full apology. That, Eisenhower refused to do.

Whatever hopes the leaders of the two superpowers had had for taming the Cold War had crashed in the flames of the U-2. Once again, U.S.-Soviet relations turned hostile. After a showy trial in Moscow, Francis Gary Powers was sentenced to 12 years in prison for espionage. (He was freed in exchange for a Soviet spy in 1962.)

The U-2 incident had shattered a number of illusions. For the first time, a U.S. President had publicly admitted that the United States engaged in spying. What was more, U.S. officials had been forced to admit to having lied.

President Eisenhower with French President Charles de Gaulle in Paris near the Arch of Triumph.

Until 1960, most Americans had assumed that their government — unlike other governments — told the truth. Such innocence was now at an end. Americans would learn to scrutinize official statements with a new realism.

A CHANGING WORLD

While wrestling with the ups and downs of U.S.-Soviet relations, the second Eisenhower administration faced a variety of other challenges and opportunities abroad. The world was changing rapidly. In 1957, British-ruled Ghana became the first colony in black Africa to gain independence. Newly independent nations began to multiply like mushrooms after a rain.

France, a U.S. ally within NATO, passed through a serious crisis. French citizens divided bitterly over their nation's colonial war in Algeria. Unable to agree on a solution, French politicians turned in 1958 to World War II hero Charles de Gaulle. De Gaulle insisted on a new constitution, ending the weak-president system of the Fourth French Republic and concentrating power in the hands of a strong president. As the first president of the Fifth French Republic, de Gaulle struggled to end the war in Algeria by negotiating Algeria's independence. (It came in 1962.)

De Gaulle also stressed France's claim to be a major power. Unwilling to depend solely on the U.S. "nuclear umbrella," he pushed a French nuclear program. In 1960, shortly before the Paris summit meeting, France tested its first atomic bomb. De Gaulle began to distance himself from the United States and NATO.

Cuban Premier Fidel Castro and United Arab Republic Gamal Abdel Nasser visit at UAR headquarters in New York.

Britain, which had had its own bomb since 1952, moved toward closer military ties with the United States. In 1958, it became the first foreign country to allow U.S. intermediate-range ballistic missiles (IRBMs) to be stationed on its soil. Two more NATO members, Italy and Turkey, accepted such missiles the following year.

The Middle East remained a hotbed of tension. Seeking to bolster pro-Western governments there, President Eisenhower in 1957 proclaimed what was called the Eisenhower Doctrine. "The existing vacuum in the Middle East must be filled by the United States before it is filled by Russia," he said. Congress gave the President the power to use U.S. military forces in the Middle East "against overt armed aggression from any nation controlled by international communism."

In 1958, Egyptian leader Gamal Abdul Nasser arranged a merger between his nation and Syria. The two countries formed the United Arab Republic. Soon after, a military coup ousted the pro-Western government of Iraq, and a leftist, pro-Nasser government took power there. When the government of Lebanon asked for help against leftist rebels, Eisenhower landed 15,000 U.S. Marines in Lebanon. The troops did not see action and remained for only a few months.

In East Asia, the United States continued to shun all forms of relations with Communist China. Meanwhile, U.S. ties with Japan went through a rocky period. U.S. and Japanese leaders worked out a new security pact to replace the one in effect since 1951. The new pact treated Japan as more of an equal. Nonetheless, Japanese leftists poured into the streets to protest. Demonstrations became so violent that President Eisenhower had to abandon a planned visit to Japan in June 1960.

RELATIONS WITH LATIN AMERICA

Hostile demonstrations were nothing new to U.S. leaders. In 1958, angry crowds had spat upon Vice President Nixon and smashed the windows of his car as he toured Venezuela and other Latin American nations. Nixon attributed the hostility to Communist agitation. "Right here was the ruthlessness and the determination, the fanaticism of the enemy that we face," he wrote later.

One part of Latin America where Americans had always considered themselves welcome was Cuba. The Caribbean nation lay only 90 miles off the coast of Florida. U.S. business people had invested heavily in Cuban sugar plantations and industries. U.S. tourists sunned on Cuban beaches and gambled at Cuban casinos.

In 1956, a former lawyer named Fidel Castro led a small band of fighters into the mountains of southern Cuba. The rebels gained many followers. On the first day of 1959, Castro's forces swept triumphantly into the capital city, Havana, as Cuba's right-wing dictator fled. Castro set up a left-wing government. He took control of plantations and industries and promised free elections.

By jerking back the welcome mat for U.S. investors, Castro set the stage for a confrontation with U.S. power. President Eisenhower applied economic sanctions on grounds that Castro had refused to pay for U.S.-owned property. Castro turned to the Soviet Union for support.

Meanwhile, Cuba went through a period of turmoil. Mobs demanded punishment for officials of the former government accused of crimes and atrocities. Many were lynched or executed without trial. News of these events horrified Americans. Some U.S. newspapers began to portray Castro as a bloody tyrant.

Cubans themselves were violently divided over Castro's policies. Many applauded the new leader and his calls for revolutionary changes. Others denounced Castro, asking why he had failed to hold the promised elections. A stream of Cuban exiles fled to Miami and other cities in the United States.

By 1960, Eisenhower had decided that Castro was either a Communist or a tool of Communists. Eisenhower authorized the CIA to form an army of Cuban exiles to invade Cuba and overthrow Castro. The invasion was set to take place in 1961 after Eisenhower left office.

SECTION RECAP

1. What was President Eisenhower's "Open Skies" plan? What was Khrushchev's objection to it?

2. How did the U-2 crash in 1960 affect the Paris Summit? Eisenhower's Soviet visit? The American public's trust in U.S. official statements?

3. In the late 1950's, how did nuclear weapons affect U.S. relations with France? with Britain?

4. On what did Nixon and Eisenhower place the blame for tension between the United States and Latin America?

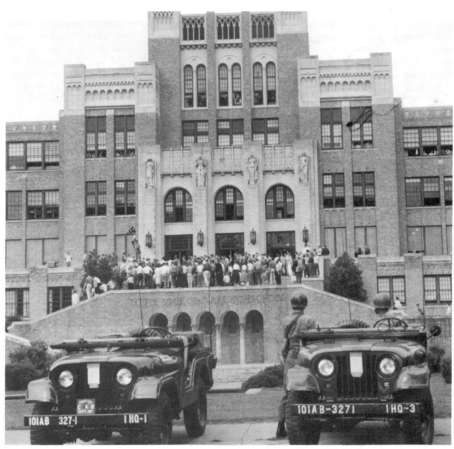

Central High School in Little Rock under federal guard.

3 Domestic Events: Hope and Turmoil

While world events often made headlines, it was day-to-day America that interested most people. What were people doing in 1957, the year when Eisenhower began his second term? Some were flipping around a new toy, a plastic disc called the Frisbee. Others had planted themselves firmly in front of a TV set.

The networks, taking a cue from the President's taste in reading, specialized in Westerns that year. If *Gunsmoke* or *Death Valley Days* didn't satisfy prime-time viewers, they could try *Have Gun — Will Travel*. Meanwhile, daytime viewers who tuned in after school saw clean-cut American teenagers dancing to the latest hit records on Dick Clark's *American Bandstand*. While the occasional performer was black, Clark and the teenage dancers were white — like the actors on TV Westerns.

CRISIS AT LITTLE ROCK

Race mattered very much in the America of 1957. It mattered to Elizabeth Eckford, a black teenager in Little Rock, Arkansas, on the morning of September 3 as she put on a new black-and-white dress and caught a bus to school. Elizabeth was one of nine black children about to be admitted to Central High School under a school board desegregation plan. But none of the students made it to class that day. Passing through a crowd of angry whites outside the school, the young people came up against grim-faced Arkansas National Guardsmen armed with rifles and bayonets. "Governor Faubus has placed this school off-limits to Negroes," a guardsman declared. He gazed straight ahead, lips tight.

Elizabeth heard ugly shouts from the crowd. A woman — a white woman — spat in her face. Another white woman comforted Elizabeth and helped her catch a bus home.

Orval Faubus, the governor of Arkansas, had called out the guardsmen to block the desegregation of the school. The governor said he acted to preserve law and order. Critics charged that Faubus' goal was to win votes by appealing to racism. The incident quickly escalated into a major confrontation between state and national power. Faubus claimed a duty to enforce state law and protect the peace. Finding no threat to peace, a federal judge ordered Faubus to remove the troops and stop hindering desegregation.

As the crisis built toward a climax, President Eisenhower avoided involvement. He did not want to anger the South. He had made clear his belief that desegregation would be a long-term process that could not be forced. On the other hand, he believed that it was his duty to enforce federal law. The Supreme Court had spoken; desegregation was now the law of the land. If a president allowed the law to be openly challenged by a governor, the result would be anarchy, perhaps even a new dissolution of the Union. Trying to buy time, Eisenhower assured southern leaders he had no wish to intervene.

Yet the crisis kept building. Obeying the federal court, Governor Faubus removed the Arkansas troops. On Monday morning, September 23, Elizabeth and the other black students slipped into school by a side door. But a mob raged outside. Its members beat up a group of black reporters. Fearing worse trouble, the mayor of Little Rock then ordered the black students removed for their own safety.

Again the next day the mob formed. This time the mayor turned to Washington for help. "The immediate need for federal troops is urgent," he wired. ". . . Situation is out of control and police cannot disperse mob." Eisenhower decided to act. Within hours, 1,000

Elizabeth Eckford, one of nine black students who integrated Central High School.

U.S. paratroopers had taken up positions in Little Rock. Meanwhile, the President federalized the Arkansas National Guard. That is, he removed it from the governor's command and put it under federal control. The guardsmen would now help to enforce desegregation rather than block it.

In a nationally televised speech that evening, Eisenhower declared: "We are a nation in which laws, not men, are supreme. . . . Mob rule cannot be allowed to override the decision of our courts." It had taken the U.S. Army to do it, but Central High School had been desegregated.

As Eisenhower had feared, the use of armed force touched a raw nerve among southern whites. "This is the darkest day in southern history since the Reconstruction," a speaker told a Kiwanis luncheon in Marshall, Texas. Those at the luncheon refused to pledge allegiance to the flag. Senator James Eastland of Mississippi declared: "The President's move was an attempt to destroy the social order of the South." Similar angry words would be heard for years to come. It was now clear however, that federal leaders took desegregation seriously. Slowly, racial barriers began to come down in schools throughout the South.

Other barriers also lowered. For many years, white officials in much of the South had manipulated laws to keep blacks from voting. In the Civil Rights Act of 1957, passed just before the Little Rock crisis, Congress made it a federal crime to try to deprive people of their voting rights. It authorized the U.S. attorney general to go to court to block any such attempts. The 1957 law was the first federal civil rights act to pass Congress since Reconstruction.

BEYOND LITTLE ROCK

Television and newspaper coverage of the Little Rock crisis carried its impact beyond Arkansas and the South. U.S. officials worried about what dark-skinned people in other

Hostile onlookers sprayed these three demonstrators with catsup, mustard, and sugar during a Jackson, MS, sit-in.

parts of the world would think of American society. Would they dwell on the violence and racism? Or would they see U.S. society as moving toward greater racial equality?

The events in Little Rock also affected Americans outside the South. Many viewers were shocked at the raw hatred they saw on their TV screens. They felt sympathy for targets of such hatred — for black people like Elizabeth Eckford. However, many northern whites mistakenly assumed that racism and discrimination were southern problems only. That was not so. In the North, blacks still faced discrimination in jobs, in housing, and in many other parts of life. Such discrimination was often informal, rather than sanctioned by local and state laws, but its impact could still be devastating. In years to come, a growing civil rights movement would target northern as well as southern racism.

The civil rights movement found new methods of dramatizing black grievances. One target was whites-only eating facilities. In much of the South, restaurants and lunch counters refused to let blacks sit down to eat a meal. For blacks there was nothing but "take-out" service.

In February 1960, four black college students bought some small items at an F.W. Woolworth store in Greensboro, North Carolina. Then they took seats at the store's lunch counter and ordered apple pie and coffee. Refused service, they remained in their seats until closing time, and the next day they were back, with friends. Soon, the tactic of "sit-ins" spread to Woolworth stores in other cities, and to the stores of other chains — S.H.

Kress, W.T. Grant, Walgreen, and more. Despite harassment from whites who gathered to jeer, the blacks eventually won out. Annoyed by the unfavorable national publicity, the chains, one by one, desegregated their lunch counters.

Meanwhile, Congress continued to address the grievances of blacks. The Civil Rights Act of 1960 gave the government new powers to enforce voting rights.

TARGETING COMMUNISM

Senator Joseph McCarthy died in 1957, having failed to discover a single Communist. Yet outspoken anti-communism did not die with him. Concerned citizens organized a number of national anti-Communist groups. Perhaps the most widely-known was the John Birch Society, founded in 1958 by a Massachusetts candy manufacturer named Robert Welch. By the mid-1960's, the society would claim 100,000 members all across the nation.

The society took its name from a U.S. intelligence officer killed by the Chinese Communists in 1945, 10 days after World War II ended. Welch viewed the officer as the first casualty of the Cold War. Targets of the Birch Society ranged from income tax to Chief Justice Earl Warren, whose Supreme Court decisions angered many conservatives. Welch also lashed out at President Eisenhower, calling him "a dedicated, conscious agent" of a worldwide Communist conspiracy. In addition, Welch attacked the civil rights movement.

Many opponents of integration were convinced that Communists were behind the civil rights movement. In 1959 an undercover agent for the state of Georgia photographed black leader Martin Luther King, Jr., with a group of people that included a columnist for the *Daily Worker*, a newspaper published by the Communist party. Later, the photograph appeared on billboards all over the South. Huge letters proclaimed that King had attended a Communist training center. Although no one ever provided any proof, accusations that King was a Communist agent circulated widely for years.

BLAZING NEW TRAILS

Americans took a series of steps toward the future in the late 1950's. Some of the steps were easy to see — and widely celebrated. Others would not be publicly perceived for years.

One advance was the introduction of jet airplanes to commercial service. For most of the 1950's, Americans who traveled by air took lumbering, propeller-driven planes. Trans-Atlantic trips took many hours and often required fueling stops in places such as Newfoundland. Time-saving jet service began between New York and London in October 1958. Two months later jets went into service on domestic U.S. flights.

Another startling change came with the introduction of a xerographic ("dry-writing") photocopier in 1960. The world came to know the machine as the Xerox 914. For the first time, offices could get instant copies on regular paper of letters, newspaper clippings, and other documents. Secretaries no longer had to spend hours retyping a document; they could

copy it in minutes. Office work changed dramatically, and so did office high jinks. Workers quickly discovered that they could make copies of handprints, cartoons, and recipes to post on walls and doors.

Medical changes were also affecting Americans' lives. Introduction of the Salk polio vaccine in 1955 (and later the Sabin vaccine) almost eliminated a much-feared childhood disease. Victims of polio often became severely crippled, and an epidemic in the early 1950's infected a record 58,000 people in one year. In 1960 only 3,277 cases were reported — the lowest total in decades.

Dr. Jonas Salk.

One medical innovation provoked great controversy. It was an oral contraceptive, or birth-control medicine, often called simply the pill. First marketed in 1960, the pill came to be used by many American women who

New York students with the lollipops they received in return for the polio shots.

wanted to decide when and if they would have children. Advocates of the pill said it would give women greater control over their own lives and prevent the birth of unwanted children. Critics said it would cause a decline in sexual morality. The Roman Catholic Church warned its members against using either the pill or other contraceptives.

Ads and news coverage ballyhooed such developments at once, but years would pass before most people heard about another innovation — the microchip. Working separately, inventors Jack Kilby and Robert Noyce came up with "the chip" in 1958. The microchip carried forward the miniaturization of electronics that had begun with the transistor. By combining several elements of electrical circuitry on a thin wafer of silicon, the microchip did away with bulky wiring. It paved the way for pocket calculators and home computers, and made space travel more practical.

THE AFFLUENT SOCIETY

With each passing year, Americans were growing wealthier. By 1961, when Eisenhower left office, one family in every six owned two or more cars. That compared with one family in 25 a decade earlier. Most families owned refrigerators, television sets, and other symbols of "easy living."

The typical family was now earning about $5,300 a year — roughly $102 a week. Compared to the $67 a week that had been the standard 10 years earlier, that seemed like a fortune. For most blacks, however, such magnificent incomes were still only a dream. Even in 1961, the typical black family earned a mere $56 a week.

More and more women, white and black, were taking jobs and bringing home paychecks. No longer did the typical job-holding woman come from a poorer family. Middle-class women in increasing numbers were serv-

American kitchens of the 1950's became showcases of new electrical appliances.

ing as breadwinners, taking jobs that in earlier years would have been filled by men.

Americans had much to brag about, and brag they did. In 1959, Vice President Nixon did his bragging in an unlikely place — the kitchen of a model American home on display in Moscow, the Soviet capital. As television cameras caught the scene, Nixon engaged Soviet leader Nikita Khrushchev in what became known as the Kitchen Debate.

Proudly, Nixon told Khrushchev that almost any American worker could afford a house like the one displayed. Khrushchev shrugged him off. Russians have nice homes too, he insisted. Nixon turned the topic to freedom of choice. In our country, he said, it is not the government that decides who shall have a new house. "We have a thousand different builders — that's the spice of life." The vice president went on to urge that two superpowers compete in washing machines — not rockets. "Yes," replied Khrushchev, "that's the kind of competition we want."

But were cars and TV sets and washing machines enough? Was America as rich and successful as it seemed? Some people were expressing doubts. One of the doubters was John Kenneth Galbraith, a Harvard economist. In 1958 he published a book called *The Affluent Society*. Yes, he declared, Americans were affluent (wealthy), but mainly in their private lives. Public needs — for schools, parks, and mental institutions, for example, — were often poorly met. Pollution fouled streams. Air was becoming unbreathable. To make matters worse, American society seemed to have neither the money nor the will to cure such ills.

Others voiced different reservations about trends in U.S. society. In *The Organization Man* (1956), magazine editor William H. Whyte, Jr., deplored a trend toward conformity in business and social life. Still other critics focused on the auto industry. Some accused manufacturers of tricking people into buying new cars by annual design changes that made older models seem obsolete, or out-dated. "Planned obsolescence," the critics said, was wasteful and only enriched the auto makers.

POLITICAL STALEMATE

Whatever the real or perceived ills of society, agreeing on solutions was difficult when control of the federal government remained split between two parties. The Republicans had successfully returned Eisenhower to the White House in 1956, but Democrats still held both houses of Congress. The congressional election of 1958, which came after *Sputnik* and in the middle of a business slump, sharply increased the Democrats' majority. Under such conditions, law-making required a spirit of compromise on both sides, leaving little room for dramatic new departures.

A key congressional concern during this period was corruption in labor unions. Senator John L. McClellan of Arkansas conducted hearings on charges of rigged elections, skimmed union funds, extortion, and racketeering. One of McClellan's prime targets was the International Brotherhood of Teamsters, whose president, Dave Beck, eventually went to prison. In 1957 the AFL-CIO expelled the Teamsters and other unions linked to corruption.

Seeking to crack down on union corruption, Congress passed the Landrum-Griffin Act of 1959. The act guaranteed fair election procedures within unions. It prescribed prison terms for officials convicted of misusing union funds. In addition, the act sought to provide further protection to employers not directly involved in labor-management disputes.

The Eisenhower administration suffered a number of embarrassments at the hands of Congress. Committee hearings drew attention to questionable gift-taking by administration officials. One of those forced to resign was White House Chief of Staff Sherman Adams, who had received a fur coat and other gifts from a businessman seeking government favors. A further embarrassment was Congress's rejection in 1959 of Eisenhower's nominee as secretary of commerce, Lewis L. Strauss. It was the first time since 1925 that Congress had rejected a cabinet nomination.

SECTION RECAP

1. Why was President Eisenhower hesitant to become involved in the Little Rock desegregation crisis? How was he eventually pressed into making a decision?

2. Name two technological and two medical advances of the late 1950's and early 1960's.

3. What point did John Kenneth Galbraith wish to make in his 1958 book *The Affluent Society*?

4 More Cultural Change

An early drive-in movie theater.

An era in American life ended in 1960, when CBS took the radio program *Amos 'n Andy* off the air. Ever since it first aired on NBC in 1929, *Amos 'n Andy* had been one of the most popular shows on radio. During the 1930's and 1940's, a stroller down an average American street at 7:00 P.M. on a summer evening seemed to hear the Negro-dialect voices of Freeman F. Gosden and Charles Correll (both white) coming from every open window on a block: "Yassuh, Andy, I's sho' happy tuh see yuh . . . ". In those days, the 15-minute program aired five nights a week.

The program fell victim to two trends in American life. First, radio was giving way to television as a medium for broadcast comedy and drama. Second, racial stereotypes were no longer deemed acceptable on the national airwaves. By 1960, programs such as *Amos 'n Andy* offended many whites as well as most

blacks. (Nonetheless, a televised version with black actors would stay on the air until 1964.)

American life was changing, and the entertainment industries reflected the new trends.

THE MOVIES FIGHT TO SURVIVE

For years, television had been cutting deeply into movie audiences. Why pay 40 or 50 cents to see a movie when you could watch a free show in your own living room? The film industry searched for ways to lure customers back.

One way was to use technology. Cinerama, CinemaScope, and other patented processes offered wider screens. The illusion of depth was created by 3-D. At the same time, new color processes provided brighter contrasts and flashier pictures.

A second way was to show movies at open-air drive-in theaters. First introduced in 1933, drive-ins reached their peak of popularity in 1958, when more than 4,000 of them were in operation. Some drive-ins seemed like miniature amusement parks, with playground slides, miniature golf courses, bingo nights, and even Ferris wheels. Operators appealed to the family trade, with carload prices that made movie-going almost as cheap as staying at home. Teenagers, too, found drive-ins an attractive place to go on dates.

Meanwhile, films were becoming bolder. Television was tending to shy away from controversy, as advertisers found that they sold more of their products if their commercials came in programs that left people feeling good about themselves rather than worrying about social problems. Films took up themes such as racial intolerance and drug addiction. They also began to use words that were too shocking and scenes that were too intimate for television. This was a major change, since the film industry had formerly exercised a severe self-censorship. Until the 1950's, the industry's Production Code not only barred certain words but required that good deeds shown on screen must be rewarded and bad deeds punished. Movies such as *Peyton Place* (1957) and *Suddenly Last Summer* (1959) marked a shift toward frankness.

WHITHER TELEVISION?

The trend away from controversy helped to make television more profitable than ever. Advertisers spent more than $1 billion on TV commercials in 1955 and more than $1.6 billion

in 1961. About half of the sum went to the three major networks, NBC, CBS, and ABC.

Technological changes were giving television producers more freedom and allowing greater versatility. Until 1958, most programs were broadcast live. If a program had to be delayed, the pictures on a TV screen were photographed on kinescope film, which then had to be processed. Videotape, introduced in the late 1950's, required no such processing. Images were recorded directly on magnetic tape and could be reused at once. Besides, videotape was easy to edit. It came into widespread use for entertainment programs and for newscasts.

Color TV, introduced in 1951, gained popularity through the 1950's, with NBC providing more color programming than the other two networks combined. Few homes had color sets, however. As late as 1960, only about 300,000 such sets were in use.

All three networks provided 15-minute nightly newscasts. But "serious" programming dropped off in the late 1950's. *See It Now*, the Edward R. Murrow program that had turned a national spotlight on Joseph McCarthy, became an occasional special in 1956. CBS dropped it for good in 1958.

In an address to TV and radio news directors in 1958, Murrow lashed out at what he called the "escapism" of television programming. He warned that television . . . "is being used to distract, delude, amuse, and insulate us." Other critics called TV an "idiot box" and turned up their noses at programs like *The $64,000 Question, Zorro,* and *Heave Ho Harrigan.*

EISENHOWER'S FAREWELL ADDRESS

Often, when people snapped on their television sets in the 1950's and early 1960's, they saw the grandfatherly figure of President Eisenhower. His press conferences were carried on television beginning in 1955. The President also made TV speeches — although at first he had resisted the idea. "I can think of nothing more boring, for the American public," he said, "than to have to sit in their living rooms for a whole half- hour looking at my face on their television screen." The most widely quoted TV speech of Eisenhower's two terms took place on January 17, 1961, three days before he left office. Eisenhower called the speech his Farewell Address.

The President's theme was the Cold War, and he echoed several of the concerns he had dwelt on in the previous eight years. The United States, he said, faced "ruthless" enemies with a hostile ideology. It needed a strong and ready military defense. Eisenhower warned against "a recurring temptation to feel that some spectacular and costly action could become the miraculous solution to all current difficulties." Rather, he argued, the United States must keep a sense of balance. In particular, it must keep "balance between the private and the public economy."

Then Eisenhower turned to what he termed the *military-industrial complex*. The term was new, and it described a close linkage between big industry and the military that dated back only to the late 1940's.

When World War II ended, U.S. leaders had sought a way to maintain war readiness during peacetime. Previously, when a military conflict ended, war industries had converted to civilian production. Factories that made tanks began making farm machinery or automobiles. If war came again, it would be simple enough to switch those factories back to making war goods.

But the complexity of modern technology now made such methods obsolete, U.S. leaders believed. This was especially so in aeronautics. If airplane makers had to depend on civilian orders, the reasoning went, many would go bankrupt. Once they had closed down, they would not be available for making warplanes for any future needs. To maintain its ability to gear up for war, then, the United States would have to plan ahead. It would have to order enough warplanes and other military necessities even in peacetime to keep its industries primed for any emergency.

Such reasoning led to major changes in the

Eisenhower reads over his Farewell Address.

relationship between government and industry. The government became a major source of funds for researching and developing new airplanes and other implements of war. Government contracts became a prime source of income for a wide range of industrial firms. The firms would prosper so long as they could renew or expand those contracts. They had a vested interest in high military budgets.

Universities also came to depend on federal funds for a growing part of their research. Even in fields like psychology, some research had military implications and was financed by the armed forces. In a sense, then, there was a "military-academic" complex as well as its military-industrial cousin — a point that Eisenhower touched on in his Farewell Address.

In the address, Eisenhower declared: "We have been compelled to create a permanent armaments industry of vast proportions . . . We annually spend on military security more than the net income of all United States corporations." He added: "We recognize the imperative need for this development. Yet we must not fail to comprehend its grave implications." He warned: "In the councils of government, we must guard against the acquisition of unwarranted influence, whether sought or unsought, by the military-industrial complex. The potential for the disastrous rise of misplaced power exists and will persist." The danger, Eisenhower said, was that military objectives might override civil liberties and democratic processes.

Eisenhower's Farewell Address would provide food for thought in the years ahead. Some people would misinterpret it as a call for the United States to cut back its military forces or to put an end to military-industrial and military-academic ties. But Eisenhower had said that such ties grew out of real needs. They were here to stay. Eisenhower wanted to alert the American people to what he saw as their potential dangers.

Eisenhower was leery of the governmental activism that the American people seemed to have been seeking since *Sputnik*. There had been calls for major new space programs, a step-up in missile building, and sweeping new domestic programs. Projects of this kind would thrust the government into new roles and entangle it more and more in everyday life. Eisenhower wanted to ward off such changes.

But his time as President was up. In November 1960 the voters had chosen a new leader who personified a taste for governmental activism. John F. Kennedy would take office on January 20, 1961, and Eisenhower's conception of limited government would go into eclipse — at least for a while.

SECTION RECAP

1. Why was the film industry suffering in the late 1950's? What methods were used to lure viewers back to movie theatres?

2. What changes in television programming in the late 1950's prompted Edward R. Murrow's criticism?

3. What did Eisenhower mean by the term *military-industrial complex*? How did this apply to the academic world of universities?

1. List the items that were American responses to *Sputnik*.

the National Defense Education Act

the summit conference

the Landrum-Griffin Act

the U-2 incident

the Antarctica Treaty

the "Open Skies" plan

xerography

Project Mercury

NASA

the Eisenhower Doctrine

Explorer I

Khrushchev's visit

Vanguard

videotape

2. Define the term *military industrial complex*. Why did Eisenhower think that Americans needed to be warned about it?

3. Describe the purpose of the U-2 overflights. What cover story was developed in case the flights were detected? Why did the cover not work when a plane was shot down? How did the incident change the view of the United States government held by most Americans?

4. What did Eisenhower do in Arkansas during the Little Rock Crisis that made it clear that the federal government intended to enforce desegregation laws? How did the reaction of many people in the South differ from those of many viewers who watched the events on television? What did the Civil Rights Act of 1957 provide?

5. How were black Americans depicted in the radio show *Amos 'n Andy*? How does it differ from the way blacks are shown in television sit-coms today? What does this tell you about the effects of the civil rights movement on the entertainment industry and American society at large?

CHAPTER 5

1961

1963

A Torch Is Passed

First Lady Jacqueline Kennedy accompanies her husband, John, to the Inaugural Ball.

O N THE EVENING BEFORE he was to be sworn in as the nation's 35th President, John F. Kennedy happened upon the text of Thomas Jefferson's first inaugural address. The speech had been printed in the program for the Inaugural Concert at Washington's Constitution Hall. Kennedy read the text in his limousine while traveling from one event to another as snow swirled through the city streets. When he had read it all, he shook his head. "Better than mine," he said.

In the third week of January 1961, the past and the future had come together in the na-tion's capital as they rarely do. The departing President, Dwight Eisenhower, had been a familiar national figure for many of his 70 years. The incoming President was only 43, the youngest person ever elected to the highest U.S. office. He had many of the advantages of youth — curiosity, attractiveness, vigor. Like Jefferson, he also had a deep appreciation of the English language and its uses.

Near dawn on January 20, 1961, the snow had stopped falling. At midday it covered roads and walkways, clung to trees and roof-tops, and glittered in the bright sun. The ceremonies at Capitol Plaza did not begin on a note of promise. First, some wires under the lectern short-circuited and began to smoke, alarming members of the Secret Service. Then the glare from the snow prevented silver-haired poet Robert Frost from reading a specially prepared verse. He announced that the poem he had written was a preface to one that he knew by heart. He thereupon recited "The Gift Outright" from memory.

At nine minutes before 1:00 P.M., Chief Justice Earl Warren delivered the oath of office. Then the new President began his address. Early in the speech Kennedy struck its keynote: "Let the word go forth from this time and place, to friend and foe alike, that the torch has been passed to a new generation of Americans — born in this century, tempered by war, disciplined by a hard and bitter peace, proud of our ancient heritage — and unwilling to witness or permit the slow undoing of those human rights to which this nation has always been committed . . . ."

"Let every nation know, whether it wishes us well or ill, that we shall pay any price, bear any burden, meet any hardship, support any friend, oppose any foe to assure the survival and success of liberty."

To the world's poor, Kennedy pledged "our best efforts to help them help themselves." To the countries of Latin America, he offered a "new alliance for progress" to help cast off "the chains of poverty." To the United Nations, "our last best hope in an age where the instruments of war have far outpaced the in-struments of peace," he gave renewed promise of support. To the Soviet Union and other adversaries, he asked "that both sides begin anew the quest for peace." He reminded Soviets and Americans alike that "civility is not a sign of weakness, and sincerity is always subject to proof." He called for the use of reason in diplomacy: "Let us never negotiate out of fear. But let us never fear to negotiate."

Finally, Kennedy returned to his earlier theme of time and place. "In the long history of the world, only a few generations have been granted the role of defending freedom in its hour of maximum danger. I do not shrink from this responsibility — I welcome it . . . . The energy, the faith, the devotion which we bring to this endeavor will light our country and all

Chief Justice Warren swears in the new President.

who serve it — and the glow from that fire can truly light the world.

"And so, my fellow Americans: Ask not what your country can do for you — ask what you can do for your country.

"My fellow citizens of the world: ask not what America will do for you, but what together we can do for the freedom of man."

Prolonged applause rang through the Capitol Plaza. The crowds who had waited in the stinging wind had heard perhaps the most idealistic inaugural address of the century. "The speech he made out there was better than Lincoln," said Speaker of the House Sam Rayburn in a moment of exuberance. Some political analysts had already speculated that the incoming administration would be marked by a new quest for excellence. Kennedy had set the tone for such a quest himself.

1 John F. Kennedy and Presidential Power

The next day, Kennedy made an early morning visit to the Oval Office in the White House west wing. He sat in the presidential chair and fiddled with the communications system on his desk. Kennedy was still getting used to thinking of himself as President. "Do you think the country is ready for us yet?" he asked with a laugh.

Kennedy was prepared to enjoy presidential power in the way that Franklin Roosevelt had once enjoyed it. The office of the presidency had never been more powerful. The

nation's greatest leaders — George Washington, Thomas Jefferson, Andrew Jackson, Abraham Lincoln, Theodore Roosevelt, Woodrow Wilson — left the office with more authority than they had found it. Presidential power had been accumulating for 170 years.

GROWTH OF THE PRESIDENCY

Some aspects of the growth of the presidency had to do with the gradual expansion of the federal government. The nation's first President, Washington, had a cabinet of five men. By 1961, the size of the cabinet had doubled. The number of employees serving in the executive branch of the federal government had multiplied many times.

The nation's founders had created a government with a separation of powers. Yet in the 20th century both Congress and the Supreme Court had placed greater responsibility in presidential hands. In two cases of the late 1930's, for example, the Supreme Court made it clear that the president's power over foreign affairs was superior to that of Congress. These rulings gave weight to later arguments that few, if any, restraints existed on the president's ability to make foreign policy.

As we have already seen, Congress also expanded presidential power in the years immediately following World War II. In 1946 it set up a Council of Economic Advisers to guide the president in the creation of national economic policies. The same year Congress approved the Atomic Energy Act, which gave the president final authority over the "development, manufacture, use, and storage of [atomic] bombs." In 1947 the National Security Act gave the president detailed power over defense and foreign policy. It also established several new tools for carrying out that power, including the CIA and the National Security Council. All three laws created a bureaucracy that became an important part of the president's general staff.

During Franklin Roosevelt's years in the White House, the staff had never numbered more than 100 people. By the second Eisenhower administration, however, it numbered some 1,200 people. Presidential power remained uniquely personal. Yet it was being executed by an ever-expanding army of federal workers.

As President, John Kennedy
used forceful oratory to press his policies.

As the Cold War continued, the presidency had come to be regarded as the most efficient branch of the federal government. It also seemed the most democratic, since only the president represented "all the people." The president had more and more control over foreign affairs and defense — and slowly took on control of the economy. Above all, the president had complete responsibility for the use of nuclear arms.

As Kennedy took office, then, the presidency seemed the central institution of American life. It had become the main political focus of television news. Kennedy did not share Eisenhower's reservations that the office had grown too powerful, or Eisenhower's restraint in using that power.

POLITICS IN THE GENES

The new President came from an Irish family in the days when the Irish loomed large in the politics of large eastern cities. His paternal grandfather, Patrick Kennedy, was a successful bar owner and minor politician. His maternal grandfather, John F. "Honey Fitz" Fitzgerald, had twice been mayor of Boston. The President's father, Joseph Kennedy, Sr., had served as ambassador to Great Britain during the 1930's. Wealthy beyond easy measure, he remained active in the Democratic party throughout his life.

Lieutenant Kennedy aboard a PT boat during World War II.

John Kennedy had three brothers and five sisters, all instilled with a strong sense of self-worth and competition. In the summers, the competition became keenest in sports such as tennis and touch football at the Kennedy home on Cape Cod. "They are the most competitive and at the same time the most cohesive family I've ever seen," said one longtime friend.

At the dinner table, discussion usually turned to public issues. "I can hardly remember a meal time," John's brother, Robert, later said, "when the conversation was not dominated by what Franklin D. Roosevelt was doing or what was happening around the world . . . . Since public affairs had dominated so much of our actions and discussions, public life seemed really an extension of family life." John recalled how his father had taken a strong interest in his children. "He held up standards for us, and he was very tough when we failed to meet those standards. The toughness was important."

At 13, Kennedy went to a boarding school in Connecticut. He then attended Choate, a New England preparatory school, and finally Harvard College, where he majored in government. For his senior thesis, he wrote a critical analysis of Britain's unwillingness to prepare for World War II. In this paper, he argued that the British in power were more interested in profits than in stopping the aggressions of Nazi Germany. With some editing, the thesis later became a book, *Why England Slept*, and won critical acclaim.

During World War II Kennedy had served as a lieutenant in the Navy, assigned to the South Pacific. In August 1943, he and 11 crewmen were aboard a patrol torpedo (PT) boat which was torn in half by a Japanese destroyer. Kennedy was thrown hard onto the deck and later recalled thinking: "This is how it feels to be killed." Kennedy saved a crew member that day by swimming through burning gasoline with the man's life-jacket belt gripped in his teeth. For his bravery he won

The Kennedy wedding party at Newport, RI. John's brother Robert claps while Edward (far left) laughs.

Navy and Marine Corps medals and the Purple Heart. He also injured his back and spent the rest of the war in a hospital.

A year after the war ended, John Kennedy won a seat in Congress as a Democrat from Massachusetts's 11th Congressional District. In 1952 he took on a popular Republican, Henry Cabot Lodge, in a race for the United States Senate and defeated him narrowly.

At about this time, he began dating a wealthy, stylish graduate of Vassar College, Jacqueline Bouvier. After a storybook courtship, the two were married in the autumn of 1953. Kennedy's back problems soon flared again, causing him ever greater torment. When he underwent risky surgery, it led to an infection that nearly caused his death. Yet he endured pain as casually as possible, and usually in silence.

Kennedy remained as cool in his politics as he was in his acceptance of pain. Among Democrats in the Senate, he was considered a "middle-of-the-roader," not always comfortable with the liberal positions of his party in Massachusetts. To be sure, he supported liberals on "bread-and-butter" issues such as Social Security, low-cost housing, and the minimum wage. He disappointed liberal colleagues, however, by his repeated failure to disavow the tactics of Senator Joseph McCarthy. Like many Irish voters, Joseph Kennedy, Sr., had taken a liking to this Republican senator of Irish descent.

In 1958 Kennedy was reelected by more than 850,000 votes, the widest margin for a Senate race in Massachusetts history. Being ambitious, Kennedy now aspired to his party's presidential nomination. So did another ambitious politician, Vice President Richard Nixon.

THE NEW FRONTIER

In the summer of 1960, the two men won the candidacies of their respective parties. In accepting his bid, Kennedy told the Democratic convention that the "frontier of the 1960's" demanded "invention, innovation, imagination, decision. I am asking each of you to be new pioneers on that new frontier."

At the opening of the campaign, television commentator Eric Sevareid saw little difference between the two candidates. He likened them to junior executives trying to get ahead in a business corporation. Although both men were attractive, Sevareid claimed, they lacked any political passion except their own personal ambition.

Within a few weeks, however, the differences between the candidates became plainer. As vice president, Nixon could show familiarity with the highest echelons of the executive branch. As a senator, Kennedy could not. Kennedy usually exuded self-confidence, even grace, in his public speeches. Nixon, by contrast, often stiffened when speaking before unfriendly audiences.

Perhaps the sharpest political mark of distinction was religion. Nixon was a Protestant, while Kennedy was a Roman Catholic. Kennedy's religion was widely viewed as a handicap. No Roman Catholic had ever been elected president.

Kennedy met the religious issue head-on in a speech before the Greater Houston Ministerial Association. "I believe in an America . . .," he told the clergymen, "where no public official either requests or accepts instructions on public policy from the Pope, the

Kennedy campaigns in Los Angeles.

National Council of Churches, or any other ecclesiastical source . . . I do not speak for my church on public matters — and the church does not speak for me." No American Catholic had ever made public his views of the role of church and state in such detail.

At first Kennedy seemed less eager to call attention to his views on civil rights. By championing the cause of black Americans too boldly, he risked a loss of support from white southerners. When Atlanta police arrested black civil rights leader Martin Luther King,

Jr., at a sit-in, however, Kennedy phoned King's wife, Coretta, to pledge assistance. His brother Robert later helped to gain King's release on bail. Nixon, meanwhile, ignored the incident. Under the circumstances, Kennedy's moves earned him hundreds of thousands of black votes across the United States.

Nixon promised to campaign in all 50 states, and he kept his word, taxing his energies to the core. Kennedy concentrated his efforts in states with large *blocs* (groups with common interests) of electoral votes such as Pennsylvania, Ohio, and Michigan. In the end, personal campaigning was less important than the way the candidates came across in four televised debates.

The 1960 campaign marked the first time that TV debates had been held in a presidential contest. In the first debate, Kennedy emerged as cool and self-confident. By contrast, a travel-weary Nixon looked drawn and haggard. He had spurned television makeup in favor of a pancake cosmetic, and as a result he looked in need of a shave. He directed his remarks to Kennedy, while Kennedy directed his to the camera. When the debate ended, most analysts believed it had helped Kennedy and damaged Nixon.

In the remaining debates, Nixon improved his performance greatly. Yet the second and third telecasts had smaller audiences than the first, and the fourth apparently did not change many minds. After the election a pollster calculated that of four million people who had watched the programs, three million had voted for Kennedy.

On Election Day, the popular vote favored Kennedy by the thinnest margin awarded any presidential candidate in this century. He won by a mere 113,000 votes out of more than 68 million cast. The electoral count gave him a wider edge — 303 to 219 — but that advantage was misleading. Several large states such as Texas and Illinois reported voting irregularities. If those two states had gone the other way, the electoral outcome would have been reversed.

How much of an affect had Kennedy's religion had on voting patterns? In every part of the country, the candidate had drawn large blocs of Catholic voters, whether of Irish, Italian, or Polish descent. (As far as can be determined, German-American Catholics were less united.) Investigations in certain precincts indicated that some Protestants had voted against Kennedy because he was a Catholic. Nonetheless, Kennedy could not have won the presidency without the votes of millions of Protestants. In fact, the Protestant vote supporting the Democrat was far larger than the combined vote of Catholics and Jews. In that sense, the 1960 campaign was a victory over prejudice.

SECTION RECAP

1. How did Kennedy's attitude toward presidential power differ from that of Eisenhower?

2. What offices did Kennedy hold before he became President? What position had his father held?

3. What campaign activity probably determined the outcome of the election more than any other? What were the results?

2 Continuing the Cold War

President Kennedy inspects
ground-to-air missiles at Key West, FL.

Unlike his predecessors in the White House, Kennedy had spent his entire political apprenticeship during the Cold War. As he had shown in his inaugural address, he cared very much about the nation's foreign policy and meant to put his stamp on it. Most of the people he chose for high office in his administration were "hard-liners" in their views toward the Soviet Union.

In his cabinet selections, Kennedy surprised some members of his own party by passing over political celebrities. For secretary of state, he rejected Adlai Stevenson and other well-known figures in favor of a more obscure and more conservative diplomat, Dean Rusk. A Georgia-born Democrat, Rusk had once served as assistant secretary of state for Far Eastern affairs and was now head of the Rockefeller Foundation. Why had Kennedy chosen him? Some insiders claimed that Kennedy wanted to be his own secretary of state and knew that Rusk would not get in his way.

For secretary of defense, Kennedy tapped Robert S. McNamara, recently promoted president of the Ford Motor Company. McNamara had a reputation as something of a "whiz kid" because of his ability to understand technology and analyze statistics. Like Kennedy, he believed in controlling events through the use of reason. Once in Washington, he took energetic command of the Department of Defense and became one of Kennedy's most loyal lieutenants.

The appointment that carried the greatest controversy was for attorney general. To head the Department of Justice, Kennedy chose his 35-year-old brother, Robert, an attorney whose government experience was limited to serving as counsel to various Senate committees. When asked by reporters how the President could justify the appointment, John Kennedy jokingly replied: "I see nothing wrong with giving Bobby some legal experience before he goes out to practice law."

Kennedy's own aides also tended to be young, practical men of ideas. As national security adviser there was McGeorge Bundy, dean of Harvard College. As Bundy's deputy, there was an economist from the Massachusetts Institute of Technology, Walt W. Rostow. The White House staff included a number of friends from past political campaigns such as Theodore Sorensen, Kennedy's speech writer, and Arthur M. Schlesinger, Jr., a Harvard historian. Journalist David Halberstam would later write a book about these aides called *The Best and the Brightest*.

THE BAY OF PIGS

Like leaders of the Truman and Eisenhower administrations, Kennedy and his people believed that the nation's security depended on its military strength and the toughness to use that strength when necessary.

As Kennedy entered the White House, he faced a lingering problem — Cuba. In March 1960 Eisenhower gave top-secret orders to the CIA to train Cuban exiles in Florida for an overthrow of the Castro government (see page 119). Kennedy knew nothing of these plans when he campaigned for the presidency.

That autumn he had repeatedly called Castro a "source of maximum danger" and referred to Cuba as "a Communist satellite." He had called for an invasion very like the one already being contemplated. Vice President Nixon had known of, and endorsed, the CIA plan, but had been sworn to official secrecy about it.

Soon after the election, Kennedy learned of the plan. In a sense, he was trapped into support of it by his campaign proposals. Moreover, some strategists believed that time was running out for any military action against Castro. Within six months, they predicted, Cuba would have MIG fighter planes and other Soviet equipment, and an invasion would be much riskier.

Then, the CIA plan acquired a sense of urgency. Yet not everyone aware of the plan supported it. Perhaps the strongest opposition came from J. William Fulbright, chairman of the Senate Foreign Relations Committee. Fulbright expressed his doubts in a confidential memorandum to the President.

Fulbright said it was hypocritical of the United States to lend support, hidden or otherwise, to any plot to overthrow another country. "After all, isn't that what the Russians do?" he pointedly asked. He also rejected the idea that Castro's Cuba threatened the United States seriously enough to prompt military action.

Fulbright's arguments did not halt the CIA plan, but they apparently made Kennedy more cautious. If the President provided U.S. military support for such an invasion, he stood to undermine confidence in American integrity around the world. But if he halted the plan, he would bear some responsibility for keeping Castro in power. Kennedy chose a middle course. He would allow the exiles to proceed, but at the last minute he cancelled an American air strike that was to have accompanied the mission.

On April 17, early in the morning, 1,400 CIA-trained Cuban commandos waded ashore at the Bay of Pigs off the southern coast of Cuba. They were fired upon by Castro's forces within minutes. The exiles had expected that an uprising would take place on the island, but Castro had already moved against Cuban dissenters. Now he quickly put down the invasion, killing nearly 500 exiles and capturing the rest.

What had gone wrong? Without the hoped-for uprising and the American air strike, the exiles were sitting ducks. As an article in *Fortune* magazine later analyzed the situation, "Bit by bit, an operation that was marginal to begin with was so truncated as to guarantee its failure."

The President took public blame for the mission's failure, though he privately criticized the CIA. Yet Kennedy showed no regret

Cuban Premier Fidel Castro shortly after the revolution.

President Kennedy with Premier Khrushchev at the American embassy in Vienna.

at having aided the mission in the first place. Instead, he pledged that his government would keep on resisting "Communist penetration" in the Western Hemisphere.

During the 1962 Christmas season, 1,113 Cuban prisoners captured at the Bay of Pigs were returned to the United States. Castro's price tag: $53 million in U.S. medicine, medical equipment, baby foods and tractors. Kennedy met the exiles in Miami's Orange Bowl on December 29. When they presented him with their banner, he promised that it would some day fly over a "free Havana."

MEETING IN VIENNA

Less than three months after the failure in Cuba, Kennedy came face-to-face with Soviet Premier Nikita Khrushchev in Vienna, Austria. Their main reason for holding a summit meeting was to discuss the future of Germany.

Sixteen years after the end of World War II, no permanent settlement had been reached with Germany. The former German capital, Berlin, was still divided into four sectors. The three western sectors had become West Berlin, a democratic outpost inside Communist East Germany. While West Berlin pulsed with energy, the Soviet sector, East Berlin, seemed as grim and lifeless as the Russian cemetery in its midst. By June 1961, some 4,000 East Germans were crossing into West Berlin each week.

Long before the Vienna meeting, Khrushchev had proposed turning Berlin into an "international city." It would no longer be controlled by the four Allies and no longer protected by Western forces. If the other Allies did not agree to set up such a city, he threatened to sign a separate peace treaty with East Germany under which East Germany would presumably control the city.

At Vienna, Kennedy reminded Khrushchev that the United States was in Berlin because it had fought its way there. To Kennedy, West Berlin was a beacon of hope to Eastern Europe, a small symbol of freedom within a totalitarian world. Kennedy's defense of the U.S. role in West Berlin seemed to cause Khrushchev to bluster all the more. "I want peace," Khrushchev claimed, "but if you want war, that is your problem."

"It is you, and not I, who wants to force a change," Kennedy responded.

CRISIS OVER BERLIN

Kennedy returned to Washington upset by the prospect of war over Berlin. Toward the end of July he announced on television that he planned to ask Congress for an additional $3.25 billion for defense. He talked of tripling draft calls and refurbishing some planes and ships in mothballs. Yet Kennedy repeated his promise to search for new paths to peace.

Meanwhile, refugees from East Germany kept fleeing westward, "voting with their feet." In July 1961, more than 30,000 of them entered West Berlin, and some 16,500 more came across in the first 10 days of August. Communist leaders were alarmed because many of these refugees were East Germany's most highly skilled workers.

Then, just after midnight on Sunday, August 13, East German tanks rumbled toward the border that divided the two Berlins. Overnight, soldiers closed nearly all of the 80 crossing points from East to West. On Monday, workers began constructing a 25-mile wall of concrete block along the perimeter. By Thursday, traffic between the two Berlins was almost halted.

Unprepared for this twist, the State Department took four days to make a formal protest to the Soviet Union. On August 18, armored trucks carrying 500 GIs lumbered through East Germany into West Berlin to demonstrate U.S. commitment, but the President made no moves to provoke war.

Once the wall was up, the crisis over Germany ended. The Soviets later signed a peace treaty with East Germany, but Allied presence in West Berlin was not affected. "Berlin is not such a big problem for me," Khrushchev cooed. "What are two million people among a billion Communists!" Kennedy observed the wall firsthand on a visit to Berlin in 1963. "All free men are citizens of Berlin," he later told a huge crowd in front of city hall, "and, therefore, as a free man, I take pride in the words 'Ich bin ein Berliner' [I am a Berliner]."

SECTION RECAP

1. Why did the United States want to invade Cuba? Why did Kennedy cancel the air strike? What were the results of the invasion?

2. Who met at the Vienna Summit? What was the main reason for meeting?

3. Why were Communist leaders disturbed about the exodus of East Germans? What ended the East-West Germany crisis?

3 Defense Strategy: Flexible Response

American jet pilots in southern Florida demonstrate their might for the President.

During the campaign of 1960, Kennedy asserted that the Republicans had been lax about U.S. defenses and had echoed earlier Democratic charges about a "missile gap" (see page 107). Once in office, Kennedy learned that no gap existed. In 1961 the United States had a formidable lead in the power of its nuclear strike force.

Even so, Kennedy and Defense Secretary McNamara fretted about Soviet efforts to catch up. After Vienna and the Berlin crisis, they stressed the need to negotiate from strength and ordered an increase of awesome proportions in the nation's nuclear storehouse. Placed on order were several hundred more solid-fuel ICBMs known as the Minuteman. Each Minuteman could carry a warhead

80 times more devastating than the atomic bomb dropped on Hiroshima.

For their part, Soviet leaders resumed nuclear testing, against protests from around the world. Soviet defense experts apparently assumed that the U.S. arms build-up was meant to give America *first-strike capacity* — the ability to ruin an adversary in one crippling round of nuclear strikes. Although the United States denied that it would ever strike the first blow, Moscow elected to match the U.S. build-up. The arms race had again accelerated.

In addition, McNamara added five army divisions and expanded the nation's air power and reserves. Kennedy himself took a personal interest in the training of Special

Forces. These forces, known as Green Berets, were paratroopers taught to survive in deserts and jungles. They were trained to blow up bridges, decipher secret codes, engage in "hit-and-run" raids, and other tactics to strengthen U.S. odds in guerrilla warfare.

The Eisenhower administration had envisioned a strategy of massive retaliation with emphasis on nuclear power. Under Kennedy defense planning was aimed at providing military alternatives in case of war.

RIVALRY IN THE THIRD WORLD

U.S. officials thought they needed to create a range of military responses. As more and more European colonies of Africa and Asia became independent nations, Soviet-American rivalry in the Third World intensified. Two weeks before Kennedy took office, Khrushchev had declared that the Soviet Union would support "wars of national liberation." Americans braced themselves for further Soviet intervention in the unindustrialized world.

Ever since World War II, the United States had supplied foreign aid to friendly nations. Now the government moved to augment such aid with several new programs. The Peace Corps sent volunteers to lend technical assistance in health, agriculture, and education. Many volunteers were idealistic young people inspired by Kennedy. Food for Peace shipped billions of dollars worth of food to countries such as Egypt and India, managing, in some cases, to stave off widespread starvation. The Alliance for Progress provided massive funds for the development of Latin American economies. Eventually, these programs brought the United States a measure of international goodwill.

Fifty Peace Corps volunteers arrive in Ghana to teach in high schools there.

Such aid was of limited value in countries threatened by civil war. One of those countries was South Vietnam where a rebel group of guerrilla fighters known as the Viet Cong was attempting to bring down the government of Ngo Dinh Diem. These warriors were now under control of Communist North Vietnam. By the autumn of 1961, the Viet Cong were expanding the number and boldness of their raids. Diem increasingly turned to the United States for help.

In 1961, few Americans knew much about Vietnam, and fewer still had ever been there. No American university offered a full-fledged course in the language or history of Vietnam. When asked about the Vietnamese civil war, Robert Kennedy brushed aside such questions with the comment: "We've got 20 Vietnams a day to handle."

The French, who had lost their colonies in Indochina in 1954 (see page 84) seemed wary of it. French President Charles de Gaulle warned John Kennedy that Vietnam would trap him and the United States in a "bottomless military and political swamp." Kennedy may have grumbled about U.S. "overcommitment" in the area, but he apparently did not believe he could reverse U.S. policy.

Kennedy had already received his share of criticism over the Bay of Pigs invasion and the Berlin crisis. Remembering the furor over the "loss" of China in 1949, he felt he had to stand firm in Vietnam. He agreed to provide Diem with millions of extra dollars in military aid. He also sent additional military advisers and Special Forces units to South Vietnam. In the first two and one-half years of his administration, the number of American "advisers" grew from 1,000 to 16,700.

This build-up worried some of Kennedy's fellow Democrats. After a trip to Vietnam in late 1962, Senate majority leader Mike Mansfield of Montana, a former professor of Asian history, advised against deeper commitments. "It is their country, their future that is at stake, not ours," Mansfield warned. "To ignore that reality will not only be immensely costly in terms of American lives and resources, but it may also draw us inexorably into some variation of the unenviable position in Vietnam that was formerly occupied by the French."

John Kennedy's response was mixed. "I got angry with Mike for disagreeing with our policy so completely," he later told an aide, "and I got angry with myself because I found myself agreeing with him." However, the build-up in Vietnam continued.

THE MISSILES OF OCTOBER

Meanwhile, all through the summer of 1962, an armada of Soviet freighters approached the island of Cuba, 90 miles from U.S. shores. When U.S. officials inquired why this traffic was so heavy, the Soviet embassy in Washington assured them that it was only business as usual.

What was happening in Cuba that summer was far from usual, however. For many months, Premier Castro had been placing his island nation more firmly in the Soviet orbit. Now he and Premier Khrushchev had hit upon a plan to install two types of nuclear missile-launching sites on the island. The freighters were delivering parts for these launching sites, and the Russian crews to put the parts together.

The plan carried considerable nuclear clout. One type of site would dispatch medium-range ballistic missiles capable of striking cities in an arc from Washington, D.C., to Houston, Texas. The other type of site could launch intermediate-range missiles bound for targets as far away as Montana. For good measure, the Soviet package included jet aircraft with a nuclear capacity. The Soviet freighters also carried nuclear warheads.

Never before had the Soviet Union allowed such warheads on foreign soil — not in Eastern Europe and certainly not in Communist China. Why, then, supply these missiles to a nation whose leader, Castro, had a worldwide reputation for erratic behavior? Reminiscing much later, Khrushchev noted that the United States had been pointing missiles at the Soviet Union for several years. He had welcomed the chance to give Americans "a little of their own medicine."

In the absence of hard information, State Department analysts guessed that Khrushchev had sized up Kennedy at Vienna and somehow decided that the President would weaken in the face of a nuclear threat. He took a calculated risk that might make the Soviet Union a nuclear equal with the United States.

For a time, Soviet military experts managed to keep the plan a secret. Then, on October 14, a U-2 spy plane photographed a field near San Cristobal. When developed the next day, the photos suggested the construction of a nuclear landing site.

Early on Tuesday morning, October 16, McGeorge Bundy, national security adviser, broke the news to the President. Greatly angered, Kennedy set up a meeting of top-level U.S. officials at the White House that morning. At the meeting, it was revealed that the site at San Cristobal would be ready for firing in about 10 days. Kennedy directed a step-up in U-2 flights and named those present as members of the Executive Committee of the National Security Council (later known simply as Ex Comm). The group met at odd times and places over the next several days. Meanwhile, further U-2 photos showed missile-launching sites being built near Havana and in central Cuba.

Kennedy and his committee agreed that the sites must be removed. But how to do it? At first, most officials favored the idea of bombing raids against the launch pads. Such air strikes would undoubtedly take a great many lives, however, probably provoking Soviet retaliation and maybe even nuclear war. At the very least, air raids by a superpower against a much smaller country would invite condemnation in the court of world opinion. Besides, surprise attacks went beyond the bounds of American defense tradition.

For these reasons, the Ex Comm gradually turned to an option suggested by Defense Secretary McNamara — a naval blockade of Cuba. Though an act of war, a blockade would avert bloodshed, at least at the outset of the crisis. A State Department official proposed calling the blockade a "quarantine." Someone else suggested asking the 20-member Organization of American States (OAS) to endorse the plan. By the end of the week, most Ex Comm members were leaning toward McNamara's idea.

Meanwhile, defense plans were moving into place. The Navy dispatched 180 ships to the Caribbean. The Defense Department gathered 90,000 Marines and paratroopers to invade Cuba if necessary. These secret operations went on all weekend and into Monday, October 22. The United States briefed allied governments on its intentions. It also asked for a meeting of the United Nations Security Council to discuss the crisis.

On Monday evening, Kennedy appeared on television to describe the Soviet threat and how he planned to meet it. He promised to make it his "unswerving objective" to rid the hemisphere of the nuclear menace by "quaran-

tining" Cuba. He said that the U.S. Navy would sink any ship attempting to run the blockade. He also warned that his government would regard any missile launched from Cuba as an attack by the Soviet Union on the United States.

DIPLOMACY OF THE MISSILE CRISIS

Thirteen hours after Kennedy's statement, the Soviet government denied that it had put missiles in Cuba for military purposes. It charged that the United States was engaging in piracy on the high seas. Meanwhile, 25 Soviet freighters continued on course to Cuba.

Photos of missile-equipped Soviet planes in Cuba were made by U.S. spy planes.

U.N. Ambassador Adlai Stevenson (right) listens as delegates discuss the evidence he has presented.

On the island itself it looked as though Russian technicians were speeding up work on the missile sites. The world teetered toward the brink of war.

United Nations Secretary-General U Thant sent letters to Kennedy and Khrushchev asking that Soviet arm shipments and the U.S. blockade be postponed, pending talks. Kennedy replied that there could be no discussions until the Soviet Union agreed to remove the bases. The same day the OAS endorsed the quarantine by an 18-0 vote.

At 10:00 A.M. on Wednesday, October 24, U.S. Task Force 136 began to block the five passageways through which Soviet ships could enter the Caribbean from the Atlantic Ocean. Two Russian merchant ships were within a few miles of the line of the blockade. No one knew what would happen when U.S. and Soviet ships met. At 10:32 the the tension broke. A report of six Soviet ships, stopped dead in the water or turned around, was verified. When Dean Rusk learned the news in Washington, he turned to McGeorge Bundy. "We're eyeball to eyeball," he said, "and I think the other fellow just blinked."

Still, Soviet technicians worked frantically on the missile sites. Other compromises were suggested but rejected by the United States.

At the U.N. Security Council, U.S. Ambassador Adlai Stevenson waged a duel of words with Soviet Ambassador Valerian Zorin. Stevenson asked Zorin to deny that his country was installing nuclear weapons in Cuba. Zorin said that Stevenson would have his answer "in due course." Stevenson's reply was icy: "I am prepared to wait for an answer until hell freezes over. And I am also prepared to present the evidence in this room — now!" He then produced enlarged aerial photos of the missile sites, greatly damaging the Soviet case.

By this time, Khrushchev knew that his calculated risk had failed. On Friday afternoon, October 26, television commentator John Scali received a phone call from a Soviet acquaintance, Alexander Fomin. Fomin was attached to the Soviet embassy and was believed to be a member of the Russian secret service. He said that he had urgent business with Scali and needed to see him at once.

The two men met within a few minutes at a Washington restaurant. Fomin inquired whether the United States would accept a settlement that allowed for the removal of the missile sites under U.N. supervision. He suggested that such an agreement might include a promise from Khrushchev never to put nuclear missiles in Cuba in return for a promise from Kennedy not to invade Cuba. Scali said he did not know but would find out.

Scali relayed these terms to the State Department, which relayed them to the members of Ex Comm. Ex Comm's response was positive, and Scali met again with Fomin to inform him. Fomin rushed off, presumably to inform Soviet leaders.

That evening Khrushchev sent Kennedy a long letter by teletype through the U.S. embassy in Moscow. Khrushchev admitted for the first time the presence of nuclear missiles in Cuba. He essentially repeated Fomin's offer. Khrushchev compared the situation to a knot in a rope. The more the two sides tugged at the rope, the tighter the knot would become. But if both sides loosened up a little, the knot could be untied. The White House decided to wait until morning to reply.

The next day another Khrushchev letter was broadcast from Moscow, this time stating stiffer terms. Kennedy and his advisers rejected the terms of the second letter and decided to answer the first. Robert Kennedy and Theodore Sorensen drafted the reply, welcoming the "desire to seek a prompt solution" and generally accepting the Soviet terms. The President's brother summoned Soviet Ambassador Anatoly F. Dobrynin to the Justice Department and gave him a copy of the letter. The attorney general told the ambassador that the United States would need assurances within 24 hours or it would be forced to take military action. In the meantime, the White House let it be known publicly that it had accepted Soviet conditions.

Khrushchev's response began to come in by radio at nine o'clock the next morning. The premier said he would dismantle the missiles and "crate and return them to the Soviet Union." He asked the United States to end its U-2 flights over Cuba. He stressed that his country would like to continue talks to prohibit nuclear weapons and relax international tension.

Khrushchev had publicly backed down, ending the crisis without significant bloodshed. Knowing how difficult it must have been for Khrushchev to give up the game, John Kennedy warned government officials against any claims of victory. That evening he went on television to praise Khrushchev's "statesmanlike" decision.

AFTERMATH OF THE CRISIS

The missile crisis marked the first time two major world powers had faced a showdown over nuclear weapons. John Kennedy's admirers applauded the way he had matched the amount of force needed to the level of the threat posed. Kennedy's biographer, Arthur Schlesinger, thought the crisis represented a high point of the administration: "To the whole world it displayed the ripening of an American leadership unsurpassed in the responsible management of power."

As tensions eased, Kennedy took a more mature look at how the United States and the Soviet Union could maintain the peace. In a speech at American University in June 1963, he reminded his audience that peace "does not require that each man love his neighbor — it requires only that they live together in mutual tolerance. . . . For, in the final analysis, our most basic common link is that we all inhabit this small planet. We all breathe the same air. We all cherish our children's future. And we are all mortal."

That same month Kennedy and Khrushchev established a telephone hot line, an instant communication link between Moscow and Washington to improve communications in

The hot line.

international emergencies. Two months later, the United States, Britain, and the Soviet Union agreed on a nuclear test ban. Their treaty outlawed nuclear weapons testing in the atmosphere, underwater, and in space (but not underground). More than 95 nations signed the pact, which went into effect in the autumn of 1963.

More recently, some historians have been more critical of Kennedy's handling of the missile crisis. Given the commanding lead of the U.S. over the U.S.S.R. in nuclear weapons, they say the President overreacted. By doing so, they claim, he contributed to the arms race he later tried to end.

SECTION RECAP

1. Why did President Kennedy feel he had to stand firm in Vietnam? What forms of aid did he provide to South Vietnam?

2. What were President Kennedy's options in removing the Soviet-backed nuclear missile sites in Cuba? What action was decided upon?

3. Upon what terms was the removal of nuclear missiles from Cuba agreed?

"Promises to Keep"

U.S. astronaut Alan Shepard
(above left)
and Soviet cosmonaut
Yury Gagarin
(with Premier Khrushchev)
made their rival
countries very proud.

On the domestic front, Kennedy's administration began at a gallop. Why were there no black Americans among the Coast Guard cadets in his inaugural parade? Were millions of Americans in urgent need of food rations? Kennedy doubled the rations in Executive Order One. His curiosity seemed insatiable, and so did his energy. One cabinet member commented that "the deadline for everything is day before yesterday."

THE RACE INTO SPACE

Of all the items on the New Frontier agenda, the most ambitious was the space program. Kennedy was convinced that a victory in space was vital to bring the nation scientific glory and to help win the hearts and minds of the world's millions in the struggle between East and West.

The space program had a great many critics. Some of them maintained that the program would cost billions of dollars better spent on earthbound projects. Others doubted that victories in space would help the nation win new friends in the Cold War. Yet these dissenting voices were drowned out in mid-April 1963 by a series of announcements from the Soviet government.

The first of them was the most dramatic: "The world's first spaceship, *Vostok*, with a man on board, has been launched on April 12 in the Soviet Union on a round-the-world orbit." The man turned out to be Russian "cosmonaut" Yury Gagarin, and he was soaring 188 miles into the atmosphere. "I am in good spirits," he told the world from his spaceship. "The machine works perfectly." He was orbiting the earth at 18,000 miles an hour.

Kennedy sent the Soviet premier a letter of congratulations. He also summoned his top space experts to discuss measures to speed along U.S. efforts. The experts agreed that the nation could start a crash program — but at a cost of several billion dollars more than planned. As the meeting broke up, Kennedy turned to the others. "If somebody can just tell me how to catch up," he said. "Let's find somebody, anybody . . . . There's nothing more important."

When the Soviets put the first human in space, NASA was preparing for its first manned Mercury flight. On May 5, a Redstone rocket carried Navy Commander Alan B. Shepard into the upper atmosphere. He stayed in space only 15 minutes, and his flight was not nearly as complex as Gagarin's. When his capsule parachuted back to earth, however, Americans welcomed him with great jubilation.

Shepard and his wife, Louise, accompanied by Vice President Johnson, on their way to the Capitol.

Twenty days later John Kennedy went before Congress to urge that Americans commit themselves to the goal of "landing a man on the moon and returning him safely to earth" before 1970. In order to meet this goal, he asked for an additional $7 billion to $9 billion over a period of five years. Congress supported Kennedy's crash program and later allocated the money he had requested.

Other Mercury flights soon followed. The most celebrated was that of Marine Lieutenant Colonel John H. Glenn, Jr., in February 1962. Glenn was the first of the U.S. astronauts to enter Earth's orbit. Serious difficulties with the capsule lent the flight great suspense before he and the capsule completed three orbits and splashed down in the Atlantic Ocean. Kennedy flew to the NASA launch site at Cape Canaveral, Florida, to greet the astronaut personally. In New York City, Glenn received a gigantic ticker-tape parade.

KENNEDY AND CONGRESS

If Senator John Kennedy had once seemed uncomfortable with liberal ideas, President John Kennedy rarely did. Many of the bills he sent to Congress were further extensions of the New Deal. His New Frontier program aimed to provide medical care for the elderly, federal aid to farmers, and various kinds of assistance to the nation's jobless. The President also asked for tax reforms to spur economic growth.

Even though Congress was controlled by Democrats, it gave many of these ambitious ideas only tepid support. For one thing, Congress was considerably more conservative than the President. For another, Kennedy's narrow margin of victory in 1960 limited his clout among lawmakers. "He had more style than power," political scientist James MacGregor Burns later wrote. "He held neither Congress nor the government in the palm of his hand. Kennedy accumulated enormous popularity, but popularity is not power."

In particular, the President had trouble raising support for aid to education and medical care for the aging. Some reform measures did become law, however, including the controversial Area Redevelopment Act of 1961. Among other things, this law provided vocational training for workers in communities where industries had shut down.

All in all, Congress enacted more than half the President's recommendations in 1961 and 1962. Lawmakers gave their most significant lift to the economy by agreeing to boost spending on defense and the space program. Congress raised the arms budget by $6 billion in 1961 alone, and it agreed to pour further billions into space technology. By 1962 it had allotted more than half of the entire federal budget to these two sectors of the economy.

The nation returned to prosperity. It seemed that the President had redeemed his promise to get the nation moving again. By the end of 1963, the rate of economic growth had doubled to 4.5 percent a year. The jobless rate had fallen, and personal income had risen by more than 10 percent. Yet much of the spending on space and defense occurred in the South and West. In the Northeast and Midwest, the unemployment pattern remained ominously high.

THE QUESTIONING OF POWER

"The men who create power make an indispensable contribution to the nation's greatness," Kennedy told an assembly at Amherst College in 1963, "but the men who question power make a contribution just as indispensable . . . for they determine whether we use power or power uses us." Some of the questions raised during Kennedy's administration led to important changes later. Among the areas in which such changes were felt were:

• **Television.** As chairman of the Federal Communications Commission, attorney Newton Minow echoed sentiments expressed earlier by Edward R. Murrow (see page 129). Minow invited television executives to "sit down in front of your TV set and keep your eyes glued to that set until the station signs off." He assured them that "you will observe a vast wasteland." Minow objected to the endless round of "game shows, violence, . . . blood and thunder, violence, sadism, murder, . . . private eyes, gangsters, more violence, and cartoons. . . And most of all, boredom." His comments nudged the networks into paying a little more attention to news and special events and a little less to commercial programming.

• **The Environment.** Until 1962, scientist Rachel Carson had written books describing nature, not trying to preserve it. In that year, however, she published *Silent Spring*, concerning a chemical used in farming, DDT. By killing insects that damaged crops, DDT helped farmers increase their crop yields. The trouble with DDT, Carson maintained, was that it stayed in the soil and in animal cells. If a bird ate a poisoned insect, some of the poison ended up in the bird's body, where it might cause sterility or death. If DDT caused such damage in birds, she asked, what did it do to humans?

Within two years after the book appeared, 40 state legislatures had passed laws limiting the use of pesticides. Carson's book also led directly to the start of the environmental movement that continues today.

• **Race Relations.** In 1963 the *New Yorker* magazine published a long article by a black novelist and essayist, James Baldwin. With persuasive power, Baldwin offered a sermon on what segregation and injustice had meant to black people and to the American conscience. He wrote that "the price of the liberation of white people is the liberation of the blacks." His article later became a book titled *The Fire Next Time*. It expressed the depth of rage in black communities and broadened the moral foundations of the civil rights movement.

CIVIL RIGHTS

Civil rights presented Kennedy with his most vexing political dilemma. On the one hand, his advocacy of the rights of black Americans had earned him 70 percent of the black vote in 1960, and he did not want to endanger that support. On the other hand, he did not dare to antagonize white southern Democrats if he wanted to carry some southern states in 1964.

At first, Kennedy tried to steer a middle course between southern white traditions and the demands of civil rights leaders. He hoped

A "freedom rider" bus ignites after being hit
by a firebomb in Anniston, AL. No one was hurt.

to repay his black supporters by appointing some of them to high positions in government. Under Robert Kennedy, the Justice Department pushed through five times the number of voting-rights suits begun in Eisenhower years. Vice President Lyndon Johnson chaired a commission to see that companies doing business with the federal government hired more blacks.

Most civil rights leaders were disappointed with the President's approach. They believed that they had to arouse him into taking a firmer stand. In 1961 the Congress of Racial Equality (CORE) returned to a tactic used during the 1940's. It organized Freedom Rides to challenge segregation on buses and in waiting rooms, restaurants, and other public places in the South.

The first of these tours left Washington, D.C., on May 4, 1961. The farther south it went, the more trouble it encountered — an arrest in North Carolina, then beatings in South Carolina. The bloodiest incidents occurred in Alabama. In Montgomery a crowd of more than a thousand staged a brawl in which 20 riders were beaten with sticks and clubs.

To preserve order, Attorney General Kennedy sent 400 federal marshals to the scene. At the same time, he pointedly refrained from intervening on the riders' behalf. After the dust had settled, however, he did ask the Interstate Commerce Commission to require the desegregation of all bus stations, train depots, and airports. The commission did so on September 22, 1961. By the end of the year, signs reading "Whites Only" had begun to come down in waiting rooms throughout the South.

The next major test of the administration's

intentions took place in Mississippi in 1962. At the time black southerners still could not attend "all-white" schools. Even so, an Air Force veteran named James Meredith had applied to enter the University of Mississippi. He had identified himself as "an American-Mississippi-Negro citizen."

More than a year after Meredith had challenged the rejection of his application in the federal courts, U.S. Supreme Court Justice Hugo Black ordered that Meredith be allowed to enter the university. Mississippi Governor Ross Barnett vowed on television never to "surrender to the evil . . . forces of tyranny." As far as Barnett was concerned, the federal government was trying to whittle away at the sovereignty of his state.

In the autumn of 1962, Meredith, accompanied by federal marshals, attempted to register four times. Four times state officials turned him away. Attorney General Kennedy tried to keep his temper, though he was determined to get Meredith enrolled. Civil rights leaders grumbled that the Justice Department was being too patient. Meanwhile, hundreds of outsiders gathered in the college town of Oxford for a showdown.

The crowds milling about the university campus became larger and uglier by the hour. Fearful of violence, the Justice Department finally called up the National Guard. The President went on television to explain the need to enforce court orders and to praise the role of Mississippi citizens in several American wars. The same night a riot broke out, leaving two men dead. The next day Meredith registered, and the crisis ended.

A similar confrontation occurred in Alabama a few months later. Federal officials faced off a defiant governor, George C. Wallace, over the desegregation of the University of Alabama. Wallace had vowed to "stand in the schoolhouse door" to prevent two black students from entering. He soon yielded to federal authority, however, and the students were admitted.

CROSSROADS IN BIRMINGHAM

By this time, the movement's leadership had mostly narrowed to one man — Dr. Martin Luther King, Jr., an organizer of the Montgomery bus boycott (see page 96). King's tactics prompted Kennedy to take an uncompromising stand on civil rights.

In the spring of 1963, the Baptist minister had gone to Birmingham, Alabama, to wage a campaign of civil disobedience aimed at ending discrimination in one of the nation's most heavily segregated cities. King knew what he was up against. His main adversary was the city's police chief, T. Eugene "Bull" Connor, known far beyond Birmingham for his unyielding attitude of hostility toward blacks.

King began his campaign on April 2 with sit-ins, marches, and efforts to integrate white churches. As enthusiasm mounted in the black community, he scheduled a major protest march for Good Friday, April 12. City officials obtained a court order to ban the march, but it came too late. King's followers marched anyway, and some were arrested, including King himself.

The civil rights leader spent eight days in jail. While there, he wrote a well-publicized

Martin Luther King, Jr., addresses
over 200,000 people
at the 1963 March on Washington.
Here he delivered
the famous words, "I have a dream."

letter stating his determination to achieve racial justice. He lashed out at the "white moderate, who is more devoted to 'order' than to justice; . . . who constantly advises the Negro to wait for a 'more convenient season.'" He also offered an impassioned argument for the morality of violating unjust laws.

Upon his release, King rallied his demonstrators again. This time, however, news teams from the wire services, magazines, and

television were poised. On May 3, civil rights activists thronged into Birmingham for another non-violent demonstration. "Bull" Connor's police met these people, many of them children, with brutal force.

Television cameras rolled as fire hoses with 700 pounds of pressure threw protesters against buildings. One news photographer snapped a shot of a police dog, fangs bared, lunging at a terrified black woman. Europeans who watched such scenes on television were horrified. Most Americans were conscience-stricken.

The nation was aroused, and President Kennedy knew it. He hastened the preparation of a new civil rights bill to submit to Congress. He also sent 3,000 U.S. troops to an Alabama air base in a show of federal power. Birmingham's city leaders agreed to meet with black representatives and talk out their differences. Eventually, King won most of his demands. Similar demonstrations spread to other southern cities and as far north as Chicago, Illinois.

On June 19, the President sent his civil rights bill to Congress. It called for an end to racial, religious, and sex discrimination in public places. In addition, it gave the attorney general the power to file lawsuits on behalf of school desegregation. Kennedy also called for programs to assure an end to discrimination in employment.

MARCH ON WASHINGTON

Kennedy's proposals stirred deep feelings throughout the nation. One survey showed a growing "white backlash" that could cost Kennedy more than four million white votes. At the same time many northern blacks were increasingly intolerant of moderate leaders. At a Harlem rally, black youths pelted Dr. King with eggs. In Chicago black militants booed James Meredith.

Partly to achieve an appearance of unity, civil rights moderates called for a demonstration in Washington to celebrate the hundredth anniversary of Lincoln's Emancipation Proclamation. The idea was that of A. Philip Randolph, head of the Brotherhood of Sleeping Car Porters. At first, Kennedy feared that it might get out of hand. He summoned civil rights leaders to the White House to express his concern. King replied that such a demonstration could serve a positive purpose by "dramatizing the issue."

On August 28, 1963, more than 200,000 Americans, including thousands of whites, gathered to sing hymns, wave placards, and show their fervor for civil rights. The demonstrators kept their dignity, and city police had nothing to handle but traffic congestion. The March on Washington was a triumph for all those Americans who believed in redressing grievances by peaceful means.

The high point of the event came when King addressed the entire throng from the steps of Lincoln Memorial. His speech rose and fell with cadences drawn from the tradition of black preaching in the South.

King appealed to the nation's conscience by noting that the ideals of the proclamation had not yet been realized. "One hundred years later," he told the assembly, "the life of the Negro is still sadly crippled by the manacles of segregation and the chains of discrimination." Yet he urged his audience not to "wallow in the valley of despair" but to conduct the struggle for freedom "on the high plane of dignity and discipline." Then he spoke of the healing power of hope:

> "I say to you today, my friends, that in spite of the difficulties and frustrations of the moment I still have a dream.
>
> "I have a dream that one day this nation will rise up and live out the true meaning of its creed: 'We hold these truths to be self-evident; that all men are created equal.'
>
> "I have a dream that one day on the red hills of Georgia the sons of former slaves and the sons of former slave owners will be able to sit down together at the table of brotherhood . . .
>
> "I have a dream that my four little children will one day live in a nation where they will not be judged by the color of their skin but by the content of their character.
>
> "I have a dream today . . .

SECTION RECAP

1. What was the New Frontier's most ambitious program? What gave it urgency?

2. How did Kennedy's proposals fare in Congress? Which encountered the most resistance?

3. What did Rachel Carson protest in *Silent Spring*? What movement did the book inspire?

4. What prompted Kennedy to take an uncompromising stand on civil rights?

5 Death of a President

View from the window of the Dallas book depository from which Kennedy was shot.

As the end of Kennedy's third year approached, he was thinking ahead to the many things he still needed to accomplish. Congress had not yet passed his recommendations for medical care for the elderly. There was the possibility of a long and bitter struggle over civil rights on Capitol Hill. French President Charles de Gaulle was planning to visit Washington in February. Kennedy and his wife Jacqueline were plannning to travel to East Asia in the spring.

Southeast Asia continued to bedevil the President. The United States was still pouring money and advisers into Vietnam without any end in sight. South Vietnamese President Ngo Dinh Diem, once regarded as a solution to the turmoil, was coming to seem part of the problem. Vietnamese of the middle and lower classes, many of them strong nationalists, criticized Diem for secluding himself from his people. Many members of the military expressed doubts about his conduct of the war. Buddhists turned against him for his favoritism toward Roman Catholics. One Buddhist monk doused himself with gasoline, then set fire to himself in a Saigon street. Photos of this immolation made the front pages of many American newspapers.

Diem even estranged himself from the new U.S. ambassador to South Vietnam, Henry Cabot Lodge. Lodge grew impatient when Diem refused to discuss possible steps he might take to improve his government.

DIEM'S OVERTHROW

Lodge became aware of rumors that Diem might be overthrown, and he reported these rumors to the State Department. Gradually, a government position emerged. The adminstration did not want to instigate a coup but it did not want to discourage one either. Lodge therefore gave tacit encouragement to the generals plotting Diem's overthrow.

The generals struck on November 1, 1963. Diem and his brother fled to a Catholic church in the Chinese section, where they fell into the wrong hands. The generals' plans spun out of control, and Diem and his brother were shot to death. U.S. officials had not anticipated an assassination. When Kennedy learned of it, he left a meeting, deeply shocked.

After Diem's death, South Vietnam would be ruled by a succession of short-lived governments, making victory against the Vietcong all the harder to achieve. In 1963, guilt over their role in Diem's overthrow led American officials to take on larger responsibilities in the war.

APPOINTMENT IN DALLAS

On Thursday, November 21, John and Jacqueline Kennedy left Washington for a brief trip to Texas. The main object of the journey was to unite two warring factions of the state's Democratic party. The President went first to San Antonio, then to Houston, receiving warm welcomes in both cities.

On Friday morning he told the Fort Worth Chamber of Commerce that the United States was "still the keystone in the arch of freedom." Then he flew to Dallas and entered the downtown area by motorcade. With him were his wife, Vice President Lyndon Johnson, and Texas Governor and Mrs. John Connally. The crowds grew larger and more enthusiastic as the motorcade approached the center of the city. As the President's car turned onto Elm Street, the governor's wife murmured approval of the greeting the President was receiving. John Kennedy turned to wave at the roadside crowd.

Kennedy rides through the Dallas streets shortly before his assassination.

Just then a crack rang out above the cheers and the applause. Some members of the presidential party thought it was the sound of a motorcycle backfiring. The first crack was followed in about five seconds by two more cracks. The President's head jerked upward, then he toppled into his wife's lap.

Kennedy had been struck by two bullets. He was rushed to Parkland Memorial Hospital, but there was nothing that the doctors could do. In early afternoon they reported that the President was dead. (Governor Connally had also been shot but eventually recovered.)

News services learned of the shooting moments after it happened. The three television networks went on the air immediately and stayed there, without commercial interruption, for three days. The nation's businesses closed, and Americans headed for home, at first unbelieving, then stricken with grief. At the President's school, Harvard, bells tolled and flags fell to half-staff. On the great lawn of the campus, under the elms, a student lay face down, sobbing.

Who had killed John Kennedy — and why? Attention quickly centered on Lee Harvey Oswald, a stockkeeper at the Texas School Book Depository. The depository was located on the President's route at almost the precise point where he had been shot. When police entered the building after the assassination, Oswald had already left. He had gone to his rooming house for a pistol, and afterward had shot a policeman who attempted to question him. Police seized Oswald in a movie theater and put him under arrest the same afternoon.

The "why" was harder to answer. There was evidence that Oswald had links to pro-Castro organizations. There were also suggestions that he was unstable enough to have done such a thing without any political motive. All chance of getting an honest confession from Oswald ended on Sunday, November 24. As the prisoner was being taken from one jail to another, a Dallas nightclub owner, Jack Ruby, shot and killed Oswald at point-blank range.

FUNERAL IN WASHINGTON

John Kennedy's body was flown back to Washington on Friday night. It remained in the East Room of the White House the next day. On Sunday, the flag-draped coffin was taken up Pennsylvania Avenue to the Capitol on a caisson led by a riderless horse with reversed stirrups — the symbol of a fallen leader. Over the next few hours, a quarter of a million Americans came to the Capitol Rotunda to pay their last respects.

Monday was the funeral, a day of muffled drums and moaning bagpipes. It began with a procession on foot from the Capitol to St. Matthew's Cathedral, where the religious services were held. Then the casket was carried to a hillside at Arlington National Cemetery, and the last guns fired a salute. A few minutes later, the casket was lowered into the earth. Throughout all these ceremonies, television cameras lingered on the widow and her two fatherless children.

Grief was worldwide. "Ah, they cried the rain down that night," said a member of the Fitzgerald family in Ireland. Countless thousands lined up at the U.S. Embassy in London to sign the condolence book. People cried in the streets of India. Indonesian flags flew at half-mast.

In the United States, the loss seemed even greater. Assistant Secretary of Labor Daniel Moynihan spoke for many when he said: "I don't think there's any point in being Irish if you don't know that the world is going to break your heart eventually. I guess that we thought we had a little more time."

The new President, Lyndon Johnson, soon chose a seven-member commission to investigate the assassination. Headed by Chief Justice Earl Warren, the panel listened to 500 witnesses give 10 million words of testimony. The Warren Commission concluded that Oswald and Ruby had both acted alone. Many Americans continued to believe that both had been part of a conspiracy. In all probability, the full truth would never be known.

Years afterward, the President's admirers would still be trying to define what had given his White House a special touch. Perhaps journalist Theodore H. White came closest when he wrote that "there began in Kennedy's time an effort of government to bring reason to bear on facts which were becoming almost too complicated for human minds to grasp . . . [Kennedy] was a realistic dealer in men, a master of games who understood the importance of ideas. He advanced the cause of America at home and abroad. But he also posed for the first time the great question of the sixties and seventies: What kind of people are we Americans? What do we want to become?"

The Kennedy funeral procession. The monument to another slain president, Lincoln, is in the rear.

SECTION RECAP

1. Whom did Ngo Dinh Diem antagonize as president of South Vietnam? What was the country's leadership like after his death?

2. Why did President Kennedy go to Dallas? Who was his assassin? Why were his motives never fully clarified?

CHAPTER

REVIEW

1. For each multiple-choice question, circle
the letter of the answer you think is best.

1. *Quarantine* was the word the Kennedy administration used to describe the action it
took in the a) Bay of Pigs invasion, b) Berlin situation, c) Cuban missile crisis, d) civil
war in Vietnam.

2. The event that spurred Kennedy to introduce a civil rights bill into Congress was
a) the March on Washington, b) the march on Birmingham, c) the freedom rides,
d) Meredith's enrollment at the University of Mississippi.

3. The factors that probably brought Kennedy the most votes in the 1960 presidential
campaign were a) the televised debates, b) his visits to all fifty states, c) his efforts to get
Martin Luther King out of jail, d) the Roman Catholic population of the United States.

4. The Alliance for Progress was a program Kennedy developed to meet Soviet challenges
in a) space, b) Germany, c) the Third World, d) weapons.

5. Which of the following was not achieved during Kennedy's administration? a) a nuclear
test ban treaty, b) a hotline connecting Washington and Moscow, c) national prosperity,
d) civil rights legislation.

6. The first man to orbit the earth was a) Gagarin, b) Glenn, c) Shepard, d) Vostok.

7. Martin Luther King, Jr. gave his "I Have a Dream" speech a) from the Birmingham jail,
b) in Mississippi, c) at the March on Washington, d) during the 1960 election campaign

8. What distinguished John F. Kennedy from other presidents was his Roman Catholicism
and his a) Harvard education, b) wealth, c) youth, d) wartime heroism.

2. Define the two following terms: *blocs*
and *first-strike capacity*.

3. Give two examples of how the presidency has grown since World War II.

4. What type of men did President Kennedy appoint to the cabinet and the White
House Staff? Name three of the men he selected for these posts.

5. Describe two of the new programs President Kennedy developed to aid friendly
Third World nations.

6. Who criticized television programming
as a "vast wasteland"? Was the criticism
justified? How did the network executives
respond?

CHAPTER **6**

1963 — 1969

The Johnson Years

Lyndon Johnson taking the oath of office as President with Jacqueline Kennedy at his left.

O N NOVEMBER 22, 1963, at 2:30 in the afternoon, Lyndon Baines Johnson took the oath of office as President of the United States. Standing at his right in the cabin of *Air Force One* — parked on an airfield in Dallas, Texas — was his wife, Claudia "Lady Bird" Johnson. On his left was Jacqueline Kennedy, widow of the slain President, her look dazed and grief-stricken, her pink suit stained with her husband's blood.

On the flight back to Washington, Johnson later recalled, "I sat in the plane and pictured it more or less as simple as if something happened to the pilot who was flying us back. We were very much in the same shape as if he fell at the controls and one of our boys had to walk up there and bring in the plane, flying at 700 miles an hour with no plans showing how long the runways were, with no maps, no notes. . . . I wasn't sure how successful I would be in pulling the divergent factions in the country together and trying to unify and unite them in order to get the confidence of the people and secure the respect of the world."

Even in the turbulent first hours of his presidency, Johnson was doing what came naturally — looking for the center, trying to find a consensus. In the years to come, he would sometimes succeed in this effort, but by the end of his presidency the nation was more sharply divided than it had been since the Civil War.

Some of the problems of the nation's eighth "accidental president" resulted from circumstances over which he had no control. But he shared more than a last name with another president, Andrew Johnson. Like Andrew Johnson, who succeeded to the presidency after Lincoln's assassination in 1865, Lyndon

Johnson followed a slain president into office. Both men were southerners, and both left the White House proud but embittered, convinced that they had done the right thing and, for their pains, been unfairly rejected by the people they had served. "How is it possible," Lyndon Johnson was to ask many times, "that all these people could be so ungrateful to me after I had given them so much?"

For Lyndon Johnson, the task was complicated by contrasts in background and style with his predecessor which he felt very keenly. JFK was a New Englander from a wealthy family, a handsome, Harvard-educated war hero who, with his beautiful wife, had maintained a European-style salon in the

Lyndon as a boy in Texas.

White House. LBJ was a rangy, rough-hewn Texan with a twang, more at ease in a 10-gallon hat than a tuxedo.

When *Air Force One* landed outside Washington, D.C., Johnson made a brief speech, raising his voice to be heard over the roar of the plane's engines: "This is a sad time for all people. We have suffered a loss that cannot be weighed. For me it is a deep personal tragedy. I know that the world shares the sorrow that Mrs. Kennedy and her family bear. I will do my best. That is all I can do. I ask for your help — and God's."

It was the beginning of a new and very different presidency — one that would be stamped with the unique personality of Lyndon Baines Johnson.

1 From Pedernales to Dallas

Lyndon Johnson was born in 1908 in the hill country of central Texas, near the Pedernales (pronounced Purd'n Alice) River. His mother, Rebekah, was one of a handful of women who had attended Baylor University. His father, Sam, was a small farmer and real estate trader. Sam had few of the refinements that Rebekah admired. His language was crude, his behavior was unpolished, and he idled away most of his time.

Lyndon's birth rekindled Rebekah's interest in learning. She taught her son the alphabet before his second birthday. Later, she encouraged him to read poetry and learn pub-

LBJ (right) as a member of the debate team at Southwest Texas Teachers College.

lic speaking. He should learn self-control, she said, and keep his promises to others. Rebekah made Lyndon feel as though nothing was beyond his reach. "Confidence of success," she often told him, "leads to real success."

After Lyndon graduated from high school, he spent two years in California picking fruit, washing dishes, and clerking in his cousin's law office. Then he returned home, confessing to his family, "All right, I'm sick of working just with my hands and I'm ready to try and make it with my brain." A week later, he went off to San Marcos to enroll at Southwest Texas State Teachers College.

Johnson soon demonstrated an ability to take advantage of his position. He turned a part-time job as a messenger to the president of the college into an appointments secretary; faculty members had to see Lyndon before they could get to the president. Johnson became a prize-winning debater and editor of the school paper.

In what would have been his senior year, Johnson left San Marcos to teach Mexican-American students in Cotulla. He later recalled: "My students were poor and they often came to class without breakfast, hungry. . . . I often walked home late in the afternoon, after the classes were finished, wishing there was more that I could do. But all I knew was to teach them the little that I knew, hoping that it might help them against the hardships that lay ahead." Johnson loved teaching, but it did not satisfy his ambition or his need to compete. He returned to college after his year at Cotulla, receiving his degree in 1930.

While in college, Johnson had driven to Houston for the 1928 Democratic National Convention. There he saw a New York politician named Franklin D. Roosevelt deliver the nominating speech for Al Smith. Johnson returned to school knowing that he wanted to be involved in national politics. His chance came in the fall of 1932 — the same fall that Roosevelt was elected President — when he became an aide to a newly elected Texas congressman. (Johnson was teaching high school at the time.) The two men were soon off to Washington. There, except for a brief period, Johnson was to remain for the next 37 years.

The mid-1930's were a crucial time for Johnson. In 1934 he married Claudia Taylor, a recent University of Texas graduate. For the next two years he served as Texas director of the National Youth Administration, a New Deal agency that provided work relief for young people rendered jobless by the Great Depression. Then, early in 1937, Johnson spotted the newspaper obituary of his local congressman. Johnson ran, and ran hard, for the vacated seat, shaking as many hands as he could find. He received twice the votes of his closest rival. In April 1937, at the age of 29, Lyndon became the representative for Texas's 10th Congressional District.

JOHNSON IN CONGRESS

Johnson ardently supported Roosevelt's New Deal. He also backed FDR's military preparedness measures, especially after the outbreak of World War II in 1939. But he was cautious when it came to racial issues, consistently voting against anti-lynching and anti-poll tax measures. His conservative constituents faithfully reelected him.

Immediately after the Japanese attack on Pearl Harbor, Johnson enlisted in the navy. He served briefly as an administrator in Australia, but Roosevelt recalled to Washington all the congressmen who had enlisted. After the war, Johnson generally supported Truman's foreign policy. On domestic issues, however, he continued to vote against all civil rights legislation. He also supported the antilabor Taft-Hartley Act.

In 1948, Johnson ran for the Senate. He drew big crowds by campaigning from a helicopter, the first ever seen by most of the Texans before whom he appeared. He won the election by the narrowest of margins — 87 votes out of 900,000 cast.

Johnson was most effective in small groups, and the 96-member Senate suited his style better than the 435-member House. He wasted little time in cultivating southern Democrats who controlled Congress, and in gaining prestigious committee memberships for himself.

Johnson aimed for a place in the Senate leadership. In 1952, after Eisenhower's election, he won the post of Senate minority leader. In 1954, when the Democrats regained control of the Senate, he became the youngest majority leader ever. Historically, majority leaders have used a variety of approaches to influence congressional votes. Johnson's method came to be known as The Treatment.

According to Rowland Evans and Robert Novak, two experienced Washington reporters, The Treatment could last 10 minutes or four hours. It came, enveloping its target, at the LBJ Ranch swimming pool, in one of LBJ's offices, in the Senate cloakroom . . . wherever Johnson might find a fellow senator within his reach: "He moved in close, his face a scant millimeter from his target, his eyes widening and narrowing, his eyebrows rising then falling. From his pockets poured clippings, memos, statistics. Mimicry, humor, and the genius of analogy made The Treatment an almost hypnotic experience and rendered the target stunned and helpless."

The Treatment worked best in private negotiations. With large groups, it often seemed crude and arrogant. For instance, it generally failed in press conferences, leaving reporters skeptical of Johnson, and the President suspicious of and annoyed with them.

Senate Leader Johnson
with fellow Texan Sam Rayburn,
who served as Speaker
of the House of Representatives for 16 years.

Johnson paid meticulous attention to details. He knew every senator's strengths and weaknesses, and remembered which committee chairman smoked which brand of cigar. All this effort earned him a reservoir of good will with his Senate colleagues. When the time came, he could collect his debts and call in his votes.

While Johnson's mastery of the Senate was unequaled in modern political history, some observers criticized his tactics. Members of his own party complained that he gave in to Eisenhower too often. But Johnson believed that only the executive branch should consistently initiate major legislation.

One of Johnson's most important achievements as Senate majority leader involved the 1957 Civil Rights Act. Since 1940, six different civil rights bills had been defeated in Congress, but times were changing. The 1954 Supreme Court decision in *Brown* v. *Board of Education* declared that segregated public schools were illegal; in 1956 Eisenhower proposed a civil rights measure aimed at ending some of the restrictions that barred black citizens from voting.

Black Americans, who had voted Democratic since the New Deal, were now willing to support any politician or party that considered their interests. Johnson realized that the Democrats in the Senate had to act favorably on civil rights or risk the loss of millions of black votes. Always looking for the practical solution, he skillfully traveled the middle road between southern segregationists and northern liberals. In spite of a record southern filibuster, the bill passed.

THE VICE PRESIDENCY

In 1960 Johnson had made an unsuccessful bid for the Democratic presidential nomination. John Kennedy, who won it, needed Texas's electoral votes to win the election, and chose Johnson as his running mate.

For Johnson, the vice presidency was a demotion from the most important position in Congress. Like every vice president before him, he became an observer. He was no longer a participant in the excitement of decision making. At best, the vice presidency exists to remind the president that his successor is only a heartbeat away. That terrible reminder became reality in Dallas in November 1963.

SECTION RECAP

1. What were the early influences in Lyndon Johnson's life? What impact did they have on him?

2. What policies did Johnson favor as a congressman from Texas?

3. How did Johnson influence fellow senators as majority leader?

4. How was Johnson different as a senator than as a member of the House of Representatives?

 # The Domestic Scene

The day after Kennedy's assassination, Johnson pledged to keep his predecessor's staff, and they assured the new President of their loyalty. It was expected, however, that there would be changes. Three top Kennedy aides left almost immediately. Robert Kennedy was the first cabinet member to resign when, in September 1964, he left to run (successfully) for the Senate from New York state.

Dean Rusk and Robert McNamara stayed on as secretaries of state and defense, respectively. As his special assistant, Johnson brought in 29-year-old Bill Moyers, a Baptist minister and former Peace Corps volunteer. Though young and inexperienced, Moyers became the driving force behind Johnson's social legislation.

Johnson was a demanding boss. He required total loyalty from his staff, controlling their private as well as their public lives. To Congress and the American public, Johnson was a walking contradiction. He wanted to be respected as a great chief of state, but he often antagonized people with his overbearing crudity. He wanted to be loved, but was prejudiced against those he felt disliked him: northerners, intellectuals, and the press. Historian Eric Goldman wrote that "his very appearance and mannerisms suggest a riverboat gambler." And yet, said Goldman, "after years of meeting first-rate minds, in and out of the university, I am sure I never met a more intelligent person than Lyndon Johnson."

Johnson shares a handshake and a pen with Martin Luther King, Jr.

EARLY ACHIEVEMENTS

The day after Kennedy's assassination, Johnson told Congress that "no memorial oration or eulogy could more eloquently honor President Kennedy's memory than the earliest possible passage of the civil rights bill." As you read in Chapter Five, this Kennedy measure — the most far-reaching piece of civil rights legislation since Reconstruction — would, among other things, outlaw racial, religious, and sex discrimination in employment and public places. As reintroduced under Johnson, it contained some additional provisions. For instance, it provided for a Fair Employment Practices Commission to oversee fairness in hiring and firing.

The civil rights bill made little progress during Kennedy's presidency, but respect for the slain President, together with LBJ's skilled persuasion, made passage more likely now. The House passed the bill 290 to 130 in February 1964. The Senate was another story, however. Southern senators tried to obstruct passage of the bill by filibustering for 57 days. Then supporters mustered enough votes to impose *cloture*, which limits debate. (Cloture had never before been imposed on a civil rights measure.) The Senate then passed, and Johnson signed, the 1964 Civil Rights Act.

Another major concern of Johnson's during his first few months in office was poverty.

Senator Goldwater's nomination was a big victory for the conservative Republicans.

According to estimates, some 35 million Americans — almost 20 percent of the population — were poor. Of this total, about a third were children. Johnson's first-hand experience with poverty in Texas made this an issue with which he could wholeheartedly identify.

In January 1964 Johnson announced that "This administration today, here and now, declares unconditional war on poverty in America," and promised that "we shall not rest until that war is won." Thus began what soon came to be called the War on Poverty. Its most important legislation, passed in August 1964, was the Economic Opportunity Act. With an initial appropriation of $945.5 million, it established 10 different programs and an Office of Economic Opportunity (OEO) to oversee them. Among the individual components were VISTA (Volunteers in Service to America), a domestic Peace Corps composed of college students who would work in poor neighborhoods to help local and state poverty programs; a Job Corps, to train young high school dropouts; Community Action Programs to increase job opportunities; and funds for loans to college students and small businesses.

The War on Poverty had its critics. Some said that there was no war; Johnson's program was just a proposal to send some unemployed teenagers to summer camp and lend money to college students. Some even doubted the poverty statistics. Many who held these views were eager to vote Johnson and his liberal programs out of office in November.

THE ELECTION OF 1964

In 1964 conservative Republicans were restless and dissatisfied. They believed that most moderate Republican candidates for the presidency — like Nelson Rockefeller of New York — were simply echoing the Democratic philosophy of big government and big spending. They wanted a candidate and a platform that upheld limited spending, low taxes, and laissez-faire economic practices. When the Republicans held their convention in San Francisco in July, conservatives triumphed and engineered the nomination of Barry Goldwater, an Arizona senator, former Air Force pilot, and a major general in the Air Force Reserve.

The Democratic convention, held in Atlantic City in August, brought no surprise in Johnson's nomination. As his running mate, Johnson chose Hubert Humphrey, a liberal senator from Minnesota who had also served as mayor of Minneapolis.

The Republicans claimed that they were offering "a choice, not an echo." Goldwater's political and economic principles, however, were not only unorthodox but, to many, frightening.

He wanted to replace the mandatory Social Security system with one offering voluntary participation. He favored right-to-work laws and opposed the union shop. He also opposed farm subsidies and federal funding for cities and education. He had voted against the Civil Rights Act of 1964. He said that he wished he could "saw off the eastern seaboard [home of the liberal establishment] and let it float to sea."

It was in foreign affairs, however, that Goldwater's views aroused the most concern. His acceptance speech stated, in words that were to become famous: "Extremism in the defense of liberty is no vice . . . moderation in the pursuit of justice is no virtue." To many Americans, these sentiments indicated a trigger-happy approach to matters of war and peace. Indeed, Goldwater did suggest that one way to locate the Vietcong in Southeast Asia was to drop a nuclear bomb and defoliate the trees. He had voted against the Test Ban Treaty in 1963, and advocated that American generals, not the president, control nuclear weapons in the field. He rejected containment, instead favoring "removal of Communists from power wherever they hold it."

The Democrats had a field day with Goldwater's "shoot-from-the-hip" style, especially his casual attitude toward nuclear weapons. They countered with one of the most powerful television commercials ever aired. In it a small girl picked petals from a daisy. She counted each one. The scene faded through her eyes to a countdown for an atomic test. Then the whole screen dissolved into a mushroom cloud. The spot mentioned neither Goldwater nor the Republicans, but the response from Republicans was strongly negative. It ran only once, during the Monday night movie on NBC. Similar spots were produced to attack Goldwater's opposition to Social Security and the Test Ban Treaty.

Because the far-right wing had captured the Republican party, the Democrats were able to broaden their appeal to include such conservative groups as bankers and business leaders. Johnson won the election by a landslide: 43 million votes to Goldwater's 27 million, with an electoral count of 486 to 52. The Democrats greatly strengthened their hold on Congress.

THE GREAT SOCIETY

As President in his own right, Johnson dedicated himself to achieving what he called the Great Society, "where freedom from wants of the body can help fulfill the needs of the spirit." His task was made smoother by big Democratic majorities in Congress — 295 to 140 in the House of Representatives and 68 to 32 in the Senate. So wide was the gap that liberal legislation could become the law of the land without a single southern vote.

This Congress enacted more social legislation than any since the New Deal. The Elementary and Secondary School Act, passed in April 1965, was designed to aid schools with poor children. The law also helped religious and other private schools by providing funds to purchase textbooks.

In July Congress amended the Social Security Act to set up two new health care systems. Medicare, paid for by Social Security deductions, provided an insurance program to cover hospital and postoperative care for those aged 65 and over. Senior citizens would also be helped in paying physicians' and surgeons' fees. Medicaid offered similar benefits for needy and disabled younger Americans not covered by Social Security taxes.

Other Great Society legislation dealt with housing and with immigration. The Omnibus Housing Act of August 1965 provided grants for community health and recreation centers, expanded urban renewal programs, and established grants for home repair. A month later a new executive department, the Department of Housing and Urban Development (HUD), was created to help deal with the growing problem of housing shortages. Johnson's appointee to head the new department, Robert C. Weaver, was the first black to become a cabinet member.

The Immigration Act, which became law in October 1965, abolished the "country by country" quota system that had favored Northern European nations since 1924. The new system allowed 120,000 immigrants from nations in the Western Hemisphere to enter the United States every year. An additional 170,000 could enter annually from other countries, but no more than 20,000 could immigrate from a country in one year. People with skills, or with relatives already living in the United States, received priority.

Johnson's administration also turned its attention to transportation. That it did so was due in large part to the efforts of a young lawyer and lobbyist named Ralph Nader. In his 1965 book, *Unsafe at Any Speed*, Nader forced automobile manufacturers and Congress to face the issue of automobile safety. In 1965 alone, almost 50,000 people lost their lives in car accidents. These accidents were the major cause of death for those under age 35.

Nader challenged the traditional idea that drivers were solely to blame for most car accidents. Auto manufacturers, he claimed, bore a big share of responsibility by producing fast, powerful cars that sacrificed safety for style. Nader named specific models whose faulty engineering contributed to highway fatalities. His case was strengthened when a congressional investigation revealed that he had been harassed by the auto industry.

Consumer advocate Ralph Nader
testifying before the House Commerce Committee.
He claimed that even the expensive
Rolls Royce had faulty door latches.

In September 1966 Johnson signed two bills into law. One provided funds to state and local governments for developing safety programs. The other set up federal safety standards for cars and tires. Soon cars were being recalled for safety violations, and new models were coming off the assembly lines with headrests, dual brakes, interior padding, and other safety features. Overseeing such innovations was one of the responsibilities of the new Department of Transportation.

CRITICS OF THE GREAT SOCIETY

As early as 1966, support for the Great Society began to slacken. In January the President admitted, "Because of Vietnam we cannot do all that we should, would, like to do." The mood of the country was also changing. Some Great Society measures were not living up to expectations. Critics argued that some plans were short-term. Others said that funding by itself was not the solution. Johnson expected "quickie" cures, they said; he made extravagant promises that neither he nor his administration could keep. One critic accused the government of being "big rather than strong, fat and flabby rather than powerful."

THE LONG HOT SUMMER OF 1964

Race relations continued to be a problem. In the South, blacks were barred from many public places and services. Freedom rides, sit-ins, and other tactics were used to integrate schoolrooms, restaurants, and transportation facilities.

In the North, the problems faced by blacks were more subtle. Blacks were not legally barred from the best jobs and neighborhoods, but they were usually excluded. Between 1945 and 1965, seven million black Americans migrated to the North from the South. Some 90 percent of them lived in large urban ghettos. Black people in the North wanted to live in decent neighborhoods, send their children to good schools, and enjoy equal employment opportunities. For example, when 460,000 black students boycotted the New York City public schools in 1964, it was not to demand the end of legally segregated schools. New York had never had *de jure* (legal) segregation. The demonstrators were calling for an end to segregated neighborhoods, which made for school segregation *de facto* (in fact) if not in law. Their protest achieved little, however. Long-established patterns of segregation and discrimination in the North were difficult to break down.

According to a survey taken in 1964, Americans named race relations as the country's most important issue. Two tragic occurrences of that year underscored their choice.

The first event began outside an exclusive apartment building on New York's Upper East Side after a janitor turned a hose on a group of black junior-high students waiting for a summer school to open. The boys then attacked him with rocks and bottles. After identifying himself, a nearby white, off-duty patrolman ordered the boys to stop. When they did not, he fired and killed one of them.

Harlem, a short distance from the shooting, reacted angrily to what seemed an unnecessary death. That night, mobs in the streets looted liquor stores, pawnshops, and other retail establishments. Rioting broke out again after the boy's funeral the next day. The destruction spread to Brooklyn; to Rochester, New York; and then to Jersey City and Philadelphia. Hundreds of people were injured and thousands were arrested. Damage was estimated in the millions.

Some observers feared that the riots of 1964 were just the beginning. Adam Clayton Powell, a Harlem congressman, referred to the riots as Revolution II, and believed them to be more dangerous than the first revolution taking place in the South. Powell predicted that the new battle cry for blacks — replacing "We Shall Overcome" — would be "Burn, Baby, Burn."

The second outbreak of violence, that same summer, occurred in the South. Civil rights organizers sponsored a drive to register black voters, especially the hundreds of thousands in Mississippi. About a thousand white volunteers went south and, with blacks, formed the Mississippi Freedom Democratic Party. Many voters were registered, but at the high cost of 15 lives. When the bodies of one black and two white volunteers were found buried under a clay dam near Philadelphia, Mississippi, the country was outraged. Seven Ku Klux Klansmen, including a county sheriff, were eventually sentenced to jail, the first time in the South that a jury of whites had convicted white defendants in a civil rights case.

A NEW VOTING RIGHTS ACT

Early in 1965, Martin Luther King's Southern Christian Leadership Conference and other civil rights groups focused their campaign on Dallas County, Alabama, and its county seat of Selma. Of Selma's 15,000 black residents, only 65 were registered to vote. On the seventh of March, several hundred protesters set out to march from Selma to Montgomery, the state capital, about 50 miles away. Local police and state troopers repulsed the marchers with clubs and tear gas. A minister leaving a restaurant with friends was so badly beaten that he died two days later.

On March 15, Johnson went before Congress to plead for a stronger voting rights bill in what many considered the best speech he ever made. "At times, history and fate meet at a single time in a single place to shape a turning point in man's unending search for freedom. So it was at Lexington and Concord. So it was a century ago at Appomattox. So it was last week in Selma, Alabama. . . . Their cause [that of black Americans] must be our cause too. Because it's not just Negroes, but really it's all of us, who must overcome the crippling legacy of bigotry and injustice. And we shall overcome."

A week later, several thousand marchers set out to walk from Selma to Montgomery. This time they were escorted by 1,800 federalized troops of the Alabama National Guard. The march was peaceful, but a civil rights worker from Detroit was shot to death later as she drove some marchers back to Selma from Montgomery.

The events in Selma inspired Congress to move quickly on the Voting Rights Act of 1965. It authorized federal examiners to supervise registration and to carry it out in districts where fewer than half of voting-age residents were registered. The law also banned literacy tests. The Voting Rights Act encouraged thousands of formerly disenfranchised (denied of the right to vote) blacks to register — almost 250,000 by the end of 1965 alone. Southern black candidates were soon being elected to state legislatures and to hundreds of local offices.

King (left of center) in a march with civil rights leaders A. Philip Randolph (far right) and Roy Wilkins (second from right).

BLACK SEPARATISM AND WHITE BACKLASH

Five days after President Johnson signed the Voting Rights Act, Americans throughout the nation learned about a black area of Los Angeles called Watts. Watts was not Harlem. Palm trees lined its streets of single-family homes, and there were no signs of decaying tenements. However, unemployment was high, incomes were low, and schools were poor. There was no community hospital. Watts was also overcrowded; its 27.3 persons per acre compared with a figure of 7.4 for the rest of Los Angeles.

The Watts outbreak began when a patrolman stopped a black man for reckless driving. When the policeman drew his gun, a crowd attacked him. Shortly afterward, rumors spread that the police had beaten three blacks nearly to death. That night, mobs swept through the streets, rocks and bottles flew, and some white motorists were pulled from their cars. The next night, 50 million Americans watched on television as Watts residents looted retail stores and burned some to the ground. Most violence was directed against white merchants, who, blacks claimed, overcharged them for shoddy merchandise. The National Guard was finally called in, and 18 men were shot as suspected looters. When the smoke cleared, 34 people were dead, 4,000 had been arrested, and damage was estimated at $50 million.

Watts was one of the worst riots in American history, but the summer of 1965 saw additional outbreaks in Cleveland, Providence, Minneapolis, Milwaukee, Detroit, and Washington, D.C. The following summer there were more. The two most damaging took place in Newark, New Jersey, and Detroit. Newark, with a 52 percent black population, had an unemployment rate four times the national average and an unresponsive city government. Detroit was different. Unemployment was low, almost half the black population owned homes, and the federal government had invested millions in antipoverty programs there. Nevertheless, both cities experienced week-long riots. The death toll in Detroit reached 43; with 1,200 buildings destroyed by arson, thousands of people were left homeless.

Although the destruction was enormous, the most harmful effect of the rioting was not physical but psychological. Fearful whites bought guns and met for target practice. Demands for "law and order" began to replace the social goals of the Great Society. The phenomenon came to be called *white backlash* — a negative reaction to black demands for equality.

Militancy was gaining ground in black society as well. An articulate group of leaders rejected nonviolence as irrelevant in such explosive times. They also spurned integration, believing that it robbed blacks of their own culture. Ho Chi Minh, Fidel Castro, and similar revolutionary leaders replaced Gandhi as models for many blacks.

One of the most passionate advocates of this new spirit was Malcolm X, a former drug dealer who became a spokesman for black separatism. While in prison, he had joined the Nation of Islam, or Black Muslims, a religious group founded in the 1930's. His intelligence and fiery rhetoric helped him move up quickly in the ranks, and he soon became second in command. In line with the Black Muslim philosophy, Malcolm X attacked whites as "devils." He also mocked the interracial civil rights movement, declaring that "an integrated cup of coffee doesn't pay for 400 years of slave labor." Convinced that violence was inevitable in the struggle for black freedom, he told his followers that "It's time for you and me to let the government know it's ballots or bullets." On a pilgrimage to Mecca (the Muslim holy city in Saudi Arabia) in 1964, Malcolm X was

The Watts section of Los Angeles didn't look like the ghettos of northern industrial cities.

converted to the traditional Islamic view of racial tolerance. Only a few months later, however, he was brutally murdered by black members of a rival Muslim group.

The threat of violence was also a prime tactic of the Black Panthers, founded in 1966. The group's chief spokesman, Eldridge Cleaver, declared the choice to be "total liberty for black people or total destruction for America." The Black Panthers frequently appeared in public heavily armed. After the FBI declared it to be a subversive organization, a concerted and successful effort was made to put most of its members behind bars.

The black slogan for the late 1960's became "Black Power." To some, it meant black separatism, especially in economic affairs. To oth-

ers, it simply meant pride in being black. A lot of black Americans began wearing their hair unstraightened in "Afros," and relaxing in loose African shirts called dashikis. Some abandoned their "slave names" for African or Muslim names. Boxer Cassius Clay, for example, became Muhammad Ali. It was at this time, too, that the term "Negro" was replaced by "black." Whatever "Black Power" meant to blacks, it estranged many whites. When white cooperation was rejected by some black civil rights groups, an era of camaraderie and shared goals seemed at an end.

THE KERNER COMMISSION

After the Newark and Detroit riots, President Johnson formed a panel of 11 distinguished Americans, headed by Governor Otto Kerner of Illinois, to investigate the causes. This National Advisory Commission on Civil Disorders (often called the Kerner Commission) issued its findings early in 1968. Behind the rioting, said the report, were "men and women without jobs, families without men, and schools where children are processed instead of educated, until they return to the street to crime, to narcotics, to dependency on welfare, and to bitterness and resentment against society." Its conclusions were summed up in a single memorable sentence: "Our nation is moving toward two societies, one black and one white, separate and unequal."

To prevent future violence, the commission made the following recommendations: create two million jobs in three years; eliminate de facto segregation in public schools; provide job training; pass open housing laws; and create six million new low-rent housing units.

Johnson called the Kerner Commission summary "a good report by good men of good will," but did not implement its recommendations because it implied that the Great Society had failed. A man whose ego bruised easily, the President commented: "We are not unaware of the problem . . . they always print that we don't do enough. They don't print what we do."

At any rate, the days of Great Society legislation were over by 1968. When asked to appropriate $2 million to exterminate rats in inner cities, one congressman laughingly offered an alternative solution: "Why not just buy some cats and turn them loose?" As far as the annual rioting was concerned, no one did anything. It simply started, and stopped, by itself.

TWO MOVEMENTS

Feminism, a movement that had been inactive since the 1920's, revived in the 1960's. Most Americans — including many women — assumed that females had equal rights under the law, but appearances were deceiving. The position of women in American society had actually been on the decline since 1920. For example, proportionately fewer women attended college in 1960 than in 1920. Women earned less money than men with the same training and experience, and the gap was widening. Studies showed that unemployment and poverty among women, especially black women, were widespread. In many states, laws discriminated against women. They

Rep. Shirley Chisholm
and NOW founder
Betty Friedan,
two outspoken feminists
of the period.

could be prohibited from serving on juries, from entering into legal contracts, from owning credit cards in their own names, and, in some instances, from holding property.

A milestone in the 1960's revival of feminism (often called women's liberation) was the publication in 1963 of *The Feminine Mystique*, a book by Betty Friedan. She pointed out the contradictions between the deference paid to women and the lives they actually led. The American home, Friedan said, was a "comfortable concentration camp" that stifled women's energy and creativity. The "feminine mystique" — that all women should find complete fulfillment as homemakers — was in reality creating legions of dissatisfied women who asked themselves "the silent question — 'Is this all?'"

Friedan's message was echoed by many other women. Shirley Chisholm, a black U.S. representative from New York City, noted that her sex had been a greater obstacle than her color. "I was constantly bombarded by both men and women," she said, "that I should return to teaching, a woman's vocation, and leave politics up to men."

In 1966 Friedan and others founded the National Organization for Women (NOW). Similar in approach to the NAACP, it used the courts and nonviolent confrontation tactics of the civil rights movement to remove many of the legal barriers to equality. NOW and other feminist organizations were aided by the 1964 Civil Rights Act, which prohibited job discrimination on the basis of sex. Women's enrollment in college increased, as did the number of women in such traditionally male professions as medicine, the law, and police work.

The 1960's also saw the rise of a Hispanic protest movement centering on migrant farm labor. This job market employed thousands of Mexican-Americans, many of them cruelly exploited by growers. One of their own, Cesar Chavez, formed the United Farm Workers (UFW) in 1963 and, after several years of organizing in California, called for a nationwide boycott of nonunion table grapes. (Pickers' annual income averaged between $2000 and $2500, with no benefits.) After five difficult years, Chavez succeeded in getting his union recognized, and in gaining some concessions for his fellow Mexican-Americans.

A rock concert audience.

THE COUNTERCULTURE

The Johnson years were the heyday of a phenomenon often referred to as the *counterculture*. It was a life-style that appealed especially to affluent middle-class whites in their late teens and early 20's. These "hippies" mostly rejected established social mores.

They embraced a casual life-style which spurned the corporate American work ethic and freed one to become a communal farmer or an artisan. Eastern religions and mysticism became popular within the hippie movement, and nonviolence, specifically anti-Vietnam war sentiment, became an identifying feature of this group as they preached the slogan, "Peace."

In a reaction against materialism, these young men and women adopted a fashion largely made up of faded jeans, army surplus clothes, and beads. Hair grew freely on both sexes. Nonconventionalism became the convention.

Also identified with the counterculture were psychedelic music and the popularization of recreational drugs. The music was anything but peaceful. In counterculture meccas such as San Francisco's Haight-Ashbury district, the loud music and open use of drugs became ugly symbols of a life-style perhaps more vulnerable than wise or practical.

SECTION RECAP

1. What two major kinds of legislation did Johnson put forward after Kennedy's death?

2. What factors aided Johnson's landslide victory?

3. What were the main programs of the Great Society?

4. How did immigration begin to change in 1965?

5. Describe the aspirations of the following groups during this period: blacks, women, migrant farmworkers, hippies.

3 The Vietnam Quagmire

U.S. Marines crouch behind a wall near Hue while South Vietnamese troops attack.

Two days after Kennedy's death, President Johnson told the American ambassador to Vietnam: "I am not going to lose South Vietnam." This determination was one of the factors that led to the transformation of the Vietnamese conflict into a full-scale war, undermined Johnson's domestic program, and, finally, forced him out of office.

Early on, Johnson was told by the CIA that more and more South Vietnamese peasants were joining the Vietcong because they hated the corrupt government in Saigon. Unconvinced, Johnson dispatched Secretary of Defense Robert McNamara to Southeast Asia in December 1963. McNamara confirmed the CIA's reports. There was also evidence that an increasing amount of American military equipment was being diverted to the North Vietnamese.

Early in 1964, Johnson responded by stepping up commando raids. South Vietnamese sabotage teams trained by American advisers were parachuted behind enemy lines to blow up bridges and destroy communications. The President also replaced the civilian ambassador to South Vietnam, Henry Cabot Lodge, with a general, Maxwell Taylor. And he appointed as commander of U.S. military forces General William Westmoreland, a strong advocate of the use of American combat troops.

A South Vietnamese soldier keeping watch under a coconut palm tree in the Mekong Delta.

THE TONKIN GULF RESOLUTION

Two incidents of late summer 1964 helped Johnson win congressional approval of increased American involvement in Vietnam. The Defense Department reported that on the second of August, North Vietnamese torpedo boats fired on an American destroyer, the *Maddox*, in the Gulf of Tonkin, off the coast of North Vietnam. The next day another destroyer, the *Turner Joy*, was also reportedly attacked.

Actually, only the *Maddox* was attacked; freak weather conditions had misled sonar technicians to believe torpedoes had been fired at them in the second incident. Furthermore, both U.S. ships were engaged in intelligence-gathering activities. But this was a crucial time — just four months before the 1964 election — and Johnson wished to appear firm. Claiming the attack was "unprovoked" and "open aggression," he authorized the bombing of North Vietnamese ports and asked Congress for a resolution allowing him to "take all necessary measures to repel any armed attack" against U.S. forces and "to prevent further aggression in Southeast Asia."

Although there was some debate in Congress, the Tonkin Gulf Resolution was adopted almost unanimously. In the House of Representatives the vote was 414 to 0. In the Senate only two men — Wayne Morse of Oregon and Ernest Gruening of Alaska — opposed the resolution. (Morse claimed that it was unconstitutional because only Congress has the right to declare war.) Johnson's actions won wide approval throughout the country. One newspaper wrote that he had "earned the gratitude of the free world."

In the campaign against Goldwater, Johnson was portrayed as a man of moderation. After his great victory in November, the "peace" President appeared willing to negotiate with the North Vietnamese, but only on condition that they cease infiltrating the South. The President knew that Ho Chi Minh would not accept this condition.

Early in 1965 a significant change occurred in the South Vietnamese leadership. Senior military officers stripped General Nguyen Khanh of his authority; he had served as both premier and chief of state. The commander of the air force, Marshal Nguyen Cao Ky, became premier, while Nguyen Van Thieu was made chief of state.

THE DOMINICAN REPUBLIC

The United States had dominated the islands of the Caribbean since the early 19th century. So powerful was American authority there that direct intervention was usually unnecessary. But events in the Dominican Republic provoked an exception to the rule.

In April 1965 a curious assortment of radicals, junior army officers, and democrats launched a coup to restore a liberal, Juan Bosch, to the presidency. (He had been overthrown by right-wing military leaders in 1963.) After the American ambassador cabled Washington that conditions were "deteriorating rapidly," Johnson ordered 23,000 marines to the Caribbean island.

At first Johnson told the world that he had sent in the marines to protect American nationals. He later claimed that 1,500 people had been decapitated by the rebels and that "a thousand American men, women, and children were pleading with their President for help." (Neither claim was true.) Finally, the administration claimed that the revolt had been subverted by "a band of Communist conspirators." What it actually feared was a leftist government that would endanger American corporate interests. Johnson's move was criticized by many foreign powers — Castro attacked him bitterly — but generally approved by the American public. By June, order was restored and a dictator friendly to the United States was back in power.

ESCALATION IN VIETNAM

While Johnson got what he wanted in the Dominican Republic, his troubles were mounting in Vietnam. Early in 1965 the Vietcong penetrated a heavily protected American camp at Pleiku. Eight Americans were killed, 100 wounded, and 10 aircraft destroyed. The one Vietcong who was killed carried a detailed map of the camp.

The Pleiku attack convinced Johnson that the United States must scrap its policy of "retaliation bombing" in favor of a more aggressive approach. The American government then launched "Operation Rolling Thunder," a continuous bombardment of targets in North Vietnam. Johnson was convinced that sustained bombing would bring the North Vietnamese to the negotiating table. "If there's one thing that the American people will not take," he said not long afterward, "it is another shooting war in Asia."

Undersecretary of State George Ball, who had cautioned Kennedy against American involvement in Vietnam, warned Johnson that bombing would not gain American objectives. North Vietnam, Ball argued, was a rural society without strategic military targets. Aerial bombardment would have little effect on people willing to die for their cause.

Indeed, bombing did not bring the North Vietnamese to the bargaining table, and the United States soon took another fateful step. In March 1965 Johnson sent 35,000 marines to protect the American air base at Da Nang. An additional 22,000 were dispatched in April after an attack on the American embassy in Saigon. As well as protecting American bases, the marines were now encouraged to undertake "search and destroy" missions — that is, to seek out and kill Vietcong.

The United States was, for the first time, using its own ground troops for offensive actions. The administration did not acknowledge the change in policy until July. There was some grumbling about what the *New York Times* called the "undeclared and unexplained war in Vietnam." But seven out of 10 Americans supported Johnson and the war. Some 80 percent believed that a troop withdrawal would lead to a Communist takeover of Southeast Asia, and thought it necessary to maintain American combat troops in Vietnam.

American escalation was also deemed necessary because of the increasing weakness of the South Vietnamese government. Since Diem's assassination in 1963, there had been 10 changes of leadership in Saigon. South Vietnam's inability to win the war on its own fueled Westmoreland's demands for additional American forces. By the end of 1965, there were 185,000 American combat troops in Vietnam. Some 1,350 had died and 5,300 had been wounded.

THE LIVING ROOM WAR

By 1965 the war in Vietnam had supplanted race relations as the most important topic for concern. Large-scale bombing and the deployment of American ground troops were arousing opposition to the war, especially on college campuses. Pacifist groups urged young men to avoid military service. There were antiwar demonstrations, parades, and teach-ins (sessions at which opponents and proponents presented their arguments in lectures and discussions).

The media played a significant role in the growing disaffection. Johnson and Westmoreland were constantly assuring Americans that victory was just around the corner — that they could "see the light at the end of the tunnel." But television news coverage, which brought the war into America's living rooms every evening, focused on devastation that seemed to have no end. Night after night brought scenes of burned-out villages, of homeless children, of American soldiers being wounded and killed. People began talking about a credibility gap — the gap between what the Johnson administration was saying and what was happening on the battlefield.

In October, 10,000 people marched down New York City's Fifth Avenue to demonstrate against the war. A growing number of senators, including Robert Kennedy, condemned the administration's policies in Vietnam. Early in 1966, J. William Fulbright of Arkansas began holding televised hearings of the Senate Foreign Relations Committee on the conduct of the war.

Those who opposed the war were called doves. The war was illegal, doves argued, because only Congress can declare war. They also claimed that the United States was betraying its own traditions of freedom and democracy by interfering in the civil war of another country. The war was immoral, doves said, because Americans were killing innocent civilians in their attempt to pacify the country. There was widespread revulsion against the use of napalm, a jellylike substance that caused horrible burns.

Americans who defended the war were labeled hawks. They rejected claims that the Tonkin Gulf Resolution was illegal. If Congress no longer supported the conflict, they said, it could rescind its resolution. The American effort in Southeast Asia was moral as well as legal, the hawks maintained. The United States was fighting to contain communism in accordance with the domino theory first propounded under Eisenhower. In this case, if South Vietnam fell to communism, then Laos, Cambodia, Thailand, and Burma would all be endangered. The United States also had a moral obligation to show that it was an ally that could be trusted. President Johnson mocked the "nervous Nellies" who broke ranks under pressure, and warned that "to leave Vietnam to its fate" would shake the confidence of people all over the world in "the value of American commitment."

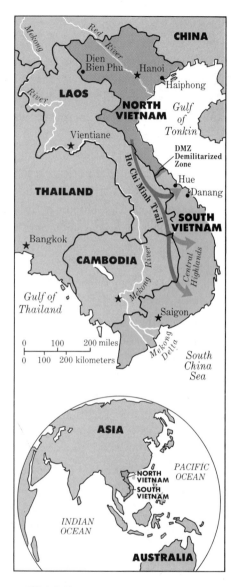

INCREASED OPPOSITION

On Christmas Eve, 1965, Johnson ordered a five-week bombing halt. He also dispatched diplomats to several capitals in Europe and Asia in hopes of finding a peaceful solution to the war. But the North Vietnamese refused to negotiate with Washington until every American soldier had left Vietnam. So bombing of the North resumed at the end of January 1966. The South Vietnamese government continued to lose support among its people, and desertions to the Vietcong increased alarmingly.

The Johnson administration was left with two choices: evacuate all American troops or escalate the war effort. For the President, the choice of escalation was obvious. By 1967 there were 385,000 American soldiers in Vietnam. The United States had also intensified its bombings. Sooner or later, military authorities believed, America's technological superiority would bring the North Vietnamese and the Vietcong to their knees.

At home, opposition to the war grew throughout 1967. Although most Americans did not favor a complete pullout, increasing numbers wanted to end the war on honorable terms — that is, under conditions that would save face for the United States without abandoning the South Vietnamese to a bloodbath. In April an organization called Mobilization to End the War in Vietnam (Mobe) sponsored demonstrations that brought out people of many different ages, occupations, and classes. Dozens of antiwar youths burned their draft cards (while others were fleeing to Canada). The antiwar movement was no longer exclusively young and radical. Among the many who spoke out was Martin Luther King, Jr.: "This madness must cease. . . . I speak as a child of God and brother of the suffering poor in Vietnam. I speak for those whose land is being laid waste, whose homes are destroyed, whose culture is being subverted. I speak for the poor of America, who are paying the double price of smashed hopes at home and death and corruption in Vietnam."

In 1967 American casualties reached 100,000. In August, troop strength reached 480,000, with an additional 50,000 on their way. Congress had appropriated another $12 billion to continue the war. Congressional doves voted in favor of funding the war because they did not want to be accused of letting down American boys in uniform.

Vietnam had turned into a quagmire — a deadly trap from which the United States could not seem to extricate itself. Bitter feeling divided doves from hawks. World opinion was turning against American involvement. Even some long-time supporters of Johnson's policy, such as McNamara, were now having second thoughts.

SECTION RECAP

1. What powers did the Gulf of Tonkin Resolution give to President Johnson? Why did Senator Morse oppose it?

2. Why did Johnson send U.S. troops to the Dominican Republic? What was public reaction?

3. How did the media influence the opinions of the American people towards the war?

4. Contrast the attitudes of the "doves" and the "hawks" towards the war. Why did the opposition to the war increase?

4 1968: The Year Things Fell Apart

Wounded U.S. Marines await assistance after a Vietcong attack on Hue.

Looking back on the year 1968, many people felt that the best thing about it was that it lasted only 12 months. It seemed impossible for so much frustration, turbulence, and grief to be compressed into such a short period.

THE PUEBLO INCIDENT

The first major news event of 1968 involved a United States ship, the *Pueblo*. Although called an environmental research ship, the *Pueblo* was a spy vessel that cruised the Sea of Japan using its electronic equipment to pick up whatever information it could about North Korea. As long as the *Pueblo* stayed 12 miles out to sea, its surveillance was perfectly legal. But North Korea claimed that the ship had violated this limit and, on January 23, seized the vessel and its 83-man crew. Before the North Koreans could board, the ship's captain, Lloyd Bucher, ordered his men to destroy all intelligence equipment and reports, but much remained undamaged for lack of time.

The *Pueblo* was the first American naval vessel to be captured since 1807. Official Washington was dismayed. One senator wanted to seize all vessels flying the North Korean flag. But Johnson had enough trouble in Vietnam without provoking trouble elsewhere in Asia. Bucher and his crew were to remain prisoners of North Korea for almost a year before being freed.

THE TET OFFENSIVE

A few days after the *Pueblo* seizure, the Vietnamese were preparing to celebrate Tet, the lunar new year. Both sides had agreed to a cease-fire, but it was short-lived. The North Vietnamese and the Vietcong realized that with people moving about visiting their relatives, Tet would be a perfect time to launch a military offensive.

On January 31, 1968, the Vietcong began the most ambitious and coordinated campaign of the war. Simultaneously, some 85,000 men struck 36 out of 44 provincial capitals, countless villages, and a dozen American military bases in South Vietnam. The most celebrated attack took place in the early morning hours at the United States embassy in Saigon. Although the building was protected by a reinforced concrete bomb shield and shatterproof windows, Vietcong commandos armed with submachine guns and rocket launchers managed to blow a hole in the embassy wall. In the course of the raid, all 19 Vietcong were killed, but they had proved that the American embassy was not impregnable.

Westmoreland called Tet the last gasp of a defeated enemy — although he would soon be asking the President for an additional 206,000 men. (His credibility had declined to such an extent that Johnson replaced him with General Creighton Abrams in April.)

While North Vietnam and the Vietcong did not gain control over the rich Mekong Delta region, Tet indicated clearly that American intelligence reports stressing the enemy's weakness had missed the mark. Vietcong fighters had shown that they could mount a sophisticated offensive against a powerful military force.

Again the American media did much to influence public opinion. Photos in *Life* magazine showed an embassy employee looking out the window holding an automatic pistol, as though he alone were charged with defending the building. Television viewers saw American marines withstanding days of shelling at their base at Khe Sanh. The Tet Offensive convinced an increasing number of Americans that Vietnam was "a lost war by a country that had never lost a war." Tet also lowered LBJ's already low credibility. America's loss of faith in its commander-in-chief was so great that the only places he could safely speak without encountering hostile crowds were American military installations. Everywhere else the President seemed to be dogged by the cruel chants of "Hey, hey, LBJ: how many kids did you kill today?"

McCARTHY IN NEW HAMPSHIRE

In the six weeks after Tet, Johnson's overall "approval rating" dropped from 48 to 36 percent. On the specific question of how he was handling the war, support for the President fell from 40 to 26 percent. Seven major newspapers that had favored Johnson's Vietnam policies became sharply critical of them, and the number of people who called themselves doves jumped from 25 to 40 percent.

In March the first presidential primary of the 1968 campaign took place, as usual, in snowy, rural, and conservative New Hampshire. Democratic voters were to choose between Johnson and Eugene McCarthy. This

Senator Eugene McCarthy after winning
the Wisconsin Democratic primary.

soft-spoken Minnesota senator, who opposed
the Vietnam War, had entered the primary
mainly to gauge the strength of antiwar sentiment. He had attracted many college students
as campaign workers — workers so enthusiastic that they traded in their jeans and
sneakers for ties and sports jackets in order to
be "Clean for Gene."

Most polls gave McCarthy an outside
chance of capturing perhaps 20 percent of the
vote. The results rocked Johnson and the nation. The Minnesotan won 42.2 percent to
Johnson's 49.5 percent. Although he lost the
primary, antiwar forces claimed a great vic-

tory. McCarthy's message had struck home
even in conservative New Hampshire.

Four days after the New Hampshire primary, Robert Kennedy threw his hat into the
Democratic ring. Distinguishing his priorities
from those of his brother John, the New York
senator said that "It is more important to be
able to walk through the ghetto than to walk
on the moon." Kennedy, who called Johnson's
policies "bankrupt," claimed that the United
States was in danger "from our own misguided policies."

LBJ'S BOMBSHELL

The New Hampshire primary was a terrible
blow to President Johnson. It seemed a bitter
end to his consensus presidency. He had not
succeeded in maintaining support for his foreign policy. His Great Society had failed to
achieve what he wanted, held hostage by the
seemingly unending cost of the war. The trust
and cooperation of the interracial civil rights
movement seemed gone. It appeared to Johnson that Americans were unwilling to believe
anything he said or did.

On March 31, 1968, President Johnson appeared before the country on a nationwide
telecast. He spoke about the chances for peace
in Vietnam, and announced his decision to
stop the bombing of North Vietnam immediately, except for an area near the demilitarized zone. He repeated his eagerness to use
diplomatic means to end "this ugly war." At
the end of his 35-minute speech, Johnson re-
viewed his 52 months in office. Then he
dropped this bombshell: "I do not believe that
I should devote an hour or a day of my time to

King's funeral cortege in Atlanta included many who had marched with him in more hopeful times.

my personal partisan causes or to any duties other than the awesome duties of this office — the presidency of your country. Accordingly, I shall not seek, and I will not accept, the nomination of my party for another term as your President. . . . Good night and God bless all of you."

Johnson's speech triggered the opening of peace talks in Paris in May. These were to drag on for years with few results, for American bombing near the demilitarized zone turned out to cover a large area and to be quite heavy. There were no signs that the Vietcong would "restrain themselves," as Johnson had hoped. The number of American troops in Vietnam reached 550,000 by April, and U.S. combat deaths totaled almost 23,000. To those who considered the war to have begun with Kennedy's dispatch of advisers in 1961, the Vietnam War became the longest in American history — exceeding the Revolutionary War — in June of 1968.

In April Vice President Humphrey announced his candidacy for the Democratic presidential nomination. Although a liberal in social policy, he had supported Johnson's conduct of the war.

ASSASSINATION IN MEMPHIS

At the time of Johnson's speech, Martin Luther King, Jr., was involved in a campaign to support 1,300 striking garbagemen — 98 percent of them black — in Memphis, Tennessee. King had been discouraged by his inability to apply his nonviolent strategies in the North (he had been attacked in Chicago in 1966). He was particularly distressed by the riots in Detroit and Newark during the summer of 1967. More militant blacks viewed him as a relic of another era. Adam Clayton Powell referred to him contemptuously as Martin "Loser" King.

At a Memphis church on April 3, a fatalistic King told his audience: "We've got some difficult days ahead. But it really doesn't matter with me now, because I've been to the mountaintop . . . I may not get to the promised land with you, but I want you to know tonight that we, as a people, will."

The next morning King was murdered by a white ex-convict's bullet as he talked to a friend on the second-story balcony of a motel. To many Americans, the slaying of the champion of nonviolence signaled the end of the nonviolent civil rights movement. One black man living within a mile of the White House exclaimed, "This is it, baby! . . . We ought to burn this place right down." In fact, within a half hour of the news of King's death, blacks throughout the country began to riot. In 168 cities, they looted and then burned thousands of stores and buildings. By the end of the week, 37 people had been killed, 2,600 fires had been set, and 21,000 people had been injured. It took 55,000 troops to restore law and order. Washington, D.C., the nation's capital and a predominantly black city, had to be protected by armed troops.

For those who believed that America might at last solve its racial problems, King's assassination was devastating. Johnson had the flags on all federal buildings flown at half-mast and proclaimed the seventh of April as a national day of mourning.

ASSASSINATION IN LOS ANGELES

King's death came just as the campaign for the Democratic nomination for president was heating up. Robert Kennedy's name and charismatic appeal helped him defeat Eugene McCarthy in Indiana, Nebraska, and South Dakota. McCarthy won in Oregon. The big test was the California primary on June 4.

Kennedy stayed in his Los Angeles hotel room that evening following the election returns. When he heard that he had won, he went downstairs to thank his cheering supporters. "Now on to Chicago and let's win there," he exhorted. Crowds forced him to exit through the kitchen. As he stopped to talk to a busboy, a Jordanian named Sirhan Sirhan fired six shots from a snub-nosed pistol. Five people were slightly injured; the sixth bullet mortally wounded Kennedy.

Kennedy's body was flown to New York City for a funeral at St. Patrick's Cathedral. His brother Ted, who lost two brothers in less than five years, ended his eulogy with a line Robert had often used: "Some men see things as they are and say 'Why?' I dream of things that never were and say 'Why not?'" From the cathedral the coffin was taken by special train to Arlington Cemetery in Virginia. The route was jammed by grief-stricken Americans, many of whom mourned not just for the man but for the promise he symbolized.

Kennedy's death was a serious setback to the chances for nominating a Democratic antiwar candidate. Now Humphrey, who had not won a single primary but who had the support of the traditional Democratic machine, became the front runner.

CAMPUS CONFRONTATION

In 1964 student protests at the University of California at Berkeley had succeeded in shutting down the school for several weeks. The unrest had initially involved free speech and then spread to other issues, most of which were resolved in favor of the protesters. Since then, America's college campuses had been the scene of many confrontations, focusing at first on the civil rights movement but finding a more compelling cause in antiwar agitation. Many students adopted the styles of the counterculture. Some were influenced by various small but vocal organizations of the so-called New Left. The best known of these was Students for a Democratic Society (SDS), which advocated a "participatory democracy" that, to many older liberals, seemed little more than anarchy.

By 1968 college protests were reaching a peak. In the first six months alone, there were 221 major demonstrations at 101 colleges, involving some 40,000 students. One of the most notable occurred at Columbia University, located not far from Harlem in New York City. The problem began when the university decided to build a new gymnasium in a nearby public park; it was intensified when students learned that Columbia had ties with the Institute for Defense Analysis, a "think tank" funded by the Defense Department.

In April the SDS called for a demonstration, and soon spearheaded the occupation of several campus buildings. When negotiations failed, the university administration called in the police. Swinging their nightsticks, they drove the students out as television cameras

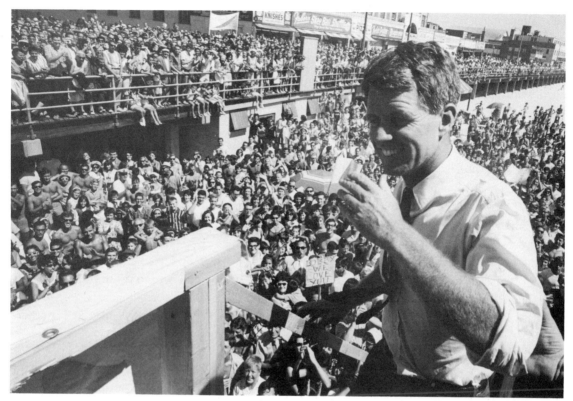

Senator Robert Kennedy campaigning on Long Island, New York.

rolled. The battle cost Columbia $300,000 — and untold thousands in alumni contributions.

The confrontations at Columbia and elsewhere had some repercussions both on campus and off. For one thing, they helped ease or eliminate altogether many university rules governing curriculum and campus life. But they did little to radicalize opinion. The SDS itself was finished as a coherent national organization by 1970.

THE REPUBLICANS AT MIAMI

The Republicans met at Miami early in August to nominate their presidential candidate. Though not warmly regarded as a person, Richard Nixon was the favorite, mainly because of the hard work he had done for the party since leaving the vice presidency. As his vice presidential candidate, Nixon chose Spiro Agnew, governor of Maryland. Conceding that Agnew was "not a household word," Nixon said he was impressed with the man's no-nonsense style.

The Nixon-Agnew ticket appealed to what some observers regarded as forgotten Americans — people who didn't break the law, didn't cheat on their taxes, raised their children to be good citizens, and generally believed minorities and criminals were being given unfair advantages. Nixon dubbed them the "silent majority." Agnew alienated about as many Americans as he pleased by attacking "pointy-headed liberals and phony intellectuals who don't understand what we mean by hard work and patriotism." Nixon had better luck with his appeals for a "new leadership" that would "end the war . . . and win the peace."

Nixon (and the Democrats too) hit hard on the theme of "law and order," correctly gauging the frustration and anger of the silent majority. Many Americans believed that crime in the streets and rioting in the ghettos should be laid at the feet of the Supreme Court, under Chief Justice Earl Warren.

Among the Warren Court decisions unpopular with conservatives, four stood out. In *Engel* v. *Vitale* (1962), the Court ruled that compulsory prayer in the public schools was unconstitutional. *Gideon* v. *Wainwright* (1963) held that poor people charged with felonies in state courts had the right to free counsel. *Escobedo* v. *Illinois* (1964) required that police allow accused persons to consult with lawyers during interrogation. *Miranda* v. *Arizona* (1966) compelled police to warn suspects that they could remain silent and have legal counsel before questioning.

TURMOIL IN CHICAGO

In sharp contrast with the bland Republican gathering, the Democratic convention in Chicago turned out to be one of the most violent and disruptive in American history. Before the convention began in late August, a loosely-knit group of radicals called Yippies (Youth International Party) announced plans to invade the city with 100,000 followers to stage a Festival of Life. There were threats, many couched in obscene language, to disrupt Chicago by such means as putting LSD in the city water supply. As a countermeasure, Mayor Richard J. Daley lined up 11,500 police officers, 5,500 national guardsmen, and 7,500 federal troops. They were joined by 1,000 FBI and Secret Service agents.

Fearing violence, only about 10,000 demonstrators showed up in Chicago. The Yippies — some 2,500 in all — brought with them a large pig, Pigasus, that they planned to nominate at their own convention. ("Pig," at this time, was a widely used insult for a police officer.) There were other demonstrators as well, including clergy and a group called Mothers for Peace.

Daley refused to issue the protesters a parade permit. When they tried to march anyway, Chicago police were poised with clubs and tear gas, eager to enforce Daley's ban. The violence peaked on the night of August 28. When some demonstrators tried to provoke attack, the police acted with ferocity, using nightsticks on many innocent spectators and reporters and indiscriminately dragging people into police wagons. Hundreds were arrested and many had to be hospitalized. (Later, an independent federal commission report described the violence in Chicago as a "police riot.")

Meanwhile, television viewers were watching not only the "battle of Chicago," in the streets but also Democratic delegates meeting to nominate a presidential candidate. One speaker, Connecticut Senator Abraham

Ribicoff, denounced "Gestapo tactics in the streets of Chicago" and Daley was seen exploding with rage. However, the convention managed to calm down long enough to nominate Humphrey. He chose Senator Edmund Muskie of Maine as his running mate.

McCarthy forces tried to get delegates to adopt an antiwar plank calling for an immediate end to the bombing and the withdrawal of all American troops, but it was defeated. In its place the convention voted for a Johnson-Humphrey resolution demanding the withdrawal of North Vietnamese troops.

THE ELECTION OF 1968

Prior to becoming vice president, Humphrey had compiled an outstanding record as mayor of Minneapolis and senator from Minnesota. He had the support of labor, many civil rights groups, and old-line party members. But many conservative Democrats were alienated by the turmoil of the Democratic convention. Their estrangement helped George Wallace's American Independent party. Wallace had been a popular Alabama governor well-known for his opposition to civil rights. His wife, Lurleen, was serving as governor in 1968 because Alabama governors were not allowed to succeed themselves. Before the convention, Wallace had never won more than 10 percent of the vote in any presidential poll. In September 1968, however, 21 percent of those surveyed showed a preference for Wallace. If elected, he promised to shoot looters on sight, return the country to law and order, win the war in Vietnam, repeal open-housing laws, and end school busing.

Chicago police move to confront demonstrators at the 1968 Democratic convention.

President Johnson in 1968.

to have a secret plan to end the war, which he would reveal after he was elected. Nixon also favored a nuclear nonproliferation treaty with the Soviet Union.

· Throughout most of the campaign, Humphrey tried to gain some support from the anti-war forces by distancing himself subtly from Johnson's position. He said that, as president, he would be willing to stop the bombing as "an acceptable risk for peace." Finally, just six days before the election, Johnson called a bombing halt. His move probably helped Humphrey, but it was too late. Although Nixon was ahead by scarcely two points the day before the election, he pulled off a narrow victory, winning by less than one percent of the popular vote.

Of Nixon's inaugural in January 1969, an observer later wrote, "Johnson stood like a caged eagle, dignified, never to be trifled with, his eyes fixed on distant heights that now he would never reach." Four years later, at his ranch on the Pedernales, he died of a heart attack.

SECTION RECAP

1. What impact did the Tet Offensive have on the war?

2. How did the results of the New Hampshire Democratic primary of 1968 affect American politics and the course of the war?

3. How was 1968 one of the most violent years in American political history?

4. Why did Nixon beat Humphrey in the 1968 presidential election?

For his running mate, he picked General Curtis LeMay, who had suggested using nuclear weapons to bomb North Vietnam "back to the stone age."

In August Nixon was comfortably ahead of Humphrey in the polls. His campaign focused on a return to law and order and an "honorable" end to the Vietnam conflict. He claimed

1. For each of the following quotes, identify the source, and the surrounding circumstances or situation:

a. ". . . saw off the eastern seaboard and let it float to sea."

b. ". . . freedom from wants of the body can help fulfill the needs of the spirit."

c. ". . . but really it's all of us who must overcome the crippling legacy of bigotry and injustice. And we shall overcome."

d. "Our nation is moving toward two societies, one black and one white, separate and unequal."

e. "Is this all?"

f. "This madness must cease . . . I speak as a child of God and brother of the suffering poor in Vietnam."

2. Define these terms: *cloture, counterculture, de facto, de jure, white backlash.*

3. Why was his election to the vice presidency a demotion for Lyndon Johnson?

4. What did the Kerner Commission recommend to put a stop to violence after the Newark and Detroit riots and why weren't its proposals adopted?

5. Why did President Johnson escalate the Vietnam War by ordering continuous bombing of North Vietnamese targets and ordering U.S. ground troops to Vietnam?

6. Why was the Vietnam War called the living room war? What effect do you think television had on the outcome of the war? Do you think the results of the Korean War would have been different if it had received the same amount of television coverage? If so, how?

7. What political and personal factors did Lyndon Johnson have going for him that practically insured his election in 1964? Do you think the outcome of the election might have been different had the Republicans nominated a more moderate candidate than Barry Goldwater? Why, or why not?

CHAPTER 7

1969 ▬◄ 1972

The Comeback of a Conservative

ON JULY 20, 1969, MILLIONS of people sat before their television sets, anxiously watching a man in a space suit climb down a ladder. He placed his left foot on a new, untried surface and proclaimed, "That's one small step for man, one giant leap for mankind." Neil Armstrong had become the first human being to walk on the moon.

Commander Armstrong, a civilian engineer, Air Force Colonel Edwin E. Aldrin, and Air Force Lieutenant Colonel Michael Collins were members of the *Apollo 11* crew. They had lifted off from the Kennedy Space Center on July 16 to embark on a 240,000-mile journey to the moon. After reaching their destination, Collins stayed aboard the command module *Columbia* while Armstrong and Aldrin descended to the moon in a lunar module, the *Eagle.* As soon as the module touched down on lunar soil, Armstrong announced to the Houston Space Center, "The *Eagle* has landed."

After Armstrong's historic walk, Aldrin joined him on the surface of the moon, collecting rocks and soil samples. Then the two astronauts lifted off and rejoined the *Columbia* for a 60-hour trip back to Earth. The *Apollo 11* mission had fulfilled President Kennedy's pledge to land a man on the moon and return him safely to Earth by the end of the decade.

Aboard the aircraft carrier *Hornet*, a proud and excited President Richard M. Nixon spoke to the astronauts in space. He described his conversation as "the most historic phone call ever made." He told the *Apollo 11* crew, "For every American this has to be the proudest day of our lives." He was on hand to greet them when they were returned to the *Hornet* after they splashed down in the Pacific. President Nixon had reason to rejoice. Ever since the 1957 Soviet launching of *Sputnik*, Americans had been determined to catch up with the Russians and then beat them in the space conquest. At last, the United States had regained the lead over the Soviet Union in the race for space.

Quarantined *Apollo 11* astronauts (from left) Armstrong, Collins, and Aldrin joke with President Nixon.

Back at Cape Kennedy, Collins captured the feelings of many Americans when he stated, "We have taken to the moon the wealth of this nation, the vision of its political leaders, the intelligence of its scientists, the dedication of its engineers, the careful craftsmanship of its workers and the enthusiastic support of its people."

The lunar landing provided a moment of shared enthusiasm among a bitterly divided people. The American public was still polarized into groups who disagreed on the course the nation should take. The war in Vietnam had split Americans into doves and hawks. Rising crime rates as well as frequent demonstrations provoked some Americans to demand sterner measures to restore law and order. In response, others became more ardent civil libertarians. Despite the War on Poverty, some Americans argued that the government was not doing enough to aid minorities or cities. Their opponents insisted that the government was doing far too much.

Polarization Politics

A people divided over national priorities could be expected to have difficulty choosing a president. In November 1968, they gave Nixon a slender majority over Hubert Humphrey, although it was not as slim as the margin by which Nixon had lost to John Kennedy in 1960. But while the voters elected a Republican President, they gave him a Democratic Congress. In the Senate, 57 Democrats faced 43 Republicans. In the House, 243 Democrats opposed 192 Republicans.

Although his margin of victory was small, Nixon's election to the presidency was an important personal triumph. It represented his return to politics after two major defeats at the polls. Eight years earlier, no one would have predicted it.

He was born on a small citrus farm in Yorba Linda, California, on January 8, 1913, the second of five sons. Nixon's father was never successful financially, and was described by neighbors as "gruff and short-tempered." His mother, a Quaker, worked hard to lift the family from poverty. Two of the boys died before reaching adulthood.

The family moved to nearby Whittier when Richard was five. He attended local schools, eventually entering Whittier College. With the help of a local scholarship, he went on to Duke University Law School where he graduated near the top of his class in 1937. On June 21, 1940, he married Thelma (Pat) Ryan, a school teacher. The Nixons became parents of two daughters, Patricia and Julie. After Pearl Harbor, Nixon enlisted in the Navy and served in the Pacific as a supply officer.

He returned home in 1946 and was elected to the House of Representatives as a Republican from the 12th Congressional District in California. Nixon was appointed to the House Un-American Activities Committee, where his role in the Alger Hiss investigation (see page 53) earned him the reputation of being a tough-minded, no-nonsense, anti-Communist. In 1950, favorable publicity helped Nixon win the U.S. Senate seat from California. In 1952 and again in 1956, Dwight Eisenhower picked Nixon to run as his vice president.

Richard Nixon as an enthusiastic member of the second-string
Whittier College football team.

In 1962, two years after losing the presidency to Kennedy, Nixon ran for governor in California. An early lead evaporated, and Nixon lost the election. Embittered by the unexpected defeat, he told reporters, "You won't have Richard Nixon to kick around anymore, because gentlemen, this is my last press conference." Nixon left politics for Wall Street and financial security.

After five years of practicing corporate law and traveling throughout the world, Nixon appeared to have changed. He seemed more contemplative and statesmanlike. No longer was he regarded as a mere tactician, interested in advancing his own career. However, he was still a very private man, elusive, hard to understand, and unwilling to share his emotions with others.

BUILDING SUPPORT

After winning the election, Nixon worked to consolidate his support. Kevin Phillips, a Justice Department aide and author of *The Emerging Republican Majority*, suggested that Nixon turn the silent majority's anger and frustration into a political advantage.

Phillips theorized that traditional Democratic voters such as southern whites, blue-collar workers, Catholics, and suburbanites, had become disenchanted with the voting records of liberal Democratic politicians. He believed that if these Democrats could join forces with traditional Republicans, Nixon would be able to isolate the liberal wing of the

Democratic party. These voters could even become the basis of a future conservative majority.

To appeal to these discontented Americans, the White House offered a variety of programs. Priority was given to the restoration of "law and order" in the streets, appointment of a more conservative Supreme Court, and the repudiation of rioters and demonstrators.

To woo southern whites in particular, the Nixon administration formulated a "Southern Strategy." It consisted of promises to slow down on civil rights, to appoint more *strict constructionists* (believers in a strict interpretation of the Constitution) to the federal judiciary, and to end involuntary busing to achieve racial integration. During the 1968 campaign, Nixon had made similar promises to Senator Strom Thurmond of South Carolina in exchange for support. The strategy had the added benefit of attracting northern blue-collar workers who felt threatened by the civil rights policies of the Johnson administration.

TAKING OFFICE

The theme of self-reliance dominated Nixon's inaugural address. Nixon claimed that his administration would be responsive to the needs of the American people. But, he cautioned, "we are approaching the limits of what government can do . . . what has to be done, has to be done by government and the people together or it will not be done at all." He wanted to encourage the private sector and personal initiative to seek solutions to the nation's ills. Many Americans were at least willing to give him a chance.

To help him carry out his plans, the President recruited a cabinet and personal staff that, for the most part, reflected his personal approach to government. He preferred to work alone, isolating himself in the Oval Office to make decisions on the major issues confronting the nation. He relied on subordinates to sift out the essential from the unessential and bring it to his attention. He did not wish to be overwhelmed by petty details which others could handle. This is why he wanted men around him whom he could trust with responsibility.

THE CABINET AND STAFF

For his cabinet Nixon chose a group who reflected his innate political conservatism. For example, the President appointed his longtime friend and wealthy corporate lawyer, William Rogers, to be secretary of state — even though Rogers had little experience in international relations. To head the Justice Department, Nixon chose John Mitchell, his former Wall Street law partner and 1968 presidential campaign manager. New York financier Maurice Stans became secretary of commerce, while George Romney, former president of American Motors and governor of Michigan, was appointed as secretary of the Department of Housing and Urban Development.

In his appointments to the White House staff, Nixon chose tough-minded, self-made go-getters. To Nixon, personal loyalty was of paramount importance. He wanted men upon whom he could rely to help him run the government. Thus, only one cabinet member,

John Mitchell, had as much influence on the President as the members of his personal staff. This was because Mitchell was a close friend and confidant.

Nixon had always regarded politics as a war to be waged against enemies rather than a game to be played against worthy opponents.

President Nixon in his San Clemente office with Henry Kissinger.

His staff had to be well-drilled subordinates, capable of carrying out presidential directives. They were required to ferret out the plans of the opposition and make sure that the President's policies prevailed.

For his chief of staff, Nixon tapped H. R. Haldeman, a former advertising executive. Haldeman was the staff member with the greatest authority. He organized the President's daily schedule, deciding who should and who should not be admitted to the Oval Office. Nixon named John D. Ehrlichman, a Seattle lawyer and former campaign aide, to serve as presidential assistant for domestic politics. All domestic activities had to be cleared through his office. Both men kept a low profile, playing down their personal importance.

As national security adviser, Nixon chose former Harvard professor and Rockefeller protégé, Henry Kissinger. Kissinger was an immigrant who escaped in 1938 from Nazi Germany. He had written extensively on nuclear weapons and diplomacy. Kissinger became more visible to the public, perhaps because at this time, prior to his marriage, he had developed a reputation for being a playboy. This made good copy for the media.

ATTACKING THE MEDIA

Richard Nixon never liked the press, and the press never liked Richard Nixon. The President was a very private man in a very public business who did whatever he could to maintain his privacy. As a result, he never allowed himself to be photographed informally, playing golf, sailing a boat, or in swim trunks, as some of his predecessors had done.

Politically, Nixon considered the major news networks to be too liberal and too critical of his domestic and foreign policy agendas. He believed that if they could be discredited, he and his administration would gain more flexibility in foreign and domestic decision making.

To test his theory, the President dispatched Vice President Agnew to Des Moines, Iowa,

Vice President Agnew tells Massachusetts reporters he does not mean to intimidate the national press.

as the main speaker at a Republican state committee meeting. In his speech, which was later broadcast on local and national television, Agnew attacked the media. He claimed that 40 million Americans were watching biased news, and he questioned whether the First Amendment guarantees of free speech should protect television.

Agnew charged that a handful of news commentators and producers decide on the "20 minutes or so of film and commentary that is to reach the public" every evening. He ac-

cused the three major networks of "packaging, presenting, and interpreting the nation's news." Agnew ended his attack by asking his audience, "How many marchers and demonstrators would we have if the marchers did not know that the ever-faithful television cameras would be there to record their antics?"

The media struck back. Network chiefs complained that Agnew's speech was an appeal to prejudice and ignorance. One television executive said the speech evoked shades of Senator McCarthy. Television journalists pointed out that between the hundreds of newspapers, weekly news magazines, and the scores of national and local television news programs, a monopoly over news programming was impossible.

Their arguments fell on deaf ears. Many Americans supported Agnew's attack on television news, and they thought his speech was long overdue. President Nixon's strategy of isolating and discrediting the media looked very promising.

SECTION RECAP

1. Why was the moon landing an especially extraordinary event in 1969?

2. How can Nixon's election to the presidency be seen as a great political comeback?

3. What qualities did people need to be appointed to President Nixon's cabinet and White House staff?

4. List some of the arguments Vice President Agnew used to attack television news programming.

2 A Pragmatic Domestic Program

At times, the rhetoric of the Nixon administration, as reported in the press, seemed at odds with its policies and programs. Attorney General Mitchell cautioned critics, "Watch what we do, not what we say." In fact, the administration's commitment to conservatism was sorely tested by concrete, practical problems. These often required a pragmatic approach, a series of trial-and-error solutions. Moreover, the administration had to win acceptance of its programs by an opposition Congress and the courts. The results were mixed.

BENIGN NEGLECT

As part of his Southern Strategy, President Nixon placed a high priority on weakening the federal government's commitment to civil rights. The battle lines were being drawn. Desegregation might not easily be reversed, but perhaps it could be slowed down. In 1969, the Department of Justice recommended that a number of school districts in Mississippi be granted a delay in meeting federal school desegregation guidelines. However, when the NAACP brought suit, the Supreme Court, led by Chief Justice Warren Burger, handed down the most important integration decision since *Brown* v. *The Board of Education* (1954). In *Alexander* v. *Holmes County Board of Education* (1969), the Court unanimously ordered an end to school segregation "at once."

In 1970, Daniel Patrick Moynihan, Nixon's urban affairs assistant, advised that the issue of race relations could benefit from a period of "benign neglect." By implication, "benign neglect" meant that the government should take a more passive role in protecting the civil liberties of blacks. That was the position Richard Nixon favored.

When the Voting Rights Act of 1965 came up for renewal in 1970, the President recommended that its provisions be applied to all states, rather than just to the South. In addition, he urged that voting rights lawsuits be tried first in state courts by local judges — an approach that would have made the act virtually useless since local judges would share local prejudices. Congress ignored Nixon's proposals and extended the act.

The President objected to court-ordered busing as a method of integrating schools. It was unpopular in the North as well as the South. He told the Justice Department to actively oppose involuntary school busing. To make neighborhood schools more attractive, he asked Congress to provide $1.5 billion in aid for school districts attempting to desegregate their facilities. Congress did pass several measures of its own, ending the use of federal funds for involuntary school busing.

However, in April 1971 the Supreme Court upheld plans to attain racial integration through busing in *Swann* v. *Charlotte-Mecklenburg*. In the Charlotte-Mecklenburg School District in North Carolina, 29 percent of the pupils were black, and most of them attended segregated schools, despite a voluntary busing plan. The court required the school district to adopt cross-town busing between the urban and suburban portions of the 550-square-mile district.

NEW JUSTICES

When Chief Justice Earl Warren resigned after the 1968-1969 Supreme Court term, conservatives were overjoyed. As part of his Southern Strategy, President Nixon had already pledged to fill Supreme Court vacancies with conservative appointees. The President's decision to nominate Warren Burger to replace the outgoing Chief Justice easily won Senate approval.

Nixon soon had another opportunity to nominate a member of the Supreme Court. In May 1969, Johnson-appointee Justice Abe Fortas was forced to resign under public pressure after *Life* magazine revealed a possible conflict of interest. Fortas had accepted and then returned $20,000. It was an installment on a lifetime grant from a charitable organization which was linked to a financier serving a prison term for stock manipulation. To fill this vacancy, Nixon placed in nomination Clement F. Haynesworth, a federal circuit court judge from South Carolina.

The NAACP quickly denounced the judge as a racist, and the AFL-CIO, the most powerful union in the country, accused Haynesworth of being antilabor. However, Haynesworth's defeat came about when Indiana Senator Birch Bayh disclosed that the nominee had ruled at least five times in favor of a firm in which he held stock. The Senate rejected Judge Haynesworth's nomination by a 45–55 vote. This was the first time in 30 years

Harry A. Blackmun just prior to being sworn in as an
associate justice of the Supreme Court.

and only the tenth time in Senate history that a Supreme Court nominee had failed to gain a majority vote.

Nixon then nominated Judge G. Harrold Carswell of Florida. Carswell's nomination was in trouble from the very moment his name was mentioned. Opponents produced a 1948 speech he had made before the American Legion. In it Carswell had said, "Segregation of the races is proper and the only practical and correct way of life in this state." Adversaries also revealed that as a member of the Tallahassee Golf Club, Carswell had voted to keep blacks from membership. Carswell's nomination was defeated 45–51.

An angered President Nixon told reporters that "as long as Democrats control the Senate, I cannot successfully nominate to the Supreme Court any federal appellate judge from the South who believes, as I do, in a strict construction of the Constitution."

Nixon turned next to the Midwest to fill the vacancy. He nominated Harvard-educated Harry A. Blackmun, a judge in the U.S. Eighth Circuit Court of Appeals in St. Louis, Missouri, who lived in Minnesota. Judge Blackmun easily won Senate approval.

By 1972, in addition to Justices Burger and Blackmun, the President also appointed Lewis F. Powell and William Rehnquist to the Court. Powell, a Virginian, was educated at Washington and Lee University and practiced law in Richmond, Virginia, until he joined the Court. Rehnquist, a graduate of Stanford University and Harvard, practiced law in Phoenix, Arizona. In 1969, he had become a member of the Department of Justice.

All four justices were selected by the President because he thought they would interpret the Constitution in a conservative manner. As a group, however, they did not always vote as the President had hoped or expected.

While President Nixon attempted to slow down the pace of civil rights for blacks, Secretary of Labor George Shultz was moving in a different direction. He developed a plan to train and employ minorities on federally funded construction projects. Both the Labor Department and the Department of Health, Education and Welfare began to use *racial quotas* (a required number or percentage representative of a minority group) and goals to advance desegregation.

CRIME AND PRISONS

By 1970 whole communities were becoming preoccupied with crime. The impact of baby boomers entering their teens and 20's could be seen in the soaring crime rate. In 1960, the national crime rate had been 294 per 100,000. Ten years later, that number had leaped to 773. During the same time period, homicides had increased by 75 percent. Between 1963 and 1973, police expenditures throughout the country went up by 800 percent. Yet, a Gallup Survey reported that four out of every 10 people were afraid to walk the streets of their towns and neighborhoods.

New York State troopers enter the prison at Attica
to put down a four-day-long uprising.
In the following weeks,
a chain reaction of disturbances occurred
in other prisons, but none with the severity of Attica.

Politically motivated crimes were also making citizens uneasy. In 1969, the Weathermen, a militant faction of the SDS, gathered in Chicago to riot in the streets. In 1970, a wave of bombings damaged large corporate offices and banks in New York City. Skyjackings also set off a wave of fear. It looked to some as if the country were heading toward anarchy.

To make matters worse, prisons were overcrowded and understaffed. Riots were commonplace, particularly in federal penitentiaries. In 1971, an uprising at the Attica Correctional Facility in upstate New York made national headlines.

Attica housed 2,254 men, 75 percent of whom were black or Hispanic. All 383 prison guards were white. Racial antagonism between the inmates and the guards was intense. The riot began when 1,200 inmates took 39 guards prisoner. They barricaded themselves in a cell block and demanded religious freedom, a decent diet, medical care, and uncensored reading material. They also asked to see Governor Nelson Rockefeller to air their grievances. The governor refused to meet with the prisoners.

When their demands were rejected, the prisoners threatened to cut the throats of their hostages. With Rockefeller's support, the warden instructed prison guards and the local police to storm the prison. In the ensuing struggle, 41 inmates and nine prison guards were killed. Tom Wicker, a *New York Times* reporter on the scene, said, "Attica was proof of the need for prison reform." To others, the Attica tragedy proved that prison officials needed to get tough with their prisoners.

THE ADMINISTRATION REACTS

It was against this background of crime statistics, demonstrations, bombings, and riots that the Nixon administration took action. In 1970, the President ordered the intelligence community and the FBI to develop a plan to combat subversives and radicals. Relying on the Omnibus Crime Control and Safe Streets Act (1968) and other legislative measures, members of the administration fought to reduce the crime rate. They met with little success. However, the administration's use of wiretapping and preventive detention to deter those they thought were criminals or subversives stirred controversy.

In 1972, the Supreme Court found that the executive branch had been overzealous in its efforts to restore law and order. The Court ruled that Attorney General John Mitchell and the Justice Department could not wiretap alleged subversives and radicals without a court order.

Justice Powell gave the majority opinion: "The price of lawful public dissent . . . must not be a dread of subjection to an unchecked surveillance power . . . Unreviewed executive discretion may yield too readily to pressure to obtain incriminating evidence and overlook potential invasions of privacy . . . We cannot accept the government's argument that internal security matters are too subtle and complex for judicial evaluation."

Law and order supporters received another setback in 1972 when the Supreme Court handed down a decision in *Furman* v. *Georgia*. The Court ruled that existing state legislation invoking the death penalty was in violation of the Eighth Amendment, which prohibits cruel and unusual punishment. They reasoned that the death penalty was prescribed in an unfair and unconstitutional manner. Too often, it was applied to crimes involving minorities, the poor, and the powerless. More carefully drafted state statutes might still be upheld.

On the other hand, the Burger Court ruled that many decisions of the Warren Court protecting the rights of accused criminals were too far-reaching. In a series of rulings issued in 1972, the Court eased some of the restrictions in criminal proceedings. In *Johnson* v. *Louisiana*, by a vote of 5–4, the Court set aside a state law requiring a unanimous vote of a jury for criminal conviction. In another 5–4 decision, *Milton* v. *Wainwright*, the Court ruled that confessions obtained by unconstitutional methods could be valid if there was enough other legitimate evidence to offset the mistake.

THE NEW FEDERALISM

In the summer after his election, President Nixon first unveiled his plans to limit the federal government's involvement in the nation's economic life. He called this idea the New Federalism. Two of his most notable proposals were the Family Assistance Plan and revenue sharing.

Between 1960 and 1972, the cost of federal welfare programs had risen from $2.1 billion to almost $18 billion. In 1961 there were 7.3 million people on the welfare rolls, while in 1972, the number increased to 14.9 million. Part of this surge in numbers can be attrib-

uted to the effects of President Nixon's anti-inflation program (see page 218).

The existing welfare programs were overburdened. Moreover, they often degraded the recipients. For example, under the terms of Aid to Families with Dependent Children (AFDC), funds would be withheld from a family if a working father lived with his wife and children, no matter how little he earned.

In 1969 Nixon proposed that AFDC be replaced by a Family Assistance Program (FAP). As originally conceived by Daniel Patrick Moynihan, FAP was designed to give the poor the right to determine their own needs. They would receive cash, or cash equivalents such as food stamps. The more traditional approach to welfare supplied the needy with special services and denied them a choice in how the money they received could be spent.

Under FAP, families earning less than $4,000 yearly would receive some federal aid. A family of four with no outside income would receive $1,600 a year and $860 in food stamps. Recipients with school-age children were required to report for work or job training. On the other hand, in 1971, the President vetoed legislation that would have established nationwide day-care centers for working mothers. He felt that it would jeopardize the stability of the family.

Conservatives objected to FAP because they thought it would raise welfare costs. Liberals thought the amount was unrealistically low — even though 20 states had lower welfare levels. They joined forces to defeat the proposed legislation in the Senate. Instead, the Congress passed welfare reform legisla-

Daniel Patrick Moynihan (right) discusses the Family Assistance Plan with reporters on *Meet the Press.*

tion that gave the administration complete control over aid to the blind, disabled, and aged, and increased annual welfare payments by $2 million a year.

Revenue sharing, a scheme first proposed during the Johnson administration, was designed to return federal funds to the states and localities. The funds would be distributed in the form of *block grants.* These were sums broadly earmarked for special purposes, such as housing or sanitation. Their chief advantage was flexibility. The administration preferred block grants over aid to specified groups of the population, such as needy children or the disabled. The former offered states and localities more discretion in determining how federal revenues would be spent. The latter ensured that certain sectors of the population would receive federal assistance, regardless of state or local priorities.

In 1972, with the passage of the State and Local Fiscal Assistance Act, revenue sharing became law. Over five years, $30 billion was distributed to state and local governments. Conservatives hailed the law as "reversing the flow of power" back to the people. Most financially troubled local governments welcomed the act. Representatives of minorities, the poor, and inner cities complained that drastic cuts in categorical grants crippled their programs. They also felt that state and local governments could not or would not provide the human services necessary to protect the civil rights of the nation's poor.

NIXON ECONOMICS

Inflation was an urgent problem facing the nation. The dollar, which was worth 100 cents in 1965, was worth 84 cents in 1969. In 1970 the consumer price index was 16 percent higher than it was in 1967, and continued to climb. The inflationary economy was a legacy of the Johnson administration.

Instead of paying for the Vietnam War by

raising taxes or cutting nonmilitary spending, President Johnson chose to borrow money from banks and pay back the principal with interest at a later date. The practice of spending more money than a government receives in revenue is called *deficit spending*.

With the additional money in circulation and no corresponding increase in production, prices tend to rise, purchasing power tends to decline, and inflation sets in. Those Americans on fixed incomes, like Social Security and pensions, are hit hardest. To slow the inflationary process, businesses raise their prices to keep their profits up. In turn, labor unions demand automatic cost-of-living raises to match rising prices. This results in a spiral of high wages and higher prices.

To slow inflation, President Nixon implemented a tight money policy. He cut federal spending on social programs and raised interest rates, forcing people to borrow less. As a result, a recession set in. Businesses could not afford the higher costs of borrowing money, so they cut back on production and delayed the purchase of new equipment. They laid off workers. Sales of goods and services declined as unemployed workers limited their purchases. Some businesses declined or went bankrupt.

The Dow Jones Industrial Average, one measurement of the stock market's health, declined from 985 in December 1968 to 631 in August 1970. During the same period, unemployment rose from 3.3 percent to six percent. Each percentage point represented the loss of 800,000 jobs. It was clear that Nixon's tight money policy was not working.

On August 15, 1971, President Nixon reversed himself and unveiled a new economic policy. Phase I of the plan was a 90-day freeze on wages, prices, and rents. The President also announced an accompanying tax cut to stimulate business and a 10 percent surcharge on imports to boost domestic industries.

The plan had mixed results. Unemployment continued to rise while wages continued to lag behind prices and profits. With a decrease in government spending and a cutback in industrial production, the recession deepened.

Phase II was a system of wage and price controls aimed at slowing rising prices to a rate of 2.5 percent a year. Many workers were opposed to the controls because corporate dividends and profits were not subject to the freeze. The corporate exemption led some of Nixon's critics to claim that the plan was Robin Hood in reverse: "You steal from the poor and give to the rich." By the end of 1971, Americans had the worst of both economic worlds, a 5.3 percent inflation rate coupled with a six percent unemployment rate. Larry O'Brien, chairman of the Democratic National Committee, blamed the problem on "Nixonomics."

In desperation, the President returned to deficit spending. The 1971 federal budget had a built-in deficit of $23 billion, only $2 billion less than the 1968 Johnson budget, which was the highest in history.

Inflation at home made American industries less competitive abroad. As a result, in 1971, the United States imported more goods than it exported for the first time since 1893. The trade deficit was due in part to an inflated

American dollar which bought fewer foreign products.

There were other reasons to explain America's loss of dominance on the world market. For example, between 1950 and 1970, America's share of the world's automobile market dropped from 75 percent to 30 percent. Similar declines took place in the shoe and textile industries.

As foreign governments accumulated more and more American dollars, they wanted to redeem them in gold. Since the United States government could no longer handle such a drain on its gold reserves, President Nixon announced that Washington would no longer redeem dollars for gold.

As a result, the dollar was devalued. That is, it became worth less compared to foreign currency. Now it took fewer foreign dollars to buy American goods, and more American goods could be purchased in foreign countries. Conversely, it became more expensive to purchase foreign goods.

ENVIRONMENTAL PROTECTION

In January 1969, a leak developed in a Union Oil Company well off the shore of California. Before it could be stopped a week later, 235,000 gallons of crude oil had flowed into Santa Barbara Harbor. It created an oil slick 800 square miles wide and blackened 30 miles of beach. Viewers of the television news were soon bombarded with images of hundreds of dead fish, and birds so soaked in oil that they could no longer fly.

Public concern about the environment had been mounting during the 1960's. Americans were learning that the fumes from their automobiles and industries were polluting the air they breathed. Chemicals from industry and untreated sewage were polluting the nation's streams, rivers, and even its oceans and underground water. In many places, fish were being killed, and the water had become undrinkable. The Santa Barbara oil spill focused public attention on all these problems and eventually forced the government to act.

Demonstrators in Sacramento protest the lack of clean air on Earth Day, 1970.

On April 22, 1970, thousands of schools and communities across the nation celebrated Earth Day. Teach-ins similar to those used against the Vietnam war were used to educate citizens to the dangers of environmental pollution. Congress adjourned for the day, and there were huge rallies in Philadelphia, Chicago, and New York.

But there was resistance to many proposed measures to clean up the nation's air and water. Business, industry, and even private individuals would be asked to make some hard choices. Solutions would cost money and force changes in the way people lived. Low-pollution fuels were often more expensive than those being used. Anti-pollution devices in factories and automobiles would raise prices. Industry leaders often argued that in order to pay for these measures, they would be forced to cut jobs or close altogether. What good was clean air to a person out of work? some asked.

Still, it was clear that support was building for a cleaner environment. In 1965, a Gallup Poll had found that only 17 percent of the public thought that air and pollution were major problems. By 1970, 53 percent showed concern.

In 1970, Congress amended the Clean Air Act of 1967 to develop uniform national air-quality standards. It also passed the Water Quality Improvement Act. This law made cleaning up off-shore oil spills the responsibility of the owner.

Since responsibility for environmental matters was scattered among many departments and agencies, the President issued an executive order on December 2, 1970 establishing the Environmental Protection Agency. The EPA was created to measure and monitor pollution, establish and enforce standards, study environmental issues, aid state and local governments in environmental matters, and provide public information.

The government also set out to improve the environment of the workplace. In 1970, approximately 14,000 people were dying each year in industrial accidents and another 100,000 were being injured permanently. The Occupational Safety and Health Administration (OSHA) was created to set safety standards and monitor compliance with them.

SECTION RECAP

1. What steps did President Nixon take to slow down the pace of civil rights enforcement? Which were successful?

2. Name President Nixon's appointees to the Supreme Court. Which were approved by the Senate? Which were not?

3. Why were people concerned about crime in the early 1970's? What did the Nixon administration do to combat it?

4. What were two notable proposals of the New Federalism? Which gained support? Which didn't?

5. What methods did Nixon use to slow down inflation? What were the consequences?

6. What purposes did the Environmental Protection Agency serve?

3 The Widening Generation Gap

A couple embrace at Woodstock, NY, at a festival that came to symbolize an era.

By 1968, the number of young people between 14 and 24 years old had swelled from 26 to 40 percent of the population. Postwar baby boomers were coming of age and making their presence known. In recognition of their growing influence and numbers, Congress granted those from 18 to 20 years old the right to vote. This was confirmed by the 26th Amendment to the Constitution, ratified in 1971.

As these young Americans did "their own thing," their parents looked on uncomprehending. They were bewildered by their children's clothing, life-styles, and music. For young people, music was a special vehicle. It set them apart from the older generation by offering them a set of rhythms and a common idiom, uniquely their own. It gave them a means for airing their feelings and making themselves heard. The folk music of protest and the more violent, sensual sounds of "acid rock" flooded the airwaves and drew audiences numbering in the hundreds of thousands to concerts.

WOODSTOCK

On a mid-August weekend in 1969, about 400,000 young people flocked to Bethel, New York, for a weekend rock concert called The Woodstock Music and Arts Fair. From every state in the nation they came, wearing their tie-dyed jeans, work shirts, headbands, and sandals. The townspeople did not know what to expect as they saw huge crowds assembling in a large pasture. But the crowds knew what was coming. They gathered to hear an all-star cavalcade of folk and rock musicians that included Joan Baez, Jimi Hendrix, the Jefferson Airplane, and Janis Joplin.

Neither the concert's promoters nor the local authorities were prepared for such large crowds. There was inadequate food and water; no shelters or bathrooms. Rain and mud added to the problems. Moreover, many in the audience had to be content to listen to the music from loudspeakers perched atop 80-foot scaffolds. No one would have been surprised if a riot broke out, but nothing of the kind happened.

Instead, people were enveloped in an uninhibited atmosphere of well-being. Some were prompted to remove their clothes or share some marijuana, but law enforcement officers looked the other way. The townspeople rose to the occasion and provided food, clothing, and shelter to those in need. To its critics, Woodstock was a spectacle of immorality, but many saw in it the possibility that young people were not all bad.

Just four months later, at a concert in Altamont, California, the worst fears of Woodstock's critics came to pass. About 300,000 young people gathered at a stock-car raceway to hear the Rolling Stones perform. In the absence of security, the rock group hired members of the Hell's Angels motorcycle gang to keep the peace. Tensions mounted, and members of the gang beat a young black man to death. Other beatings followed. Some lives were lost in accidents. The concert offered a violent, terrifying counterpoint to the Woodstock experience.

THE VIETNAM MORATORIUM

Music wasn't the only way in which young Americans made themselves heard. Many young people, especially college students, joined in marches, demonstrations, and protests to condemn policies with which they did not agree. After all, their future and the future of their country were at stake. What disturbed them most was America's continuing involvement in the war in Indochina. They were determined to voice their opposition.

On October 15, 1969, over two million Americans throughout the nation participated in teach-ins, rallies, parades, and church services to mark Moratorium Day, the largest antiwar demonstration in the nation's history. While primarily directed toward young people, a surprising number of older Americans took part in the events. A highlight of the day was a candle-lit march past the White House led by Coretta Scott King.

Vice President Agnew dismissed the protesters as "an effete corps of impudent snobs who characterize themselves as intellectuals." But *Time* magazine said the moratorium infused "new respectability and popularity into the antiwar resistance." The President remained unswayed. He warned Americans to remain united against defeat: "Let us understand: North Vietnam cannot defeat nor humiliate the United States. Only Americans can do that."

KENT STATE

On April 30, 1970, President Nixon announced that South Vietnamese and United States troops were crossing into Cambodia, a neutral nation, to wipe out enemy sanctuaries. His statement sparked an angry reaction on the nation's college campuses. Many students believed that the President was increasing American involvement in the war

instead of ending it, as he had promised. The protest ultimately spread to over a thousand campuses and included 1.5 million students.

On the campus of Ohio's Kent State University, protest turned to tragedy. Saturday night, May 2, an antiwar rally went out of control. Someone on campus threw railroad flares through the window of an ROTC (Reserve Officers' Training Corps) building, burning the wooden structure to the ground. Then a few Kent State students hampered local fire fighters by throwing rocks and slashing fire hoses. At the mayor's request, Governor James Rhodes called out the Ohio National Guard. By midnight on Sunday, the campus was peaceful.

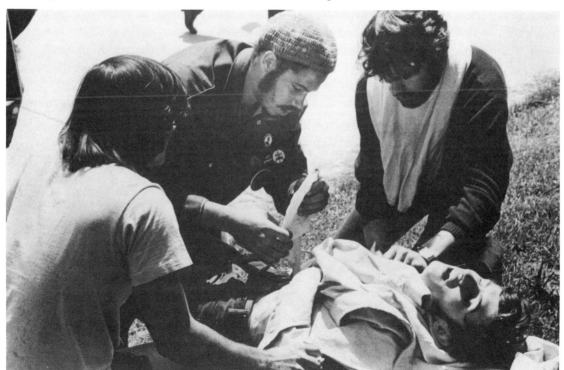

An injured student at Kent State University receives medical treatment.

Monday, May 4, began as an ordinary day with a nonviolent antiwar demonstration involving about a thousand students. The National Guard arrived on campus, dressed in full battle gear, armed with M-1 rifles, pistols, and tear gas. They directed the protesting students "to evacuate the campus," informing them, "You have no right to assemble." The students shouted back, "Pigs off campus! We don't want your war."

The guardsmen then fired tear gas canisters to disperse the crowd. Some students threw rocks in return. Other students fled with about a hundred guardsmen in pursuit. Those guardsmen soon found themselves out of tear gas and trapped between two buildings. Seeing their predicament, the students began to jeer at the guardsmen. Suddenly, a single, unidentified rifle shot was heard. The anxious guardsmen panicked and started shooting at the students who were about 150 feet away.

Meanwhile, other students, not involved in the demonstration, were crossing the campus on their way to class. They were completely unaware of what was going on. Then, one girl screamed, "Oh my God, they're killing us." Thirteen seconds later, four students lay dead, and nine others were wounded.

Antiwar protests resulted in further loss of life. Only 10 days after the deaths at Kent State, two students were killed and 11 were wounded at Jackson State, a black college in Mississippi. White policemen and highway patrolmen had fired 150 rounds of ammunition into a women's dormitory.

The deaths of college students at the hands of police and the National Guard shocked the sensibilities of most Americans. In the aftermath of these tragedies, the Scranton Committee was set up to investigate the shootings. It concluded that at Kent State, "the soldiers' lethal volley was unnecessary, un-

Demonstrators wave the peace sign outside the funeral of Kent State student Jeffrey Miller.

warranted, and inexcusable." However, the Justice Department chose not to call a federal grand jury to review the circumstances of the shootings. Regarding events at Jackson State, the Scranton Committee stated: "The 20-second burst of buckshot, rifle, and machine-gun fire was an unreasonable, unjustified overreaction." But, a Mississippi grand jury placed the blame on the students for "engaging in civil disorders and riots."

At more than 250 American campuses, enraged students left their studies to gather in Washington for a demonstration in front of the White House. At dawn on May 9, President Nixon paid a surprise visit to the Lincoln Memorial where students were assembling. He told the students that he was interested in them and their ideas. He suggested that they send a delegation to the White House to talk things over or call on special phone lines that had been set up. (The President had chosen some of his youngest, most articulate aides to answer the phones. It was their job to convince the students that the President's invasion of Cambodia would bring the war to a speedy conclusion.) However, the President's overture did not bring an end to student protests and demonstrations against the war.

SECTION RECAP

1. What problems arose during the Woodstock festival and how were they overcome?

2. List some of the events that took place on Moratorium Day.

3. What caused the tragedy at Kent State University?

4 A Change of Directions in Foreign Policy

Nixon unfurls more than 20,000 signatures of Coloradans supporting his plan to get out of Vietnam.

As a superpower, the United States had global concerns. Policies worldwide had to be reevaluated and adjusted as new personalities came to power and new problems arose. For example, in 1970, the United States had to reformulate Middle Eastern policies. The death of the nationalist president of Egypt, Gamal Abdel Nasser, brought Anwar Sadat to power. In Jordan, the Palestine Liberation Organization (PLO) was formed for the purpose of destroying the nation of Israel.

In 1970, changes also occurred in other parts of the globe. In South America, the people of Chile elected an avowedly Marxist president, Salvadore Allende. In Africa, the Portuguese colony of Angola was struggling for independence. While each of these developments required a response from the United States government, the government had already begun to reappraise its overall responsibilities. Of greatest priority to the Nixon administration were new initiatives to end the war in Vietnam, to begin diplomatic exchanges with the Communist government of mainland China, and to negotiate a series of understandings with the Soviet Union.

Seeking a balance between being the policeman of the world and returning to a fortress America, Nixon told Congress in July 1968: "America cannot and will not, conceive all the plans, design all the programs, execute all the decisions and undertake all the defense of the free nations of the world." However, the President pledged to continue existing treaty obligations to allies and economic and military aid to anti-Communists. This statement became known as the Nixon Doctrine.

ATTEMPTING TO WIND DOWN THE WAR IN VIETNAM

A cornerstone of the Nixon Doctrine was *Vietnamization*, an idea originating with Defense Secretary Melvin Laird. Laird was a former congressman from Wisconsin who had a reputation for being flexible and pragmatic. Vietnamization involved the replacement of American fighting troops with South Vietnamese forces who would gradually assume responsibility for their country's defense. From a high of 541,000 in March 1969, there were less than 70,000 combat troops in South Vietnam by May 1972.

Polls indicated that the American people endorsed the President's position. Almost 60 percent of Americans had favored phased troop withdrawal, but only one in five supported immediate and unconditional withdrawal.

However, the results of Vietnamization were disappointing because South Vietnamese troops were not effective. As a result, the President authorized air raids by B-52 bombers on North Vietnamese sanctuaries in neighboring neutral Cambodia. The raids were intended to destroy Communist supply depots along the thickly forested border that divided Cambodia and Vietnam. He kept these raids secret from the American public.

Planes were also dispatched to bomb the Ho Chi Minh trail, an enemy supply route in Laos. In addition, the President ordered a resumption of bombing over North Vietnam during the spring of 1970. In doing so, he reversed President Johnson's 1968 policy.

Ground warfare soon spread beyond South Vietnam's borders. Since 1969, troop actions in Laos doubled. In March 1970, while the neutralist Cambodian leader Norodom Sihanouk was visiting the Soviet Union, Lon Nol, a pro-American, right-wing general, seized power. This change in government encouraged President Nixon to send American and South Vietnamese soldiers into Cambodia. On April 30, he gave a televised speech informing the public that ground forces were invading

U.S. helicopters carrying troops of the First Air Cavalry in South Vietnam.

neutral Cambodian territory to destroy enemy sanctuaries.

Besides demonstrations like the one at Kent State, the invasion of Cambodia provoked a huge public outcry. Congress also took the President to task. The Senate repealed the Gulf of Tonkin Resolution it had approved under President Johnson. It also debated an amendment sponsored by Democratic Senator Frank Church of Idaho and Republican Senator John Sherman Cooper of Kentucky to deny funds for American ground troops or military advisers in Cambodia. The war in Vietnam presented other difficulties for the President as well.

Earlier in the Nixon administration there had been criticism of the way the war in Vietnam was being waged. In 1969, disturbing rumors began to circulate about the brutal conduct of American troops in Vietnam. In November, *New York Times* reporter Seymour Hersh broke the story that one year earlier, American army troops had slaughtered civilians at My Lai, a small Vietnamese village. The American public was shocked and outraged.

My Lai was thought to be giving sanctuary to the enemy. In March 1968, United States Army Commander Ernest Medina ordered his infantry company to clear out suspected Vietcong. Lieutenant William L. Calley, Jr. was the officer in charge. Calley's unit had been in Vietnam for three months. During that period, sniper fire and booby traps had claimed the lives of 150 of the recruits.

The enemy was everywhere, yet nowhere to be found. In My Lai, all the unit found were old men, women, and children. These they rounded up. Calley commanded Private First Class Paul Meadlo to kill them. He later said, "Well, we kept right on firing. They was [sic] waving their arms and begging."

In March 1971 Lieutenant Calley was convicted by an Army court martial of the premeditated murder of 22 South Vietnamese civilians. Others were charged with murder, but only Calley was convicted and sentenced to life imprisonment. Generally, conservatives were sympathetic to Calley, believing that he was carrying out his orders and therefore innocent of any crime. Liberals insisted that Calley was a scapegoat for higher-ups in the Pentagon. In view of public sympathy for Calley, Nixon ordered him released from prison while the case was appealed. Subsequently, his sentence was reduced, and in six months, he was freed on parole.

The My Lai Massacre called attention to the demoralized condition of American forces in Vietnam. In addition to brutal actions against South Vietnamese citizens, enlisted men were accused of *fragging*, throwing fragmentation grenades at officers to kill those they felt they could no longer obey. Soldiers openly defied orders to fight the enemy. Evidence of drug abuse surfaced. Troop morale was low. However, many soldiers did carry out their orders and maintained military discipline.

Ten weeks after the My Lai verdict was handed down, the *New York Times* began to print a series of top-secret Defense Department documents, known as the Pentagon Papers. They traced the origins of U.S. involvement in Vietnam. The newspaper had received photocopies of the documents from Daniel Ellsberg, a defense analyst who had become disillusioned with American policies in Indochina.

The Pentagon Papers revealed that each escalation of the Vietnam War came after a previous military decision had failed. They showed that President Johnson made military decisions to increase U.S. participation in the war long before he informed Congress or the American people. The documents also provided evidence that all of the presidents had been reluctant to negotiate with the enemy.

The papers portrayed civilian and military decision makers as confused and harried men forced to make life-and-death choices under pressure, and with limited information. No one in authority had an overview of the entire situation in Indochina. Instead, a top Defense Department aide listed the U.S. military objectives in the following order: "Seventy percent to avoid a humiliating defeat for the United States, 20 percent to keep South Vietnam out of China's grasp, 10 percent to permit the people of South Vietnam to enjoy a better, freer way of life."

After the first installment of the Pentagon Papers was published, the Justice Department obtained a temporary court order to prevent the *Times* from publishing any more of the classified materials. Government lawyers argued that the documents would reveal information that could be harmful to national security.

Three weeks later, the Supreme Court, in a 6-3 vote, rejected the government's arguments. "Paramount among the responsibilities of a free press," declared Justices Hugo Black and William O. Douglas, "is the duty to prevent any part of government from deceiving the people and sending them off to distant lands to die."

The *Times* (and later the *Washington Post*) immediately resumed publication of the study. A Gallup Poll taken shortly after the Supreme Court's decision found that almost 60 percent of those polled favored the newspapers' right to print the Pentagon Papers. Congress was predictably displeased with what was revealed about presidential use of its war powers.

In May 1968, peace talks began in Paris between the United States and North Vietnam. National Security Adviser Kissinger represented the United States, and Le Duc Tho was North Vietnam's negotiator. The partici-

pants met several times but were unable to accept each other's proposals. Both sides were holding out for victory.

In March 1972, the North Vietnamese made a final effort to knock out South Vietnam. Washington responded by escalating B-52 bombing raids over Hanoi. Then the United States launched a massive air and sea blockade of North Vietnam's ports, including the mining of Haiphong harbor. This effort was aimed at stopping Soviet supplies from reaching North Vietnam.

The bombing brought Kissinger and Le Duc Tho back to the Paris peace table. This time the North Vietnamese dropped their demand to be part of a coalition government in South Vietnam. But the talks broke down again.

A Saigon street after a Vietcong raid.

President Thieu found the terms for peace unacceptable.

In mid-December the United States again bombed Hanoi and Haiphong. At the end of the month Kissinger and Le Duc Tho resumed their talks. In mid-January, 1973, all sides reached an "Agreement on Ending the War and Restoring Peace in Vietnam." In return for the release of war prisoners, the United States agreed to remove its military personnel from Vietnam within 60 days. A cease-fire was to take effect on January 27. Direct U.S. involvement in Vietnam was finally nearing an end.

RESUMING DIPLOMATIC RELATIONS WITH CHINA

For two decades, the United States had refused to extend diplomatic and trade relations to the People's Republic of China. During that interval, the world's most populous nation had become a nuclear power and a major role model for Third World Asian and African countries. By 1970, the United States was the only major power to withhold diplomatic recognition.

In an article published in the October 1967 issue of the prestigious journal, *Foreign Affairs*, Richard Nixon had gone on record favoring diplomatic recognition of the People's Republic. He had written that "we simply cannot afford to leave China forever outside the family of nations, there to nurture its fantasies, cherish its hates, and threaten its neighbors. There is no place on this small planet for a billion of its potentially most able people to live in angry isolation." In February

1969, President Nixon recommended to Henry Kissinger that the initiative be taken for a presidential trip to China.

There were several advantages to reopening diplomatic relations with China. In addition to fostering *détente*, or a relaxation of international tensions, Americans hoped that the trip would keep the Soviet Union wondering about America's motives. The Soviet Union and the People's Republic of China had been engaged in a series of border disputes. Also, they had long disagreed about the direction international communism should take. China hoped to gain a neutral position between the Soviet Union and the United States.

For the United States, trade with the People's Republic offered 740 million customers, the largest export market in the world. For the Chinese, it could mean recovery from a decade of political upheaval that had left their economy in terrible shape.

Kissinger set up a series of diplomatic exchanges that eventually brought Nixon to Beijing, the capital of China. Early in 1971, Washington began to relax trade and travel restrictions. The Chinese reciprocated by inviting a group of Americans to participate in a table tennis tournament in April. The team was greeted by Premier Zhou En-lai. Later, a Chinese team visited the United States as part of this Ping-Pong diplomacy. In July, Kissinger secretly flew to Beijing to arrange for a summit meeting. In August, Secretary of State William Rogers announced that the United States would withdraw its opposition to the seating of China in the United Nations. In October 1971, the General Assembly of the

President Nixon reviews Chinese troops with Premier Zhou En-lai and an interpreter.

United Nations voted to oust Taiwan and to admit the People's Republic as the legitimate government of China.

On February 21, 1972, President Nixon's plane touched down in Beijing. Nixon and Kissinger were met by Premier Zhou. Together they sped off to chat with an ailing Mao Zedong, the legendary father of the Chinese revolution. The cordial and frank meeting lasted an hour. Kissinger later remarked that Mao "had the quality of being at the center of wherever he stood."

On the day before the President left for home, he and Premier Zhou signed a statement summing up their divergent but not irreconcilable differences. The Shanghai Communiqué stated that there was only one government of China and that the issue of Taiwan would have to be settled peacefully. The United States was ultimately committed to withdraw its long military support from the Taiwan government.

Nixon's visit to China had a big impact on American television audiences. For those who had followed Nixon's long career as an unbending foe of communism, it seemed rather strange to watch the President and the premier walking along China's Great Wall and toasting each other's countries. But a Harris Poll showed that 68 percent of Americans approved of the trip. Before the summit conference, Americans routinely called the People's Republic "Red China" and described its people as cruel, ignorant, and warlike. Afterward, many more Americans viewed the Chinese as intelligent, hard-working, and progressive.

Although more symbolic than practical, the summit meeting established President Nixon's reputation as a world statesman and pleased most U.S. allies. Even Democrats who had long called for a resumption of normal relations with China had to applaud.

SMOOTHING RELATIONS WITH THE SOVIET UNION

Before the China visit, President Nixon and Soviet General Secretary Leonid Brezhnev agreed to a summit meeting in Moscow. The two nations were interested in reducing international tensions, despite the ongoing war in Indochina. Moreover, both were finding that the costs of an uncontrolled arms race were becoming exceedingly high.

Nixon and Brezhnev's limousine speeds past an image of revolutionary leader V.I. Lenin in Moscow.

For example, the 91st Congress had become so irritated by Pentagon cost overruns that it was reluctant to appropriate funds for an antiballistic missile system. Antiballistic missiles (ABMs) were defensive weapons intended to knock incoming enemy missiles from the skies. The Pentagon argued that an ABM system would make it less likely that the Russians would attempt a first strike, or nuclear offensive designed to wipe out a country in one blow. The Pentagon's proposed ABM system was estimated to cost over $100 billion. It passed the Senate by a single vote.

In May 1972, the two most powerful men in the world sat across the table from each other. Brezhnev dismissed Nixon's trip to Beijing as ceremonial and symbolic. The Moscow summit, he claimed, would be businesslike and productive. The meeting did produce concrete results. Both leaders accepted a series of arms-reduction proposals known as the Strategic Arms Limitation Treaty (SALT). Each party agreed to (1) limit deployment, or placement, of ABMs to two sites, (2) freeze existing ABMs at their current levels for five years, (3) hold off deployment of the remaining 12 sites.

The agreement left the Soviet Union with more offensive weapons than the United States. Their missiles could carry heavier payloads. However, the American missiles were considered to be more accurate, and soon they were to be equipped with multiple warheads, which would further increase their effectiveness. A single missile carrying multiple warheads would be able to strike several targets at one time.

Both countries were permitted to maintain enough offensive weapons to launch a first strike or respond to the other's first strike. In other words, if either country were to launch a nuclear attack on the other, the victim would still have the means to strike back. As a result, neither nation would find it worthwhile to initiate a nuclear attack against the other. Thus, the SALT agreement perpetuated the nuclear stalemate but limited the arms race.

At the summit conference, the two nations also agreed to collaborate on space exploration, health research, and environmental protection. The Soviet Union agreed to buy $750 million worth of U.S. grain over several years. Also, the governments pledged themselves to solve their disputes peacefully. Finally, they arranged to hold a conference on European security in 1973 at Helsinki.

Shortly after he returned home, Nixon reported to a joint session of Congress. Speaking of the Beijing and Moscow summits, the President said, "An unparalleled opportunity has been placed in America's hands. Never has there been a time when hope was more justified and complacency more dangerous."

SECTION RECAP

1. What military strategies did President Nixon use to try to end the war in Vietnam ?

2. How did U.S. policy toward the "two Chinas" change under President Nixon? How did his trip to China affect the American public?

3. What did the SALT agreement accomplish? List some of the other topics discussed at the summit meeting in Moscow.

5 The 1972 Election Campaign

Senator George McGovern campaigns in Brooklyn, NY for the presidency.

In January 1972, Democratic front-runner Senator Edmund Muskie of Maine and President Nixon were tied in the popularity polls. Then, a few days before the New Hampshire primary, a mysterious letter appeared in the ultraconservative New Hampshire *Union Leader*. The letter charged Muskie with making insulting remarks about "Canucks," people of French-Canadian ancestry. The "Canuck" letter so angered the senator that in a tearful scene in front of television cameras, he accused the newspaper's publisher of lying.

Later, the letter was proved to be a forgery. However, Muskie's emotional outburst crippled his chances of winning the Democratic nomination. Although Muskie won the New Hampshire primary, he failed to do well in successive primaries and soon withdrew his candidacy.

In 1968 George Wallace, running as an Independent, had won 13.5 percent of the presidential popular vote. It was enough to encourage him and his supporters. By 1971, Wallace was appealing to others besides a handful of segregationists for support. He billed himself as a "law and order" populist. In the process, he became a serious contender for the Democratic nomination. Wallace won the Florida primary and came in a respectable second in Wisconsin.

While campaigning in Maryland, Wallace heard a voice in the crowd call out, "Hey, George, aren't you gonna shake my hand?" Wallace turned and froze as Arthur Bremer fired five bullets into his body. One bullet lodged in the candidate's spine, paralyzing him from the waist down.

McGOVERN'S CANDIDACY

Almost by default, Senator George McGovern of South Dakota became the Democratic favorite. After 10 years of protest and dissent, it appeared to McGovern supporters that a coalition of liberals, students, women, and blacks, might win the election.

McGovern, a World War II bomber pilot and former college professor, was one of Nixon's most persistent critics. The South Dakota senator opposed the war in Vietnam. He favored *amnesty* (a general pardoning) for draft-resisters and approved of reducing the penalty for smoking marijuana to a noncriminal offense. As his solution to the welfare problem, Senator McGovern endorsed a proposal to give each welfare recipient a grant of $1000 yearly.

McGovern won the Democratic nomination on the first ballot. He chose Senator Thomas Eagleton of Missouri as his running mate. However, that choice turned into a political nightmare. It was soon revealed that the vice presidential candidate had once been hospitalized for nervous exhaustion. Eagleton had been given electro-shock therapy in partial treatment for his depression. At first, McGovern said he supported Eagleton "1000 percent." But, political realities forced McGovern to ask Eagleton to step down. Sargent Shriver, a former Peace Corps director and brother-in-law to John and Robert Kennedy, replaced him.

In the minds of Americans, the damage had been done. Before the Eagleton affair, McGovern trailed Nixon by an acceptable 10 percent. Afterward, the margin widened to 35 percent. To add to his woes, McGovern had managed to antagonize influential Chicago Mayor Richard Daley. He also lost the support of George Meany, president of the AFL-CIO. His labor union, the largest in the country, opted to remain neutral throughout the campaign. In addition, McGovern's liberal Democratic party platform cost him needed votes.

NOMINATING NIXON FOR A SECOND TERM

President Nixon's status at home and abroad had never been higher. He had recently returned from very successful summit meetings in Beijing and Moscow. The Senate had ratified the SALT agreement, and the last of the American ground forces in Vietnam returned home.

When the Republican National Convention opened in Miami, there was little question as to who would be nominated. The Republican platform did not offer many surprises either. President Nixon continued his attack on involuntary school busing to achieve school integration. He also pledged that if reelected, he would put an end to "this age of permissiveness." Translated into action, this meant: opposing the legalization of marijuana; keeping defense spending at its present levels, or higher, and rejecting amnesty for draft-resisters whom the Republicans called draft-dodgers.

THE WATERGATE BREAK-IN

All indicators pointed to an overwhelming victory for Nixon in November. However, Nixon still viewed politics as a war rather than a game against respected opponents. Although his political enemies seemed a distant threat, if a threat at all, the President could not sit back and enjoy his lead. He had to make his victory a certainty. The President and those who surrounded him were more concerned with ensuring the opposition's defeat than playing the game by the rules.

In 1971, White House staffers had set up a Special Investigations Unit to stop leaks to the press about government operations. This group included men who had served in the CIA and FBI and came to be known as the Plumbers. After Daniel Ellsberg released the Pentagon Papers, they broke into his psychiatrist's office in search of information that would discredit Ellsberg.

Later, White House staffer G. Gordon Liddy suggested that the Plumbers might be used to gather information that would be useful in Nixon's campaign for reelection.

The campaign was headed by John Mitchell, who had resigned as attorney general to take the job. His operation was called the Committee to Re-elect the President (CRP), and it would eventually raise $60 million for the campaign. Mitchell rejected Liddy's proposals to wiretap the phones of several Democrats and to try to disrupt the opposition's convention. But eventually he approved Liddy's plan to break into the Democratic headquarters in the Watergate apartment and office complex in northwest Washington.

On June 18, a short article appeared on the front page of the *Washington Post*. It described the arrest the previous evening of five men wearing rubber gloves and outfitted with wiretapping equipment. They had been caught in the headquarters of the Democratic National Committee. Police found 45 crisp $100 bills and a notebook with the message "E. Hunt W. H."

White House Press Secretary Ron Ziegler characterized the break-in as a "third-rate burglary," and Mitchell denied that the incident was in any way connected with CRP. Senator McGovern called President Nixon "the most deceitful President in history." But to most Americans the Watergate burglary seemed unimportant. For nine months, it was considered a trivial event.

COUNTING THE BALLOTS

In November, President Nixon received 60.7 percent of the popular vote, only slightly less than Lyndon Johnson's landslide victory in 1964. Nixon ran strong among traditionally Republican groups. He also gained votes from blue-collar workers, union families, and Catholics, who usually voted Democratic.

In the electoral college, McGovern managed to win only the state of Massachusetts and the District of Columbia. McGovern did well among blacks, liberals, and low-income voters. However, his liberal platform lost him the support of moderate Democrats.

Never had Nixon been stronger nor his opponents weaker. But as the President moved toward a second term, he knew that his involvement in the events following a simple burglary could destroy his political career. For a man as remote and secretive as Nixon, hiding the truth became a necessity and an obsession.

The Watergate complex
where burglars broke into
the headquarters
of the Democratic National Committee.

SECTION RECAP

1. To which groups of voters did the President, Senator McGovern, and Governor Wallace try to appeal in 1968? What happened to the Muskie and Wallace campaigns?

2. What were the objectives of the Watergate burglary? Who approved it?

3. Which groups of traditionally Democratic voters did Richard Nixon manage to win over?

1. On a separate sheet of paper, make a list of letters A through L. Next to each of the letters on your paper corresponding to the domestic activities pursued by the Nixon administration, mark an S for successful or a U for unsuccessful.

a. Family Assistance Plan

b. Haynesworth nomination

c. Environmental Protection Agency

d. ending involuntary school busing

e. trying voting-rights cases in local courts

f. using wiretapping to fight crime

g. delaying compliance with school desegregation deadlines

h. tight money

i. revenue sharing

j. occupational safety

k. Blackmun nomination

l. wage and price controls

2. Define the following terms: *block grants, deficit spending, détente, fragging, first strike, revenue sharing, strict constructionists, Vietnamization.*

3. What aspects of Woodstock would make it a symbol of "permissiveness" for some Americans?

4. Why did the measures the President took to end the war in Vietnam spur protests and demonstrations?

5. What did the United States hope to gain by recognizing the People's Republic of China? What would it have to give up?

6. Why did the break-in at Democratic National Headquarters take place?

7. Richard Nixon's election was seen as a great political comeback for him. How might it also be seen as having been a great comeback for the Republican party as a whole?

8. In Chapter Three, you read about the invention of the teenager. Was the youth of 1968 different from the youth of 1958? If so, in what ways, and what factors do you think might have "changed" teenagers in those 10 years?

CHAPTER 8

1972 — 1977

The Watergate Scandal and its Aftermath

ALL THROUGH THE SUMMER of 1972, small groups of Republicans closeted themselves in Washington, D.C. Although they were only supposed to be planning campaign strategy, they sometimes uttered desperate thoughts. The "President's men," as reporters called them, had as their goal the reelection of Richard Nixon. They guessed that the task would be easy but for one thing — the burglary at Watergate (see page 236).

These officials realized that CRP Chairman John Mitchell had authorized the Watergate break-in to spy on Democratic campaign planning. They knew that a CRP member, James McCord, had been arrested at the Watergate on the night of Saturday, June 17. They were aware that a White House consultant, E. Howard Hunt, may have been implicated in the burglary by the notebook taken into police custody. They believed they would have to hide the trail of the Watergate burglary before it could do great damage to Nixon's presidency.

What the President's men were doing, then, was covering up links between Watergate and the White House. Near summer's end, Richard Nixon gave the public an indication of his concern. On August 29 he told the nation that he had directed his counsel, John Dean, to investigate all leads that might involve anyone in his administration. He said that Dean's work had turned up nothing. He added: "What hurts in matters of this sort is

The Watergate Committee begins

its investigation.

not the fact that they occur, because overzealous people in campaigns do things that are wrong. What hurts is if you try to cover it up."

Nonetheless, his campaign managers tried and succeeded at a cover-up — for a time anyway. In November, Nixon won reelection in a landslide, carrying 49 out of 50 states. At the start of 1973, he should have been basking in glory. In the polls his ratings had reached new heights. But Nixon could not rest easy. Like a worried picnicker on a summer afternoon, he could see the first flickers of lightning on the far horizon and hear the distant hint of thunder.

The Watergate affair was not the passing cloud the President had hoped it would be. Instead, it would build into a great storm that would lash at the institutions of American government and batter the President and many of his closest aides. The storm would keep pounding away for many months, until finally it had swept President Nixon from office. But at the start of 1973, the flashes of lightning were still scattered and distant.

 A Crisis of Faith

The Watergate affair was not really about a burglary, although it began with a burglary. Investigators would uncover many other crimes — illegal wiretaps, violations of election laws, interception of private mail, perjury, blackmail, and more. The Watergate incident was about the abuse of power by those entrusted with the conduct of the nation's affairs. As the story of that abuse of power became public, it touched off a crisis of faith among the American people. Was the President bound by law — or was he above the law? How could democracy work if Americans lost faith in their leaders?

President Nixon seems not to have known about the Watergate burglary in advance. He became involved almost immediately after, however, by helping to organize a cover-up. Hiding a crime is itself illegal.

President Nixon did not seem to have realized the seriousness of what he was doing. Months later, he would puzzle over the sequence of events. He would ask what he had done wrong. As he saw it, he had done what anyone else would have done in the same circumstances — shown loyalty toward his aides by trying to protect them.

Nixon and his advisers had good reason to fear a thorough investigation of the Watergate burglary. Many of those linked to the burglary had taken part in other secret deeds on behalf of the White House. Some deeds were designed to plug leaks of sensitive information. Some were to raise money for undercover operations against the Democrats. Several of the deeds were probably illegal. Of special concern were the Plumbers. Not only had they broken into Daniel Ellsberg's psychiatrist's office, they had placed taps on phone lines belonging to journalists whose names appeared on a White House "enemies list."

Nixon and his advisers did not want such actions to become public. A few days after the Watergate burglary, the President met with the White House chief of staff, H. R. Halde-man. Nixon agreed to have the CIA block an FBI investigation of Watergate. The CIA was to say that "national security" was at stake. "Play it tough," said Nixon. "That's the way they play it and that's the way we are going to play it."

However, CIA leaders refused to play along. Seeking to buy time, White House officials paid hundreds of thousands of dollars in "hush money" to the men charged with the Watergate burglary. But it was not enough. By March 1973 one was demanding $130,000 more to keep his mouth shut.

DIGGING OUT THE TRUTH

The FBI made little headway in uncovering the truth about Watergate. In fact, its acting director burned some of the evidence on orders from the White House. But others were on the case.

First came the newspaper reports. They dug out tantalizing tidbits, one after the other. Piece by piece they gradually formed a coherent story. Many newspapers played a part, but one that stood out was the *Washington Post* — a liberal daily that Nixon had many reasons to dislike. *Post* reporters Carl Bernstein and Bob Woodward turned out a string of reports that helped to build pressure for an official investigation.

In February 1973 the U.S. Senate voted, 77 to 0, to set up a Select Committee on Presidential Campaign Activities, headed by Senator Sam Ervin, a North Carolina Democrat. The Watergate Committee, as it came to be called, hired a large staff and prepared to hold public hearings.

Washington Post reporters Woodward (left) and Bernstein.

In March the White House cover-up began to fall apart. Two of the men charged in the Watergate burglary, James McCord and CRP counsel G. Gordon Liddy, had been convicted. The five others had pleaded guilty, apparently expecting light sentences. But U.S. District Judge John T. Sirica set sentences of 30 or 40 years. Sirica said he suspected that more than a simple burglary was involved. Lighter sentences might be possible, the judge suggested, if the men would tell for whom they had been working. And some of the men began to talk. (Eventually, their sentences were reduced.)

Others began to talk, too. People who worked for CRP had stories to tell. People on the White House staff joined in. Each knew some aspect of the big picture. Each wanted to tell his or her story first, hoping to bargain for a light sentence or no sentence at all.

President Nixon realized that matters had grown very serious. He and his staff debated what to do. Should they tell the whole truth? No, it was too late for that. Should they refuse to cooperate with investigators? No, that would make it seem that they had something to hide. Instead, they chose to tell part of the truth and hope that would be enough.

But it would not work. Investigators already knew too much. Haldeman had warned another staff member: "Once the toothpaste is out of the tube, it's going to be very hard to get it back in." He was soon proved right.

In April 1973 Nixon learned that the Department of Justice had solid evidence against John Mitchell and Nixon's two top aides, Haldeman and John Ehrlichman. Regretfully, Nixon asked Haldeman and Ehrlichman to resign. Nixon publicly proclaimed his own innocence. He insisted he was trying to find out the truth.

Nixon appointed a new attorney general, a respected lawyer named Elliot Richardson. Richardson, in turn, named a special prosecutor to assume control of the Justice Department's investigation of Watergate. The prosecutor, Archibald Cox, was assured that he had full authority to carry the investigation wherever it might lead. Cox's investigation proceeded side-by-side with the Senate committee's.

Meanwhile, Daniel Ellsberg had gone on trial for leaking the Pentagon Papers. During the trial, reporters learned of the Plumbers' burglary of Ellsberg's psychiatrist's office. When the news became public, a judge dismissed charges of conspiracy and espionage against Ellsberg, saying the government's misconduct made a fair trial impossible.

WHAT DID THE PRESIDENT KNOW?

People all across the nation turned on their televisions on May 17, 1973, to watch the start of the Watergate Committee's public hearings. In the weeks that followed a stream of witnesses told of participating in many abuses of power. They told of attempts to harass White House "enemies" through the tax system. They told of "dirty tricks" in political campaigns. They told of "laundering" secret

CRP Chairman John Mitchell during his testimony before the committee.

contributions through banks in other countries so sources could not be traced. But had these deeds been ordered by overzealous staff members, or by the President himself?

Committee members struggled to fit the many stories into one clear picture. Again and again, Senator Howard Baker, a Tennessee Republican, hammered away at a crucial question: "What did the President know, and when did he know it?"

Two months into the hearings, the Watergate Committee learned a startling fact: In 1971, President Nixon had hidden tape recorders in his offices. Ever since, he had been recording conversations with his advisers. The Watergate Committee immediately asked to hear the tapes of specific conversations that had been mentioned in the hearings. Special Prosecutor Cox asked for tapes too. Nixon said no to both the committee and Cox. A monumental court battle began, testing some of the fundamental principles of government in the United States.

DEBATING EXECUTIVE PRIVILEGE

President Nixon claimed a constitutional right to protect the confidentiality of his private conversations. Without such a right, he argued, a president's advisers would not feel free to give open and candid advice. The president would be unable to carry out the duties of a chief executive.

Other presidents, including Eisenhower, had claimed executive privilege. Often, Congress and the courts had yielded to such arguments. But now President Nixon's claim of executive privilege clashed with the claims of two other branches of the federal government. The Watergate Committee claimed a right to hear the tapes on behalf of the legislative branch. The special prosecutor claimed that the tapes were needed as evidence in criminal cases before the judicial branch.

Judge Sirica ruled that the need for criminal evidence overrode the President's claim of executive privilege. He ordered Nixon to give him the tapes. Sirica would review them for evidence, and pass on any relevant sections to Cox, the special prosecutor. (But Sirica would not pass any tapes to the Senate committee, since he rejected the committee's claim.)

Next, President Nixon took his case to the U.S. Court of Appeals. In October 1973, that court also ordered him to give up the tapes. It said: "Though the President is elected by nationwide ballot, and is often said to represent all the people, he does not embody the nation's sovereignty. He is not above the law's commands."

Defying the court, the President tried a desperate tactic. First, he offered to let John Stennis, a Democratic senator from Mississippi, listen to the tapes and verify a summary for the Watergate Committee. Then, he ordered Special Prosecutor Cox to drop all court proceedings aimed at getting the actual tapes. Cox refused, saying it would violate his pledge to the Senate and the country.

Nixon's angry response on October 20, 1973, became known as the Saturday Night Massacre. The President ordered Richardson to fire Cox. Richardson refused. The attorney general had publicly promised not to interfere with the special prosecutor's duties. Richardson resigned. So did his assistant, Deputy Attorney General William Ruckelshaus. Finally a third official, Solicitor General Robert Bork, agreed to fire Cox. That evening, FBI agents moved in to take control of Cox's files. The office of special prosecutor had been abolished.

To many Americans, the President's actions were an outright attack on the rule of law. Outside the White House, the blaring of horns responded to a protester's sign: "Honk for Impeachment." Leading newspapers and magazines joined in demanding Nixon's impeachment. Others called on the President to resign.

CLOSING IN

In the months that followed, events closed in on President Nixon. The House Judiciary Committee announced plans for impeachment hearings. Under pressure, the President agreed to the appointment of a new special prosecutor, Leon Jaworski.

New revelations were embarrassing. Critics charged the President had slashed his tax bill by overestimating the value of vice-presidential papers he had donated to the National Archives. Others accused Nixon of granting favors to corporations and dairy groups that had contributed illegally to his campaign.

Stunned by the reaction to the Saturday Night Massacre, Nixon handed over seven tapes to Judge Sirica late in 1973. One contained an unexplained gap of 18 and one-half minutes. The President's secretary said she had erased it by accident.

In March 1974, a federal grand jury *indicted* (formally accused) several close Nixon associates. Among those indicted were Mitchell, Haldeman, and Ehrlichman. They were accused (and eventually found guilty) of perjury and conspiracy to obstruct a criminal investigation into the Watergate burglary. The special prosecutor had advised the grand jury that Nixon could not be indicted while in office, but he was named as a co-conspirator.

Additional facts about the cover-up continued to surface. Jaworski and the House Judiciary Committee both demanded more tapes. President Nixon tried to seize the initiative. On April 29, 1974, he went on national television to announce that he was releasing 1,200 pages of edited transcripts of important tapes. Viewers could see, stacked on a table beside the President, 38 bound volumes of transcripts — one for each member of the Judiciary Committee. "Everything that is relevant is included," said the President, "the rough as well as the smooth. . . . I want there to be no question remaining about the fact that the President has nothing to hide."

Newspapers printed long excerpts from the transcripts and paperback publishers printed three million copies of the complete text. Readers were dismayed. It was not so much the President's profanity that shocked. It was his whole attitude — the cynicism that showed through so many of the private conversations.

The text convinced many members of Congress — including some leading Republicans — that the President would have to resign. Said Representative William Hungate, a Missouri Democrat: "If this is what he thought he *could* release, I'd like to hear what else is on those tapes." Representative Peter Rodino, the New Jersey Democrat who was chairman of the House Judiciary Committee, demanded the full tapes.

DEBATING IMPEACHMENT

While the battle for the tapes moved through the courts, the Judiciary Committee held three months of private sessions. Twenty-one Democrats and 17 Republicans carefully weighed the evidence. They debated the grounds on which a president might be impeached.

Under the Constitution, *impeachment* is a process by which the House of Representatives brings formal charges against a U.S. official. A vote of impeachment is the first of two steps. The second step is a trial before the Senate, with the Chief Justice presiding. The Senate decides whether or not to convict the accused official. If convicted by the Senate, the official is automatically removed from office.

Some said the President could be impeached only if he had actually committed a crime. Didn't the Constitution specify that removal would take place upon conviction for "treason, bribery, or other high crimes and misdemeanors"? Others said "high crimes and misdemeanors" included abuses of power short of an actual crime. Representative

Ehrlichman (top) and
Haldeman (bottom).

President Nixon with selected transcripts.

Rodino held the second position. He argued that the President could be impeached for "the kind of conduct that brings the whole office [of the President] into scandal and disrepute, the kind of abuse of power that subverts [undermines] the system we live in."

In July 1974, the Judiciary Committee held dramatic public hearings. It presented three articles of impeachment. Article One charged Nixon with obstruction of justice for participating in a cover-up of the Watergate burglary. Article Two charged Nixon with abuse of power. It said he had violated people's constitutional rights by misusing such federal agencies as the FBI, the CIA, the Secret Service, and the Internal Revenue Service. Article Three charged that Nixon had "willfully disobeyed" *subpoenas* (legal orders) from the House of Representatives. Each article was adopted.

While President Nixon's public support had eroded, some Americans still clung to a belief in his innocence. Or, alternately, they argued that Democrats as well as Republicans "played dirty" at times. Hadn't Lyndon Johnson been accused of stealing elections? Hadn't Franklin Roosevelt spied on his "enemies"? What had Nixon done that was worse? Wasn't the whole Watergate affair merely a vendetta by Democrats and liberals against a conservative Republican President? Such questions overlooked the sweeping scope of Nixon's deeds. They also overlooked the mounting evidence that Nixon had blatantly used the powers of his office to suppress a criminal investigation.

Some members of Congress argued that a vote of the full House for impeachment would open the way for some future Congress to impeach a president for purely political reasons. The President's defenders said no one had produced a "smoking gun" that might link Nixon directly to deeds such as the cover-up.

And then the "smoking gun" turned up. As the impeachment hearings took place, the Supreme Court had ordered the President to release still more tapes. "The . . . assertion of [executive] privilege must yield to the demonstrated specific need for the evidence in a pending criminal trial," said Chief Justice Warren Burger. The President turned over the tapes on August 5, revealing the "smoking gun." On a tape for June 23, 1972, Nixon could plainly be heard ordering Haldeman to block the FBI investigation of Watergate. The President had been part of the cover-up from the very beginning.

Now many of Nixon's former supporters called on him to resign. Three high-ranking Republicans from Congress met with Nixon in the White House. Senator Barry Goldwater of Arizona spoke first. "Mr. President," he said, "if it comes to a trial in the Senate, I don't think you can count on more than 15 votes." Nixon turned to Representative John Rhodes of Arizona. "And not more than 10 in the House, John?" said the President. "Maybe more," Rhodes replied, "but not many more." The reality of the numbers sank in. Nixon's choice seemed to be either impeachment and conviction — or resignation.

On August 8, 1974, Nixon appeared on television to announce that his resignation would be effective at noon the following day. It was a sadly historic moment. No U.S. president had ever resigned.

In his resignation speech the President said he had made mistakes in the belief that he was acting "in the best interest of the nation." Nixon admitted no guilt. He was resigning, he said, because his support in Congress had withered.

AN UNELECTED PRESIDENT

Ordinarily, President Nixon's successor would have been the vice president elected in 1968 and 1972, Spiro Agnew. But a scandal unrelated to Watergate had brought Agnew down. He was accused of taking payoffs from construction company executives while he was governor of Maryland and even after becoming vice president. Agnew insisted on his innocence, but in October 1973 he resigned. He pleaded "no contest" to a charge of having evaded federal income taxes while serving as governor. Agnew paid a $10,000 fine but did not go to jail.

The 25th Amendment, ratified in 1967 after President Kennedy's assassination, provided for the replacement of a president or vice president. Nixon had chosen House minority leader Gerald R. Ford of Michigan as his new vice president. Congress confirmed the nomination by a majority vote, and in December 1973, Ford became vice president.

Now, in August 1974, Ford became President. He had served 25 years in Congress, eight of them as leader of House Republicans. He was the first President appointed under the U.S. Constitution. Ford eventually nominated for vice president Nelson A. Rockefeller, a former governor of New York. Congress would again give its approval.

Outside the White House,
August 8, 1974.
The headlines tell of
history in the making.

Ford, a former college football star, brought a more open, approachable style to the White House. In Congress he had been a loyal party man, moderately conservative, part of the Republican mainstream. He expected to be able to work easily with Congress. "My motto," he told a joint session of Congress, is "communication, conciliation, compromise, and cooperation. . . ."

Ford wanted to put the Watergate scandal in the past and get on with the business of running the country. Upon taking office, he declared: "Our long national nightmare is over." Even so, the nightmare could not just be wished away. Many people were calling for criminal charges against Nixon, now that he was an ordinary citizen again. Ford rejected that course, saying it would stir up "ugly passions" once more. One month after assuming the presidency, Ford gave Nixon a formal pardon, excusing all federal crimes that Nixon "committed or may have committed" while President.

The pardon stirred an angry uproar. Critics said it was unfair to let Nixon go free while his associates served jail terms. Some accused Ford of having made a deal with Nixon, of joining in the Watergate cover-up. Ford's ratings in opinion polls dropped sharply. Still, many people defended the new President for ending the scandal without further political upset. The furor over the Watergate scandal did subside. In 1979 the last of Nixon's convicted associates was freed from prison. Some of them wrote best-selling books about their adventures and their remorse.

SECTION RECAP

1. With what specific act did Nixon's role in the Watergate cover-up begin? What purpose did the cover-up serve?

2. What was the Saturday Night Massacre?

3. On what grounds did the Supreme Court reject Nixon's claim of executive privilege in withholding the White House tapes?

4. How did the United States come to have an appointed president in 1974?

The Urge to Reform

The scandals of the Nixon years focused attention on a number of political problems. Some people argued that the President had become too powerful. Others said federal agencies like the CIA and the FBI had abused their powers. Still others pointed to corruption in election campaigns. As scandals unfolded one after another, a mood of reform swept through the nation. Congress passed a number of new laws aimed at curbing serious excesses.

THE IMPERIAL PRESIDENCY

Richard Nixon's claim to executive privilege and other sweeping powers went much further than that of his predecessors. His actions threatened the constitutional balance between Congress and the president.

That, at least, was the argument of historian Arthur M. Schlesinger, Jr. In his 1973 book *The Imperial Presidency*, Schlesinger traced the growth of presidential power from the days of George Washington to the 1970's. He noted how earlier presidents had claimed powers that went beyond a strict interpretation of the Constitution. Abraham Lincoln had "ignored one law and constitutional provision after another" in fighting the Civil War. Franklin D. Roosevelt had signed important agreements with other nations without the advice and consent of the Senate. Dwight Eisenhower had made sweeping claims of executive privilege. Lyndon Johnson had asserted the right to commit U.S. forces to battle without the prior approval of Congress.

Bit by bit, the powers of the president had grown larger and the powers of Congress had diminished. Schlesinger saw this trend as partly a response to changed conditions — but dangerous if carried too far. Nixon, he said, had carried matters to alarming extremes.

In addition to the abuse of executive privilege, argued Schlesinger, Nixon acted as if his powers as commander in chief of the armed forces were almost limitless. And he used many other techniques to usurp congressional powers. He impounded (refused to spend) almost $19 million appropriated by Congress for specific purposes such as pollution control.

Congress took a number of actions designed to curb "the imperial presidency":
• The War Powers Act of 1973 limited the authority of the president to commit U.S. troops to situations that involve actual fighting or the threat of fighting. Presidents who order U.S. troops into action must receive the approval of Congress within 60 days, or else withdraw the troops within 90 days.
• In 1974 Congress established procedures by which it could order a president to spend impounded funds.
• In 1974 Congress amended the Freedom of Information Act (1966) to permit greater access to government documents. It gave courts the power to order government agencies to release information covered by the law.

CONTROLLING THE CIA AND FBI

The Watergate investigation had turned a spotlight on activities of the CIA and the FBI. Major controversies swirled about the agencies through the mid-1970's.

In December 1974, the *New York Times* uncovered what it called "a massive, illegal domestic intelligence operation" by the CIA "against the antiwar movement and other groups." Seymour M. Hersh reported that the agency had compiled files on at least 10,000 citizens. He said it had opened mail, tapped wires, and conducted break-ins.

President Ford appointed a high-level commission to investigate. House and Senate committees started investigations of their own. The investigations confirmed Hersh's charges, and made more.

The CIA, it turned out, had hired mobsters to try to murder Cuban Premier Fidel Castro and plotted to assassinate other foreign leaders. It had used mind-altering drugs on unsuspecting people. Its agents had infiltrated activist groups and compiled computerized files on more than 300,000 people.

The FBI, too, was cast in a harsh light. During the 1960's it had conducted a secret campaign to discredit Martin Luther King, Jr., who it considered "dangerous." The FBI tapped King's phones and bugged his hotel rooms. It passed around stories about alleged details of King's private life. FBI infiltrators had used blackmail and outright violence in seeking to disrupt a wide range of black and antiwar groups between 1956 and 1971. Many of the questionable operations had been carried out on the orders of J. Edgar Hoover, who headed the FBI and its predecessor agency from 1924 until his death in 1972. For generations of Americans, Hoover *was* the FBI. Stories of his petty vendettas and racial prejudices made grim reading.

Some people reacted strongly. Senator Philip A. Hart, a Michigan Democrat, said he had not believed his own children when they told him the FBI was carrying out illegal actions. "It couldn't happen. They wouldn't do it," Hart said he told himself. Hart added that now, after years of hearing the FBI warn about "subversive organizations" that would "threaten our liberties," he was convinced that the FBI itself was such an organization. "How," Hart asked, "shall we insure that it will never happen again?"

Congress sought to prevent future abuses by the two agencies. Members agreed that the nation needed the CIA to collect information about threats from abroad and the FBI to investigate violations of federal law and to catch criminals. But it also needed to make sure that these agencies did not become secret police forces that threatened the rights and liberties of all Americans.

President Ford appointed a board of three private citizens to keep a close watch on the CIA. In 1976 the Senate set up a permanent Select Committee on Intelligence. The House set up a similar committee in 1977. Both agencies got new leaders who promised to make sure their agents stayed within the law.

Conservatives, in particular, argued that Congress had placed dangerous "shackles" on the two agencies. In the years that followed, there would be political pressure to loosen the new controls.

CAMPAIGN REFORMS

The Watergate investigations had suggested an unhealthy relationship between pol-

FBI headquarters in Washington, D.C.

itics and money in the United States. President Nixon's 1972 campaign committee had received substantial sums from top business leaders. Often, the contributions came directly from corporate funds — although that was illegal under federal law. To some corporate officers, the Nixon campaign's requests for money seemed rather like shakedowns.

The Nixon campaign had rushed to get donations before a new campaign law went into effect in April 1972. The new law required a public listing of the names and addresses of all people giving more than $100 to a congressional or presidential campaign.

Congress tightened and extended the campaign law in 1974 and again in 1976. These measures were intended to reduce chances for corruption and limit the influence of big spenders over federal officials. In the most sweeping innovation, Congress began public funding of presidential campaigns. Since 1976, the taxpayers have paid for the campaigns of major-party candidates (and some independent candidates) for president and vice president. Federally-funded candidates must also agree to spending limits.

SECTION RECAP

1. How did the War Powers Act of 1973 limit presidential power?

2. Name one abuse of power by each the FBI and the CIA revealed in the 1970's.

3. What was the most sweeping change Congress made in federal election funding?

3 Patching Up the Economy

President Nixon's New Economic Policy of 1971 provided only temporary relief from inflation and other problems. By 1974, major new problems were buffeting the economy.

The first news stories in 1972 were easy to overlook. Shifting ocean currents and overfishing had caused a drastic drop in anchovy populations off the coast of Peru. This directly affected feed companies which ground up anchovies and mixed them with grain to boost the protein content of cattle and chicken feed. When anchovy supplies dwindled, feed prices rose. The result was higher meat prices for U.S. consumers.

About the same time, crop failures struck farmers in India, the Soviet Union, and other parts of the world. World food supplies shrank. For U.S. farmers, who were churning out food surpluses, that was good news. Exports of U.S. crops increased sharply. Farmers earned high prices for their wheat, corn, and soybeans, but consumers paid much more for their groceries. In 1973, food prices were up 12, 15, and eventually 19 percent over the year before.

THE OIL SHOCK

No one had paid much attention in 1960 when a group of oil-producing countries formed the Organization of Petroleum Exporting Countries, or OPEC. A major goal was to boost oil prices. For more than a decade, OPEC's policies had little effect on U.S. consumers.

Meanwhile, U.S. wells were not pumping out the oil as fast as U.S. factories, homes, and cars were using it. In 1960 the United States had imported less than 10 percent of the oil it used. By 1973 imports had grown to

New cars did not move in 1974.

almost 20 percent — and were predicted to climb steadily higher. A big part of these imports came from OPEC nations.

In late 1973 and early 1974, OPEC nations took advantage of world events to force oil prices sharply higher. In October 1973 a new Arab-Israeli war broke out (see page 259). Arab oil producers — including Saudi Arabia and Iraq — declared an oil boycott against the United States and Western European nations they claimed sided with Israel. Non-Arab OPEC members like Iran continued to sell oil, but the demand was far greater than the supply. Prices shot to four times their previous level.

Even before the boycott, U.S. filling stations had been running short of gasoline. Now shortages became common. Long lines of cars formed during the few hours each day when filling stations opened for business. During the bitter winter of 1973–1974, many factories and schools in the Midwest had to close for lack of heating fuel.

The Arab nations called off their boycott in March 1974. But oil prices did not fall. OPEC nations set ceilings on their production and kept the price of a barrel of oil at record levels. They now had the clout to make their prices stick.

THE RIPPLE EFFECT

The skyrocketing prices of food and oil rippled through the whole economy. Oil shortages caused a rise in demand for coal and other fuels, and coal prices began to rise. Auto makers had to pay more for the fuel they used in manufacturing, and this raised their costs,

so they charged more for autos. Other manufacturers did the same. Consumers paid more for furniture, clothing, shoes, and many other products.

The "ripple effect" touched off a new round of inflation. In 1974, price rises totaled 11 percent. Such inflation made it hard for individuals to save for the future and for businesses to plan their investments.

In 1974 and 1975, the economy plunged into the worst recession since the Great Depression of the 1930's. Unemployment reached nine percent in the spring of 1975. In the past, periods of inflation had usually been accompanied by a spurt of business activity. Now, however, inflation seemed to have made the economy stagnate. Economists coined the term *stagflation* to describe the situation.

THE ENERGY CRISIS

Americans had tended to consider energy supplies as cheap and virtually limitless. Early settlers had found plenty of wood in the forests of North America. Later they had tapped vast reserves of coal, oil, and gas. But from 1953 onward, Americans used more energy than they produced domestically. Energy was becoming less cheap — and it was obviously not limitless.

People began to speak of an energy crisis. They pointed out that the United States had only six percent of the world's population yet consumed 40 percent of its energy resources. Couldn't Americans manage with less energy?

U.S. leaders urged Americans to find ways of saving energy. People reset their thermostats to use less heat in winter and less air conditioning in summer. President Nixon had proposed relaxing environmental regulations so that industries could use high-sulfur coal in place of oil. The federal government offered tax credits to people who insulated their homes or installed solar heating. Congress lowered the speed limit to 55 miles per hour.

Meanwhile, the United States took steps to boost production of energy. President Nixon proposed various steps that he said would help the United States regain energy self-sufficiency by 1980. Many observers said the target date was unrealistic and questioned whether the goal was attainable at all. Nixon's plan called for a stepped-up production of oil, natural gas, coal, and nuclear power. To get at the huge oil reserves in northern Alaska, Congress authorized an 800-mile Trans-Alaska Pipeline (completed in 1977).

Politicians began a long debate over price controls on energy, which remained in effect even after other price controls ended in 1974. Energy companies argued that such controls should be removed quickly. They said the lure of higher prices would bring heavy investment in new oil and gas wells, thus increasing U.S. energy supplies. President Ford proposed an immediate end to price controls on energy, but Congress refused. Many Democrats argued that controls should be lifted gradually so as not to touch off a new round of inflation.

The debate on the energy crisis grew testy at times. Some members of Congress suggested that major oil companies had connived with OPEC nations to "fake" a crisis. Perhaps the crisis was merely a pretext to grab bigger profits by forcing competing oil companies ("the independents") out of business. Perhaps someone was manipulating events so as to pressure Congress to lift environmental restrictions or to grant new tax subsidies to the oil industry. News that oil company profits had risen as much as 400 percent helped to feed such suspicions. Opinion polls had indicated that many Americans blamed U.S. oil companies and the U.S. government more than foreign oil interests for the crisis.

But others maintained that the crisis was indeed real. Oil executives argued that U.S. policies had discouraged energy companies from investing in new domestic oil and gas wells. They said the United States could end the energy crisis by boosting production. Environmentalists, on the other hand, said the world was reaching the limit of its energy resources. They called for more careful use of existing supplies.

RESTORING THE ECONOMY

Upon taking office, President Ford declared: "Inflation is domestic enemy number one." He sought to fight inflation first by reducing federal spending. He also called for a temporary tax boost of five percent for corporations and wealthy individuals. President Ford devised the slogan "Whip Inflation Now" for the inflation-fighting plan he submitted to Congress in October 1974. Soon the acronym "WIN" appeared on shiny red and white buttons worn by administration officials.

Cutting spending and raising taxes is a traditional conservative approach to fighting in-

The Trans-Alaska Pipeline helped ease the oil crisis.

flation, but it had little effect on stagflation. The recession deepened. Prices kept going up. In January 1975, President Ford changed his strategy. Instead of tax increases, he called for tax cuts, which Congress quickly approved. The theory was that tax cuts would boost consumer spending and cause business to pick up.

By the end of 1975, the recession was over, but lower taxes contributed to much bigger budget deficits. The deficit shot up from $6 billion in 1974 to $53 billion in 1975 and almost $74 billion in 1976. Inflation slowed but remained a serious problem.

SECTION RECAP

1. Why did U.S. food and oil prices rise sharply in 1973 and 1974?

2. Why was the United States especially vulnerable to disruptions of its oil supplies?

3. How did the solutions to the energy crisis proposed by President Nixon and those of environmentalists differ?

4. What twin economic problems did President Ford face? What finally ended the recession?

4 Troubles Abroad

A German policeman guards an Israeli airliner after the terrorist attack at Munich.

The peace accords of January 1973 led to the withdrawal of U.S. troops from the Vietnam War but did not end the war itself. Both Communist and anti-Communist Vietnamese kept fighting. Warfare persisted elsewhere in Indochina as well. Meanwhile, U.S. leaders were distracted by other arenas of conflict, such as the Middle East.

U.S. foreign policy remained in the same hands during the transition from President Nixon to President Ford. Henry Kissinger, Nixon's national security adviser, had upstaged Secretary of State William Rogers ever since 1969. In August 1973 Kissinger took over his job, and remained secretary of state through the Ford years.

WAR IN THE MIDDLE EAST

Arab-Israeli tensions had first flared into war in 1948, when Israel came into existence. War erupted again in 1956. In 1967 Israel made major territorial gains in a third war that lasted just six days. This Six-Day War left Israel in control of three important territories. First was the Sinai Peninsula, which was part of Egypt. Second was the West Bank, land claimed by the Kingdom of Jordan west of the Jordan River. Third was the Golan Heights, a small but strategic corner of Syria. The occupied territories gave Israel a large buffer zone.

After 1967, a number of Arab states broke off diplomatic relations with the United States. They turned to the Soviet Union for economic and military aid. Egypt's President Nasser brought in thousands of Soviet advisers and set up Soviet-made missiles along the Suez Canal. But Nasser died in 1970, and two years later his successor sent the Soviets home. The new Egyptian president, Anwar Sadat, claimed that the Soviets had been unwilling to supply enough modern weapons to ensure Israel's defeat.

Meanwhile, Arab Palestinians, who had lacked a strong leader since losing their homeland to Israel in 1948, had organized the Palestine Liberation Organization (PLO) in 1964. The PLO combined many separate factions that disagreed about political and military goals and tactics. But all wanted an official Palestinian homeland. The problem was that the PLO and Israel both claimed the same land. Each refused to recognize the other or to negotiate.

In September 1972, eight Arab terrorists murdered 11 Israeli athletes competing in the Olympic Games in Munich, West Germany. The attack touched off a new cycle of violence. Israeli forces raided Palestinian camps in Lebanon and Syria. Palestinian commandos struck across the Israeli border. Arabs and Israelis girded for a new war.

On October 6, 1973, as the first court battle over the Watergate tapes raged in Washington, Egyptian tanks rumbled into the Sinai Peninsula. Syrian planes attacked Israel from the north on Yom Kippur, the holiest of Jewish holy days. The Yom Kippur War was the fourth Arab-Israeli war. Although the coordinated attack took Israel by surprise, the Israelis managed to hold the line.

The Soviet Union rushed help to Syria. President Nixon sent 80 Phantom and Skyhawk jet fighters to Israel, along with tanks and other aid. Nixon did not want the Soviets to think U.S. foreign commitments would suffer because of a domestic crisis over the Watergate affair. The Arab oil boycott was one response to Nixon's actions.

The 1973 war ended in a United Nations-sponsored truce after Israeli troops drove the Egyptians back across the Sinai Peninsula and the Suez Canal. Afterwards, U.S. diplomats stepped up efforts for an Arab-Israeli settlement. Secretary Kissinger made repeated trips among the capitals of Egypt, Israel, Jordan, and Syria. His so-called *shuttle diplomacy* resulted in an agreement in January 1974 that allowed Egyptian forces to reoccupy a narrow strip east of the Suez Canal. U.S.-Egyptian relations warmed considerably.

More shuttle diplomacy led to disengagement agreements for the Golan Heights (May 1974) and the Sinai Peninsula (September 1975).

COMMUNIST VICTORIES IN INDOCHINA

The United States continued trying to shore up the anti-Communist forces in Indochina. Laos attained relative peace through a cease-fire early in 1973. However, fighting between Communist and anti-Communist armies went on in South Vietnam and Cambodia.

Cambodia was not covered by the peace accords signed by the United States and the Communists. U.S. planes continued bombing Communist bases and trails there until Congress ordered a halt in August 1973.

The pro-U.S. governments of Lon Nol in Cambodia and Nguyen Van Thieu in South Vietnam were too weak to hold off Communist forces for long. Cambodian Communists, known as the Khmer Rouge, seized power in 1975. In South Vietnam, Vietcong and North Vietnamese troops marched into Saigon, the capital. Shortly afterward, Communists also gained control of Laos.

Decades of war had taken a heavy toll in Vietnam. The United States had 55,000 dead and 300,000 wounded. An estimated 1.2 million Vietnamese soldiers and guerrillas on the opposing sides had died.

In the final days before Saigon's fall, hundreds of American non-combatants and thousands of anti-Communist Vietnamese sought to flee. U.S. helicopters lifted many would-be refugees from the roof of the U.S. embassy.

Altogether, the helicopters evacuated 1,373 Americans and 5,600 South Vietnamese to U.S. Navy ships in the nearby South China Sea. Hundreds of thousands more Vietnamese fled by other means.

In 1954, President Eisenhower had predicted that if Indochina fell to the Communists, neighboring countries would topple too — like a series of dominoes. Yet, while most of Southeast Asia fell into Communist hands, it was far from unified. All of the new governments had serious problems.

The Khmer Rouge sought to remake Cambodia into a "pure" Communist state. The new government ordered a mass evacuation of the capital, Phnom Penh. Brutal forced-marches and other oppressive measures took up to two million lives in the years after 1975.

The Vietnamese Communists reunified the two halves of their country, achieving Ho Chi Minh's goal of a fully independent, though desperately poor, Vietnam. The new Vietnam was a totalitarian state. Saigon took a new name, Ho Chi Minh City, in honor of the revolutionary leader who had died in 1969.

FLEXING U.S. MUSCLES

U.S. leaders worried that their failure to rout the Communists from Southeast Asia had made the United States look weak. Thus, when Cambodians seized the U.S. merchant ship *Mayaguez* and its 39-man crew in May 1975, President Ford ordered a military response.

U.S. planes bombed the Cambodian mainland and attacked Cambodian gunboats. Meanwhile, more than 100 U.S. Marines braved intense ground fire to land on an island in the Gulf of Siam and search for the captured crew. They found no one. Soon after, however, the crew members turned up on a small boat, waving a white flag.

The operation cost the lives of at least 38 Americans (including 23 who died in a helicopter crash during preliminary maneuvers in Thailand). It also provoked a protest from the Thai government over the use of U.S. bases in Thailand for the attack. Some Americans criticized President Ford for "overreacting"; others praised him for "showing U.S. resolve." The President's rating in opinion polls rose sharply.

Thousands of Americans and South Vietnamese fled Saigon just before its fall.

KEEPING TENSIONS DOWN

President Ford continued the Nixon-Kissinger policy of détente (relaxation of strained relations) with the Soviet Union. Ford and Kissinger met with Soviet leader Leonid Brezhnev in November 1974 near the city of Vladivostok in Soviet East Asia. The two leaders — one a former football star, the other a former soccer player — seemed to hit it off. Upon leaving, Ford gave Brezhnev a heavy Alaskan wolf coat.

The Vladivostok meeting produced a preliminary agreement on further U.S.-Soviet arms control measures. It also helped to smooth the way for a 35-nation conference in Helsinki, Finland, the following year.

The Helsinki Conference was attended by the leaders of the United States, Canada, and 33 European nations. It was the largest summit meeting in European history. The conference produced a 30,000-word document — the Helsinki Final Act — that recognized the permanence of the changes in European borders after World War II. The Soviets had been urging such a document for many years. The Helsinki Final Act also contained a pledge to respect individual rights and human liberties. By getting European Communist governments to sign that pledge, Western nations hoped to increase pressures for change in Eastern Europe. The Communist authorities continued to repress *dissidents* (critics of the government), but Western nations would use periodic "Helsinki review meetings" to call attention to various abuses.

SECTION RECAP

1. What territories changed hands in the Six-Day War of 1967?

2. What part did the United States play in the Yom Kippur War of 1973 and its aftermath?

3. What happened to South Vietnam after the U.S. troop withdrawal of 1973?

4. Why did U.S. planes bomb Cambodia in 1975?

5. What were two important provisions of the Helsinki Final Act?

5 Women and Minorities

The turbulent 1960's had raised many issues. Blacks had demanded a share of the American dream. Indians, Hispanics, and other minorities had raised their own voices. Women had called attention to discrimination against them in opportunities and income. New laws had responded to some of the demands. New attitudes had begun to replace old stereotypes in people's minds. But many of the old problems had simply taken new forms.

EQUAL RIGHTS FOR WOMEN

Civil rights laws of the 1960's had outlawed job discrimination based on sex. But it was easy to see that employment opportunities were still not equal. The 1970 census found that women who held factory jobs earned an average $3,634, compared to $6,737 for men. Among professionals, the gap was $6,030 to $10,617. The average college-educated woman earned about as much as the average man with an eighth-grade education.

To take advantage of newly won opportunities in the work place, women's groups pressed for free day-care centers, financed with public funds. In 1971 President Nixon vetoed a bill that would have created a national system of day-care centers. He said such a system would adversely affect the "family-centered approach . . . the keystone of our civilization."

**Phyllis Schlafly,
a leader of
anti-ERA forces.**

Women's groups had more luck in winning further laws against sex discrimination:
• The Equal Employment Opportunity Act of 1972 gave the government increased powers to enforce laws against job discrimination.
• Title IX of the Federal Education Amendments of 1972 opened school activities, including sports programs, equally to females and males.
• The Fair Housing Act of 1974 barred sex discrimination in the sale or rental of housing.
• The Depository Act of 1974 and the Equal Credit Opportunity Act of 1975 allowed women to obtain loans and credit cards under the same conditions as men.

The National Organization for Women (NOW) and other groups championed an Equal Rights Amendment (ERA) to the Constitution. Such an amendment, first put forward in the 1920's, had languished for years. Now the time seemed ripe. Congress gave enthusiastic approval in 1972. The amendment read: "Equality of rights under the law shall not be denied or abridged by the United States or by any state on account of sex."

Submitted to the states for ratification, the ERA made rapid progress. Within three years, 34 of the necessary 38 states had ratified it. NOW founder Betty Friedan and other women spoke out in favor of the amendment. Many women's groups worked feverishly to win final approval.

But some women, like author Phyllis Schlafly, considered the ERA a threat to the traditional family and to historic differences in sexual roles. Schlafly denounced ERA supporters as "a bunch of bitter women seeking a constitutional cure for their personal problems." She organized a group called Stop ERA, which worked with other groups to try to defeat the amendment.

CONTROVERSY OVER ABORTION

A second women's issue that whipped up controversy was abortion. Abortion is the act of ending a pregnancy before a baby is born. For much of U.S. history, abortion was sharply restricted by law. To be legal, an abortion usually had to be deemed necessary to save the life of the mother. Some states barred abortion under any circumstances.

In 1962, an Arizona woman named Sherry Finkbine learned that the drug thalidomide, which she had taken earlier in her pregnancy, might cause her baby to be deformed. Unable to get an abortion in the United States, she went to Sweden to get one. A movement for change began to gain strength. Between 1967 and 1970, 12 states revised their laws to permit abortion in special cases (for example, if a pregnancy resulted from rape).

By 1970, some portions of the women's movements were pressing for more far-reaching changes. In effect, they supported "abortion on demand." Those who held this view argued that it was a woman's right to decide for herself whether to end a pregnancy or to bear a baby. Laws against abortion, they claimed, forced many women to seek out illegal abortions, from which they often died.

Many people opposed abortion on moral grounds. They argued that human life begins at the moment of conception, and that abortion is therefore murder. Once a fetus (unborn baby) exists, the argument goes, it has the same "right to life" as a baby that has left its mother's body. That was the position of the Roman Catholic Church and of many Protestant and Jewish leaders. But religious authorities were divided on the issue, and so were many Americans. Bitter arguments developed between people who called themselves *pro-choice* (pro-abortion) and people who called themselves *pro-life* (anti-abortion).

The pro-choice forces gained a major victory in 1973, when the U.S. Supreme Court ruled that the right to have an abortion was part of a woman's constitutional right to privacy. The decision, in the case of *Roe* v. *Wade*, was by a majority of seven to two. For the first time, "abortion on demand" became part of American life. In many cities, women's groups or private doctors set up abortion clinics. Many hospitals changed their rules to allow for abortions.

But the abortion debate had just begun. Advocates of abortion rights cited polls showing broad support for their position in specific situations. On the other hand, critics of abortion mounted a national campaign to reverse the Court's decision by amending the Constitution. They helped to persuade Congress to bar the use of federal funds for most abortions.

BLACKS AND THE AMERICAN DREAM

Despite governmental efforts to wipe out racial discrimination, many black Americans of the 1970's saw themselves as excluded from the American dream. Racial rebuffs were still an everyday experience for U.S. blacks. The small town of Kaufman, Texas, had two self-service laundries — one for blacks, one for whites. Race bias was not just a southern phenomenon. When a black family moved into the mostly white subdivision of Oak Valley, near Philadelphia, in 1974, someone burned a cross on the family's lawn.

Discrimination against blacks contributed to both economic and social problems. Blacks had lower incomes than whites. Thus, black children were four times as likely as white children to live in poverty. Black families were more likely to be receiving welfare. Blacks were twice as likely to drop out of high school, three times as likely to be unemployed, and five times as likely to be murdered.

Some people argued that the government's own welfare programs were contributing to blacks' problems. They said misguided welfare regulations contributed to the persistence of poverty and to the rising numbers of fatherless black families. Was "the system"

perpetuating an "underclass" — a new generation of deprived black Americans? Many thought so. Conservatives and liberals alike looked for solutions, but they had little success in finding any that most people would support.

Some of the news was positive, however. Increasing numbers of blacks were graduating from college. More blacks were moving into better jobs, earning higher incomes, building up bank accounts. As a consequence, more blacks were moving into the middle class — which often meant moving out of city centers to the suburbs.

Some suburbs took active measures to integrate blacks into the community. Oak Park, Illinois, a village of 62,000 on the outskirts of Chicago, adopted a policy in 1973 of making sure that new black residents were scattered about the village rather than concentrated in one area. The village banned "For Sale" signs. It adopted strict rules against *blockbusting* (a practice used by some real-estate firms to panic whites into selling out to blacks). It also

Youth programs were one way the government tried to help black Americans.

started a program of low-interest loans for home and apartment improvements.

Blacks were also making gains in politics. By 1977, 16 blacks were serving in the House of Representatives and one in the Senate. The number of blacks holding elective office in the 50 states and the District of Columbia had risen from 1,185 in 1969 to 3,979 in 1976. Blacks served as mayors of such large cities as Los Angeles, California; Washington, D.C.; and Newark, New Jersey. But while blacks made up 11 percent of the nation's population, they still held less than one percent of its elective offices.

An Indian militant stands guard at Wounded Knee.

INDIAN ACTIVISM

Indians — or Native Americans, as many preferred to be called — were also demanding attention. The nation's 800,000 Native Americans were not a single, unified group. Disagreements often broke out between "traditionalists" and "modernists." Traditionalists sought to preserve tribal culture. They stressed communal values and tribal togetherness. Modernists accepted modern technology and the culture of mainstream society. They included many Indians who had taken jobs as civil servants, teachers, and scientists.

Federal policy toward Indians had passed through many twists and turns. In 1953, Congress had adopted a policy of *termination*. The idea was to put an end to special federal policies for Indians and encourage them to become fully integrated into the general society. A few attempts at termination resulted in economic hardship and bitter protests, so the policy was dropped.

Many Indian communities were severely poor. Native Americans had the highest unemployment rate of any ethnic group in the country. They also had the highest rates of alcoholism, tuberculosis, and suicide. During the 1960's and 1970's, federal antipoverty programs improved Indian living standards a little. During the 1970's, the federal government tried to strengthen the Indian role in managing tribal affairs. For the first time in U.S. history, Indians made up a majority of the employees in the Bureau of Indian Affairs.

A spate of Indian activism had begun in the 1960's, seeking to assert Indian claims of various sorts. Many actions, such as "fish-ins" in streams claimed as traditional Indian fishing grounds, drew upon the black civil rights movement for inspiration.

Some protest actions turned violent. In 1973, members of a group called the American Indian Movement (AIM) took over a trading post and church at the Sioux Pine Reservation in Wounded Knee, South Dakota. The activists sought federal respect for an 1868 treaty. They also sought changes in the way the reservation — the site of an 1890 massacre by U.S. troops — was governed. At least two people died during a 71-day siege. Finally, the Indian activists surrendered.

HISPANICS

The fastest-growing of all minority groups were the Hispanics, people of Spanish-speaking heritage. A few U.S. Hispanics could trace their families back to the earliest Spanish settlers, who came to California and the Southwest before the Pilgrims landed in New England. Others had more recently come from Mexico, Puerto Rico, and Cuba.

In the mid-1970's, some 11 million Americans identified themselves as Hispanics. Six million Mexican-Americans, living mainly in the Southwest were the largest group. Next came some 1.5 million Puerto Ricans, concentrated in and around New York City. (In the 1970's an estimated three million people lived in Puerto Rico, a commonwealth of the United States. Puerto Ricans are born U.S. citizens, whether they live in Puerto Rico or on the mainland.) Cubans made up the third-largest group, numbering close to a million. Most lived in Florida and in cities along the East Coast. Smaller groups of Hispanics hailed from other countries of Latin America, the Caribbean, and elsewhere.

Considering their numbers, Hispanics had very little such power at the start of the 1970's. But Hispanic activists were beginning to gain national recognition. One was Cesar Chavez, a Mexican-American (see page 186), who had organized California farm laborers into unions in the 1960's. Another was Herman Badillo, a Puerto Rican who served as a member of Congress from the Bronx, a part of New York City.

SECTION RECAP

1. What was the ERA and how did it fare in the early 1970's?

2. Why was the Supreme Court's 1973 decision in *Roe* v. *Wade* controversial?

3. What is blockbusting and how did it affect blacks?

4. What was the policy of termination, and why did the government give it up?

5. What are three main groups within the Hispanic community in the United States?

6 The 1976 Election

Gerald Ford, the first appointed president.

President Ford announced in 1975 that he would run for the presidency in 1976. He wanted to be more than an "unelected President." But winning election would not be easy.

Ford had gained considerable public sympathy for his efforts to restore respect for the office of president. He attracted further sympathy in September 1975, when he was the target of assassination attempts on two separate trips to California. In one case, a woman pointed a gun at the President, and a Secret Service agent grabbed the gun. Seventeen days later, another woman actually fired a shot and missed.

Ford's trips to Vladivostok and Helsinki, to China, and to other places had helped polish his image as a statesman. But many people had another image of Ford — that of an ineffective bumbler.

Ford had stumbled and fallen while descending the steps of the presidential plane *Air Force One*. He had bumped his head. He had sliced golf balls into other people's heads. Television comedians Johnny Carson and Chevy Chase had made exaggerated imitations of Ford and his presidential gaffes.

Ford also had come under fire for some of his policy decisions. Soon after assuming office he had offered what he called an earned amnesty for draft-evaders and deserters during the Vietnam War. Ford declared that the amnesty was not a pardon. It required those affected to take an oath of allegiance and make a two-year commitment of public service. Many draft-resisters refused the offer, saying it implied guilt on their part. Some liberals called for a full pardon. Yet many Americans argued that amnesty of any kind was morally wrong. Some conservatives said that draft-evaders and deserters should take their punishment for refusing to fight for their country.

Conservative Republicans mounted a major challenge to Ford's election hopes. They rallied behind Ronald Reagan, a former California governor. Reagan and Ford waged a close battle through the primaries, with Ford winning by a narrow margin at the Republican National Convention in Kansas City. As his running mate, Ford chose Senator Robert Dole of Kansas.

JIMMY CARTER, THE OUTSIDER

The big surprise on the Democratic side was the emergence of Jimmy Carter, a former governor of Georgia. One of Carter's chief assets was that he was a Washington outsider. In 1976, many American voters wanted a president not tainted by the Watergate scandal. He campaigned on the theme of restoring morality and integrity to the presidency. "I will never lie to you," Carter told crowd after crowd.

Carter did so well in the primaries that he won on the first ballot at the Democratic National Convention in New York City. The issue of the war in Vietnam no longer divided the party, as it had in 1968 and 1972. Carter chose Senator Walter Mondale of Minnesota to be his running mate.

THE CAMPAIGN

Both Ford and Carter campaigned against big government. They tried to capitalize on the disillusionment that seemed to grip the country.

Ford stressed the achievements of his administration. He claimed credit for ending the recession, slowing inflation, and promoting peace. Carter called for a "time of healing" to replace a "time of torment." He promised to help the poor at home and work for human rights and arms control abroad.

The candidates participated in three televised debates — the first by major presidential candidates since 1960. For many years, incumbent presidents had refused debates, figuring a president had more to lose than to possibly gain. But Ford lagged behind Carter in the opinion polls, and the debates helped him to close the gap.

However, Carter won a narrow victory on election day, taking 51 percent of the votes to Ford's 48 percent, and 297 electoral votes to Ford's 240. The Democrats maintained their power in Congress, and for the first time since 1969, occupied the White House.

SECTION RECAP

1. How did President Ford propose to deal with people who had been draft-evaders or deserters during the Vietnam War?

2. What theme did both presidential candidates stress in 1976? How was being an "outsider" helpful to Jimmy Carter in his campaign for president?

3. Why did President Ford agree to televised campaign debates when earlier presidents had refused?

1. Match the following people with their roles in the Watergate Affair.

_____1. John T. Sirica

_____2. H.R. Haldeman

_____3. Sam Ervin

_____4. G. Gordon Liddy

_____5. E. Howard Hunt

_____6. Bob Woodward

_____7. John Mitchell

_____8. Archibald Cox

a. *Washington Post* reporter

b. Head of the Senate Watergate Committee.

c. White House consultant whose notebook was found at the burglary.

d. U.S. District judge trying the Watergate burglars.

e. White House Chief of Staff told to block FBI investigations of the burglary.

f. CRP chairman who authorized the break-in.

g. Special Prosecutor for the Watergate investigation.

h. CRP counsel convicted as a Watergate burglar.

2. Define these terms: *blockbusting, dissidents, impeachment, indicted, pro-choice, pro-life, shuttle diplomacy, stagflation, supoenas, termination.*

3. What purposes were served by laws to reform federal election campaigns?

4. What were some of the objections to President Ford's handling of the *Mayaguez* incident?

5. What were the goals of members of the Hispanic community in the United States?

6. Why did some people perceive President Ford to be an ineffective bumbler?

7. What political reforms occurred as a result of the Watergate scandal? Do you think the same reforms would have occurred eventually, regardless of Watergate? Why, or why not?

8. What disadvantages do you think President Ford faced as successor to Richard Nixon? What obstacles did he face in his bid for the presidency in 1976?

CHAPTER 9

1977 ▬ 1981

Facing Trials and Frustrations

The Carter family on Inauguration Day, 1977.

IT WAS JANUARY 1977. A cold spell gripped the nation. Huddled in front of their televisions, 130 million Americans — more than half of the people in the country — watched the saga of a black youth named Kunta Kinte. Two centuries earlier he had been wrenched from his home in western Africa and carried off into slavery to America.

Kunta, a member of the Mandinka people, left his village to gather wood to make a drum.

Slavers seized him. They threw him into the hold of a ship, along with other men, women, and children — Mandinkas, Wolofs, Fulanis, Sereres. In chains, the captives were transported to Annapolis, Maryland. Many did not survive the voyage, and those who did went on the auction block. Kunta became the property of a John Reynolds of Spottsylvania County, Virginia.

On eight nights over a two-week span, the

largest television audience in history (up to that time) followed the life of Kunta Kinte and the generations that succeeded him. The viewers saw a moving story, pieced together by a descendant of Kunta Kinte, a writer named Alex Haley. As a boy, Haley had heard his grandmother tell of an ancestor called the African. She told of his capture while looking for wood to make a drum. Years later, hoping to trace his family's history, Haley traveled to western Africa. In a village in Gambia, he heard an old man, a story teller, describe the tale of the ancestor who went to look for wood and never returned. For Haley, it was a thrilling moment. He had found his family's roots. And *Roots* is what he called the best-selling book that he wrote as a result of his research.

The TV miniseries based on *Roots* allowed a vast audience to relive the agony of slavery and to savor the power of a family's determination to build a better life. Americans were showing a keen interest in such stories in 1977. One year earlier, the United States had celebrated its bicentennial. It was a time

Alex Haley with his mother.

when many Americans were delving into genealogy — family history. They were looking for their roots, to get a sense of their own place in history.

Jimmy Carter, former governor of Georgia, had spoken of this need in 1976 while campaigning for the presidency. "One of the real problems in this country these days," Carter had said, was "the lack of roots, the mobile society, the constant moving from here to there . . . the absence of anything that lasts in people's lives." Carter had won the presidential election in November 1976, narrowly defeating President Gerald Ford. One week before *Roots* ran on television, Carter became President.

Americans were living through a confused and unsettling time. The Vietnam War, the Arab oil boycott, surging inflation, the Watergate affair — all these had buffeted Americans' lives. What people wanted now was a sense of stability.

1 Stability and Change in American Society

For most Americans, the center of activity and support had traditionally been the family. This couldn't have been truer of the new First Family. The Carters whirled into Washington and the White House, from Amy, the nine-year-old daughter who roller-skated down the corridors, to Miss Lillian, the spunky matriarch who at the age of 67 had served a two-year tour of duty with the Peace Corps in

India. And of course, Rosalynn Carter, Jimmy's strongest supporter during the campaign, continued her activism by becoming deeply involved in programs for mental health and the aged, all with the support of the new President.

Yet many American families of the 1970's lacked the stability of years past. Many homes had been broken by divorce.

THE FAMILY IN FLUX

About 2.1 million American couples married in 1977. More than half that many — just under 1.1 million couples — divorced. The divorce rate had doubled since 1965, and was five times what it had been in 1910. Most divorced people married again within three years — but often ended up back in divorce court. Comedians joked that American marriages were fashioned on the principle of the revolving door.

Observers offered many explanations for the rising divorce rate. Divorce laws had been eased. The growing tendency of women to hold jobs gave them greater independence and a better chance to make lives of their own. Divorced men and women faced less social prejudice than in the past. (In 1980, American voters for the first time would elect a divorced man to be president.)

One result of high divorce rates was that more and more parents were bringing up children alone. Occasionally (as in the 1977 novel *Kramer Versus Kramer* by Avery Corman) the father won custody of the children. Nine times out of 10, however, the mother did. It was not easy for a single parent to raise children while at the same time holding a job, even a part-time job. Single-parent families often lived at or below the poverty level.

Many children had only one parent at home from the start. Births to unmarried women accounted for 15.5 percent of all births in 1977, almost triple the 1960 rate. More than half of all black babies were now born to single women. But the rate of illegitimate births was rising faster among whites than among blacks. Nearly half of the single mothers were teenagers.

Statistics showed a sharp rise in the number of couples cohabitating — living together but not married to each other. One fourth of such couples had children. But what happened if an unmarried couple broke up? Who got the kids? Was one parent entitled to financial help such as alimony from the other?

Few could doubt that the American family was changing. But were the changes for better or for worse? On the positive side, some said it was good that women had a way out if their husbands abused them. In the past, they said, many more women had endured brutality in silence, often because of social and religious pressures against divorce.

But others, however, emphasized the negative side of the changes. Some interpreted high divorce rates as a sign that people were becoming too self-centered, less willing to consider a spouse's wishes or needs. (The 1970's, after all, were being called the Me Decade.) Many argued that traditional family values were breaking down. They called for a return to strict moral codes and stronger religious training.

Another family-related issue which continued to stir debate in the late 1970's was the proposed Equal Rights Amendment. When Congress submitted the ERA to the states in 1972, it set a deadline of seven years for ratification. As the deadline approached, only 35 of the necessary 38 states had ratified. In 1978,

The Carters worshiped at Plains Baptist Church.

the amendment's supporters in NOW and other groups persuaded Congress to extend the deadline until 1982.

Sexual roles were also at issue in an emotional debate over homosexuality. Homosexuals (or "gays," as many now called themselves) were less likely than in the past to hide their same-sex preference. Many formed and joined pressure groups to demand laws preventing discrimination against homosexuals in jobs, housing, and other areas.

The new visibility and assertiveness of homosexuals met a sharply divided reaction from "straight" (heterosexual) Americans. Some showed sympathy and understanding. The American Psychiatric Association, for example, decided in 1973 to drop its former position that homosexuality was a mental disorder. Some religious leaders went out of their way to help homosexuals who sought religious guidance. Others cited Scripture in support of their view that homosexuality violated God's law.

MATTERS OF FAITH

Religious considerations received much attention in the late 1970's. In running for office, Jimmy Carter had made frequent reference to his own Southern Baptist upbringing and to the "born-again" character of his Christian faith. As President, he sometimes made weekend trips to his hometown of Plains, Georgia. There he might teach a Sunday school class or help to direct a religious service.

Americans had long been a religious people. Sixty percent of the population belonged to a church or synagogue. Forty-one percent attended on a weekly basis. Although Roman Catholics numbered more than 48 million, Jews more than 6 million, and Eastern Orthodox Christians about 4 million, most American believers (71 million) were Protestants.

During the late 1970's, U.S. religious practices were becoming more diverse than ever before. "Mainstream" denominations were losing members. At the same time, Mormons, Seventh Day Adventists, and smaller, fundamentalist churches were growing rapidly. In some cities, Muslim mosques and Buddhist temples added to the rich religious mix. Moreover, new churches, such as the Unification Church founded by Korean missionary Sun Myung Moon, had begun to attract a following.

In times past, American parents had rejoiced when their children "got religion." However, some parents of the 1970's showed alarm when their children became followers of *cults*, or unorthodox religious groups of questionable origin and purpose. Why had Stephen

Followers of Rev. Sun Myung Moon (right) at the Unification Church's mass wedding.

shaved his head and begun begging for alms like an Asian monk? Why had Suzie left home to enter a religious retreat in the mountains? To some people, the cults were a menace. Parents began to complain that their children had been brainwashed, taught to despise their families, turned against their friends. In desperation, some parents "kidnaped" their children from these groups and confined them for a period of "deprogramming."

Concern about cults peaked in November 1978, when 911 members of the People's Temple, a U.S.-based cult, died in a mass suicide in Guyana. The group had left California to follow its leader, the Reverend Jim Jones, in making a new home in the South American jungle. When a California congressman went to check out conditions at the new community, called Jonestown, he and members of his party were killed. Then Jones led his followers in drinking poisoned soft drink.

A happier event was the visit of Pope John Paul II to the United States in 1979. Crowds of admirers greeted the leader of the Roman Catholic faith in Boston, Philadelphia, Chicago — wherever he went. In New York's Madison Square Garden, an exuberant group of students adapted their school cheer to salute the Pope: "Rack 'em up, stack 'em up, bust 'em in two. Holy Father, we're for you!"

The Pope renewed his earlier denunciations of divorce and abortion. He urged young people to turn away from drugs and other forms of escapism. "I propose to you the option of love," he said, "which is the opposite of escape . . . the love of God and of your neighbor."

Pope John Paul II with Carter at the White House.

DEBATE OVER MINORITY RIGHTS

Americans who were inclined toward social activism in the 1970's also confronted other issues. Some of them concerned programs designed to meet demands for equality on the part of blacks and women. One of the most controversial programs was called *affirmative action*. It began as an effort by federal authorities to enforce civil rights laws of the 1960's.

Those laws barred discrimination against blacks, other minorities, and women. Affirmative action further sought to encourage the hiring and promotion of such people, as well as improve their educational opportunities.

A company that adopted an affirmative action program set a series of goals for giving minorities or women a more equal share of jobs, especially in higher positions. One large organization set 38,000 separate targets. Each outfit had its own way of enforcing the policy. For example, one company cut the bonuses of managers who failed to hire or promote enough women or members of minority groups.

Under federal rules, two groups of companies were expected to adopt affirmative action programs. One group included firms that were found to have had a past policy of discrimination. The other group included all firms that sought contracts to do work for the government. Most major U.S. companies were in one or both groups. Affirmative action programs also applied to areas other than employment — for example, to school sports programs or college admissions.

Supporters of affirmative action argued that it was necessary to make up for past discrimination. They compared life to a footrace. In the past, they said, minorities and women had been forced to run with their feet tied together. They were far behind. They needed special help to get back in the race.

Critics argued that affirmative action amounted to discrimination against whites and males. It was, they claimed, nothing but "reverse discrimination." Among the critics were many business people who resented the red tape involved and many union members who wanted job advancement to be based strictly on seniority. Some blacks and women claimed that affirmative action programs insulted them by implying that they couldn't make it on their own.

Allan P. Bakke, a Norwegian-American and a Vietnam veteran, decided to test the legality of affirmative action after his application to the School of Medicine of the University of California at Davis was rejected in 1972. The medical school had 100 openings, of which it had set aside 16 for minority applicants — blacks, Hispanics, and Asians. Bakke had scored higher on admissions tests than some minority applicants who were admitted.

He took his case to the Supreme Court. In 1978, a closely divided Court ruled in *Regents of the University of California* v. *Bakke*, that the school's affirmative action program was inflexible. The school had violated the Civil Rights Act of 1964 by discriminating against Bakke because he was white, the Court held. At the same time, the Court declared that carefully-tailored, more flexible affirmative action programs were permissible under the Constitution, as long as they aimed to remedy past discrimination.

Just as controversial as affirmative action were school desegregation plans that involved busing children from one part of town to another to equalize the racial mix in different schools. Some communities, like Berkeley, California, did so voluntarily. Others, like Boston, did so under court order.

Supporters said busing schemes were a way

Desegregation plans still met with mixed success in the late 1970's.

of remedying intentional discrimination, such as drawing school district boundaries to exclude blacks. Critics said busing destroyed neighborhood schools and took away people's rights. They pointed out that children being bused sometimes had to leave home as early as 5:30 A.M. Many black parents joined whites in criticizing busing. In a 1975 Gallup Poll, only four percent of those questioned said they favored busing.

Many critics charged that busing only made the problem of "white flight" worse. In many cities, especially in the North, whites had been leaving central areas and moving to the suburbs. By 1980, whites made up only 27 percent of the people in the school district of Los Angeles, 18 percent in Chicago. Not even busing could have integrated those school districts.

Despite the controversy they stirred, affirmative action programs and busing re-

mained as two of the many means Americans were using to create a society in which people treated one another as equals. Great changes had taken place since the 1950's. Figures showed a dramatic rise in the numbers of black elected officials and in black education levels. Many new job opportunities had opened up for blacks, Hispanics, Asians, and members of other minorities.

Still, people of different races held contrasting views about how far the nation had come. A 1978 poll conducted by the *New York Times* and CBS News found that two thirds of the whites questioned said blacks had made "a lot of progress" in erasing discrimination. Fewer than one half of the blacks agreed. Fifty-one percent of blacks said there had not been "much real change."

GETTING INVOLVED

The surge of social activism that had begun in earlier decades crept into the 1970's with a variety of goals. Conservative farmers in Minnesota organized bitter protests against a high-voltage power line. In 1977 critics of nuclear power staged a massive sit-in on the site of a proposed nuclear plant in Seabrook, New Hampshire. Police hauled more than 1,400 protesters to jail.

Perhaps the most far-reaching protest of the period grew out of middle-class resistance to high taxes. A "tax revolt" began in California and swept like wildfire across much of the nation. Two men, Howard Jarvis and Paul Gann, started the revolt by circulating a petition to limit the property taxes that cities, counties, and school districts in California could impose. California was one of 22 states (mostly in the West) that had adopted the *initiative* process. Under that process, citizens who collect enough signatures can place a proposal on the ballot for voters to adopt or reject. Jarvis, Gann and their supporters collected 1.2 million signatures — twice as many as they needed. In 1978 their proposal went on the state ballot as Proposition 13.

Homeowners who had been hit by one tax increase after another warmly embraced the proposal. Many put signs on their lawns: "Vote For Proposition 13." The measure passed by a two-to-one margin. As a result, California property taxes dropped by nearly 60 percent.

Howard Jarvis, cosponsor of California's Proposition 13.

At first, the state distributed money from a budget surplus to help cities and counties meet their needs. Soon, however, governing bodies ran out of money. They laid off teachers, cut the hours for parks and swimming pools, and reduced social services.

The drive to cut property taxes eventually spread to other states and cities. Supporters of tax restrictions tended to be conservatives who argued that governments had been spending too much money. They said many of the services that had to be cut back were either unnecessary or better handled through private enterprise. Liberals generally opposed the tax restrictions, saying they hurt all citizens, but especially schools and the needy. Still, the liberals were on the defensive. A conservative tide seemed to be rising.

SECTION RECAP

1. What were two changes affecting family life in the 1970's? What did some people say were the positive and negative aspects of these changes?

2. What was the goal of affirmative action? What did the Supreme Court say about Alan Bakke's experience? What did it say about such programs in general?

3. What is the initiative process, and where is it used? What was the goal of Proposition 13?

2 New Directions in Political and Economic Life

Direct-mail fund-raising had an overwhelming effect on U.S. politics.

By the late 1970's, Richard Viguerie had become one of the U.S. Postal Service's best customers. From a high-rise office building in Falls Church, Virginia, Viguerie sent out letters to millions of Americans. The letters usually included a strongly worded statement such as the following: "You and I must choose — and the Senate must decide — whether we will personally accept the White Flag of Surrender as America's banner." At the end came an appeal for money on behalf of a conservative candidate or cause. In response, donations poured in. Most were small — $10 from a church deacon, $25 from a retired Army colonel, $5 from a widow on Social Security. But the gifts added up to millions of dollars.

TURN TO THE RIGHT

The success of Viguerie's fund-raising was a sign of strong conservative sentiment among many Americans. With the vast sums of money he raised, Viguerie helped to defeat liberal Democrats and Republicans alike, and elect conservative candidates. Other fund-raisers were doing the same.

Direct-mail fund-raising mushroomed after

1974, when congressional liberals pushed through a campaign-reform law in response to abuses uncovered during the Watergate scandal. The law placed a $1,000 limit on donations by any individual to any candidate.

To meet their need for campaign funds, politicians turned to an obscure device called the political action committee (PAC). Often PACs hired direct-mail fund-raisers to bring in the money.

PACs had been used for years by committees, labor unions and business interests to pool their money for political purposes. But the number of PACs soared after 1974. Many new PACs focused on single issues, such as promoting a pro-life policy on abortion or opposing gun control. Single-issue PACs could be stunningly effective in defeating a candidate who voted "wrong" on a particular issue, and this gave them a great deal of political clout.

Some of the most dynamic single-issue PACs were part of what was now being called the New Right. Like the "old right," or conservatives in general, the New Right favored strict limits on government and preservation of traditional values. What set the New Right apart was its focus on the family, sex-related issues, and religion. Groups within the New Right also favored tougher measures against pornography, a constitutional amendment to permit prayer in public schools, and defeat of the ERA.

By tapping new sources of campaign money, the rise of PACs and direct-mail appeals had a dramatic effect on U.S. politics. The changes sparked considerable controversy. Some political activists, like Viguerie, saw PACs as a victory for true democracy. "Direct mail has allowed conservatives to bypass the liberal media," he said. "There really is a silent majority in this country, and the New Right now has learned to . . . mobilize them." Liberals said the success of single-issue PACs was distorting the political process. Yet they also turned to direct-mail appeals on issues such as arms control and laws against pollution.

A CHANGING ECONOMY

It's part of the American dream. An individual invents a new product, sets up a business, and becomes a millionaire. For two college dropouts who knew how to tinker with electronics, the dream came true during the 1970's. Steven P. Jobs and Stephen Wozniak tinkered around in Jobs's parents' garage until they came up with a personal computer, or PC. The PC was small yet versatile, to serve the needs of a person rather than a large business.

Jobs and Wozniak founded Apple Computer Inc. in 1976 and helped to set off a rapid growth in the computer industry. In a few short years, Apple became one of that industry's giants.

Apple was one of a cluster of electronics companies that gave the name Silicon Valley to a section of Santa Clara County in northern California. (Silicon is a key ingredient of modern electronic devices.) The electronics industry was on the rise in the late 1970's, while "smokestack" industries — steel and textiles, for example — were in decline. This trend had

Apple Computer Inc. founders
Steven Jobs (left) and Stephen
Wozniak (right) introduce a new PC.

wider implications, for electronics and other high technology industries tended to be highly automated. They needed relatively few workers. Factory hands who lost a job in a steel plant were unlikely to find another in an electronics plant.

In other ways, also, the American economy was going through a historic transformation. In the years after World War II, the United States had mainly dominated world trade. U.S. industries sold billions of dollars worth of goods abroad as the United States helped nations in Europe and elsewhere to rebuild their shattered economies. Now, that dominance was at an end. Europe, Japan, and a growing number of Third World nations exported large quantities of high-quality, low-cost products. Many American customers were buying watches from Switzerland, cars from Japan, and jogging shoes from South Korea.

One result was that the U.S. trade balance often slipped into the red. That is, in some years the United States paid out more for imported goods than it earned from exported goods. This happened occasionally in the early 1970's, then every year from 1976 on. In 1978, the worst year of the decade, the United States imported $31.1 billion more merchandise than it exported.

A merchandise trade deficit was one of many economic problems afflicting the United States. Prices were rising rapidly. Unemployment, although declining, remained above seven percent. In 1979 the OPEC nations gave the world a second "oil shock" by again raising prices, although not so steeply as in 1974. The new shock sent U.S. inflation levels

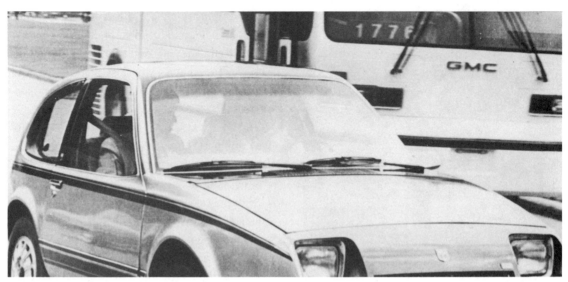

Small cars became popular in the late 1970's.

shooting into double digits; overall consumer prices jumped by 13.5 percent from 1979 to 1980. The American economy dipped into a recession in 1980, with businesses cutting back and more people losing their jobs.

Congress and the Carter administration struggled to repair the damage and restore the economy's vigor. The Humphrey-Hawkins Full Employment Act of 1978 said that unemployment should be cut to four percent or below, but didn't say how. Meanwhile, Congress cut taxes, hoping to stimulate new investment.

In 1979, the management of the nation's third-largest auto manufacturer, Chrysler, appealed for federal help. Car sales were sagging. The company was losing money. If it went out of business, thousands of workers would lose their jobs. Some people argued against federal help. Said Senator William Proxmire, Democrat of Wisconsin: "You just

can't have a free enterprise system without failures." Chrysler's new president, Lee Iacocca, argued that if Chrysler collapsed, many other firms would go too, like falling dominoes.

In the end, Congress agreed to a bail-out. The federal government would stand behind $1.5 billion in loans that Chrysler negotiated with banks and other private lenders. The loan guarantee proved successful. In the 1980's Chrysler paid off its loans and earned a profit once more.

Federal spending continued its steady rise under the Carter administration. To save money, President Carter trimmed back some domestic programs, over liberal opposition. Meanwhile, he boosted defense spending. The net effect was to increase the level of budget deficits. By the end of Carter's term, the national debt was poised to top $1 trillion for the first time.

AN OUTSIDER IN WASHINGTON

President Carter had an uneasy relationship with Congress. As a consequence, he had only limited success in getting his programs adopted. Carter liked to picture himself as an outsider in Washington — a simple peanut farmer who had come to the nation's capital to shape up the professional politicians. He was indeed a peanut farmer, if not a simple one. His family business also ran to cotton gins and peanut warehouses. His political record showed that he was no amateur.

Carter had grown up in Plains, Georgia, a town so small that the main street was only two blocks long. After one year at a nearby college, he had won an appointment to the United States Naval Academy at Annapolis,

U.S. Naval Academy student Jimmy Carter.

Maryland. During his years in Annapolis, he had shown special interest in electronics and naval tactics. After graduation in 1946, he had entered training in submarine navigation.

Within a few years he had joined a new Navy elite — the team developing the world's first nuclear-powered submarines. The team was led by Captain (later Admiral) Hyman Rickover, the project's pioneer and a demanding taskmaster. "He expected the maximum from us," Carter later wrote, "but he always contributed more."

When Carter's father died in 1953, the young naval officer felt obliged to return to the family business. Back in Georgia, he eventually became involved in local politics. In 1962 he was elected to the Georgia Senate. Eight years later, he became the state's governor. By the time he sought the presidency, then, Carter had broad experience in politics at both state and local levels.

Carter brought several unusual qualities to the presidency. He was the first president from the Deep South in this century. He was one of the very few to have been raised in a small town. Far more than recent presidents, he was a master of small details, particularly technological ones. "With his excellent memory," wrote White House aide Hedley Donovan, "he could show a dazzling command of facts and figures in a press conference, town meeting, or a session with congressmen."

In his speeches, Carter described Americans as "basically decent, basically honest," people of "great common sense." There were indications that he saw himself in the same way. "The president's use of the nickname

'Jimmy' rather than the more formal 'James' as his official signature epitomized [summed up] his conception of himself and his presidency," his first secretary of state, Cyrus Vance, later wrote. "He could not abide pomposity and inflated egos. He emphasized his desire for a 'team spirit' among his advisers. He looked for personal compatibility in every candidate for a cabinet-level post."

Yet neither modesty nor personal magnetism kept the Carter White House from flip-flops and zigzags in decision making. As time went on, some of the President's own aides criticized him for creating a "leadership crisis" of his own. One of his speech writers, James Fallows, charged that Carter spent too much time on unimportant details and neglected the broader aspects of policy-making. According to Fallows, Carter lacked "the passion to convert himself from a good man into an effective one, to learn how to do the job. Carter often seemed more concerned with taking the correct position than with learning how to turn that position into results . . . He did not devour history for its lessons, surround himself with people who could do what he could not, or learn from others that fire was painful before he plunged his hand into the flame."

Carter was an outsider, then, in the sense that he lacked experience in national politics. His chief advisers were Georgians who lacked a power base in Washington. Within a month of taking office, Carter had angered Democratic leaders of Congress by cancelling public works projects in a number of important states. That soured the President's relations with many of his natural political allies.

Allegations of scandal further weakened Carter's position. His budget director, Bert Lance, resigned in 1977 after being accused of loose financial practices as a banker in Georgia. (A federal jury later found Lance innocent of bank fraud.) The President's brother, Billy Carter, had troubles of his own after accepting money from the government of Libya in North Africa. Although Billy Carter agreed to register as a foreign agent, talk of a "Billygate" scandal persisted.

GRAPPLING WITH ENERGY PROBLEMS

The oil price rises of the 1970's had shifted billions of dollars from American pockets to Arab pockets. Arabs came to the United States to invest in businesses of many kinds. A second effect of the oil shocks was more far-reaching. That was a growing feeling that the world's energy supplies were dwindling and that energy shortages would haunt the United States for years to come.

President Carter devoted a great deal of attention to the energy crisis. Solemnly, the President warned Americans to "face the fact that the energy shortage is permanent." He stressed two goals. One was to increase the nation's domestic energy supply. The other was to cut energy usage through conservation. Wearing sweaters to dramatize his point, the President urged Americans to turn down their thermostats to save heating oil.

Carter's energy proposals stirred great controversy. Many people suggested that it was somehow un-American to try to use less energy. "This country did not conserve its way

Long lines at service stations were one result of the 1979 gas shortage.

to greatness. It produced its way to greatness," said one Texan.

Congress turned down many of Carter's proposals. It declined to create a standby system for rationing gasoline sales in case of an emergency. Other proposals fared better, however. The oil and gas industry supported the idea of gradually lifting price controls that had been placed on U.S.-produced fuels during the first oil shock. Congress approved, on the theory that higher prices would encourage more production — and more conservation. Congress also agreed to create a new Department of Energy, which went into operation in 1977. Moreover, Congress voted for a federal program to help industry create synthetic (artificial) fuels. In addition, Congress created a "strategic petroleum reserve," storing oil in underground caverns in readiness for a new Arab boycott.

Energy shortages touched every American's life. Many service stations ran short of gasoline during the summer of 1979 and limited their hours. Long lines of cars formed at the few stations that were open. That year, the price of gasoline, which had been hovering around 70 cents a gallon, shot over one dollar for the first time. At such prices, more people turned to smaller cars that got better mileage. Industry, too, sought to economize. Factories installed new, more efficient heating plants and found other ways to cut energy costs. Americans were conserving energy whether they liked it or not.

Meanwhile, the nation had felt a new shock. In March 1979 an accident struck a nuclear power reactor at Three Mile Island, near Har-

Three Mile Island (top) looms over the town of Goldsboro, PA. President Carter (right) toured the plant soon after the accident.

risburg, Pennsylvania. The trouble began with a breakdown in the reactor's cooling system. Deprived of the water it needed to carry away heat, the reactor core became hotter and hotter. Small bursts of radiation escaped into the environment. Fortunately, engineers got the cooling system working again before a dreaded "meltdown" and massive radiation releases could occur. But the accident, the worst ever to hit the nuclear power industry in the United States, had caused 144,000 people to be evacuated from the area. It had sent shudders of fear through the nation and revealed cracks in the Nuclear Regulatory Commission's system of safety checks.

Experts took comfort from the fact that the accident had been kept under control. A presidential commission said that even if a meltdown had occurred, a rugged containment building and an underlying layer of rock would most likely have prevented a massive radiation release. Even so, the accident had dealt a new blow to a nuclear power industry that was already reeling. Even before Three Mile Island, electric utilities had been cutting back orders for nuclear reactors. Energy conservation had reduced the demand for more electricity, and high interest rates and expensive safety measures had raised the costs of building nuclear plants. After Three Mile Island, the nuclear power industry faced years of uncertainty and public skepticism. Among those shaken by these developments was President Carter. The President had counted on nuclear power as a key element of his plan for boosting energy production.

To President Carter, energy problems were a major headache. In a speech to the nation in July 1979, he said they contributed to a "crisis of confidence" that was rattling Americans' faith in the future. Although Carter declared that firm action could resolve the crisis, much of the public seemed unconvinced. His domestic efforts earned him persistently low ratings in public-opinion polls. When he turned to foreign affairs, Carter faced an even greater challenge.

SECTION RECAP

1. What are PACs? Why did they become so popular after 1974?

2. What problems did the American economy face in the late 1970's? How did Congress and the Carter administration try to repair the damage?

3. Which of President Carter's energy proposals did Congress approve? Why was the nuclear accident at Three Mile Island such a blow to President Carter's energy plan?

President Carter in 1979.

3 Accomplishments and Frustrations in Foreign Policy

Afghan rebel raiders prepare to conduct a raid into Afghanistan's Doab Valley.

President Carter had high hopes that his direction of U.S. foreign policy could help to ease international tensions and promote human rights. He did attain two major goals, negotiating a new Panama Canal treaty and nudging the Middle East peace process forward. However, U.S.-Soviet relations took a turn for the worse. More dramatically, an unforeseen crisis in Iran came to dominate the final year of Carter's term and shatter his hopes for reelection.

DEALING WITH THE SOVIETS

When President Carter took office, the policy of détente had drained much of the bitter enmity from U.S.-Soviet relations. The SALT treaty of 1972 had tempered the arms race.

The Helsinki accords of 1975 had brought at least surface agreement on the issue of human rights. Nonetheless, the underlying rivalry between the two superpowers was as sharp as ever. U.S. officials were studying intelligence reports that suggested an alarming buildup of Soviet power.

The Carter administration was divided over how to deal with the Soviets. Secretary of State Vance wanted to negotiate a new, more sweeping SALT treaty. In the interest of arms control, he sought to play down U.S.-Soviet differences. National Security Adviser Zbigniew Brzezinski thought the United

States could attain its goals only if it asserted its power forcefully. On a number of occasions, he pressed for a stern U.S. response to what he saw as bad behavior by the Soviets. The friction between Vance's "soft" line and Brzezinski's "hard" line often produced sparks within the Carter administration.

U.S. arms negotiators were hampered by a lack of agreement in the public at large. A small but vocal "peace movement" argued that the more weapons the two superpowers built, the greater the danger of nuclear war became. Those who held this view often argued that the 1972 SALT treaty had little effect in taming the arms race. They blamed both U.S. and Soviet leaders for refusing to compromise. Supporters of arms control included some government officials who said it was important to halt the arms race while the two sides were relatively equal in strength. If one side gained an edge, they said, agreement would be far more difficult to achieve, and the risk of war would grow.

On the other hand, critics of arms-control negotiations warned that U.S. leaders were in danger of falling into a Soviet trap by agreeing to cut back on arms. Some said the Soviets could not be trusted to keep their word. If a new arms treaty should be signed and the Soviets then cheated, war would become more likely. They argued that a Soviet military buildup had already put the United States at a disadvantage, and that the United States should concentrate on building up arms, not cutting back.

With President Carter's approval, SALT talks resumed in 1977. Two years later Carter flew to Vienna, Austria, to meet Soviet leader Leonid Brezhnev and sign a treaty known as SALT II. The 1979 treaty went beyond the earlier SALT accord. It set limits on the size and number of offensive nuclear weapons each side could have. Carter claimed that the treaty would advance U.S. security. But critics warned of the danger of "appeasement." (The term referred to policies of the 1930's in which Britain and France sought peace with Hitler's Germany at almost any price.)

SALT II faced stiff opposition in the Senate, which must approve all treaties. In December 1979, just before senators were to vote on the treaty, Soviet troops intervened in the Asian nation of Afghanistan. The Soviet action brought strong protests from the United States. President Carter announced that he was asking the Senate to suspend action on the SALT II treaty. Yet both U.S. and Soviet leaders said they would observe treaty provisions as long as the other side did so too.

Although Soviet leaders claimed their troops had been invited into Afghanistan by the legal government, news reports showed that a sudden change of government had come just before the "invitation." U.S. leaders accused the Soviets of an outright invasion.

Afghanistan is a largely Muslim country lying between Iran and Pakistan, on the Soviet Union's southern border. A coup had ousted its king a few years before. In 1979, a pro-Soviet government was already in power, but its two factions quarreled. Soviet intervention was met with widespread rebellion in the valleys, deserts, and mountains of Afghanistan. The Muslim rebels sought aid and refuge in border areas of Pakistan (a U.S. ally). Before long, U.S. agencies were secretly funneling arms to the rebels. Soviet leaders sent more than 100,000 soldiers to fight the rebellion, which would drag on for many years.

Almost all the world's nations condemned the Soviet intervention. With support from most of the "non-aligned" nations, the United Nations General Assembly voted to demand the withdrawal of outside troops. A Soviet veto blocked action in the U.N. Security Council, however.

Détente seemed to be over, as the events in Afghanistan plunged U.S.-Soviet relations into a new chill. U.S. leaders pointed out that Soviet troops and aircraft had moved closer to the oil-rich Persian Gulf area. They said Soviet actions posed a threat to Western interests in the region — interests that had already been set back by a 1979 revolution in Iran (see page 301). In January 1980 the President announced what became known as the Carter Doctrine. He said the United States would resist "any attempt by any outside force to gain control of the Persian Gulf region."

As a direct sanction, President Carter cut off U.S. grain sales to the Soviet Union. Later, he declared a U.S. boycott of the 1980 Olympic Games in Moscow. Several other Western nations joined the boycott.

In his budget for 1981, Carter urged an increase in military spending to close what he called a gap between Soviet and U.S. power. The United States was developing a number of new weapons. One was a mobile intercontinental missile called the MX. Its mobility would presumably make it harder for Soviet planners to target. Another was a device called the cruise missile that hugged the ground as it zigzagged toward its target. A third was the Stealth system that used electronic technology to make planes and missiles almost invisible to enemy radar. Soviet planners too were developing new weapons. With or without SALT II, new technology was keeping the arms race alive.

NEW PARTNERSHIP IN ASIA

While U.S. relations with the Soviet Union got worse, those with China improved. The first step came in late 1978, when the United States broke off diplomatic relations with Taiwan. American supporters of the Nationalist Chinese on Taiwan were angered. But the China lobby (see page 49) had lost much of its strength, and protests were ineffective. Early in 1979 Washington exchanged ambassadors with the Communist government in Beijing for the first time.

By improving relations with China, the Carter administration hoped to gain an advantage over the Soviet Union. The two Communist giants were bitter rivals. U.S. and Chinese leaders had a mutual interest in countering Soviet influence in Asia. Both the United States and China saw the Soviet-backed regime in Vietnam as an enemy.

A second reason for improving relations with China was trade. As the most populous country in the world, China was potentially a major customer for American products. Ever

Russian surface-to-air rockets poised near Kabul, Afghanistan.

since the late 18th century, American merchants had plied the China trade. The U.S. government had promoted such trade through a policy known as the Open Door. After the Communists came to power in 1949, however, China had been closed to this trade. The door began to open again in the early 1970's. U.S. and Chinese diplomats signed a trade treaty in July 1979, and the door opened wide.

Shirts made from Chinese cotton appeared in U.S. stores. Chinese tea poured from U.S. teapots. U.S. oil companies helped drill for oil off China's shores. A U.S. firm made plans to open one of the world's biggest coal mines in China. And American soft drinks became popular among Chinese.

Both the United States and China watched with concern as war broke out in Kampuchea (formerly Cambodia) in 1978. Kampuchea was a neighbor of Thailand, a U.S. ally. The United States did not want fighting to spill over the Thai border.

Vietnam sent troops into Kampuchea to help overthrow one Communist regime and install another. The ousted regime, led by Pol Pot, was widely condemned for brutal policies that had taken millions of lives. China supported the Kampuchean resistance against the Vietnam-backed regime. In 1979 China and Vietnam began a series of border clashes. Vietnam kept large numbers of troops in Kampuchea.

The turmoil in Southeast Asia created at least one million refugees. As Vietnamese citizens had done a few years earlier, Kampucheans fled to escape war and political repression. Many became refugees in Thailand and China. Others — called boat people — set sail to places like Singapore. An estimated 600,000 refugees came to America.

Vietnamese boat people await help to come ashore in Malaysia.

A NEW LOOK AT IMMIGRATION LAWS

Like earlier waves of immigrants, the newcomers sought jobs and new lives. They became fishers, factory workers, grocers, and shopkeepers. In some places, Asian immigrants met hostility and prejudice. Elsewhere, civic and religious groups offered them help and friendship.

The surge of Asian immigrants came at a time of economic trouble, when many Americans had lost their jobs. Other boat people were arriving from Haiti and Cuba, and still others were coming from Mexico, India, and elsewhere.

Some people said that the United States should shut off the flow of immigrants. This, they argued, would help to preserve scarce jobs for Americans. Others rejected such arguments. They said the United States should continue to be a haven for victims of persecution and poverty. Besides, they argued, immigrants often took low-paying jobs that U.S. citizens did not want.

Especially alarming to many Americans was a reported rise in illegal immigration. Many people snuck across the Mexican border, and managed to get fake identification papers that helped them to get jobs or, in some cases, public assistance. U.S. officials had no way of counting these illegal aliens but were sure the number was very high.

Congress began a sweeping reassessment of U.S. immigration laws. The Refugee Act of 1980 changed a law dating to the 1950's that gave preference to immigrants fleeing Communist countries. The new act removed that preference, which had been adopted at a time when refugees from communism came mainly from Europe, not Asia or Latin America.

Despite heated debate, Congress could not agree on a way of resolving the problem of illegal aliens. Proposals to punish employers who hired such people met stiff opposition from Hispanics. The critics argued that such a law would punish all Hispanics, citizens and non-citizens alike. Their reasoning was that employers might turn away Hispanic citizens and legal immigrants rather than risk hiring someone with false documents.

PANAMA CANAL TREATIES

President Carter fought to achieve a new status for the Panama Canal, one of his major foreign policy goals. Built by the United States between 1904 and 1914, the waterway had been under U.S. ownership ever since. It linked the Atlantic and Pacific oceans across the narrowest part of Central America.

For the United States, the canal served vital military and economic needs. U.S. military leaders considered the canal as an essential link in U.S. defenses. For many people in Latin America, however, the waterway was a symbol of U.S. imperialism. They resented the high-handed manner in which the United States had gained Panama's permission to build the canal. They also bridled at a clause in a 1903 treaty that excluded Panama from exercising any authority in the canal zone — for all time. After a spasm of rioting in the 1960's, the canal had become a major source of friction between Panama and the United States.

Presidents Johnson and Nixon had tried to negotiate a new treaty that would satisfy both Panamanians and Americans. Both presidents faced charges that a new treaty would amount to a giveaway of vital U.S. interests. Presidents Ford and Carter tried again. In 1977 President Carter submitted two treaties for Senate approval. One allowed Panama to share in operation of the canal for a time and to assume full ownership in the year 2000. The other guaranteed the canal's neutrality and specified that the United States could use military force to defend the waterway.

Once more critics warned against a giveaway. With the help of New Right fundraisers such as Richard Viguerie, conservatives mounted a massive campaign against the two treaties. Said former California governor Ronald Reagan about the canal: "We built it, we paid for it, it's ours, and we should . . . keep it."

With many senators inclined to oppose the treaties, President Carter went all out to win ratification. He marshaled support from military commanders who testified that the treaties would make defense of the canal easier by improving relations with Panama's government and citizens. He won endorsements from former President Ford and Ford's secretary of state, Henry Kissinger. He offered political favors to fence-sitting senators. (To win one senator's vote, the President even sat up late reading a textbook the senator had written. His praise of the book the next day may or may not have played a part in the senator's last-minute support for the treaties.) After weeks of suspense, both treaties squeaked by on votes of 68 to 32, one vote more than the required two-thirds majority.

President Carter considered the treaties a key step in cementing relations with Latin America. As a second step, he sought to demonstrate U.S. opposition to dictatorship and oppression.

HUMAN RIGHTS

"I want to see our country set a standard of morality," President Carter declared in 1977. "I feel very deeply that when people are put in prison without trial and tortured and deprived of basic human rights that the President of the United States ought to . . . do something about it."

President Carter made a point of speaking out against what he considered to be violations of human rights. His administration criticized right-wing dictatorships in Chile, Brazil, and Paraguay. It also criticized Communist regimes in the Soviet Union and Poland. In some cases, the Carter administration cut back aid to friendly governments that had poor human-rights records.

Some critics said the administration was harder on allies than adversaries. They accused the administration of having a "double standard" — of holding right-wing govern-

ments to stricter rules than Communist governments. By its actions, said critics, the Carter administration was giving aid and comfort to the enemy.

Others defended the administration. They argued that the United States could not persuade the world's people of its commitment to democracy if it supported dictatorships that tortured and killed their own citizens.

TURMOIL IN CENTRAL AMERICA

Complaints of human rights violations were widespread in Nicaragua and El Salvador. Both teetered on, then over, the brink of civil war.

Since 1936 Nicaragua had been ruled by right-wing dictators of the Somoza family, who had close ties to the United States. During the 1970's, leftist rebels organized a guerrilla army to fight the Nicaraguan government. The rebels called themselves Sandinistas, after a guerrilla leader named César Augusto Sandino. During the 1920's and 1930's, Sandino had led an uprising against U.S. Marines who occupied Nicaragua. To many Nicaraguans, he was a symbol of resistance against "Yankees." He was also a martyr, having been assassinated by the first Somoza.

Backed by peasants, workers, priests, and many business people, the Sandinistas launched a civil war in May 1979. Seven weeks later, after bitter fighting and great destruction, dictator Anastasio Somoza-Debayle fled the country. The Sandinistas took power. They promised land reform, democracy, and social justice with a leftist tilt.

The Sandinista junta parades in Managua, Nicaragua.

The Carter administration offered economic aid to the new regime, hoping to strengthen moderate forces among the Sandinistas. But many in the administration worried that the Sandinistas were under Cuban or Soviet influence. U.S. officials did not want revolutions to spread to other parts of Central America.

The United States took steps to shore up the government of nearby El Salvador, where unrest had been brewing for years. Rival bands of leftist guerrillas had been trying to stir up a rebellion. In 1979, a military coup had ousted El Salvador's rightist government and brought in a moderate *junta* (ruling group). With U.S. support, the new military-civilian junta began a program of land reform.

Yet leftists condemned the reform as "too little," and rightists condemned it as "too much."

Meanwhile, incidents of terror multiplied in El Salvador. Leftist guerrillas abducted and murdered a variety of opponents. Right-wing officers and wealthy families formed "death squads" to kill leaders of labor unions and moderate or left-wing politicians. In March 1980, rightists shot and killed the country's Roman Catholic archbishop while he said Mass.

President Carter offered to send military aid and advisers to help the government maintain order. But signs that military officers were behind some of the terror alarmed U.S.

leaders. In December 1980 the United States suspended its aid after four U.S. women, three nuns and a Catholic lay worker were murdered — apparently by Salvadoran soldiers. The Carter administration resumed its aid when a civilian moderate, José Napoleón Duarte, assumed leadership of the junta.

It was too late, however, to prevent civil war in El Salvador. A number of moderate and leftist groups joined forces and adopted a unified policy of all-out warfare. By the time President Carter left office, El Salvador's U.S.-backed government was struggling against a growing guerrilla movement.

SHADOWS OVER AFRICA

Conflicts in Africa drew much attention during the Carter years. U.S. officials worried about Soviet and Cuban support for left-wing governments or movements in Ethiopia, Angola, and elsewhere. Was Africa to become an arena for all-out East-West competition? That was a danger U.S. officials wanted to avoid. Therefore, they worked to promote settlements of a number of conflicts in southern Africa.

The United States supported efforts to bring majority rule (that is, black rule) to Britain's breakaway colony of Southern Rhodesia. A white government in the colony had revolted against British rule and declared independence in 1965. Blacks had then organized guerrilla armies and fought to overthrow the Rhodesian government. Britain and the United States put pressure on the Rhodesian government. Finally, British officials arranged a settlement. Southern Rhodesia

South African apartheid separates whites from non-whites.

changed its constitution to give blacks the right to vote. The colony held elections and changed its name to Zimbabwe in 1979. One of the black rebel leaders became prime minister the following year.

Zimbabwe and other nations of southern Africa lived in the shadow of prosperous, powerful, white-ruled South Africa. The United States had joined most of the world's other nations in condemning South Africa's rigid *apartheid* system of racial separation. Nonetheless, U.S. officials had little hope of changing that system in the near future. Their immediate goal was to persuade South Africa to abandon its grip on the territory of Namibia.

A guerrilla movement was battling for Namibian independence. At times, fighting had spilled over into neighboring nations like Angola, and U.S. officials feared that the war might spread. As far as the United States was concerned, the choice facing southern Africa was a stark one. Either there would be peaceful change, or bitter and perhaps uncontrollable warfare. Despite repeated diplomatic maneuvers, however, the Carter administration did not succeed in bringing peace to Namibia. The war there continued.

Part of the reasoning behind such U.S. policies was summed up by Secretary of State Vance after he left office. He wrote: "If the United States did not support social and political justice in Rhodesia, Namibia, and South Africa itself, Africans would correctly dismiss our human rights policy as mere cold war propaganda, employed at the expense of the peoples of Africa."

Not all Americans agreed with that reasoning, however. Some argued that guerrilla movements like the one in Namibia were part of a Communist-inspired campaign to destabilize southern Africa. In this view, the United States needed to secure its economic and political interests in the region. The best way to do that was to support the white government of South Africa while nudging it toward reform of apartheid. Debate over U.S. policies in Africa was beginning to heat up.

TRIUMPH AT CAMP DAVID

President Carter helped to achieve a major breakthrough between Israel and Egypt. After 30 years in a state of war, the two nations agreed to make peace. The breakthrough began with a dramatic visit by Egyptian President Anwar Sadat to Jerusalem, the Israeli capital, in November 1977. This was followed by a December trip to Egypt by Israeli Prime Minister Menachem Begin.

President Carter, eager to help work out a settlement, invited Sadat and Begin to join him at Camp David, Maryland. The three men and their advisers met there in September 1978 for 13 days. Carter, acting as mediator and participant, used U.S. influence and promises of aid to prod the two Middle East leaders to settle their differences. Finally, Sadat and Begin reached agreement on the framework for a peace treaty. Then lower-level delegations worked for many more weeks to settle the details.

Sadat and Begin returned to the United States for a treaty-signing ceremony at the White House in March 1979. "We have won, at last, the first step of peace — a first step on a

Egypt's President Sadat, President Carter,
Israeli Prime Minister Begin.

long and difficult road," Carter declared. The
treaty ended the state of war between Israel
and Egypt. It led to Israeli withdrawal from
the Sinai Peninsula, occupied in the 1967
Arab-Israeli war (page 259). But the treaty
did nothing to settle Israel's differences with
its other Arab neighbors — Syria, Jordan,
and Lebanon, in particular. Those nations,
and most other Arab governments, cut off
diplomatic relations with Egypt. Many Arabs
denounced Sadat as a traitor, saying he had
harmed the cause of the Palestinian Arabs by
signing a separate peace.

As Carter had said, the treaty was only one
step. If it was to be more than a hollow victory, it would have to be followed by further
steps in the years ahead.

SECTION RECAP

1. What was SALT II supposed to achieve?
Why did President Carter ask the Senate to
suspend action on the treaty?

2. What were two benefits of the improved
relations with China during the Carter administration?

3. What was the purpose of the Immigration
Act of 1980? What were the arguments for
and against allowing the flow of immigrants
into the United States to continue?

4. How did President Carter finally win support for ratification of the Panama Canal
treaties?

5. What two things did the 1979 treaty between Egypt and Israel accomplish? How did
it affect relations between Egypt and other
Arab nations?

4 Upheaval in Iran

For many years, the Middle Eastern nation of Iran had been closely allied to the United States. Under a strong-willed emperor, Shah Mohammed Reza Pahlavi, Iran had been a firm supporter of U.S. foreign policy. In return, the United States had supported the shah's efforts to make Iran the dominant power in the Persian Gulf region.

One U.S. president after another had affirmed U.S. support for the shah. Under President Eisenhower, the CIA had helped him keep his grip on power (see page 88). President Nixon had offered large-scale military aid. President Carter had welcomed the shah at the White House and paid a return visit to Tehran, the Iranian capital. During his visit over the New Year holiday of 1978, Carter toasted Iran as "an island of stability in a turbulent corner of the world."

BACKGROUND TO INSTABILITY

Yet Iran was far from stable. Its surface tranquility, maintained by a powerful secret police force called SAVAK, masked a deep and growing discontent. The shah had angered many Iranians by pushing his nation into rapid modernization and aligning it with the United States. A new class of wealthy Iranians had sprung up, but many poor people had been pushed aside. The shah's efforts to promote women's rights had helped some Iranians, but shocked many others. Traditionalist Muslims viewed the shah's reforms as an attack on religion and tradition.

Shiite Muslim leaders called *ayatollahs* helped to mobilize opposition to the shah. During 1978, riots and disorders swept Iran. The shah tried unsuccessfully to crush the rebellion. Early in 1979, he fled the country. Soon after, the most respected of the Muslim leaders, Ayatollah Ruhollah Khomeini, returned from exile and assumed leadership of the revolution.

Khomeini sought to turn Iran into an Islamic state, run according to strict religious rules. His goals conflicted with the goals of Iranian moderates and leftists, who wanted a *secular* state (one that was not specifically religious). For months, struggles between religious and secular forces kept Iran in turmoil.

Ayatollah Ruhollah Khomeini.

U.S. leaders had been surprised and shocked by the shah's sudden downfall. They tried to salvage some influence by supporting moderates in the new government. However, a crisis erupted in the fall of 1979, when U.S. leaders allowed the deposed shah to enter the United States to be treated for a serious illness. Angry Iranians demanded that U.S. leaders hand over the shah so that he could be punished. President Carter refused to do so.

Early in November 1979, Iranian militants stormed into the U.S. embassy in Tehran and seized 52 Americans as hostages. The militants offered to release their captives in exchange for the shah. Ayatollah Khomeini, who had denounced both the United States and the Soviet Union, supported the hostage-taking. His stand proved popular with Iranians and eventually helped the Islamic traditionalists rise to power over their secular opponents.

AMERICA HELD HOSTAGE

Embroiled as it was in Iran's internal politics, the hostage crisis proved very difficult to end. A number of world leaders demanded that Iran's government force the militants to let the hostages go, but nothing happened. The crisis dragged on for weeks, then for months. One U.S. television network offered nightly updates under the title *America Held Hostage*. Many Americans voiced outrage at the inability of the Carter administration to free the embassy personnel.

The administration ordered U.S. banks to "freeze" some $8 billion in Iranian accounts. It expelled Iranian students. It sent Iran's ambassador home.

When nothing else worked, U.S. officials sent a small military force into Iran on a rescue mission in April 1980. The mission failed when three U.S. helicopters malfunctioned and two aircraft collided at an Iranian desert rendezvous. Eight crew members died in the crash. Secretary of State Vance had argued against the use of military force. When Carter, Brzezinski, and other officials approved the mission, Vance resigned in protest.

Not even the death of the shah in July 1980 ended the crisis. President Carter's inability to free the hostages fatally damaged his hopes for reelection. As the 1980 presidential election grew closer, Carter's rivals deplored what they called U.S. weakness. They urged further action to end the impasse.

The Republicans nominated Ronald Reagan, who had strong support among traditional conservatives and members of the New Right. Reagan promised to restore respect for the United States abroad. He assailed Carter's economic policies as the chief cause of high unemployment, inflation, and budget deficits. Promising to step up defense spending, cut taxes, balance the budget, and slash federal regulations, Reagan said he would "take government off the backs of the great people of our country."

Carter turned back a challenge from Senator Edward Kennedy of Massachusetts to become the Democratic candidate. Carter defended his policies, saying there were "no simple answers to complicated questions." He accused Reagan of "insensitivity" to poverty and other social problems, and called Reagan's tax-cut plan "completely irresponsi-

Freed American hostages are greeted by the Reagans.

ble." The President claimed Reagan was too inclined to use force rather than diplomacy to solve world problems.

Reagan won an overwhelming victory. He and his running mate, George Bush of Texas, won 51 percent of the popular vote and the electoral votes of 44 of the 50 states. Carter and Vice President Walter Mondale won 41 percent of the popular vote. An independent candidate, Representative John B. Anderson of Illinois, won seven percent.

In the weeks following the election, the Carter administration finally negotiated a settlement of the hostage crisis. The hostages flew to freedom on the very day of Reagan's inauguration as President, January 20, 1981. "God is great! Death to America!" shouted an Islamic militant as the hostages left Tehran.

Americans rejoiced and cut yellow ribbons that they had tied around trees as a reminder of the captivity. In New York, jubilant construction workers put up a sign that had its roots in the civil rights movement: "Free at last! Free at last! Thank God they are free at last!" Then, at the bottom: "Never again."

SECTION RECAP

1. What were the traditionalist Muslims' objections to the shah of Iran's alliance with the United States?

2. What event preceded the hostage-taking in the U.S. embassy in Tehran? What were the Iranian militants' terms for release of the hostages?

3. How did the hostage crisis affect the 1980 U.S. presidential election?

1. For each sentence, select the correct word.

a. In the late 1970's the number of single-parent households was (increasing/decreasing).

b. During the late 1970's, "mainstream" religious denominations were (gaining/losing) members.

c. Busing children to school was becoming (more/less) acceptable to many Americans in the late 1970's.

d. Passage of Proposition 13 meant that the amount of property taxes that cities, counties, or school districts in California could impose would be (limited/unlimited).

e. The New Right used direct-mail fund-raising to gain many (large/small) contributions.

f. As the American economy underwent a transformation, it became (more/less) automated.

g. During the late 1970's, the U.S. trade balance was more often in the (black/red).

h. Under President Carter, the budget deficit substantially (increased/decreased).

i. President Carter felt that the energy shortage was (temporary/permanent).

j. At Three Mile Island, a meltdown (did/did not) occur.

2. Define these terms: *affirmative action, apartheid, ayatollahs, boat people, cults, initiative, junta, secular.*

3. Describe three qualities that made Jimmy Carter an unusual president.

4. Why did some Americans object to the Panama Canal treaties and why did others support them?

5. What did the United States do to try to secure the release of the American hostages held by Iran?

CHAPTER **10**

1981 — 1987

The Reagan Revolution

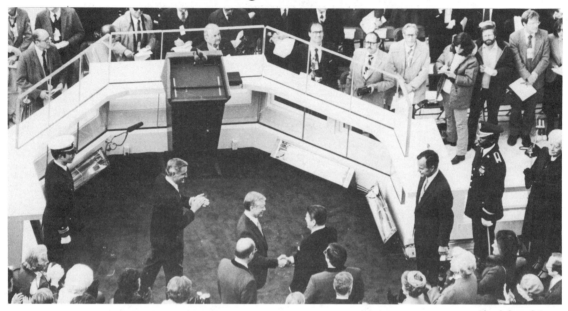

The defeated Carter congratulates the new President.

RONALD REAGAN HAD a favorite subject and an endless string of stories to illustrate it. The subject was government — big government. In Reagan's view, government had grown too big. It was time to trim it back.

One story dealt with Reagan's teenage years, back in the 1920's. Coming from a family of modest means, Reagan needed a job to save money for college. He worked for a building contractor. "At the end of the week, all the boss had to do was reach in his pocket and take out the cash to pay me," Reagan recalled. "No auditors, no bookkeeping, no withholding of any funds [for taxes] . . ." Then Reagan drew the moral of the story: "Much of [the government regulation] we have today is what has made teenage unemployment, particularly lack of summer jobs, so great."

When Reagan was a teenager, the Great Depression had not yet struck. Franklin D. Roosevelt had not yet become President. Roosevelt's New Deal had not yet begun to attack the nation's economic woes by providing a broad new array of government programs.

Looking back from the 1980's, Reagan contended that the New Deal and other activist government programs had gone too far. "Government is not the solution to our problem," Reagan declared in his inaugural address of 1981. "Government is the problem."

President Reagan set out to make drastic cuts in federal programs. His cuts were so broad and so deep that they amounted to a fundamental shift in the way the United States was governed. Not since New Deal days had Americans seen such sweeping changes. The Reagan Revolution, as people called it, would affect American life for many years to come.

Of course, the Reagan Revolution stirred controversy. Conservatives generally applauded the President's moves, although some said Reagan did not go far enough. Liberals loudly protested. They said Reagan was gutting social programs and shifting money from poor people to rich people. Still, the lines between conservatives and liberals were shifting. Many people who considered themselves somewhere in the middle seemed to like what Reagan was doing. In 1986, as Reagan neared the middle of his second term, a Gallup Poll gave him the highest approval rating of any second-term president since World War II. Sixty-eight percent of those questioned said they approved of the way the President was handling his job.

Foreign policy played a part in the President's popularity, too. Reagan cranked up military spending and took an assertive stance toward the Soviet Union and other adversaries. Some Americans accused Reagan of having an itchy trigger finger. Yet Reagan's popularity rose when he sent U.S. troops to invade Grenada, a Caribbean island, in 1983. It rose again when he ordered the bombing of the North African nation of Libya in 1986.

Because of his popularity, Ronald Reagan was able to restore confidence in the office of the presidency. Not since before the Vietnam War and the Watergate scandal had Americans held the presidency in such high esteem. Even some people who deplored Reagan's policies tended to agree that he was a strong and effective leader. Under Reagan, the "crisis of confidence" that had festered for years seemed to be drawing to an end.

1 Reshaping the National Agenda

Ronald Reagan had to overcome a good deal of skepticism to win Americans' hearts. He had first come to public attention as a movie actor. Recalling such films as *Knute Rockne — All American* (a 1940 drama) and *Bedtime for Bonzo* (a 1951 comedy), political critics scoffed that Reagan was a grade-B actor and a grade C politician. But Reagan would prove that his political skills, at any rate, were first class.

REAGAN AND HIS IDEAS

Ronald Reagan had definite ideas about where the United States should be headed. He believed that government should be smaller and taxes lower. He believed that America was still a land of opportunity, and that people could better themselves if they really tried. Reagan's vision of America was of a land where people depended on their own grit and initiative, not on government aid.

Reagan took the same do-for-yourself attitude about foreign affairs. The world was a dangerous place, and the United States must look out for itself. That meant a readiness to use military force. It meant building ever-stronger defenses against the Soviet Union. Reagan minced no words: the Soviet Union was an "evil empire" and had to be firmly resisted.

Reagan called his main ideas "basic principles" and vowed to stick to them rigidly. His basic principles amounted to an *ideology*, a systematic body of beliefs. Laurence I. Barrett, a chronicler of the Reagan years, called Reagan "the most overtly ideological President in the nation's history."

If so, Reagan was not completely rigid. He knew the art of compromise. When necessary — usually after holding out until his opponents had made important concessions — President Reagan would agree to concessions of his own.

Reagan is helped into his car after an assassination attempt.

Reagan came to his sharply conservative ideology fairly late in life. During his acting career he was a liberal Democrat. Later, he would say he had been "a near-hopeless hemophiliac liberal," bleeding for every cause that came along.

Reagan's attitudes began to shift during the late 1940's, when he was a union activist, and then president of the Screen Actors Guild. As you read in Chapter Two, that was turbulent period in the motion picture industry. Reagan resisted communism in the film industry on the one hand, and the use of fear tactics to deal with communism on the other. Later, anti-communism became a central strand in Reagan's ideology.

In the 1950's, when leading-man roles no longer came Reagan's way, he became a spokesman for General Electric. For a salary of $150,000 a year, Reagan toured the country making speeches to GE employees and civic groups. Gradually, Reagan's speeches took on a more conservative cast. He denounced high taxes and government regulation and won enthusiastic applause from his audiences.

After leaving GE, Reagan appeared for a time on a television program called *Death Valley Days*. He also joined the Republican party, dazzling conservatives with a forceful television speech just before the 1964 election. Reagan urged voters to support Barry Goldwater, the Republican presidential candidate. After Goldwater's crashing defeat, Reagan succeeded him as the hero of the Republican party's conservative wing.

Reagan became a full-time politician. Californians elected him governor in 1966 and reelected him in 1970. Meanwhile, Reagan sought the Republican presidential nomination in 1968 against Richard Nixon and in 1976 against Gerald Ford. Both times he lost. Success finally came in 1980, when Reagan won both the nomination and the presidency.

President Reagan's style combined a winning smile, a quick wit, and effective leadership with an inclination to delegate responsibility to his staff. This earned him the nickname Teflon President, as he repeatedly escaped blame for some controversial or embarrassing actions of his administration. His popularity and credibility suffered in 1986 when it was discovered arms had been secretly sold to Iran. The revelation that profits from the sale had been used to support contras in Nicaragua further hurt his reputation.

In March 1981 a 25-year-old drifter fired six shots at President Reagan as he left a hotel in Washington, D.C., after making a speech. Rushed to a hospital, the President was found to have a .22 caliber bullet lodged in his lung. Despite the pain, Reagan kept smiling and delivering one-liners. ("Please tell me you're Republicans" he told surgeons who were about to remove the slug.) Reagan recovered quickly, winning new admiration for his bravery and pluck.

Reagan was the first divorced man to become President. His first marriage, to actress Jane Wyman, broke up in the late 1940's. In 1952 Reagan married an aspiring actress named Nancy Davis. In her role as homemaker, Nancy Reagan gave strong support to her husband's political aspirations. According to one Reagan aide, she was "as much responsible for his success" as he was.

Lieutenant Reagan and family in 1942.

CUTTING BACK GOVERNMENT

President Reagan's attack on "big government" began one month after he took office. With the assistance of his budget director, David Stockman, the President sent Congress 84 proposals for slashing programs that ranged from food stamps to Coast Guard services. The President asserted that his cuts were aimed only at "fat." He said he had no intention of removing the "safety net" or taking benefits away from the "truly needy."

The Reagan proposals brought howls of outrage from liberals. Some accused Reagan of trying to "repeal the New Deal." Others said his programs would erase the progress made in the 1960's and 1970's in reducing poverty and promoting equal rights.

Nevertheless, liberals were on the defensive. The 1980 elections had swept a Republican majority into the Senate and narrowed the Democratic majority in the House. Moreover, many Democrats shared Reagan's belief that something had to be done to reduce budget deficits and turn the rising tide of federal spending. The Democratic party was split among liberal, moderate, and conservative factions. They could not agree on any clear alternative to Reagan's proposals.

Thus, the President succeeded in framing the debate in his own terms. Congress would cut back social spending. Debate focused mainly on which programs to cut and by how much. A group of conservative southern Democrats, nicknamed the Boll Weevils, sided with the Republicans on key issues. In the end, Congress approved about 50 of the President's 84 proposals in one form or another.

The programs that were cut back affected both middle-class and poor Americans. Congress limited low-cost loans to college students. It made it harder for poor people to qualify for food stamps. It trimmed welfare rolls and reduced benefits. It cut back Social Security payments to children whose parents had died. It shaved subsidies for school lunches and for Amtrak passenger trains. It cut back unemployment insurance, aid to housing, aid to education, job training, and many other programs.

Critics charged that the cuts had a devastating effect on people with low incomes. Especially hard hit, they said, were "the working poor." Because of changes in eligibility rules, some 700,000 families lost all or part of the benefits they had been receiving. The poverty rate, which had been declining since President Johnson's Great Society programs of the 1960's, began to rise again.

Year after year, President Reagan returned to Congress with new proposals for cutbacks. After 1981, Congress put up more resistance, but cutbacks continued nonetheless.

The many deep cuts did not halt the rise in federal debt. In fact, spending continued to increase because:
• A rapid increase in military spending offset the reductions in social spending.
• Massive budget deficits forced stepped-up government borrowing at unusually high interest rates.
• A large part of the government's domestic spending was locked up in entitlement programs.

Reagan's advisers found the last point particularly frustrating. *Entitlement programs* are those whose benefits are available to all people, rich or poor, who meet certain requirements set by law. The best-known example of this is Social Security. Other entitlement programs include veteran benefits and military and civil service pensions. The law provides formulas for determining who is entitled to benefits and how much each person will receive. Once the formulas are set, spending is automatic. Costs may be significantly affected by changes in economic conditions that are beyond the government's control.

Powerful interest groups support the entitlement programs. The elderly, who make up the largest group of Social Security recipients, form a significant voting bloc — and are more likely to vote than other Americans. Early in his term, President Reagan proposed some modest cuts in Social Security spending.

The idea stirred such a storm that Reagan quickly backed down. After that, Social Security was off limits to budget cutters.

In fact, the Reagan team concentrated its cutbacks on programs that accounted for a mere 15 percent of the total budget. Given Reagan's priorities, they had little choice. They could not touch entitlement programs without stirring massive opposition. They could hardly cut military spending while Defense Secretary Caspar Weinberger was advocating increases. Yet the two "untouchable" items — entitlement programs and military spending — made up by far the largest part of the budget.

The net result of President Reagan's initiatives was the greatest redirection of public purpose since the New Deal. Instead of starting new programs, the government was cutting back old ones. Critics accused the Reagan administration of "icy indifference to human

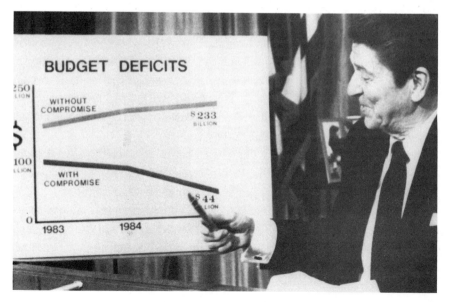

Reagan often used visual aids in televised speeches.

Deregulation encouraged fare wars.

needs." But Reagan and his supporters took a different view. "Back in the New Deal days," said Reagan, "many critics of Franklin Roosevelt accused him of trying to destroy the free enterprise system . . . Like FDR, may I say that I'm not trying to destroy what is best in our system of humane, free government. I'm doing everything I can to save it, to slow down the destructive rate of growth in taxes and spending, to prune nonessential programs so that enough resources will be left to meet the requirements of the truly needy."

DEREGULATION

President Reagan also sought to cut back the broad array of government regulations. Over the years, Congress had created a network of regulatory agencies. Some agencies set rules for truckers, for bus companies, for airlines. Some set rules to control pollution. Some set rules to protect workers' safety or to assure consumers that their food and drugs were wholesome and effective.

Americans were sharply divided over the merits of government regulations. Supporters said regulations were essential to protect the public or the environment and to restrain the excesses of businesses. Critics said regulations interfered with free enterprise and placed added costs on consumers, businesses, and taxpayers.

The critics began to make headway during the 1970's. President Carter got Congress's approval to reduce or end regulation of the transportation and communication industries. This process, known as *deregulation*, began in 1978. Carter also encouraged regulatory agencies to be more flexible in applying their rules.

President Reagan pushed for further deregulation, especially in banking. His appointees to some regulatory agencies made no secret of their desire to see the agencies abolished entirely. The Reagan administration cut back regulations to protect the environment, to fight discrimination, to protect consumers and workers, and to control business practices.

Deregulation meant different things to different people. To a group of wheat growers in Montana, it meant higher freight rates on the state's only railroad. To people in small-town America, it meant fewer buses or airline flights each day. Sometimes it meant no service at all. But other people benefited from deregulation. Airlines engaged in fierce competition on busy routes. Between cities like New York, Miami, and Los Angeles, fare wars slashed prices. Enthusiastic travelers took more frequent trips and still saved money.

While businesses generally favored deregulation, some business people and many union members disliked it. Truckers found themselves hustling more and earning less. Airline and bus companies sometimes went bankrupt in the face of stiff new competition. As companies struggled to cut costs to the bone, union and nonunion workers often found themselves taking pay cuts. Consumer groups argued that companies were now more likely to cut corners on safety and service.

REAGANOMICS

"It's time to try something different," President Reagan had said, when talking about how the nation's economy should be run. What Reagan and 34-year-old Budget Direc-

tor David Stockman came up with, Reaganomics, was indeed different.

The traditional conservative approach to balancing the budget is to cut spending, raise taxes, or both. President Reagan cut spending in social programs, such as education and welfare, and even tried to eliminate some departments altogether. But at the same time, military spending had been increased, and the result was an increase, rather than a decrease in overall spending.

When it came to taxes, the President and Stockman promoted a theory known as *supply-side* economics. It called for a tax cut, rather than an increase. They argued that this approach would stimulate the economy by allowing workers to bring home more of what they earned. Since consumers would — theoretically — spend, save, and invest more, businesses would benefit by being able to increase their investments. With the boom in spending, earnings would increase, and the taxes on the increased earnings would increase government income and help to balance the budget.

Supply-side economics, with its focus on providing incentives to those who supply goods and services to the economy, was not without its critics. George Bush, who was to become Reagan's vice president, dismissed the theory as "voodoo economics" in 1980 as he campaigned against Reagan for the Republican presidential nomination.

When it came down to the bottom line, Reagan's and Stockman's program had proved a failure. Businesses were not as eager as had been anticipated to invest their tax savings in new improvements. The stock market fell as interest rates remained high. In 1981 and 1982, the economy went through a deep recession. Government income did not rise as had been expected. Reagan was forced to ask Congress for more budget cuts.

Stockman embarrassed the administration by expressing his doubts in some aspects of the economic program. In an interview, he claimed the program had been put together too fast, and said "the administration didn't add up all the numbers." Stockman was called to the Oval Office. He emerged with a public apology and a reaffirmation of his confidence in Reaganomics.

However, even Reagan's devotion to the supply-side theory would waver. By 1982 it was obvious that budget deficits were rising even faster than Reagan's advisers had forecast. Reagan consented to small tax increases in 1982 and 1984. One measure forced people to pay a higher percentage of their earnings in Social Security taxes, thus warding off a looming crisis in Social Security financing.

Meanwhile, the budget deficit got bigger and bigger. In its first six years the Reagan administration spent about $1 trillion more than it took in. That meant a doubling of the national debt. The deficit now exceeded the combined deficits of all U.S. presidents from Franklin D. Roosevelt through Jimmy Carter. Democrats did not hesitate to point out the irony. Ronald Reagan, the avowed foe of budget deficits, was the biggest deficit spender of all time.

Political leaders groped for a way to reduce the budget deficits. President Reagan sup-

ported a balanced-budget amendment that would bar deficit spending except in times of war. While the amendment won widespread support, Congress chose an alternate way of attacking deficits.

The Gramm-Rudman-Hollings Act of 1985 set targets for reducing the deficit in annual steps and eliminating it entirely by 1991. Under the act, Congress would have to cut spending or raise taxes to meet the targets. If it failed to do either, or if a president vetoed Congress's efforts, spending cuts would be imposed automatically. The act was designed to break a deadlock between Congress and the President, both reluctant to make choices that were bound to be unpopular. In 1986 the U.S. Supreme Court ruled part of the Gramm-Rudman-Hollings Act unconstitutional. However, the act's main provisions remained in effect.

Deficits were one of many problems that plagued the Reagan administration. Unemployment was another. It touched levels it had not reached since the Great Depression, topping 10 percent during 1982.

Despite those troubles, the Reagan administration scored economic successes on other fronts. Most important, it tamed inflation. Sharply rising prices had been a problem since the late 1960's. Businesses had trouble planning for the future. Workers found that their wages sometimes bought less than the year before. In 1980, the last year of the Carter administration, consumer prices rose by a shocking 13.5 percent. By the mid-1980's, however, the inflation rate had dropped to between three and five percent. Economic

The President, Vice President Bush (left), and House Speaker O'Neill.

TAX REFORM

In 1984 a liberal group published a report saying that 128 large corporations paid no federal income taxes. The list read like a who's who of big business. Many people who learned of the report were outraged. David H. Pryor, a Democratic senator from Arkansas, recalled: "We'd all go home to town meetings and you'd see some postal clerk get up and say, 'Why is General Dynamics paying no taxes and I'm paying 30 percent of everything I make to the government?' You couldn't answer a question like that except by saying, 'I'm going to go back to Washington and do something about that. I'm going to plug those loopholes.'"

A *loophole* is any tax rule that gives specific taxpayers a tax reduction. For example, one loophole provided that companies paid lower taxes when they bought energy-saving equipment. The argument for loopholes is that they allow the government to encourage practices that it deems socially useful. The argument against loopholes is that they favor one set of taxpayers over all the others.

Complaints about loopholes had been made for years. Periodically, members of Congress would vow to defy "special interests" and remove the loopholes. But somehow nothing much changed. Each new tax bill seemed to have more loopholes than the one before.

In the mid-1980's, however, a populist "tax revolt" was gaining strength. Equally important, the solidarity that business people had shown in supporting the loophole-riddled system was breaking down. Many of the existing loopholes favored traditional industries like oil

experts said that the administration seemed to have broken the back of inflation, for the time being at least.

and steel. Relatively few of them helped the new service and high-tech industries. Leaders of those newer industries supported reform of the tax system.

A number of tax-reform plans vied for support. At first, experienced observers thought the plans had little chance. Lobbyists pestered Congress to restore one loophole after another. Tax reform seemed to be dead or dying. Malcolm Wallop, a Republican senator from Wyoming, compared tax-reform legislation to a sick horse. "If we had a horse this sick back home," he said, "we'd take it out and shoot it."

Support for tax reform was so strong, however, that the "horse" recovered. The Senate and House passed roughly similar bills in 1986 and set to work on a final draft. The tax reform had many important features. It wiped out numerous loopholes (although it did retain others). It simplified the tax structure. (Instead of 15 "rate brackets," with taxes ranging from 11 percent to 50 percent, depending on income level, it had just a few broad brack-

ets.) It excused millions of "working poor" people from paying any income tax at all. Said one economist: "There will be pain from these changes, but it's worth the pain because it levels the playing field."

Both the Republicans and the Democrats claimed credit for the most sweeping tax reform in a generation. In fact, reform was only possible because both parties worked together. The result was a net gain for the President, however, because it furthered his goal of reducing the federal government's influence over the nation's economy.

U.S. COURTS: CHANGING THE GUARD

Like other presidents, Ronald Reagan used the power of appointment to make sure that his ideas would affect U.S. policy long after he had left office. He appointed hundreds of federal judges who shared his own vision. Perhaps of greatest importance were his appointments to the U.S. Supreme Court. As the pinnacle of the federal judicial system, the

Justice O'Connor is sworn in by Chief Justice Burger (left).

Supreme Court has the last word in interpreting laws and the Constitution.

During the 1980 campaign Reagan had promised to appoint a woman to the Court. He kept his word. When Justice Potter Stewart retired in 1981, the President chose Sandra Day O'Connor, a judge on the Arizona Court of Appeals, to take his place.

It was a historic moment. No woman had ever served on the Supreme Court. Although O'Connor's record suggested she held conservative views that were compatible with the President's vision, many liberals praised the appointment. Members of the New Right, however, criticized O'Connor for having supported abortion rights in certain cases.

O'Connor joined what was called the Burger Court — after Chief Justice Warren Burger. When Burger had been appointed by President Nixon in 1969, he was expected to lead the Court in a sharp trend away from the liberal decisions of the 1950's and 1960's. But some of its decisions were called liberal, because they expanded individual rights (as in the abortion rights decision of 1973). Other decisions were called conservative because they strengthened the powers of the police or other authorities. It was hard to pin a clear label on the Burger Court, or on many of the individual justices. For example, while O'Connor often sided with the Court's conservative wing, she occasionally switched to the side of the liberals on a specific issue like women's rights. On such occasions, she formed part of the Court's middle, or "swing," faction.

In 1986, President Reagan got a second chance to impose his own stamp on the Court.

Chief Justice Burger retired. President Reagan nominated one of the Court's most forceful conservatives, Justice William Rehnquist, to become Chief Justice of the United States. Reagan named a judge from the U.S. Court of Appeals, Antonin Scalia, to the seat that Rehnquist vacated. Scalia, the first Italian-American to be chosen for the Court, was widely praised for his sharp mind and legal skills. He was also an outspoken conservative.

Reagan's supporters hoped the new Rehnquist Court would take a sharp turn toward conservatism. At first glance, that did not seem likely. After all, Burger had been a conservative. The Court's conservative wing was neither larger nor smaller than before. Predictions about future Court trends are notoriously risky. History shows that Supreme Court justices have often surprised even the presidents who appointed them.

SECTION RECAP

1. What were the main reasons federal spending increased under the Reagan administration, despite the spending cutbacks? Give an example of an entitlement program.

2. What are regulatory agencies? What did their supporters and critics have to say about them?

3. How did supply-side economists propose to stimulate the economy? What was the actual effect of this strategy?

4. What were three important features of the tax reform bills passed in 1986? How did the reform finally became possible?

2 Reasserting U.S. Power

Nicaraguan children play on a Soviet tank.

When President Reagan took office in 1981, Americans were still debating the lessons of the Vietnam War. Some said the United States lost the war because of a failure of will. According to this view, if Americans had united behind their leaders and if they had "fought to win," the U.S. side would have prevailed. Others said the war showed that U.S. power had definite limits. Many who held this view argued that Congress should restrain the presidents' war-making powers to help avoid "another Vietnam."

In campaigning for office, Ronald Reagan declared the Vietnam War to have been "a noble cause." As President, he sought to increase presidential power to act forcefully in what a chief executive believes to be the national interest. Reagan did not always get his way with Congress, but he gave the United States a more activist foreign policy. Reagan's supporters said he had ended a "paralysis" that dated to Vietnam. Critics said he had taken risks that might plunge the United States into future wars.

TAKING SIDES IN CENTRAL AMERICA

President Reagan went farther than President Carter in seeking to block the spread of leftist revolutions in Central America. He stepped up aid to the pro-U.S. government in El Salvador. He called the Sandinista government in Nicaragua a Communist dictatorship. First secretly and then openly, President Reagan armed rebels who sought to overthrow the Sandinistas. The United States conducted a series of military maneuvers in Honduras, which borders Nicaragua and El Salvador. It forged closer ties with Honduras, Costa Rica, and Guatemala. It stepped up naval activity in the Caribbean.

President Reagan accused the Soviet Union and Cuba of using Nicaragua's government to funnel military aid to leftist rebels in El Salvador. He argued that Nicaragua threatened to become "a Soviet military beachhead inside our defense perimeters." The President's warnings were grim. If Americans did not help Central Americans to block the threat at once, the Communist tide would soon be lapping at the United States' southern border. "Desperate Latin peoples by the millions would begin fleeing north into the cities of the southern United States, or to wherever some hope of freedom remained," said Reagan.

Many Americans doubted the President's theories and questioned his policies. Some said the Sandinistas were not Communists at all, but leftists who were struggling to build a democracy under desperate circumstances. They argued that Nicaraguan elections held in 1984 were freer than elections held by the pro-U.S. government of El Salvador. Others argued that even if the Sandinistas were Communists and even if they had rigged the elections, they were no threat to their neighbors.

Members of Congress were divided. Some warned that U.S. actions were driving the Sandinistas closer to the Soviets. They said the more President Reagan committed the United States to opposing the Sandinistas, the greater the risk that U.S. troops might eventually have to be sent. Did Americans really want "another Vietnam?" they asked. Others strongly supported the President. They said the United States must overcome "the Vietnam syndrome" and fight for what it believed in.

The anti-Sandinista rebels were generally called *contras*, from the Spanish for "counter-revolutionaries." President Reagan called the rebels "freedom fighters" or "the democratic resistance." The rebels included people from all walks of life and former Sandinistas who had switched sides. They also included Nicaraguan military officers who had served the old Somoza dictatorship. In Congress, critics charged that some contra leaders smuggled drugs on the side. Other members insisted that the contra leaders were men of principle who wanted only to rid their country of a cruel dictatorship.

At first, Congress resisted the President's policies. After learning that the CIA was secretly supporting contra groups, Congress voted in 1982 to ban U.S. aid from being used to overthrow Nicaragua's government. In 1985 Congress lifted that ban and approved $27 million in aid to the contras. But Congress specified that the aid must be non-military. Not until 1986 did President Reagan win congressional support for military aid.

What made Congress change its mind? Some members cited reports of repression within Nicaragua. Sandinista leaders had closed down the main opposition newspaper and cracked down in other ways. Others cited administration reports of stepped-up Soviet military aid to Nicaragua. Just as important, perhaps, was a fear of the political fallout if Nicaragua's revolution should spread. No one wanted to be accused of having "lost" Central America.

Nicaragua's government, accusing the United States of aggression, had taken its case to the World Court, an arm of the United Nations. U.S. leaders argued that the court had no power to hear the case. They declined to take part — a decision that some Americans criticized as "an admission of guilt." In 1986 the World Court ruled that the United States had broken international law by arming the contras and taking part in military attacks. It said the United States had an obligation to pay for the damages it had caused. U.S. officials rejected the verdict, saying it was based on misinformation and faulty reasoning. Since the court had no way to enforce its verdict, Nicaragua seemed unlikely to collect on its claim.

Despite the activist U.S. policy, Central America remained mired in conflict. In El Salvador, the U.S.-backed government seemed to have grown stronger, but civil war continued. Four Latin American nations (called the Contadora group) sought to promote a peace settlement involving the United States, Nicaragua, El Salvador, and other parties. But talks dragged on with little progress.

EYES ON THE CARIBBEAN

President Reagan sought to link Central America and the Caribbean more closely to the United States. He offered a package of trade and aid to 28 countries of the region. The President's Caribbean Basin Initiative passed Congress in July 1983.

Under the legislation, the United States abolished *duties* (taxes on trade) for 12 years on a wide range of products that might be sold here by Caribbean and Central American nations. (Some products, such as textiles and footwear, were left out in order to protect U.S. producers.) The idea was to encourage U.S. and other companies to invest in the region. Supporters said the program would boost private enterprise and raise standards of living. It might also undermine Cuban influence in the region.

The initiative had side effects, however. It ended a special preference enjoyed by the Caribbean island of Puerto Rico. As a U.S. commonwealth whose people are U.S. citizens, Puerto Rico has had duty-free access to U.S. markets for a long time. After 1983 it had to share that access with independent nations of the region. At the same time, Puerto Rico was losing federal funds under President Reagan's cutbacks. Puerto Rican leaders struggled to make the island more self-sufficient in the face of severe economic troubles.

Meanwhile, violence flared in the Caribbean island nation of Grenada, about 100 miles

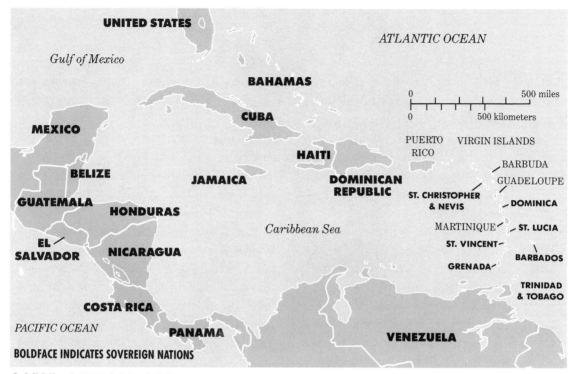

LATIN AMERICA AND THE CARIBBEAN

north of Venezuela. On October 19, 1983, military rebels killed the country's Cuban-backed, leftist prime minister and several members of his cabinet. A new government, further to the left, took power.

Six days later, about 7,000 U.S. troops staged a predawn invasion of Grenada. Troops from seven small Caribbean nations took part. Grenadan soldiers and Cubans fought back, but within four days the invaders had won. Officials put the death toll at 20 Americans, 24 Cubans, and 44 Grenadans.

At first, U.S. officials said their goal had been to protect the lives of some 1,000 Americans on the island. But they set out to give Grenada a new, pro-American government. Most Grenadans seemed to welcome the intervention.

On the international scene, however, the U.S.-led intervention met wide condemnation. The United Nations General Assembly passed a resolution deploring the invasion.

Late in 1984, Grenadans elected a new, moderate government. In 1986 cheering crowds welcomed President Reagan to the island nation.

CONFRONTING THE SOVIETS

President Reagan turned up the heat on U.S.-Soviet relations. He accelerated the U.S. arms buildup that began under President Carter. He spoke out strongly against Soviet policies and against the very nature of the Soviet system. He played down — for a time — efforts to reach new agreements with Soviet leaders.

The arms buildup was crucial to Reagan's strategy. Like Carter, Reagan argued that the Soviets had pulled ahead in the arms race. He talked of a "window of vulnerability" — a risky period during which a Soviet attack might wipe out so many U.S. weapons that the United States could not strike back effectively. Critics questioned whether such a "window" really existed. If it did, a massive U.S. buildup quickly closed it. By 1983 a presidential commission was saying that the United States had sufficient power to deter any Soviet attack.

President Reagan's most spectacular move was to step up research on space-based defenses. As Reagan described them, such defenses might include orbiting satellites that could aim powerful laser beams to knock out Soviet missiles soon after launch. In announcing the plan in 1983, President Reagan described space-based defenses as a "shield" that would make nuclear weapons "impotent and obsolete." He called his plan the Strategic Defense Initiative, or SDI. Because of its futuristic trappings, most people called the plan Star Wars.

Scientists were not at all sure that Star War defenses were possible. But thousands of researchers set to work on an array of different projects. Experts said the program would not advance past the research stage until at least the mid-1990's. Estimates of the cost ranged from $26 billion to $90 billion and up. That was for research alone. Actually building the system would cost far more.

Star Wars was only one of many military programs that caused U.S. defense spending to skyrocket in the 1980's. The defense budget rose five to eight percent a year — not counting inflation. By 1987 the annual defense budget had grown to about $300 billion, almost twice what it had been in 1980.

As the U.S. military buildup went on, President Reagan lashed out verbally at the Soviet Union and its leaders. "They are the focus of evil in the modern world," the President declared in a speech to a convention of evangelical Protestants in 1983. Later that year, when a Soviet jet shot down a South Korean airliner that crossed Soviet territory in East Asia, Reagan accused the Soviets of a massacre.

The airliner incident was one of the most serious of the Reagan years. Korean Air Lines Flight 007, a jumbo jet, was flying from New York to Seoul, South Korea, by way of Alaska. It carried 269 men, women, and children. Among the passengers was U.S. Representative Lawrence P. McDonald, a Georgia Democrat, chairman of the rightist John Birch Society. All 269 were killed. Soviet leaders charged that the plane was on a spy mission, helping the U.S. military to probe Soviet defenses. U.S. leaders dismissed the charge as preposterous, and the International Civil Aviation Organization concluded that the plane had strayed over Soviet territory by accident.

As he entered his second term, President Reagan expressed more interest in arms control and other talks with the Soviets. But progress was slow. The Soviets seemed eager to reach an agreement that would slow down U.S. Star Wars research. U.S. proposals stressed other goals, such as a sharp reduction in offensive weapons.

U.S.-Soviet relations were complicated by a rapid turnover in Soviet leaders. Leonid Brezhnev died in November 1982. His successor, Yuri V. Andropov, died in February 1984. The next leader, Konstantin U. Chernenko, died in March 1985. Finally a younger man, 54-year-old Mikhail S. Gorbachev, took over. Gorbachev had a new, less-ponderous style. He sought to pep up the lagging Soviet economic system and establish new contacts with Western leaders.

President Reagan met Gorbachev for the first time in Geneva, Switzerland, in 1985. While the Geneva summit led to no sudden improvement in U.S.-Soviet relations, U.S. leaders felt it had been worthwhile. The two leaders met again at Reykjavik, Iceland, in the autumn of 1986. This time the discussions focused almost entirely on the issues of arms control. President Reagan proposed the elimination of all ballistic missiles by 1996, and the two sides appeared close to an agreement. Yet at least one sticking point remained: U.S. insistence on pursuing SDI, and Soviet opposition to this plan. The two sides continued their negotiations.

PROBLEMS FOR SOVIET LEADERS

Soviet leaders grappled with several major problems in the 1980's. Two problems in particular drew U.S. attention.

One was the continuing war in Afghanistan. Soviet troop strength there climbed to

Gorbachev and Reagan conclude a summit conference.

120,000 as Soviet and Afghan government forces fought the U.S.-backed Muslim resistance. Disunity hampered the rebels' effectiveness. In 1985, the seven main rebel groups formed an alliance. The United States stepped up its aid to the rebels. But neither side seemed to be able to wear down the other.

A second Soviet worry was caused by unrest in the East European country of Poland. Under pressure from striking workers, Poland's Communist government announced in 1980 that workers could form their own independent labor unions. Previously, all unions had been controlled by Communist authorities. A number of new unions sprang up. The largest, called Solidarity, gained massive support from the public and from leaders of Poland's powerful Roman Catholic Church. Solidarity demanded sweeping changes in Poland's way of life.

For a time it seemed that Poland's Communist system was tottering. U.S. leaders sought to encourage the trend to freer institutions. But they worried that Soviet troops might sweep into Poland in a repeat of the 1968 crackdown on Czechoslovakia's Communist government. That did not happen. Polish authorities acted on their own. In December 1981 they banned Solidarity and arrested its leaders, including a shipyard worker named Lech Walesa. (Later released, Walesa won the Nobel Peace Prize for 1983.)

Events in Afghanistan and Poland drew varied U.S. reactions. You will recall that the Soviet move into Afghanistan in 1979 had led President Carter to ban U.S. grain sales to the Soviets (page 292). U.S. farmers pro-

tested that the ban cost them dearly. Keeping a campaign pledge, President Reagan lifted the ban in 1981. But he applied new sanctions the next year, saying that Soviet pressure had forced Poland's crackdown on Solidarity. This time the sanctions banned the sale of oil and gas equipment that the Soviets wanted for a major new pipeline.

COMBATING TERRORISM

The 1980's saw an apparent surge in the use of *terrorism* in international affairs. Terrorism is the use of violence to spread fear in advancing a political cause. Terrorists use such methods as assassinations, bombings, and hijackings.

Several world figures — including the leaders of Egypt (1981), India (1984), and Sweden (1986) — died at the hands of assassins. Another assassin wounded Pope John Paul II in 1981. The Pope recovered. Those four incidents appear to have been unconnected, although in some cases the motives were unclear. Why, for example, would a right-wing Turkish gunman have wanted to kill the Pope? The gunman, convicted by an Italian court, later charged that Bulgarian (and probably Soviet) intelligence agents had masterminded a plot against the Pope. Supposedly, this was to snuff out resistance to Communist rule in the Pope's homeland of Poland. A sensational trial ended in Italy in 1986 without confirming the gunman's charges.

Terrorism was employed by groups of the right and of the left, by small groups and by governments. Terrorism attributed to right-wing groups included bombings of abortion

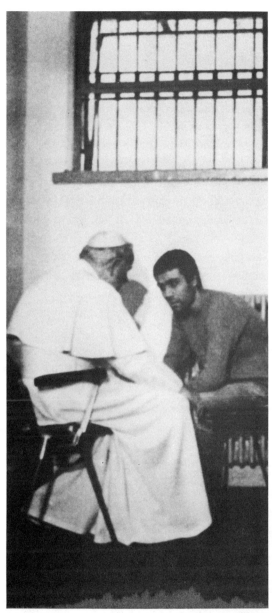

Pope John Paul II
and his convicted attacker
meet in prison.

clinics and attacks on Arab-Americans in the United States. Terrorism attributed to left-wing groups included attacks on U.S. diplomats and soldiers in Latin America, Europe, and elsewhere.

Many highly publicized incidents of terror were organized by groups fighting for the Arab cause against Israel. In 1983, a truck packed with explosives demolished a U.S. Marine headquarters in Beirut, Lebanon. Some 240 Marines died in the rubble. In 1985, hijackers seized an Italian cruise ship, the *Achille Lauro*, in the Mediterranean. The one casualty among the 80 passengers and crew members was an American tourist, shot in the head and dumped over the side of the ship. At Christmastime that same year, gunmen firing automatic weapons sprayed travelers with bullets in simultaneous attacks on airports in Rome and Vienna. Fourteen people, including an 11-year-old American girl, were killed.

U.S. leaders were frustrated by their inability to protect Americans abroad. They wanted to strike back at terrorists who harmed Americans, but it was hard to know where to strike. A number of separate groups carried out terrorist attacks. Some seemed to have links to Palestinian guerrillas or to the governments of nations like Iran, Syria, and Libya. Others operated from bases in France, West Germany, and other European countries. All these groups saw the United States as a supporter of Israel and as an "imperialist" power. Most were shadowy organizations that had no fixed bases.

U.S. leaders believed many of the terrorist groups worked together from time to time.

But proof was hard to come by. Finally, U.S. leaders focused on the North African nation of Libya as a key supporter of terrorist networks. Libya's ruler, Muammar Qaddafi had often praised terrorist acts. He had denounced the United States and offered refuge to ultra-leftist forces.

The United States and Libya had many reasons for conflict. Before Qaddafi came to power in a coup in 1969, the United States had a major air base in Libya. Qaddafi had been supporting a rebel movement against the Western-backed government of Chad, Libya's neighbor to the south. Moreover, the United States had rejected Libya's claim to a part of the Mediterranean called the Gulf of Sidra, along Libya's northern coast. In 1981, Libyan warplanes attacked two U.S. Navy F-14s in the disputed zone. The U.S. warplanes shot down the Libyan planes. Later that year,

U.S. officials claimed Qaddafi had sent "hit squads" to the United States to assassinate top government officials.

That was the background to a new confrontation that followed a terrorist attack in 1986 on a German discotheque frequented by U.S. military personnel. U.S. officials said they had "indisputable" evidence of a Libyan connection. Denouncing Qaddafi as a "mad dog," President Reagan ordered bombing raids against the Libyan capital and four other sites. U.S. warplanes struck at night and caused extensive damage. When the smoke had cleared, more than 50 people were dead. Among them were Qaddafi's adopted infant daughter and two U.S. airmen.

U.S. polls showed strong public support for

Libyan officials show off a bomb dropped during the U.S. air raid.

the President's action. Some called for further moves. But the U.S. air raids sparked an outburst of anti-American feeling in countries like Britain, where marchers carried portraits of Reagan labeled "Mad Dog No.2." The British government supported the U.S. strikes and had authorized the use of U.S. fighter-bombers based on British soil. On the other hand, France had denied permission for the warplanes to fly across its territory. It was ironic, then, that polls showed strong support for the U.S. action in France and strong opposition in Britain.

U.S. officials had no illusions that the strike against Libya would put an end to terrorism. They declared that Libya was only one of the many countries backing international terrorism. But officials hoped that the U.S. attack would make terrorists think twice before harming Americans. Said President Reagan: "We have done what we had to do. If necessary, we shall do it again."

THE SEETHING MIDEAST

Terrorism was one of a number of problems confronting U.S. policy-makers in the Middle East. Two other problems drew special attention.

One was a bitter war that started in 1980 between the Arab ally of Iraq and the Persian nation of Iran. Neither was friendly with the United States. But U.S. officials feared that the war might spread and disrupt oil production all along the Persian Gulf. Arab oil-producing countries like Saudi Arabia and Kuwait, allies of the United States, were backing their Arab neighbors in Iraq. U.S.

officials had a second fear, too. They worried about the stability of the Saudi Arabian and other Arab monarchies. They did not want Iranian-style Islamic fundamentalism (see page 301) to overthrow more pro-U.S. rulers.

The Persian Gulf War began when Iraq invaded Iran. By the end of the war's second year, Iranian troops had driven back the Iraqis. Fighting raged back and forth along the border. From time to time, both sides sent planes to strike merchant ships — even "neutral" ships — in the Persian Gulf. Iraq wanted to stop Iran from shipping oil to earn money to continue the war. Iran wanted to stop military supplies from reaching Iraq. U.S. officials protested when their ships were struck or when gunboats stopped ships for inspections. But all sides seemed to want to avoid open confrontations that might expand the war.

A second and bigger Mideast problem was Israeli-Arab hostility. Despite its 1979 accord with Egypt (page 299), Israel faced many enemies. In 1981 Muslim fundamentalists assassinated Egyptian President Anwar Sadat, whom they considered a traitor to the Arab cause. Sadat's successor, Hosni Mubarak, seemed notably cooler toward Israel. However, Israel and Egypt remained at peace.

U.S. leaders stepped up aid to Israel and Egypt while seeking ways to widen the "peace process." But Mideast tensions built up, fed by chaos in the small Arab nation of Lebanon, just north of Israel. Civil war between Lebanese Christian and Muslim factions had been raging since 1975. Syria and Palestinian groups also had fighting forces in Lebanon. Conditions verged on anarchy.

Seeking to calm the chaos and put an end to Palestinian attacks on Israeli border villages, Israel invaded Lebanon in 1982. Israeli troops drove all the way to the capital, Beirut. They trapped Palestinian forces loyal to Yasir Arafat, head of the Palestine Liberation Organization (PLO). The PLO had to abandon its Lebanese bases and move to the more distant nation of Tunisia.

U.S. officials denounced the Israeli invasion, but thought it opened new prospects for peace. President Reagan called for negotiations between Israel and Jordan, with Jordan's government representing Palestinians. The aim, said Reagan, would be some sort of self-government in association with Jordan for the part of Palestine known as the West Bank. (The West Bank was under Jordanian rule until Israeli troops occupied it in 1967.)

Reagan's plan faced many obstacles. The PLO and other Palestinian groups insisted on a fully-independent Palestine centered on the West Bank. Many Israelis, on the other hand, vowed never to give up the West Bank, and their government permitted large numbers of Israelis to settle there.

To help persuade Israel to withdraw its troops from Lebanon, the United States and other Western nations agreed to send token forces to police a cease-fire there. The U.S. Marines who had been killed in Beirut in the 1983 truck bombing were part of that force. Criticized at home, President Reagan decided not to subject U.S. troops to further danger. He pulled the last U.S. forces out of Lebanon early in 1984. The Lebanese civil war raged on. The Middle East cauldron kept boiling.

WHAT ABOUT SOUTHERN AFRICA?

Turmoil in southern Africa grew worse in the 1980's. Rebels continued battling for the independence of Namibia (page 299). Meanwhile, the white-run government of South Africa faced growing resistance from blacks.

The Reagan administration said President Carter had been ineffective in influencing South Africa because he had taken a hostile stance toward the white government. Reagan officials said they would use persuasion rather than coercion to prod South Africa to make reforms. Officials called their policy "constructive engagement."

The United States sought to link the conflict in Namibia to a civil war in neighboring Angola. Angola had a leftist government that supported Namibian rebels fighting for independence from South Africa. The Angolan government had invited in Cuban troops to help protect a key oil-producing area of Angola. U.S. leaders wanted the Cuban troops to leave Angola. The Americans decided on a "carrot-and-stick" policy. They would offer the "carrot" of trying to get South Africa to agree to Namibian independence. That was something Angola's government wanted. U.S. officials would use the "stick" of sending aid to a rebel group called UNITA that was fighting against Angola's government. That was something Angola's rulers did *not* want.

But the Reagan administration faced a problem. In 1976, Congress had voted to bar U.S. aid to the UNITA rebels. President Reagan asked for a change in the law. In 1985 Congress agreed. The next year UNITA leader Jonas Savimbi visited the United

Bishop Desmond Tutu, outspoken critic of South African apartheid.

While it was trying to influence events in Angola and Namibia, the U.S. government denounced South Africa's cruel apartheid system and quietly urged the South African government to make changes. Critics said U.S. urgings were too quiet. One outspoken critic was a black Anglican bishop (later archbishop) named Desmond Tutu, who won the Nobel Peace Prize for 1984. Tutu said black South Africans saw the United States as "collaborating with this racist regime."

In 1983, South Africa's white leaders began a series of steps designed to ease the rigors of apartheid. Such steps included political rights for Asians and people of mixed race, but not for blacks. They included an end to "pass laws" that had been used to keep whites and blacks almost totally separate. But the changes seemed to satisfy no one. White South African rightists were outraged. Blacks called the changes insignificant. Rioting spread through many of the country's black townships. Opponents of the government planted bombs and mines to blast military and civilian targets.

Meanwhile, an international movement against apartheid gained strength. In the United States, blacks and whites carried signs ("Apartheid Kills") outside the South African embassy. They staged sit-ins at the offices of U.S. companies operating in South Africa. They boycotted brands of gasoline and soft drinks that had links to South Africa. They demanded that universities and other institutions sell stocks in companies that did business in South Africa.

Congress began to debate official measures

States and got a hero's welcome. Top officials hailed him as a "freedom fighter." Once again, CIA funds began to flow to the Angolan rebels. In a speech announcing what came to be called the Reagan Doctrine, President Reagan promised to support "freedom fighters" around the world.

against apartheid. Many countries of the world called for sanctions, such as an *embargo* (cut-off) of all trade with South Africa. Stiff sanctions won support from many members of Congress, including a majority in the House. Supporters said sanctions were the most effective method of forcing the South African government to give up apartheid. President Reagan ordered limited sanctions in 1985. But he and others criticized all-out sanctions, saying such measures would hurt South African blacks more than whites. They also said sanctions would anger South African whites and stiffen resistance to change.

The debate over sanctions helped to point up the strong U.S. presence in South Africa. Some 280 U.S. companies did business there. U.S.-owned factories made products that ranged from cars to cookies, from drill bits to textbooks.

The debate also highlighted South Africa's importance as a source of strategic metals. The United States gets much of its platinum, chromium, and manganese from South African mines. Those metals are vital to the production of steel, airplanes, computer components, and other products. Aside from South Africa, the main supplies of such materials lie within the Soviet Union.

Perhaps most of all, the debate raised questions about the future of South Africa itself. Was slow, peaceful change still possible? Was violent, revolutionary change inevitable? In either case, where did U.S. interests lie and how could those interests be advanced? And what about the people of South Africa — black and white, Asian and mixed-race? How

could *their* interests best be served? There were many hard questions, and no easy answers.

THE THIRD WORLD: SINKING DEEPER IN DEBT

Other hard questions concerned the Third World, made up of the many countries that were struggling to climb out of poverty. During the 1980's many Third World countries slipped backward. Their populations grew larger. Their incomes grew smaller.

Most Third World countries depended for income on sales of primary products, largely minerals and agricultural crops. But prices of primary products swung up and down — often down. They did not keep pace with prices of manufactured products that Third World countries imported from industrial nations.

Some Third World countries received help through foreign-aid programs of industrial nations. But the United States and other countries had cut back many of the aid programs started in the 1960's. More and more, Third World countries had to borrow the money they needed to build up their economies. Sometimes they borrowed from international bodies such as the World Bank and the International Monetary Fund (IMF). Sometimes they borrowed from governments or from big banks.

The largest loans went to the countries with valuable resources like oil, iron, and rich farmland. Lenders figured such countries were good risks because they had good prospects for building up industry. The money they earned from new industries would help pay back the loans in future years. Countries like Mexico, Brazil, and Venezuela borrowed billions of dollars in the 1970's.

But hard times hit in the 1980's. Industrial nations in North America and Europe went through recessions. They bought less from the Third World. Prices of primary products dipped lower. Even oil prices, which had soared to record heights in the 1970's, plunged to very low levels. The drop in oil prices had disastrous effects on Mexico, Venezuela, and other oil-producing nations.

Many Third World countries were unable even to pay interest on existing loans. When they asked for new loans to help them keep up payments, lenders balked. But something had to give. If Third World countries *defaulted* (did not keep up payments) on their debts, banks and other lenders would lose money — big money. The resulting crisis might harm the industrial nations as well as the Third World. In fact, industrial nations were already losing, because debt-stricken nations could no longer afford to buy the industrial nations' goods.

In 1985, U.S. Treasury Secretary James A. Baker III proposed one possible solution. It was a solution that emphasized the Reagan administration's free-market ideology. First, said Baker, borrowing nations would have to change policies that interfered with free enterprise. Then, the industrial nations would get the World Bank and other agencies to make new loans totalling $9 billion to bail out the debt-ridden nations. Those loans would reassure private bankers, who would chip in

another $20 billion or so. By pumping more money into struggling economies, Baker hoped to revive prosperity not only in the Third World but in industrial nations as well.

Baker's plan did not please everyone. Some people, especially in Third World countries, said the industrial nations seemed to be trying to dictate how others should run their economies. Many said the policies would add to the hardship and suffering among the poorest people in the countries involved. But the industrial nations seemed willing to try Baker's plan, or something like it. Unless there was effective action, the world's debt crisis threatened to grow worse and worse.

SECTION RECAP

1. Who were the contras? What made Congress change its mind in supplying military aid to the contras?

2. List at least three reasons for conflict between the United States and Libya. What did U.S. officials hope would be the result of the strike against Libya?

3. Why did Israel invade Lebanon in 1982? What was the U.S. reaction, and what did President Reagan do after the invasion?

4. Why did President Reagan criticize the idea of all-out sanctions against South Africa for its apartheid system? What were some of the U.S. interests in South Africa?

5. Why did recessions in industrial nations hurt the economies of Third World nations? What was James Baker's proposed solution to the problem?

3 Facing the Future: The Great American Debate

The Statue of Liberty, restored and celebrated.

Americans of many colors and many national origins flocked to New York City over the Fourth of July weekend of 1986. They sang "God Bless America," watched spectacular fireworks, bought souvenirs, cheered the "grand old lady," the 100-year-old Statue of Liberty. Liberty Weekend was an old-fashioned, patriotic celebration of its newly-restored splendor. In one of the weekend's many speeches, President Reagan declared: "Our work as Americans can never be said to be truly done until every man, woman, and child shares in our gift — in our liberty."

"Never truly done," the President said, and it was true — nothing was *ever* "truly done." Decisions made one year might be changed the next. Problems solved today might erupt again tomorrow. As the Reagan years drew to a close, Americans contemplated an array of unsettled questions that beckoned them toward the future.

AFTER REAGAN: MORE REAGANISM?

The Reagan Revolution sent new energy pulsing through the Republican party. Party leaders interpreted Reagan's 1980 victory as a "mandate for change." When Reagan won by an even larger margin in 1984, Republican leaders said a fundamental realignment in U.S. voting patterns was underway. Ever since the New Deal, a majority of the nation's voters had identified themselves as Democrats. Now, even in the traditionally Democratic South, the Republican party was making major gains.

The Republicans gained a boost from the New Right, often called the Religious Right. Made up mainly of white, fundamentalist Protestants, the New Right was especially strong in the South. Ronald Reagan had won solid backing from the New Right for his stands against abortion and in favor of school prayer. Republican leaders looked to the New Right for continued support once the Reagan era had ended.

The Democrats, meanwhile, seemed to be going through a period of soul-searching. The party had always been noted for its many bickering factions — liberal and conservative, pro-labor and pro-business, northern and southern. In the face of the Reagan Revolution, many leading Democrats shifted rightward. But others argued that the apparent shift to conservatism among American voters was only temporary. They urged the Democratic party to support liberal policies as it had often done in the past.

In 1984, the Democrats nominated Walter Mondale as their candidate for president. Mondale had served as vice president under Jimmy Carter. He offered a liberal alternative to many of Reagan's policies. Mondale called for maintaining many social programs of the Great Society and New Deal variety. Some critics within the Democratic party said Mondale was too liberal — too tied to "special interests" like labor unions. Others said he was too conservative, that his policies did little to serve the needs of blacks, Hispanics, and poor whites.

As his running mate, Mondale chose a woman — U.S. Representative Geraldine A. Ferraro of New York. Ferraro was the first woman to run on a major-party ticket in a presidential election. (Victoria Claflin Woodhull had been the first woman to run for president. She ran in 1872 on behalf of the Equal Rights party.) Mondale and Ferraro won only one state, Minnesota, and the District of Columbia. They got 13 electoral votes to Reagan's 525.

Were the Democrats on a permanent downhill slide? Some people thought so. But others saw possible troubles ahead for the Republicans. They pointed to polls showing that Americans who liked President Reagan often disliked Reagan's conservative policies. The 1986 elections bolstered this argument. After six years as the minority in the Senate, the Democrats took control, 55-45. Although the Democrats pledged to seek bipartisan solutions to national problems, it was hard to tell whether Reagan's ideology would remain a vital force after he left office.

FREE TRADE OR PROTECTIONISM?

A second question hanging over the future was how the United States would deal with its serious trade problems. Under Carter, the United States had run up large trade deficits. Under Reagan, those trade deficits doubled and then tripled. Year after year, U.S. purchases of foreign goods kept climbing. U.S. manufacturers were losing sales, U.S. workers were losing jobs, and industries were crying out for trade protection.

Trade protection, or *protectionism*, is the use of restrictive measures such as tariffs to shield a country's businesses from foreign competition. Protectionism is the opposite of *free trade*, which is the exchange of goods among nations without significant restrictions. Throughout its early history the United States followed a policy of protectionism to help nurture infant U.S. industries. In recent years, and especially since World War II, the United States has had a policy of free trade. It has encouraged other nations to follow free-trade policies, too, in order to open up as many markets as possible for U.S. goods.

In the late 1970's and 1980's, Americans renewed the debate over protectionism and free trade. Industries like automobiles, textiles, and steel were being hurt by imports. Managers and workers in such industries called for a variety of protective measures. They argued that other industrial nations often used government subsidies and other measures to give their industries and farmers an unfair advantage. They especially criticized Japan, which sold a great deal to the United States but bought little.

Other Americans argued for continued free trade. They warned that if the United States adopted protective measures, other nations might respond by shutting out U.S. goods. A "trade war," they said, would help no one. Companies making products like aircraft and computers still enjoyed large sales abroad, and managers and workers in those industries tended to favor continued free trade.

In the trade debates of the 1980's, the lines were blurred. Ronald Reagan ardently defended free trade, which he described as an essential part of free enterprise. Yet he sometimes fudged and approved of protective measures. For example, Reagan persuaded Japan to put quotas on its auto exports to the United States for a few years. He could argue that the measure was not protectionist because it was "voluntary" on Japan's part. But Japan had to be convinced to act.

Many Democrats, meanwhile, spoke out for stronger protective measures. They accused President Reagan of doing too little to help beleaguered U.S. industries and end large trade deficits. Trade restrictions gained broad support in Congress. But the trade debate was far from settled.

CRISIS IN FARMING

On July 4, 1986, a parade snaked through a small town in western Illinois. An 85-year-old farmer, watched. Despite the festivities, the man was troubled. "You know," he said sadly, "I sold corn in 1948 for $2.50 a bushel. My neighbor sold some the other day for $2.35.

Rock singer Lionel Richie at the Live Aid concert.

Something's out of line somehow."

Indeed it was. U.S. farmers were in their worst crisis since the Great Depression of the 1930's. Farm incomes nosedived during the recession of 1981-1982. The rest of the economy began to recover in 1982, but farmers went from one bad year to another. Crop prices stayed so low that many farmers could not make payments on their debts. Some lost their farms. On more than one occasion, angry farmers tried to prevent forced sales of their neighbors' land, but rarely succeeded.

The federal government took active measures to try to help farmers. At a time when the Reagan administration was cutting back the government's role in other areas, it poured a record amount of money into agriculture. Federal farm programs soared from $8.8 billion in 1980 to $22.9 billion in 1983.

Congress approved a major new farm act in

1985. The act began a new program of direct payment to farmers. The program aimed to boost farmers' income without requiring a rise in the price of farm products. Congress wanted to keep the prices low so that U.S. farm products could compete on world markets. U.S. farmers had been selling a large part of their corn, wheat, and soybeans to foreign buyers. But the U.S. farmers had to compete against farmers in Western Europe, Australia, and South America who also had grain for export. U.S. prices had to be low enough to attract buyers.

The fact was, the world had more food than it knew what to do with. More precisely, it had more food than it knew how to sell. At the same time people were starving in places like Ethiopia, where drought and war caused massive suffering. In the summer of 1985, dozens of rock stars and other performers put on a 17-hour concert in Philadelphia and London to raise money to fight starvation. The concert, carried live on television and radio all over the world, was called Live Aid. It raised an estimated $70 million. Performers also staged Farm Aid concerts to raise money for hard-pressed U.S. farmers, but the money was only a drop in a very large bucket.

Despite the concerts and despite the money the government pumped into rural areas, the farm crisis continued. Each year, about 100,000 U.S. farmers left the land for good. By the mid-1980's only 2.2 million farms were left — down from 6.8 million in 1935. Middle-sized family farms were rapidly disappearing. What remained were some very big farms (often run by corporations) and some very small farms (often run by men and women who held other jobs and farmed in their spare time).

Looking to the future, observers predicted more changes in U.S. farming. Many of those changes were expected to come from *biotechnology* — the application of scientific advances to biology. For example, scientists were mixing hereditary material from different plants to create stronger, more productive crop varieties. They were developing cows that give more milk than ever before. Advances in biotechnology do not come cheap. In many cases, only the largest farms can afford the new techniques. By the year 2000, according to one study, about three fourths of U.S. food may come from a mere 50,000 large farms.

That study troubled many people. Was the family farm dying? How would the trend to bigger farms affect the many small towns dotted about Illinois and other farm states? Would consumers end up paying higher prices for their food? Or would biotechnology bring prices down to lower and lower levels? Nobody could know for sure.

IN SPACE: REACHING OUT?

The excitement with which Americans had greeted the dawn of the space age had faded in the 1970's. From time to time, unmanned spacecraft sent back spectacular photographs of distant planets and their moons. Even so, manned space flight had become relatively humdrum.

The main project for U.S. astronauts was a *space shuttle* program that had its first flight in 1981. Designed to be used over and over, three space vehicles shuttled between earth and earth orbit. They took off with the aid of booster rockets. They landed like airplanes on landing strips.

The space shuttles had both military and commercial applications. For a price, they would launch satellites for communications companies or carry out experiments for researchers. Some of their flights stirred little interest. Others made history. For example, a flight in 1983 carried Sally K. Ride — the first U.S. woman to fly in space — into orbit. A flight later that same year carried Guion Bluford, Jr., the first black American in space.

In January 1986, the shuttle program suffered a crushing blow. A fiery blast destroyed the shuttle *Challenger*, 73 seconds after take-

The space shuttle *Columbia,*
one of three used by NASA.

off. All seven astronauts died. The tragedy was especially poignant for two reasons. First, one of those killed was Christa McAuliffe, a social-studies teacher from Concord, New Hampshire. She was to have led "ordinary" Americans into space. Second, the crew of the *Challenger* represented the very diversity of the nation. Members included a black American, a Jewish American, and an Asian American, people from every major region of America.

Investigators said a flawed booster rocket had caused the blast. They sharply criticized NASA for mistakes in engineering and management, and said the companies that built the rocket had shared in the fault. The explosion set back the shuttle program by at least two years. To the despair of U.S. officials, other NASA and Air Force space launches failed in the months that followed. At least temporarily, the nation's ability to launch commercial, scientific, and military satellites was severely crippled.

Meanwhile, the Soviet space program seemed to be picking up speed. It was the Soviets who had put the first woman (a Russian) and the first black (a Cuban) into space. By the 1980's the Soviets were launching five times as many rockets each year as the United States. While the Soviets had not developed a space shuttle, they had made advances in other areas such as space platforms and experimental space "factories."

Americans had to answer some crucial questions. Should the United States place greater reliance on unmanned missions to minimize the danger of space exploration to human lives? Should private enterprise take over NASA's commercial space projects? Should NASA go ahead with its next project — a permanently manned space station for the mid-1990's? Does the United States need a new goal as dramatic as the "man-on-the-moon" goal of the 1960's in order to stir public support for space exploration? Is space exploration worth its high cost, or could space money be put to better use in other programs?

CIVIL RIGHTS: MORE TO DO?

In the 1980's, the debate over equal rights entered a new era. Some questions seemed to have been settled, others remained unsettled, and new ones kept appearing.

The Reagan administration cut back federal programs on civil rights, as it cut regulations in other areas. Officials went to court to argue against busing and affirmative action. They limited the scope of rules barring discrimination in federally-aided programs. Spokespersons for blacks, women, handicapped people, and others who had benefited from such programs denounced the administration's moves as "turning back the clock" on civil rights. But President Reagan defended the actions. He said: "I think that we must have a color-blind society. Things must be done for people neither because of nor in spite of any differences between us in race, ethnic origin, or religion."

The United States Supreme Court sometimes backed and sometimes rejected the administration's arguments. The Court continued to support busing and affirmative action in certain cases.

Congress and state governments sent out mixed signals, too. Congress passed a new, stronger Voting Rights Act in 1982. It also approved a new federal holiday on January 15 to honor the birthday of civil rights leader Dr. Martin Luther King, Jr. However, other rights measures went down to defeat. The Equal Rights Amendment to bar sex discrimination died when the 1982 deadline passed and too few states had ratified it.

The nation seemed to be in a holding pattern, uncertain of the future. A national commitment to equal rights had come up against a widespread desire to limit the involvement of government in daily life. There was no clear way to reconcile those two values.

LIFE AND LEISURE: WHAT NEXT?

On a Thursday night in July 1984, a handful of viewers in New York City watched the first U.S. network broadcast (NBC's "The Tonight Show") to be transmitted with stereo sound. At first, only one station and a few receiving sets were equipped for TV stereo, but the phenomenon quickly spread.

TV stereo was one of many changes that affected U.S. life and leisure in the 1980's. Cable TV, which had made slow gains in the 1970's, mushroomed in the next decade. Along with the traditional four broadcast networks (three commercial, one public), Americans could choose from a smorgasbord of channels — music videos, Christian soap operas, Spanish-language sitcoms, sports events, round-the-clock weather, movies, and many other options. People in areas that had no cable service or who wanted to avoid paying a monthly cable fee began to set up "satellite dishes" in their yards. They received programs in even greater abundance, direct from satellites. However, in 1986 many cable networks began to scramble their satellite signals. That way they could block unauthorized reception.

Cable networks brought both entertainment and public affairs programs into the home. A network called C-Span began regular coverage of sessions of the U.S. House of Representatives in 1979. In 1986 the U.S. Senate also opened its sessions to television.

The 1980's also saw the spread of computer games, video recorders, compact disc players, and other electronic devices. The broadcast TV networks suffered in the competition for people's leisure time. Fewer people were watching broadcast programs. The networks lost advertising revenue. Budgets began to pinch, and the networks laid off employees. Observers predicted many more changes in U.S. television in the years ahead.

Technological advances changed much more than Americans' leisure pursuits. Computers revolutionized office work. Industrial robots took over an increasing number of tasks in factories. Heart and other organ transplants, once largely experimental, gained increasing acceptance as tools of medical science. Advances in biotechnology led to new vaccines and treatments.

President Reagan recovered rapidly from cancer surgery.

For all its progress, however, medical science remained baffled by certain diseases. The search for a cure for various cancers went on. Meanwhile, a new and deadly disease called AIDS (acquired immune deficiency syndrome) spread rapidly in the 1980's, especially among homosexuals and intravenous drug users. Federal officials predicted that by the early 1990's AIDS would kill as many people each year as motor vehicle accidents. Scientists struggled to develop a vaccine, while U.S. Surgeon General C. Everett Koop raised controversy by advocating education about AIDS, starting at grade-school level, as a means of preventing its spread.

Technology was bringing many benefits while raising a host of new questions. Modern industry gave America an unprecedented array of products for easier living. But where would industry dump its toxic wastes? Computers helped the authorities fight crime. But what threat, if any, did crime-fighting computers pose to the ordinary citizen's privacy? Chemical pesticides helped farmers raise better crops. But what were they doing to the environment? Were all the new technologies creating more problems than they solved?

The questions seemed almost endless. But Americans could take heart from their knowledge of history. Earlier generations had faced equally pressing questions. They had done their best to answer them. Perhaps the task was never truly finished. But now it was a new generation's turn to puzzle over questions, some new, and others that puzzled the previous generations, and try to come up with the answers.

SECTION RECAP

1. What trade problems did the United States face in the 1980's? Which U.S. industries favored free trade? Which favored protectionism?

2. How was biotechnology predicted to affect farming and agriculture in the United States? Why was this alarming to many people?

3. What gains were made in the 1980's in the cause of civil rights? What losses did it suffer?

4. What advances were made in the 1980's in the fields of television? Industrial technology? Medicine?

1. Match the items in column A with the resultant foreign policy moves made by the Reagan administration in column B.

_____ 1. Window of vulnerability
_____ 2. German discotheque bombing
_____ 3. Israeli invasion of Lebanon
_____ 4. Iran-Iraq war
_____ 5. New more-left wing government in power
_____ 6. Sandinista repression
_____ 7. Polish crackdown on Solidarity
_____ 8. South African apartheid
_____ 9. Third World loan defaults
_____10. Angolan civil war

a. Protests against ship inspections
b. Invasion of Grenada
c. Baker's bail-out program
d. Limited sanctions
e. Aid to UNITA
f. A Middle East peace plan
g. Strategic Defense Initiative
h. Banned sale of oil and gas equipment to U.S.S.R.
i. Airstrike against Libya
j. Military aid to contras

2. Define these terms: *biotechnology, contras, default, deregulation, duties, embargo, entitlement programs, free trade, ideology, loophole, protectionism, space shuttle, supple-side economics, terrorism.*

3. Give some of the arguments used to criticize deregulation.

4. What was the effect of the Caribbean Basin Initiative on Puerto Rico?

5. What were the effects of the *Challenger* explosion?

INDEX